Personnel Selection

SIXTH EDITION

Personnel Selection

Adding Value Through People – A Changing Picture

SIXTH EDITION

Mark Cook

WILEY Blackwell

Contents

Preface to the sixth edition

Every chapter of this sixth edition has been revised to incorporate new research and new ideas, so that amount of change in each chapter gives an indication of much new research has been reported in each area. The chapters on personality and assessment centres have needed the most revision. In order to keep the book within a manageable and affordable length a lot of older material has had to be removed, but I have tried to keep some historically important material. Chapter 11 covers a new topic: the contribution of social networking sites to selection. Two chapters have needed much less revision. One is Chapter 9, on biodata, where conventional paper and pencil measures may have been supplanted by interactive equivalents, which, however, do not seem to have been researched much, if at all. The other is Chapter 5, on the letter of reference, which has never been researched adequately, despite being so widely used. Every chapter has been rewritten even where there is not all that much new research to describe.

Established truths, or beliefs, continue to be questioned. Issues formerly described as finally settled and not needing any further discussion have been reopened, notably differential validity (whether the correlation between test and work performance might be different for different sections of the population, most particularly for white and non-white Americans). Another 'closed' issue that has been reopened is the importance, or unimportance, of specific abilities compared with general mental ability. There certainly seems to be a trend for things that were formerly described confidently as *not a problem* to be appearing perhaps to pose a problem after all.

There is growing awareness of how different selection tests correlate, which tends to cast doubt on approaches that emphasize the paramount importance of matching the test to the job. Emphasis on identifying separate aspects of work performance, notably organizational citizenship, counterproductive work behaviour and adaptability, runs in parallel with the suggestion that there might be a tendency for all measures of work performance to be positively correlated, the 'monolithic' hypothesis.

To keep the list of references to a reasonable length, references are not necessarily given for points that are not central to selection, e.g. heritability, or personality theory.

The key references sections at the end of each chapter are selected to be accessible, meaning they are written in English, and so far as possible obtainable through PsychInfo or other online systems. This tends to mean journal articles are included, whereas chapters in books are not.

Certain types of material I have generally not included, including simulations of work using students, and 'Monte Carlo' simulations in which sets of data are generated according to certain rules, then analysed as if they were 'real' data. I have always thought these an example of *getting out what you put in*, and not very useful.

One area that might be moving towards becoming important, but also controversial, could be the roles of commercial interests in general, and test publishers in particular. To declare my interests in this area, I have been involved in the publication of psychological tests in the past, but am not now.

I would to thank Swansea University for all their help with library and other facilities, and Karen Howard for her invaluable continuing support.

Department of Psychology
Swansea University
2015

Preface to the first edition

When I first proposed writing this book, I thought it self-evident that personnel selection and productivity are closely linked. Surely an organization that employs poor staff will produce less, or achieve less, than one that finds, keeps and promotes the right people. So it was surprising when several people, including one anonymous reviewer of the original book proposal, challenged my assumption, and argued that there was no demonstrated link between selection and productivity.

Critics are right, up to a point – there has never been an experimental demonstration of the link. The experiment could be performed, but it might prove very expensive. First, create three identical companies. Second allow company A to select its staff by using the best techniques available, require company B to fill its vacancies at random (so long as the staff possess the minimum necessary qualifications), and require company C to employ the people company A identified as least suitable. Third, wait for a year and then see which company is doing best, or – if the results are very clear-cut – which companies are still in business. No such experiment has been performed, although fair employment laws in the USA have caused some organizations to adopt at times personnel policies that are not far removed from the strategy for company B.

Perhaps critics only meant to say that the outline overlooked other more important factors affecting productivity, such as training, management, labour relations, lighting and ventilation, or factors which the organization cannot control such as the state of the economy, technical development, foreign competition, and political interference. Of course all of these affect productivity, but this does not prove that – other things being equal – an organization that selects, keeps and promotes good employees will not produce more, or produce better, than one that does not.

Within-organization factors that affect productivity are dealt with by others writings on industrial/organizational psychology. Factors outside the organization, such as the state of world trade, fall outside the scope of psychology.

Swansea, 1995

CHAPTER 1

Old and new selection methods

We've always done it this way

WHY SELECTION MATTERS

Clark Hull is better known, to psychologists at least, as an animal learning theorist, but very early in his career he wrote a book on aptitude testing (Hull, 1928), and described ratios of output of best to worst performers in a variety of occupations. Hull was the first psychologist to ask how much workers differ in productivity, and he discovered the principle that should be written in letters of fire on every HR manager's office wall: *the best is twice as good as the worst*.

Human resource managers sometimes find they have difficulty convincing colleagues that HR departments also make a major contribution to the organization's success. Because HR departments are neither making things, nor selling things, some colleagues think they do not add any value to the organization. This represents a very narrow approach to how organizations work, which overlooks the fact that an organization's most important asset is its staff. Psychologists have devised techniques for showing how finding and keeping the right staff adds value to the organization. Rational Estimate technique (described in detail in Chapter 14) estimates how much workers doing the same job vary in the value of their contribution. One 'rule of thumb' this research generated states that *The value of a good employee minus the value of a poor employee is roughly equal to the salary paid for the job*. If the salary for the job in question is £50,000, then a good employee, in the top 15%, is worth £50,000 more each year than one in the bottom 15%. Differences in value of the order of £50,000 per employee mount up across an organization. Hunter and Hunter (1984) generated a couple of examples, for the public sector in the USA.

- A small employer, the Philadelphia police force (5,000 employees), could save $18 million a year by using psychological tests to select the best.
- A large employer, the US Federal Government (4 million employees), could save $16 billion a year. Or, to reverse the perspective, the US Federal Government was losing $16 billion a year, at 1980s prices, by not using tests.

Personnel Selection: Adding Value Through People – A Changing Picture, Sixth Edition. Mark Cook.
© 2016 John Wiley & Sons, Ltd. Published 2016 by John Wiley & Sons, Ltd.

Some critics see a flaw in such calculations. Every company in the country cannot employ the *best*, for example, computer programmers; someone has to employ *the rest*. Good selection cannot increase national productivity, only the productivity of employers that use good selection methods to grab more than their fair share of talent. At present, employers are – largely – free to do precisely that. The rest of this book explains *how*.

RECRUITMENT

Traditional methods

Figure 1.1 summarizes the successive stages of recruiting and selecting an academic for a British university. The *advertisement* attracts applicants, who complete and return an *application form*. Some applicants' *references* are taken up; the rest are excluded from further consideration. Applicants (As) with satisfactory references are shortlisted, and invited for *interview*, after which the post is filled. The employer tries to attract as many As as possible, then pass them through a series of filters, until the number of surviving As equals the number of vacancies.

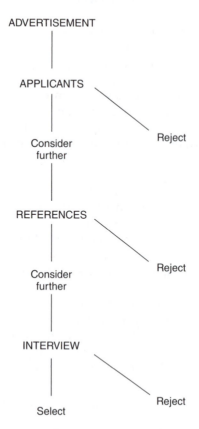

Figure 1.1   Successive stages in selecting academic staff in a British university.

Recruitment sources

There are many ways employers can try to attract applicants: advertisements, agencies – public or private, word of mouth, 'walk-ins' (people who come in and ask if there are any vacancies), job fairs, and the Internet. Employers should analyse recruiting sources carefully to determine which find good employees who stay with them. Employers also need to check whether their recruitment methods are finding a representative applicant pool, in terms of gender, ethnicity, and disability. Newman and Lyon (2009) investigate targeted recruiting, through the wording of advertisements for job. They suggest that saying the organization is 'results oriented' will tend to attract more As high in conscientiousness, and saying the organization is 'innovative' will attract more As high in mental ability. Later chapters will describe research showing As high in conscientiousness and mental ability tend to make better employees. Newman and Lyon suggest the right advertisement can attract such applicants, both overall and from minorities, so meeting the twin aims of many employers: good employees *and* a representative workforce.

Realistic job previews

Any organization can paint a rosy picture of what is really a boring and unpleasant job because they fear no one would apply otherwise. In the USA realistic job previews (RJPs) are widely used to tell applicants what being, for example, a call-centre worker is really like: fast-paced, closely supervised, routine to the point of being boring. Earnest, Allen and Landis's (2011) analysis confirms the results of several earlier reviews that there is a very modest link with reduced turnover, suggesting RJPs may be worth using, given that RJPs cost employers very little whereas turnover costs them a lot. Earnest *et al.* suggest RJPs work by making As see the employer as more honest.

Informal recruitment

Applicants are sometimes recruited by word of mouth, usually through existing employees. Besides being cheaper, the grapevine finds employees who stay longer (low *turnover*) possibly because they have a clearer idea what the job really involves. Zottoli and Wanous (2000) report informal recruits on average do slightly better work; the difference is small (d = 0.08; page 31) but is achieved very cheaply. However, fair employment agencies, for example the (British) Equality and Human Rights Commission, generally frown on informal recruitment; they argue recruiting an all-white workforce's friends is unfair because it tends to perpetuate an all-white workforce. Weller *et al.* (2009) report data from the German Socio-Economic Panel Study, nearly 3,000 people, representative of the whole German working population, tracked over five years. Weller *et al.* confirm that informal recruitment results in lower turnover: more employees recruited through agencies or advertisement leave in the first two years, and leave sooner, departures peaking at 9 months compared with 17 months for employees recruited through informal contacts.

New technology and recruitment

Advertising, making applications, sifting applications and even assessment can now be carried out electronically, which can make the whole process far quicker. People even talk of making 'same-day offers'. More and more jobs are advertised on the Internet, through the employer's own website or through numerous recruitment sites. People seeking jobs can post their details on websites for potential employers to evaluate, which gives the job seeker an opportunity that did not exist before. Most employers now use electronic application systems, eliminating the conventional paper application form. Internet recruitment can greatly increase the number of As, which is good for the employer if it broadens the field of high-calibre As, but it does also create work sorting through a mountain of applications.

APPLICATION SIFTING

The role of the application form (AF), or its new technology equivalent, is to act as first filter, choosing a relatively small number of applications to process further, called *sifting*. Sifting can take up a lot of time in HR departments so any way of speeding it up will be very valuable, so long as it is fair and accurate. Research suggests sifting is not always done very effectively. Machwirth, Schuler and Moser (1996) used *policy capturing* analysis, which works back from the decisions HR make about a set of applications to infer how HR decides. Machwirth *et al.* showed what HR *do* often differs from what they *say*. Managers said they sifted on the basis of proven ability and previously achieved position, but in practice rejected applicants because the application looked untidy or badly written. McKinney *et al.* (2003) analysed how US campus recruiters used grade point average (GPA; college course marks) to select for interview. Some chose students with high marks, which is the logical use of the information, given that GPA does predict work performance to some extent, and that it is linked to mental ability, which also predicts work performance. A second large group ignored GPA altogether. A third group selected for lower GPA, screening out any As with high grades, which does not seem a good way to sift, given the link between work performance and mental ability. The choice of strategy seemed essentially idiosyncratic, and not linked to type of job or employer.

Accuracy and honesty

Numerous surveys report that alarming percentages of AFs, résumés and CVs contain information that is inaccurate, or even false. These surveys often seem to have a 'self-serving' element, being reported by organizations that offer to verify information supplied by As; not much independent research has been reported. Goldstein (1971) found many applicants for nursing vacancies exaggerated both previous experience and salary. More seriously, a quarter gave a reason for leaving that their previous employer did not agree with, and 17% listed as their last employer someone who denied ever having employed them. McDaniel, Douglas, and Snell (1997) surveyed marketing, accounting, management and computing professionals, and found that 25% to 33% admitted misrepresenting their experience or skills, inflating their salary, or suppressing damaging information, such as being sacked. Keenan (1997) asked British graduates which answers on their application forms they had 'made up … to please the recruiter'. Hardly any admitted to giving false information about their degree, but most (73%) admitted they were not honest about their reasons for choosing that employer, and 40% felt no obligation to be honest about their hobbies and interests. Electronic media, such as the Internet, do not bypass these problems. It is just as easy to lie through a keyboard as it is on paper or in person.

RESEARCH AGENDA

- The accuracy of CV and application form information.
- What sort of information is wrongly reported.
- What sort of people report false information.
- Why people report wrong information.
- Whether the amount of incorrect information is increasing.
- The role of careers advice, coaching, self-help books and websites.

Fairness and sifting

Equal opportunities (EO) agencies in the USA have produced long lists of questions that application forms should not ask for one reason or another. Some are obvious: ethnicity, gender, and disability (because the law forbids discrimination in all three). Others are less obvious: for example AFs should not ask about driving offences, arrests or military discharge, because some minorities have higher rates of these, so the question may create indirect discrimination. Questions about availability over holidays or weekends may discourage some religious minorities. A succession of surveys (reviewed by Kethley & Terpstra, 2005) have consistently shown that most US employers seem unaware of, or unconcerned by, this guidance and continue to ask questions the agencies say they should avoid. Kethley and Terpstra review 312 US Federal cases involving AFs, and find complaints centred on sex (28%), age (25%), and race (12%). Some questions listed as 'inadvisable' – military discharge, marital status, arrest – have never been the subject of a court case. Internet recruitment and selection could raise another set of 'fairness' issues, because not everyone has access to the Internet. In 2014 a UK government-run recruitment system caused some embarrassment – to itself and the government – by advertising vacancies as suitable for 'recent graduates', alleged to be a code word for 'young'.

Bias in sifting

Many studies have used the *paper applicant* method, which prepares sets of equally suitable As who differ in one key feature – gender, age, having a beard, etc. – then has HR staff rate their suitability. This is an easy type of research to do, and one that usually 'gets results', by finding evidence of bias:

- Davison and Burke (2000) reviewed 49 studies of gender bias, and found both male and female sifters biased against female As. The less job information is given, the greater the bias.
- Ding and Stillman (2005) reported New Zealand data showing overweight female As tend to be sifted out.
- Correll, Benard and Paik (2007) find women with children tend to be sifted out, but men with children are not, and may even be favoured.

Paper applicant research has a flaw, however: the sifters know they are being scrutinized by psychologists, so may be on their best behaviour. Also they are not really hiring As, and will not have to work with the people they 'select'.

Research on sifting in the USA had reached the reassuring conclusion that it seemed free of racial bias, but a study by Bertrand and Mullainathan (2004) suggested there may be a problem after all. They used a different approach, called the *audit* technique. They sent their 'paper applicants' to real employers, applying for real jobs, and counted how many were shortlisted for interview. Choice of first name identified A as white or African American. (Americans will assume 'Brad' and 'Carrie' are white, while 'Aisha' and 'Leroy' are African American). For every 10 'white' As called for interview, there were only 6.7 'African Americans'; African Americans were being sifted out by ethnicity. Bertrand and Mullainathan could argue their data show what is really happening in the real US job market, which justifies the slightly unethical practice of sending employers fake job applications. The International Labour Organization seems to approve, for it publishes a manual on how to conduct 'natural experiments' to test for discrimination. Some research, described in Chapter 4, takes this method a step further, by accepting invitations to interview, and noting how the interview proceeds. The audit method is in one respect even easier than the paper person method, because HR do not have to agree to participate. Hoque and Noon (1999) wrote to British employers enquiring about possible vacancies, not applying for a specific job, calling themselves 'Evans', implying a white person, or 'Patel', implying a South Asian person. 'Evans' got on average slightly longer and more helpful replies. McGinnity and Lunn (2011) find Irish applicants in Ireland twice as likely as African, Asian or German applicants to be interviewed. McGinnity and Lunn note the effect seemed stronger than found elsewhere and suggest this may reflect the low number of non-Irish people in Ireland, and a strong feeling of national identity. The data were collected between March and September 2008, just before the financial crisis that started the recession; a replication today would be interesting. In the Netherlands, applicants with Arab-sounding names are four times less likely to be called back by the employer (Derous, Ryan & Nguyen, 2012). Agerström *et al.* (2012) get the same result in Sweden. It is sometimes argued that providing more information about people will avoid 'snap' judgements based on apparent race or nationality, but Agerström *et al.* find that providing information about Erik's coldness and lack of commitment or Hassan's warmth and high commitment did not prevent discrimination. Research has widened to include other possibly discriminated-against classes of applicant.

Social class

Jackson (2009) confirms the continuing importance of social class in Britain. Applicants with high-status names (Charles Bartle-Jones vs Gary Rodgers) or with high-status pastimes (polo vs darts), or who have been to public (i.e. private) rather than state schools get (slightly) more favourable responses from employers.

Pregnancy

Morgan *et al.* (2013) list four elements of some US employers' perception of pregnant women as job applicants: lower competence, lack of commitment, inflexibility, and as needing 'accommodation' (changes in working conditions or hours etc.). Morgan *et al.* employ a variant of the 'audit' approach, in which women go into a department store and ask if it has any jobs, and to complete an application form. Sometimes they wear a pregnancy prosthesis that makes them look about five months pregnant, and they are provided with four different scripts to counter one of the four stereotypes listed above: for example, 'I have the help I need so I can work whenever you need me'. The scripts had some effect in reducing discrimination.

Age

Ng and Feldman (2012) list six common stereotypes of older workers: that they are less motivated, less trusting, less healthy, more resistant to change, more vulnerable to work-family imbalance, and less willing to participate in training and development. All would tend to result in older As being sifted out at the shortlisting stage. Ng and Feldman also review evidence on actual age differences and conclude the first five stereotypes are false, but there is evidence that older workers are less willing to participate in training and development. In an earlier paper Ng and Feldman (2008) examined the actual correlation of age with a range of work performance measures, and found no age differences in most: core task performance, creativity, training programme performance, safety performance, and counterproductive work behaviour (ranging from taking too long a break to wrecking machinery). In some respects older workers perform better: less often late, less often absent, more likely to go beyond the letter of their job description. The correlation of age with (avoiding) absence and lateness is 0.26–0.28, which is as good as many selection tests achieve. Ng and Feldman's results suggest the stereotyped view of older workers is incorrect, and that in some ways they are better employees.

Weight

Agerström and Rooth (2011) report an audit study from Sweden. Pairs of parallel real applications were sent to employers advertising a range of jobs through the Swedish Employment Agency, one with a photo (face only) of an obese person, one with a photo of a similar but not obese person. The obese person was less than half as likely to be invited for interview. Two months later some of the HR managers who had done the sifting agreed to do an implicit association test (described in detail in Chapter 8) which showed they tended to think of obese persons as ineffective, slow, lazy, incompetent, and lacking in initiative. The implicit association test does not ask sifters to rate, for example, obese people on, for example, energy, but aims to uncover automatic associations sifters have, but may be unaware of.

Gender and 'backlash'

'Agentic' people are ambitious, task-oriented and assertive, whereas 'communal' people are caring, helpful and collaborative. In Western countries gender stereotypes expect men to be agentic, and women to be communal. Carlsson *et al.* (2014) report an audit study on CVs that conform to this stereotype, or do not: caring, helpful men, and ambitious, assertive women. They test the hypothesis that there will be a 'backlash' against applicants who do not fit the stereotype. However over 5,000 real applicants to 3,000 real jobs in Sweden showed no evidence of 'backlash'.

IMPROVING APPLICATION SIFTING

Behavioural competences

Applicants are asked to describe things they have done which relate to key competences for the job. *Ability to influence others* is assessed by A describing an occasion when A had to persuade others to accept an unpopular course of action. This method might improve the AF as a selection assessment, but there is no research on whether it does.

Weighted application blanks and biodata

Application forms can be converted into weighted application blanks (WABs) by analysing past and present employees for predictors of success (Chapter 9). One study found American female bank clerks who did not stay long tended to be under 25, single, to live at home, and to have had several jobs (Robinson, 1972), so banks could reduce turnover by screening out As with these characteristics. (Robinson's list probably would not be legal today, however, because it specifies female bank clerks.) Most WABs are conventional paper format, but the technique would work equally well for electronic applications. Biodata also uses biographical items to select, but collects them through a separate questionnaire, not from the AF.

Training and experience (T&E) ratings

In the USA application sifting used to be assisted by T&E ratings which sought to quantify applicants' training and experience by various rating systems, instead of relying on arbitrary judgements. T&E ratings seem to have been overtaken in the USA by various Internet application coding systems. Note, however, that T&E ratings had extensive research (McDaniel, Schmidt and Hunter, 1988) showing they do actually predict work performance; similar research for Internet application coding has yet to be reported.

Minimum qualifications (MQs)

The advertisement says As need a civil engineering qualification plus a minimum of five years' experience, the intended implication being that people who lack these will not be considered, so should not apply. MQs are generally based on education and experience. However, educational MQs may exclude some minorities, while length of experience may exclude women, who tend to take more career breaks. Hence in the USA MQs may be challenged legally, and so need careful justification. Buster, Roth and Roth (2005) described elaborate systems of panels of experts, discussions and rating schedules for setting MQs. (As opposed to setting an arbitrary MQ, or using the 'one we've always used', or the 'one everyone uses'.) For example the experts might be asked to 'bracket' the MQ; if it is suggested that three years' experience is needed, then ask the experts to consider two and four years as well, just to make sure three years really is the right amount.

Background investigation, aka positive vetting

Application forms contain the information applicants choose to provide about themselves. Some employers make their own checks on As, covering criminal history, driving record, financial and credit history, education and employment history, possibly even reputation and lifestyle. Background checking is rapidly growing in popularity in the USA, from 51% of employers in 1996 to 85% in 2007 (Isaacson *et al.*, 2008), possibly driven by several high-profile cases where CEOs have been caught falsifying their CVs. In Britain, background investigations are recommended for childcare workers, and used for government employees with access to confidential information (known as *positive vetting*). Presently there is little or no research on whether background checks succeed in selecting 'good' employees and rejecting unsuitable ones.

Isaacson *et al.* compare As who failed a background check with those who passed, and find those who failed score slightly higher on a test of risk-taking. The closest they could get to work performance was a realistic computer simulation of manufacturing work, where the failed group worked slightly faster but slightly less well. Roberts *et al.* (2007) report a long-term follow up of a New Zealand cohort of 930 26-year-olds, which found no link between criminal convictions before age 18 and self-reported counterproductive work behaviour.

Internet tests

Many employers are replacing their conventional paper application forms by short tests completed over the Internet. Some assess job knowledge; it can be useful to screen out people who know little or nothing about about subjects, for example, Microsoft Excel, they claim expertise in. Testing can improve the whole selection process by screening out, early on, As who lack the mental ability necessary for the job. (Chapter 6 will show that mental ability is generally a good predictor of work performance.) In conventional selection systems, tests are not normally used until the shortlist stage, by which time many able As may have been screened out. It is theoretically preferable to put the most accurate selection tests early in the selection process, but the cost of conventional paper-and-pencil testing tends to prevent this. Some Internet tests assess personality or fit. Formerly HR inferred, for example, leadership potential from what As said they did at school or university. Some Internet sifting systems assess it more directly by a set of standard questions. No research has been published on how well such systems work.

Application scanning software

Numerous software systems exist that can scan applications and CVs to check whether they match the job's requirements. This is much quicker than conventional sifting of paper applications by HR. Automated sifting systems can eliminate bias directly based on ethnicity, age, disability or gender, because they are programmed to ignore these factors. However they will not necessarily ignore factors *linked* to ethnicity, disability, age or gender, such as sports and pastimes. Sifting software will do the job consistently and thoroughly, whereas the human sifter may get tired or bored and not read every application carefully. Sifting electronically is not necessarily any more accurate. Accuracy depends on the decision rules used in sifting, which in turn depend on the quality of the research they are based on. Reports (Bartram, 2000) have suggested some scanning systems do nothing more sophisticated than search for key words; once applicants realize this, they will take care to include as many as possible. There is an urgent need to know what application sifting programs actually do. Psychologists tend to be rather sceptical, for one fairly simple reason. If these systems are doing something tremendously subtle and complex, where did the people who wrote them acquire this wisdom? There is no evidence that human application sifters are doing anything highly complex that software can model, nor is there any body of research on application sifting that has described any complex, subtle relationships to put into software. Stone *et al.*'s (2013) survey concludes that little or no research has been reported on several fairly important questions, including keyword searching in applications.

RESEARCH AGENDA

- The link between various application sifting systems and later work performance, for competence based applications, background investigations, Internet testing, application scanning and sorting software systems.
- Policy capturing research on application scanning and sorting software systems.
- Investigation of how application sifting software operates, and what it can achieve.

OVERVIEW OF SELECTION METHODS

The first column in Table 1.1 lists the main techniques used to select staff in North America, Europe, and other industrialized countries. The list is divided into traditional and 'new', although most 'new' methods have been in use for some time. Table 1.1 also indicates which chapter contains the main coverage of each method.

WHAT IS ASSESSED IN PERSONNEL SELECTION?

The short answer to this question is: ability to do the job. A much more detailed answer is provided by job analysis, which lists the main attributes successful employees need (see Chapter 3). Table 1.2 lists the main headings for assessing staff.

Mental ability

divides into general mental ability (or 'intelligence'), and more specific abilities such as problem solving, clerical ability, or mechanical comprehension. Some jobs also need sensory abilities: keen hearing, good balance, or good eye-hand co-ordination

Physical characteristics

Some jobs need specific physical abilities: strength, endurance, dexterity. Others have more implicit requirements for height or appearance.

Table 1.1   Traditional and new(er) selection assessment methods.

Traditional methods	Chapter	Alternative names
Application form/CV/résumé	1	
Traditional interview	4	
References	5	
New(er) methods		
Electronic application	1	
Structured interview	4	
Peer rating	5	
Mental ability test	6	Aptitude test
Personality questionnaire	7	Personality inventory
Honesty test	7	Integrity test
Projective test	8	
Graphology	8	Handwriting analysis
Biodata	9	Weighted application blank
Assessment centre	10	Extended interview
Emotional intelligence	11	Situational judgement Social intelligence
Work sample test	11	Trainability test, in tray/basket
Physical ability test	11	
Drug use testing	11	

Table 1.2   Seven main aspects of applicants assessed in selection.

Mental ability
Personality
Physical characteristics
Interests and values
Knowledge
Work skills
Social skills

Personality

Psychologists list from five to 30 underlying dispositions, or personality traits, to think, feel and behave in particular ways. An extravert person likes meeting people, feels at ease meeting strangers, etc. The employer may find it easier to select someone who is very outgoing to sell insurance, rather than trying to train someone who is presently rather shy.

Interests, values and fit

Someone who wants to help others may find charity work more rewarding than selling doughnuts; someone who believes that people should obey all the rules all the time may enjoy being a traffic warden. People cannot always find work that matches their ideals and values, but work that does may prove more rewarding. 'Fit' means the applicant's outlook or behaviour matches the organization's requirements. These can be explicit: soldiers expect to obey orders instantly and without question. Fit may be implicit: the applicant may not sound or look 'right for us', but there is no written list of requirements, or even a list that selectors can explain to you.

Knowledge

Every job requires some knowledge: current employment law, statistical analysis, or something much simpler, how to use a telephone, how to give change. Knowledge can be acquired by training, so need not necessarily be a selection requirement. Mastery of higher-level knowledge may require higher levels of mental ability.

Work skills

The ability to do something quickly and efficiently: bricklaying, driving a bus, valuing a property, diagnosing an illness. Employers sometimes select for skills, and sometimes train for them. Mastery of some skills may require levels of mental or physical ability not everyone has.

Social skills

These are important for many jobs; and essential for some. They include communication, persuasion, negotiation, influence and leadership, teamwork, etc. Hogan, Chamorro-Premuzic and Kaiser (2013) argue that the changing nature of work in the developed world means social skills are now much more important, especially in the service sector, and in teamwork. Hogan *et al.* also suggest that being able to get on with colleagues in general has always been overlooked in selection.

Construct and method

Arthur and Villado (2008) note that many reviews fail to distinguish clearly between *construct* and *method*. Construct refers to *what* is being assessed, for example, personality; method refers to *how* it is assessed, for example, personality questionnaire.

NATURE OF THE INFORMATION COLLECTED

Discussions of selection methods tend to focus on the merits of personality questionnaires (PQs), or structured interviews, or work samples; they do not usually address the issue of what sort of information the method generates. Table 1.3 sorts selection methods by five qualitatively different types of information.

Table 1.3   Five categories of qualitatively different information, obtained by selection tests.

Self-report	Information provided by the applicant *Application form, including online application, T&E rating, biodata, personality questionnaire, honesty test, projective test, interest questionnaire, interview.*
Reported	Information provided by other people about the applicant *References, peer rating.*

Demonstrated
  a) Test
 	
  b) Behavioural
	The applicant performs a task or demonstrates a skill
	Work sample, mental ability test, job knowledge test, physical ability test.
	Group exercise, behavioural test.

Recorded	Information that is recorded somewhere *School marks, degree class, professional qualification, published work*
Involuntary	Information the applicant may not be able to control consciously *Graphology, drug use testing, polygraph, psychophysiology, voice stress analysis.*

Self-report evidence

Information that is provided by the applicant, in written or spoken form, on the application form, in the interview, and when answering personality questionnaires, attitude measures, and biographical inventories. Some self-reports are free-form or unstructured, for example some interviews or application forms. Other are more structured, such as personality questionnaires, biodata, or structured interviews. Some self-reports are fairly transparent, notably interviews and personality questionnaires. (Transparent in the sense that As will have little difficulty working out what inference will be drawn from what they say.) Other assessments may be less transparent, such as biodata, or projective tests; As may find it less easy to decide what answer will be seen as 'good' or 'poor'.

Self-report data have some compelling advantages in selection. The system is generally very cheap and very convenient; applicants are present, and eager to please, so collecting information is easy. Self-report can also be justified as showing respect and trust for applicants. It can be argued that some questions can only be answered by the person him/herself. It is not usually very sensible to start an argument with someone about whether they are satisfied with their job. If they say they are, then they should know. Unless, however, there is any reason to think they are not telling the truth, which may be a possibility in the context of personnel selection. In fact self-report has a fundamental disadvantage in selection: As provide the information, and the employer generally has no way of verifying it. Self-report has two other limitations: coaching, and lack of insight. There are many books on how to complete job applications; career counselling services advise students what to say at interviews. The second problem is lack of self-insight. Some As may genuinely think they are good leaders, or popular, or creative, and incorporate this view of themselves into their application, PQ, or interview. However by any other criterion – test, others' opinion, or achievement – they lack the quality in question. This issue has not been researched much, if at all, in the selection context. These problems make it important to confirm what applicants say about themselves by checking information from other sources. Kruger and Dunning (1999) note that people who score badly on tests often greatly overestimate their performance, suggesting that people may lack the ability to recognize their own shortcomings. This has been dubbed the Dunning Kruger effect.

Self-report can also create *common method variance* problems. If all the information about Jones's personality, and Jones's job performance, comes from Jones him/herself, there is a risk that a correlation might reflect something other than a true link between the two, such as a general optimism, or general pessimism, or simply not telling the truth. Research should try to avoid common method variance problems by getting information about aspects of Jones from different sources, or by having some way of checking what he or she says.

Other report evidence

Information about the applicant is provided by other people, through references or ratings. Other reports vary in the degree of expertise involved. Some require no special expertise, such as peer ratings and the letter of reference. Others use experts, generally psychologists.

Demonstrated evidence

The applicant performs a task or demonstrates a skill. Tests include general mental ability (GMA)/intelligence tests, as well as tests of aptitudes, and specific knowledge (trade or job knowledge or achievement tests). These are real tests, with right and wrong answers. Demonstrated evidence also includes work samples, group exercises, simulations and other behavioural exercises typically included in assessment centres. Demonstration evidence has fewer limitations than self- or other reports. Ability tests cannot generally be faked. On the down side, demonstrated evidence tends to be more difficult and expensive to collect.

Recorded evidence

Some information used in selection can be characterized as recorded fact. The applicant has a good degree in psychology from a good university. The information is recorded, and verifiable. (Although some employers make the mistake of relying on self-report data, and failing to check applicants' qualifications at source.) Work history can also provide a record of achievement, for example the applicant was CEO/MD of organization XYZ when XYZ's profits increased. Published work, grants obtained, inventions patented, prizes and medals also constitute recorded evidence.

Demonstrated and recorded information tends to have an asymmetric relationship with self- or other reported information. Evidence that someone cannot do something disproves the statement by the applicant or others that he/she can. However the converse is not true: being told that someone cannot do something does not disprove demonstrated or recorded evidence that he or she can. To this extent, demonstrated and recorded evidence is superior to self- and other reported evidence.

Involuntary evidence

Some evidence is provided by applicants, but not from what they tell the assessors, nor from things they do intentionally. The classic example is the polygraph, intended to assess A's truthfulness from respiration, heart rate and electrodermal activity, not from the answers A gives. In fact the polygraph is used to decide which of A's self-reports to believe, and which to classify as untrue. Two other involuntary assessments are graphology and drug use testing. The former seeks to infer As' characteristics from the form of their handwriting, not from its content. Drug use testing assumes that drug use can be more accurately detected by chemical analysis of blood or urine than by self-report. DNA tests of mental ability or personality might – or might not – be devised at some future time. Some types of demonstrated evidence seem to have an almost magical quality about them which appeals to some.

WORK PERFORMANCE

Selection research compares a *predictor*, meaning a selection test, with a *criterion*, meaning an index of the person's work performance. This can be very simple when work generates something that can be counted: widgets manufactured per day, or sales per week. It appears very simple if the organization has an appraisal system whose ratings can be used. The supervisor rating criterion is widely used, because it is almost always available (in the USA), because it is unitary, and because it is hard to argue with.

On the other hand finding a good criterion can soon get very complex, if one wants to dig a bit deeper into what constitutes effective performance. Questions about the real nature of work, or the true purpose of organizations soon arise. Is success better measured objectively by counting units produced, or better measured subjectively by informed opinion? Is success at work unidimensional or multi-dimensional? Who decides whether work is successful? Different supervisors may not agree. Management and workers may not agree. The organization and its customers may not agree.

Objective criteria are many and various. Some are more objective than others; *training grades* often involve some subjective judgement in rating written work. *Personnel criteria* – advancement/promotion, length of service, turnover, punctuality, absence, disciplinary action, accidents, sickness – are easy to collect (but can be hard to interpret). Analyses of selection research (Lent, Aurbach & Levin, 1971) have shown that a subjective criterion – the global supervisor rating – was clearly the favourite, used in 60% of studies. Criteria of work performance are discussed in greater detail in Chapter 12.

FAIR EMPLOYMENT LAW

Most people know it is against the law to discriminate against certain classes of people when filling vacancies. These protected classes include women, ethnic minorities, and disabled people. Most people think discrimination means deciding not to employ Mr Jones because he is black or Ms Smith because she is female. Direct discrimination is illegal, but is not the main concern in personnel selection. The key issue is indirect discrimination, or *adverse impact*. Adverse impact means the selection system results in more majority persons getting through than minority persons. For example some UK employers sift out applicants who have been unemployed for more than six months, on the argument that they will have lost the habit of working. The former Commission for Racial Equality (CRE) argued this creates adverse impact on some ethnic minorities, because their unemployment rates are higher. Adverse impact assesses the *effect* of the selection method, not the *intentions* of the people who devised it. Adverse impact means an employer can be proved guilty of discrimination, by setting standards that make no reference to ethnicity or gender. Adverse impact is a very serious matter for employers. It creates a presumption of discrimination, which the employer must disprove, possibly in court. This will cost a lot of time and money and may generate damaging publicity. Selection methods that do not create adverse impact are therefore highly desirable, but unfortunately are not always easy to find. Fair employment issues are discussed in detail in Chapter 13.

CURRENT SELECTION PRACTICE

Surveys of employers' selection methods appear quite frequently, but should be viewed with some caution. Return rates are often very low: Piotrowski and Armstrong (2006) say 20% is normal. There is also the grey (and black) side of selection. Some methods are not entirely legal or ethical, so employers are unlikely to admit to using them. Rumours suggest that some employers gain unauthorized access to criminal records by employing former police officers, or use credit information to assess applicants (forbidden by credit agencies in the UK). There are even rumours of secret databases of people to avoid employing, because they are union activists or have complained about unsafe working conditions. Many organizations forbid the use of telephone references, but Andler and Herbst (2002) suggest many managers nevertheless both ask for them, and provide them.

Selection in Britain

Table 1.4 presents three recent UK surveys, by IRS (Murphy, 2006), CIPD (2006), and Zibarras and Woods (2010). Table 1.4 confirms earlier UK surveys, showing that most UK employers are still using interviews of various types, that most still use references, that most use tests at least some of the time, but less frequently online. Only half use assessment centres or group exercises, while few use biodata. Two surveys gave no information about return rate. Zibarras and Woods survey organizations of various sizes from a handful of

Table 1.4   Three surveys of UK selection, by CIPD (2006), IRS (Murphy, 2006) and Zibarras & Woods (2010).

	CIPD	IRS	Z&W
% Return rate[a]			10
Sample size	804	100	579
Application form		85	60
CV		20	85
Criminal check			27
Interview			
Unstructured IV			42
Face to face IV		98	
Panel IV		28	
Structured IV			69
Structured panel	88		
Structured one to one	81		
Competency based	85		
Telephone	56	32	
References			
References		85	72
Employment ref (pre-interview)	49		
Academic ref (pre-interview)	36		
Tests			
Tests for specific skills	82		
General ability tests	75		39
Literacy/numeracy	72		28
Personality/aptitude Qs	60		26
Psychometric tests (mostly PQs)		64	
Online test	25		
Biodata		4	27
Work sample			19
Behavioural assessments			
Assessment centre	48	35	17
Group exercise	48		15

[a]CIPD % are employers who use that method (rarely/occasionally/frequently). IRS and Zibarras & Wood % are employers who use that method (extent/frequency unspecified).

employees to more than 1,000, and find no significant differences in choice of selection methods. They find differences between different sectors, which they characterize as the public and voluntary sectors more being likely to use formalized methods, for example application forms rather than CVs, and structured interviews rather than unstructured ones.

Selection in Europe

European countries favour a social negotiation perspective on selection, which emphasizes employee rights, applicant privacy, and expectation of fair and equitable treatment. Salgado and Anderson (2002) concluded that mental ability (MA) tests are now more widely used in Europe than in the USA. The most recent comprehensive survey of European practice remains the Price Waterhouse Cranfield survey from the early 1990s (Dany & Torchy, 1994) which covered 12 western European countries and nine methods. Table 1.5 reveals a number of interesting national differences:

- The French favoured graphology but no other country did.
- Application forms are widely used everywhere except in the Netherlands.
- References were widely used everywhere but less popular in Spain, Portugal and the Netherlands.

Table 1.5   Summary of surveys of selection test use in Europe (Dany & Torchy, 1994; Schuler *et al.*, 2007; König *et al.*, 2010).

		AF	IV	Psy	Gph	Ref	Apt	AC	Grp
UK	1994	97	71	46	1	92	45	18	13
Ireland	1994	91	87	28	1	91	41	7	8
France	1994	95	92	22	57	73	28	9	10
Portugal	1994	83	97	58	2	55	17	2	18
Spain	1994	87	85	60	8	54	72	18	22
Germany	1994	96	86	6	6	66	8	13	4
	1993[a]	98	60/63	21	9	71	34	39	51
	2007[a]	99	73/42	20	2	57	30	58	42
Switzerland	2010[b]	100	99	32[c]	16	89	19	26	nr
Netherlands	1994	94	69	31	2	47	53	27	2
Denmark	1994	48	99	38	2	79	17	4	8
Finland	1994	82	99	74	2	63	42	16	8
Norway	1994	59	78	11	0	92	19	5	1
Sweden	1994	na	69	24	0	96	14	5	3
Turkey	1994	95	64	8	0	69	33	4	23

Methods: AF – application form; IV – interview panel; Psy – psychometric testing; Gph – graphology; Ref – reference; Apt – aptitude test; AC – assessment centre; Grp – group selection methods.
[a] Data from Schuler *et al.* (2007).
[b] Data from König *et al.* (2010).
[c] Personality test.

- Psychometric testing was most popular in Spain and Portugal and least popular in West Germany and Turkey.
- Aptitude testing was most popular in Spain and the Netherlands and least popular in West Germany and Turkey.
- Assessment centres were not used much but are most popular in Spain and the Netherlands.
- Group selection methods were not used much but were most popular in Spain and Portugal.

Schuler *et al.* (2007) report a survey of 125 German HR managers, which they compare with a similar survey from 1993. Methods that have become less popular include references, unstructured interviews, biographical question-naires, and medical examinations. Methods that have become more popular include structured interviews and assessment interviews. The 2007 survey also collected data on perceived validity, and perceived acceptability to applicants. Methods seen as having high validity include structured interview, assessment centre, group discussion and work sample; methods perceived as having low validity include graphology and online PQ. This indicates the German HR people seem generally well informed about selection test validity, with the possible exception of tests of mental ability. The 2007 survey includes some information linking selection methods to type of vacancy. Use of references seems to be linked very closely to status; references are most likely to be used for executives, are rarely used for clerical and retail jobs, and are not used at all for unskilled or skilled workers. Assessment centres are used for apprentices, trainees and management. MA tests are only used for selecting apprentices.

Selection in the USA

Piotrowski and Armstrong (2006) report the most recent US survey, of 151 companies in the Fortune 1000. US employers used application form, résumé and reference check virtually without exception. Half used 'skills testing', and a substantial minority used personality tests and biodata. A few employed drug use testing. Piotrowski and Armstrong did not enquire about use of interviews.

Selection further afield

Less is known about selection in other parts of the world. Surveys of New Zealand (Taylor, Keelty & McDonnell, 2002) and Australia (Di Milia, 2004) found a very similar picture to Britain; interview, references and application were virtually universal, with personality tests, ability tests and assessment centres used by a minority, but gaining in popularity. Arthur *et al.* (1995) described selection in Nigeria and Ghana; interviews were nearly universal (90%), references widely used (46%); paper-and-pencil tests were less frequently used, as were work samples (19%) and work simulations (11%). Ryan *et al.*'s (1999) survey covered no fewer than 20 countries, although some samples were rather small. Mental ability tests were used most in Belgium, the Netherlands, and Spain, least in Italy and USA. Personality tests were used most in Spain, least in Germany and USA. Projective tests were used most in Portugal, Spain, and South Africa, and least in Germany, Greece, Hong Kong, Ireland, Italy, and Singapore. Drug tests were used most in Portugal, Sweden, and USA, and least in Italy, Singapore, and Spain. Ryan suggested the data confirmed a prediction from Hofstede's (2001) discussion of national differences in attitudes to work: countries high in *uncertainty avoidance* (see Box 1.1) used more selection methods, used them more extensively, and used more interviews. Huo, Huang and Napier (2002) surveyed 13 countries including Australia, Canada, China, Indonesia, Taiwan, Japan, South Korea, Mexico, USA, and Latin America. They found interviews were very widely used, but less so in China and South Korea. Some countries, including Mexico, Taiwan, and China, based selection partly on connections (school, family, friends, region, or government). Selection in Japan emphasized ability to get on with others, possibly because Japanese employers traditionally offer people lifelong employment.

Economic climate

A very plausible hypothesis states that high unemployment will mean that employers need worry less about what applicants think of selection methods, so some might feel free to use less popular methods, such as mental ability (intelligence) tests, or personality questionnaires. The years from 2007 to the present (2015) would have been a good time to test this, an opportunity, however, that seems to have been missed.

Box 1.1   Uncertainty avoidance

Uncertainty avoidance means organizations do not like unpredictable situations, and maintain predictability by adhering to formal procedures and rules. Countries that tend to be high in uncertainty avoidance include Greece and Portugal, while countries low in uncertainty avoidance include Singapore.

REASONS FOR CHOICE OF SELECTION METHOD

One survey (Harris, Dworkin & Park, 1990) delved a little deeper and asked why personnel managers choose different selection methods. Factors of middling importance were fakability, offensiveness to the applicant, and how many other companies use the method. Interviews, although very widely used, were recognized to be not very accurate, as well as easy to fake; Harris *et al.* suggest personnel managers are aware of the interview's shortcomings, but continue using it because it serves other purposes besides assessment. Terpstra and Rozell (1997) by contrast asked personnel managers why they did *not* use particular methods. Some they did not think useful: structured interviews, mental ability tests. Some they had not heard of: biodata. They also avoided mental ability tests because of legal worries. Muchinsky (2004) noted that the commonest questions American managers ask about selection tests are *How long will this take?* and *How much will it cost?* not *How accurate is it?*

Box 1.2   Role Repertory Grid

The Role Repertory Grid is method of finding out what people think about things, such as selection procedures, or the nature of work (Chapter 3), that seeks to dig a little deeper than simply asking *Do you use interviews to select, if so why?* HR people are given a list of selection methods, and asked to consider them in sets of three at a time, for example interview, reference and personality questionnaire. They are then asked to say which two differ from the third, for example PQ differs from interview and reference. They then have to say *how* they differ, to which one answer might be that interviews and obtaining references are traditional ways of selecting staff while PQs are a recent invention. This is repeated, with different sets of three selection methods up to 20 times. Respondents are usually forbidden to give the same reason twice, and are usually asked to apply the distinction they have drawn, for example *traditional/recent invention*, to all the other selection methods in the list. The Repertory Grid method is intended to discover the person's own conceptual framework for thinking about selection, rather than to impose the researcher's.

König, Jöri and Knüsel (2011) use the Repertory Grid method (Box 1.2) to uncover ideas about 11 selection methods in 40 Swiss HR practitioners. Some of their distinctions are purely descriptive, even practical: *spoken* vs *written; need to bring in outside people to do it* vs *can do it ourselves.* Other distinctions show a concern with the nature of the information: *candidate's view of him/ herself* vs *other people's view of candidate.* Things the work psychologist might think very important were mentioned by only a few HR people: five of the 40 mentioned validity, while only four mentioned fakability. Most surprising perhaps are the things not one of the 40 mentioned: law, applicant reaction, or cost. Koenig *et al.* speculate (their word) that Swiss HR may be unconcerned about cost because of a 'generally good economic situation', and less worried about legal problems because Switzerland is 'relatively free of legal pressure'. Eleven of the 40 viewed selection methods in terms of *the present* vs *long-term axis into the past.* Koenig *et al.* suggest some may be influenced by psychoanalysis. As Koenig *et al.* note, there is much scope for more research here.

Asking applicants

All the surveys discussed so far ask HR how they select. Billsberry (2007) presents 52 UK accounts of selection procedures by those on the receiving end. The accounts amply confirm the hypothesis that some of the 80% of employers who do not reply to surveys have something to hide. Applicants describe rudeness, unprofessional behaviour, blatant lying, obvious bias, and sexual harassment. The most generally favoured form of assessment seems to be the interview, often conducted very incompetently. Billsberry's data suggest that a large survey of job applicants is an urgent necessity to find how many employers are behaving badly towards applicants.

RESEARCH AGENDA

- Employers' reasons for choosing selection methods, and more use of repertory grid methods.
- Information from applicants about use of selection methods.

KEY POINTS

In Chapter 1 you have learned the following:

- Employees vary greatly in value so selection matters.
- How employees are recruited may be linked to turnover.
- Deciding which application to proceed with and which to reject is called sifting and is often done inefficiently or unfairly.
- Sifting can be improved by T&E ratings, and careful setting of minimum qualifications.
- Conventional paper application methods can be improved.
- The Internet may greatly change the application process.
- Sifting software is something of an unknown quantity.
- Selection uses a range of tests to assess a range of attributes.
- Information used in selection divides into five main types.
- Selection methods must conform with fair employment legislation.
- The problem with fair employment is not deliberate or direct discrimination, but adverse impact meaning the method results in fewer women or minority persons being successful. Adverse impact will create problems for the employer so should be avoided if possible.
- Selection in developed countries follows broadly similar patterns, with some local variations.

KEY REFERENCES

Agerström *et al.* (2012) describe possible unconscious bias against overweight applicants in Swedish HR staff.

Bertrand & Mullainathan (2004) describe discrimination in selection in the USA.

Billsberry (2007) presents 52 accounts of how applicants experienced selection.

Buster *et al.* (2005) describe a system for setting minimum qualifications.

Davison & Burke (2000) review research on gender bias in application sifting.

König *et al.* (2011) analyse thinking about selection methods in Swiss HR personnel.

McKinney *et al.* (2003) describe how information on college grades is used in sifting.

Ng & Feldman (2012) analyse six common stereotypes of older employees.

Stone *et al.* (2013) review research on electronic selection and recruitment systems.

USEFUL WEBSITES

checkpast.com. A (US) background checking agency.
zerochaos.com. Another (US) background checking agency.
hrzone.com. Offers advice on range of HR issues in the USA.
incomesdata.co.uk. Income Data Services, a UK company that reports interesting research on HR issues, including survey of selection tests.
siop.org. (US) Society for Industrial and Organizational Psychology, includes details of conferences, and The Industrial/Organizational Psychologist.

CHAPTER 2

Validity of selection methods

How do you know it works?

Assessment methods need themselves to be assessed, against six main criteria; an assessment should be:

- *reliable*   giving a consistent account of applicants (As)
- *valid*   selecting good As and rejecting poor ones
- *fair*   complying with equal opportunities legislation
- *acceptable*   to As as well as the organization
- *cost-effective*   saving the organization more than it costs to use
- *easy to use*   fitting conveniently into the selection process

Selection methods do not automatically possess all these qualities; research is needed to show which possess what. Few assessment methods meet all six criteria so choice of assessment is always a compromise. Chapter 15 will offer an overview.

RELIABILITY

Reliability means consistency. Physical measurements for example, the dimensions of a chair, are usually so reliable their consistency is taken for granted. Most selection assessments are less consistent. At their worst they may be so inconsistent that they convey little or no information. Several different sorts of reliability are used in selection research.

1. *Retest reliability* compares two sets of scores obtained from the same people, on two occasions, typically a month or so apart. The scores may be interview ratings, or ability test scores, or personality questionnaire profiles. If the test assesses an enduring aspect of applicants, as selection tests are meant to, the two sets of information ought to be fairly similar. Reliability is usually given as a correlation (Box 2.1). Retest reliability is also calculated for work performance measures, such as monthly sales figures, or supervisor ratings. These too ought to be fairly consistent month by month.

Personnel Selection: Adding Value Through People – A Changing Picture,
Sixth Edition. Mark Cook.

Box 2.1   Correlation

Height and weight are correlated; tall people usually weigh more than short people, and heavy people are usually taller than light people. Height and weight are not perfectly correlated; there are plenty of short fat and tall thin exceptions to the rule. (Figure 2.1).

The correlation coefficient summarizes how closely two measures like height and weight go together. A perfect one-to-one correlation gives a value of +1.00. If two measures are completely unrelated, the correlation is zero – 0.00. Sometimes two measures are inversely, or negatively, correlated: the older people are, the less fleet of foot they (generally) are.

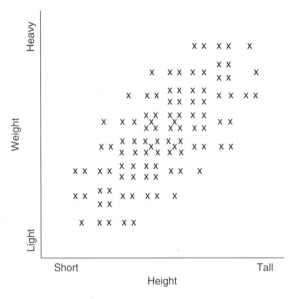

Figure 2.1   Height plotted against weight, showing a positive correlation of 0.75.

2. *Inter-rater reliability* is calculated by comparing ratings given by two assessors for people they have both interviewed, or both supervised at work. If the assessors do not agree, one at least of them must be wrong, but which? Inter-rater reliability should be calculated from ratings that have not been discussed (a requirement not likely to be met in the case of real supervisor ratings in real organizations).

Box 2.2   Split half reliability

The test is divided in two, each half scored separately and the two halves correlated, across a large sample. If the test is too short, the halves will not correlate well. The usual way of splitting the test is to separate odd-numbered items from even numbered.

3. *Internal consistency reliability*. Psychological tests usually have a dozen or more component questions or 'items'. Internal consistency reliability checks whether all questions are measuring the same thing. Suppose a personality test asks 10 questions each of which actually assesses a different trait. Calculating a score from the 10 questions will generate a meaningless number. Internal consistency reliability for this 'test' will give a value near zero. The same will happen if a test consists largely of questions that do not assess anything at all. One reason why employers should avoid 'home-made' tests is the risk of finding they do not measure anything. Poor internal consistency reliability can also mean the test is too short. Earlier research used split half reliability (Box 2.2), but modern research uses the alpha coefficient (Box 2.3).

Box 2.3   Alpha coefficient

Based on examining the contribution of every item of the test to the total score. Mathematically equivalent to the average of every possible split half reliability. This procedure gives a coefficient that does not vary according to how the test is split.

Retest reliability requires the same people to do the test twice, whereas internal consistency reliability can be computed from a single set of data. Hence internal consistency data are more popular with test publishers. However the two types of reliability provide different sorts of information about the test, so are not really interchangeable. Where supervisor ratings have more than one scale, covering more than one aspect of work performance, internal consistency reliability can be calculated, and is considerably higher than inter-rater reliability.

Box 2.4   Standard deviation

The standard deviation does two things: (1) it describes how one person compares with other, and (2) it summarizes the variability of the whole distribution. Standard deviation is usually abbreviated to SD.

A distribution is completely summarized by its mean and SD, so long as it is normal, i.e. bell-shaped and symmetrical. (Distributions of some natural scores, like height, are normal; distributions of constructed scores, like IQs, are made normal.)

The SD can be used to describe someone's height, without reference to any particular system of measurement. A man 6'2" high is 2 SDs above the mean. Anyone who understands statistics will know how tall that is, be the local units of height metres, feet and inches, or cubits.

Error of measurement

A simple formula based on reliability and standard deviation (Box 2.4) of scores gives the test's error of measurement, which estimates how much test scores might vary on retest (Box 2.5). An 'IQ' test with a retest reliability of

0.90 has an error of measurement of five IQ points, meaning one in three retests will vary by five or more points, so clearly it would be a mistake for Smith who scores IQ 119 to regard himself as superior to Jones who scores 118. If they take the test again a month later, Smith might score 116 and Jones 121. One of many reasons psychologists avoid using IQs is they tend to create a false sense of precision. One reason untrained people should not use psychological tests is they tend not to understand error of measurement.

Box 2.5   Standard error of measurement (s.e.m.)

s.e.m is calculated by the simple formula SD X $\sqrt{(1-r)}$, where SD is the standard deviation of test scores, and r is the test's reliability.

VALIDITY

A valid selection method is one that measures what it claims to measure, that predicts something useful, one that works. A valid test is based on research and development. Anyone can string together 20 questions about accepting diversity; it takes patient research, studying large groups of people, collecting follow-up data, to turn the list of questions into a valid selection test. Up to 11 different types of validity can be distinguished (Table 2.1). They differ in convincingness, suitability for different sample sizes, legal acceptability, and their centrality to selection.

Table 2.1   Core and marginal types of validity in selection research.

Core types of validity in selection	
Criterion	Test predicts work performance.
Content	Test looks plausible to experts.
Construct	Test measures something meaningful/important.
Convergent/divergent	Tests that 'should' correlate do correlate, while tests that 'should not' correlate do not.
Cross validation	Test predicts work performance in two separate samples.
Incremental	Test measures something not already measured.
Differential	Test predicts better for one class of person than another.
Synthetic	Tests measure component traits and abilities that predict work performance (covered in Chapter 3).

Marginal types of validity in selection	
Face	Test looks plausible.
Factorial	Test measures five separate things.
Mythical	People think research has shown the test is valid.

CRITERION VALIDITY

The test predicts productivity. Nearly 100 years ago Link (1918) published the first selection validation study, for American munitions workers, using a battery of nine tests. The most successful test, the Woodworth Wells Cancellation test, correlated very well – 0.63 – with a month's production figures for 52 munitions inspectors. Criterion validation looks for evidence that people who score highly on the test are more productive, no matter what the test is called, what the questions are, how they are selected, or how plausible the test looks. What matters is predicting the criterion – work performance. Since 1918 thousands of similar studies have been reported: early validation research was summarized by Super and Crites (1962). Criterion validity has two main forms: predictive and concurrent.

- *Predictive validity.* The test predicts who *will* produce more. This parallels real-life selection: HR select today, and find out later if their decisions were correct.
- *Concurrent validity.* The test 'predicts' who *is* producing more. Test and work performance data are collected at the same time, i.e. concurrently. Also referred to as present employee validity.

Concurrent validation is much quicker and easier than predictive validation, because there is no need to wait for the outcome. Consequently a lot of validation research is concurrent. Fifty years ago Guion (1965) said the 'present employee method is clearly a violation of scientific principles'. Morgeson *et al.* (2007) agree: 'only studies that use a predictive model with actual job applicants should be used to support the use of personality in personnel selection'. Concurrent validation has three possible problems, and one possible advantage.

Problem 1 – missing persons In concurrent studies, people who have left or who were dismissed are not available for study. Nor are people who proved so good they have been promoted, or left for a better job somewhere else. In concurrent validation both ends of the distribution of performance may be missing, which may restrict range and reduce the validity correlation (see page 44). Roth and Huffcutt (2013) say data on this type of attrition are 'seldom, if ever, reported in primary studies'.

Problem 2 – unrepresentative samples Present employees may not be typical of applicants, actual or possible. The workforce may be all white and/or all-male when As include, or ought to include, women and minorities.

Problem 3 – direction of cause Present employees may have changed to meet the job's demands. They may have been trained to meet the job's demands. So it may be trivial to find present successful managers are dominant, because managers learn to command influence and respect, whereas showing dominant

As become good managers proves dominance matters. This is a particular problem with personality, but could affect abilities as well. Would 10 years spent doing numerical or financial analysis work produce an increase in scores on a numerical ability test? Lay opinion tends to say Yes. Test constructors assume the answer is No.

Advantage – avoiding faking Present employees may be less likely to fake PQs and other self-reports than applicants, because they already have the job and so have less need to describe themselves as better than they are. Chapter 7 looks at predictive and concurrent validity for PQs.

The applicant/present employee distinction is also important when analysing adverse impact. Finding no difference in test scores between white and non-white present employees can look like 'good news', but can be very misleading if more low scoring non-white persons have been excluded at the application stage. Roth, Buster and Bobko (2011) complain that analyses of adverse impact sometimes take no account of whether people are present employees or true applicants, which might be termed the *Bobko–Roth fallacy*.

Selective reporting and 'fishing expeditions'

Psychologists have traditionally relied on tests of statistical significance to evaluate research. A result that could arise by chance more often than one time in 20 is disregarded, whereas one that could only be found by chance one time in 100 is regarded as a real difference, or a real correlation. However this system can be misleading, and can sometimes be used to mislead. Suppose research is using the 16PF personality questionnaire, and 10 supervisor ratings of work performance. This will generate 160 correlations. Suppose eight correlations are 'significant' at the 5% level, i.e. larger than would arise by chance one time in 20. Researchers should conclude they have found no more 'significant' correlations that would be expected by chance, given so many have been calculated. But researchers have been known to generate plausible explanations of the link between, for example, 16PF dominance and supervisor rating of politeness, and add their results to the 16PF literature. This is called a 'fishing expedition'; it would usually be rejected by a refereed journal, but might be cited by, for example, a test publisher as evidence of validity. Unscrupulous researchers have also been known to omit tests or outcomes that failed to 'get results', to make the research look more focused.

Box 2.6   Variance

Variance refers to the variability of data. Workers vary in how good their work is. The aim of selection to predict as much of this variation as possible. Variance is computed as the square of the standard deviation.

Effect size

Wiesner and Cronshaw's (1988) review reported a correlation of 0.11 between the traditional selection interview and work performance. What does a correlation of 0.11 mean? Correlations can be interpreted by calculating how much variance they account for, by squaring and converting to a percentage: $0.11^2 = 0.01$, i.e. 1% of the variance (Box 2.6) in later work performance. The other 99% remains unaccounted for. This type of interview does not tell the employer much about how employees will turn out.

The 0.30 barrier?

Critics of psychological testing argue that tests rarely correlate with 'real-world' outcomes, such as work performance, better than 0.30. The intended implication is that tests are not very useful. Critics seem to have chosen 0.30 because a 0.30 correlation accounts for just under 10% of the variance. Harpe (2008) notes that in the USA the principal fair employment agency, the Equal Employment Opportunities Commission, tends to consider a correlation below 0.30 as failing to establish validity, which certainly makes 0.30 a barrier for American employers. The very largest correlations obtainable in practice in selection research (0.50 to 0.60) account for only a quarter to a third of the variance in performance. It may not be realistic to expect more than 0.50 or 0.60. Performance at work is influenced by many other factors – management, organizational climate, co-workers, economic climate, the working environment – besides the assessable characteristics of the individual worker. Sulea *et al.* (2013) report Romanian data that illustrate this point. They find that personality tests give a modest prediction (0.14–0.24) of whether employees will engage in counterproductive work behaviour (CWB), ranging from taking two minutes' extra tea break to sabotaging machinery. However, a far more important correlate of CWB turns out to be 'abusive supervision' (bullying, ridiculing, unfairness, etc.) which correlates 0.46.

The *d* statistic

The *d* statistic describes the size of a difference between groups of people. Chapter 1 (page 3) noted there is a small difference in work performance between employees recruited informally by word of mouth and those recruited formally through press advertisement. The *d* statistic computes how many SDs separate the means. For informal vs. formal recruitment, *d* is 0.08, meaning less than a tenth of an SD separates the averages, so the difference is not very great. Very small effect sizes, such as a correlation of 0.11, or *d* statistic of 0.08, mean the selection or recruitment procedure does not make much difference. This tends to be a reason to look for something better. However, it can sometimes be worth using something that achieves only modest results; informal recruiting only makes a small difference in subsequent output but this improvement is achieved very easily and cheaply, and can mount up across a lot of vacancies filled. (But recall also from Chapter 1 that fair employment agencies generally disapprove of informal recruiting.)

CONTENT VALIDITY

The test looks plausible to experts. Experts analyse the job, choose relevant questions, and put together the test. Content validation was borrowed from educational testing, where it makes sense to ask if a test covers the curriculum, and to seek answers from *subject matter experts*. Content validation regards test items as *samples* of things employees need to know, not as *signs* of what employees are like. Devising a content valid test for firefighters might have three stages.

1. An expert panel, of experienced firefighters, assisted by HR and psychologists, write an initial pool of test items – things firefighters need to know, for example, *Which of these materials generate toxic gases when burning?* or be able to do, for example, *Connect fire appliance to fire hydrant.*
2. Items are rated by a second expert panel for how often the problem arises or the task is performed, and for how essential it is.
3. The final set of knowledge and skill items are rewritten in a five-point rating format for example, *Connect fire appliance to fire hydrant. 5 (high) quickly and accurately assembles all components … 1 (low) fails entirely to assemble components correctly.*

Content validation has several advantages: it is plausible to applicants, and easy to defend because it ensures the selection test is clearly related to the job. It does not require a large sample of people presently doing the job, unlike criterion validity. Content validation also has limitations. It is only suitable for jobs with a limited number of fairly specific tasks. Because it requires people to possess particular skills or knowledge, it is more likely to be suitable for promotion than for selection. Content validity is subordinate to criterion validity. Content validation is a way of writing a test that ought to work. The organization should also carry out criterion validation to check that it really does.

CONSTRUCT VALIDITY

The test measures something meaningful. When a new selection system is devised, people sometimes ask themselves 'What is this assessing? What sort of person will get a good mark from it?' One answer should always be 'People who will do the job well.' But it is worth going a bit deeper and trying to get some picture of what particular aspects of applicants the test is assessing: abilities, personality, social background, specific skills, etc. There are several reasons why it is important to explore construct validity:

- If a new test is mostly assessing personality, and HR already use a personality test, HR may well find the new test is not adding much. The new test may not be called a personality test; it may be labelled emotional intelligence or sales aptitude.

- If a two-day assessment centre measures the same thing as a 30-minute ability test, it would be much cheaper to use the 30-minute test.
- If the new test turns out to be mostly assessing mental ability, HR will be alerted to the possibility of adverse impact on certain groups.
- If As complain about selection methods, and HR have to defend them in court, HR may want to be able to say exactly what the test assesses, and what it does not. They may be made to look very silly if they cannot do this.

Construct validity is usually assessed by comparing one selection method for example, interview ratings, with other methods for example, psychological tests. Construct validity reveals what a method is actually assessing (which is not necessarily what it is intended to assess). For example, the traditional unstructured interview turns out to be assessing mental ability to a surprising extent (Chapter 4).

CONVERGENT/DIVERGENT VALIDITY

Assessment centres (ACs) (Chapter 10) seek to assess people on a number of dimensions for example, problem-solving ability, influence, and empathy, through a series of exercises; for example, group discussion and presentation. Figure 2.2 illustrates three types of correlations:

- Those at AAA are for the same dimension, assessed in different exercises, which 'ought' to be high; this is *convergent validity*.
- Those at bbb are for different dimensions, assessed in the same exercise, which 'ought' to be lower; this is *discriminant validity*. (They need not be zero, because the dimensions may be correlated.)
- Those at ccc are for different attributes, assessed in different exercises, which 'ought' to be very low or zero.

	A - group discussion			B - presentation		
Dimensions	1	2	3	1	2	3
A-group discussion						
1 - influence						
2 - empathy	bbb					
3 - planning	bbb	bbb				
B - presentation						
1 - influence	AAA	ccc	ccc			
2 - empathy	ccc	AAA	ccc	bbb		
3 - planning	ccc	ccc	AAA	bbb	bbb	

Figure 2.2 Three types of correlation in an assessment centre with three dimensions (1 to 3) rated in each of two exercises (A and B).

In AC research in particular, and in selection research in general, it often turns out that both convergent and divergent validity are low. Low convergent validity means that different measures of the same dimension do not correlate: influence measured by PQ does not correlate with influence assessed by group discussion, which implies one or other measure is not working, or that something complex and unexpected is happening. Low divergent validity means that a test intended to measure several conceptually different dimensions is failing to differentiate them, and that all the scores derived from, for example, a group discussion are highly correlated.

Method vs construct

The same distinction – *how* versus *what* – applies to other selection tests, but under a different name: *method* (how) and *construct* (what). Arthur and Villado (2008) suggest these are often confused, but should be clearly distinguished. Some accounts talk about the usefulness of 'the interview', or 'the assessment centre', which Arthur and Villado consider a serious mistake because interview and assessment centre are methods that can be used to assess all sorts of different constructs: ability, personality, social skill, knowledge of accounting, ability to deceive, etc. The method–construct confusion is made in discussions of validity, adverse impact, and acceptability of methods to candidates. It is true that meta-analytic league tables of selection test validity since Hunter and Hunter (1984) have often presented a single value for 'the validity' of, for example, the assessment centre (AC), without any reference to what the AC is intended to assess. Arthur and Villado suggest differing estimates of AC validity offered in five successive analyses, starting with Hunter and Hunter (1984), may reflect this. Some methods are more all-purpose than others; interviews can be used to assess almost anything, but mental ability tests assess only mental ability (general, specific, verbal or non-verbal etc.). Some constructs are usually assessed by only one method: personality by questionnaire for example. Later sections of this book will consider alternative methods, when the 'standard' method seems to have a lot of problems.

CROSS-VALIDATION

This means checking the validity of a test a second time, on a second sample. Cross-validation is always desirable, but it becomes absolutely essential for methods likely to capitalize on chance, such as personality questionnaires that generate a lot of scores, and empirically keyed biodata (Chapter 9). Locke (1961) gave a very striking demonstration of the hazards of not cross-validating: he found students with long surnames (7+ letters) were less charming, happy-go-lucky, and impulsive, liked vodka, but did not smoke, and had more fillings in their teeth. Locke's results sound quite plausible, in places, but all arose by chance, and all vanished on cross-validation.

INCREMENTAL VALIDITY

A selection test for example, a reference, may not be very accurate in itself, but it may improve the prediction made by other methods, perhaps by covering aspects of work performance that other selection methods fail to cover. On the other hand, a method with good validity, such a job knowledge test, may add little to selection by mental ability test, because job knowledge and mental ability tests are highly correlated, so cover the same ground.

Figure 2.3 illustrates incremental validity, showing two predictors, and an outcome, work performance. Where the predictor circles overlap the outcome circle, the tests are achieving validity. In Figure 2.3a, the two predictors – mental ability test and reference – do not correlate much, so their circles do not overlap much, whereas in Figure 2.3b the two predictors – job knowledge and mental ability – are highly correlated, so their circles overlap a lot. Note the effect on the overlap between predictor and outcome circles. In Figure 2.3a the predictors explain more of the outcome, whereas in Figure 2.3b they explain less, because they both cover the same ground.

Incremental validity is very important when assembling a set of selection tests; it is too easy otherwise to find the selection procedure is measuring the same thing over and over again. Incremental validity needs data on the

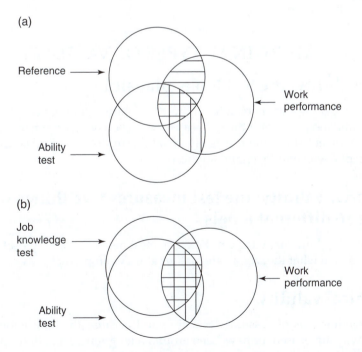

Figure 2.3 Schematic representation of the relationship between two predictors, e.g. mental ability test and interview, and work performance, where (a) the predictors are not highly correlated and (b) they are highly correlated.

intercorrelation of selection tests, which is very patchy in its coverage. Sometimes there is a lot – for example, mental ability tests and interviews; sometimes there is hardly any – for example, references. Schmidt and Hunter (1998) offered estimates of the correlation between mental ability and other tests, and of likely incremental validity, discussed in Chapter 14.

DIFFERENTIAL VALIDITY

This means the test works better for one group of people than another, for example that it predicts work performance in men better than in women. This is something personnel selection absolutely does not want; differential validity could make a test unusable in selection. It has been supposed that differential validity does not occur: Schmidt and Hunter (1998) said emphatically that '85 years of research had shown no differential validity by race or sex', that differential validity in selection is *not a problem*. However recently the issue has resurfaced: the evidence is discussed in Chapter 13. Note the distinction between *adverse impact* and *differential validity*. Adverse impact means one section of the population for example men, score higher on a test for example physical strength. Differential validity would mean strength predicts work performance for men, but not for women, or not as well for women. This has happened in British military research (Rayson, Holliman & Belyavin, 2000) described in Chapter 11.

MARGINAL TYPES OF VALIDITY

Face validity: the test looks plausible

Some people are persuaded a test measures dominance, if it is called 'Dominance Test', or if the items all concern behaving dominantly. Face validity does not show the test really is valid, but does help make the test more acceptable to employer and applicants.

Factorial validity: the test measures five things but gives them 16 different labels

Knowing how many factors (Box 2.7) a test measures is very useful, but does not reveal what the factors are, nor what they can predict.

Mythical validity

Sometimes people assume tests are valid because they are widely used, or heavily advertised, or have been around a long time. Sometimes people think validity data are better than they really are, because research evidence is not very accessible, or is seldom or never read. Zeidner, Matthews and Roberts (2004) say Goleman (1995) describes a study at Bell Laboratory showing that

Box 2.7   Factor analysis

Table 2.2 shows (fictitious) correlations between performance on six typical school subjects, in a large sample. The correlations between English, French and German are all fairly high; people who are good at one tend to be good at the others. Similarly the correlations between Maths, Physics, and Chemistry are fairly high. However correlations between subjects in different sets – e. g. English × Physics – are much lower. All of which suggests that people who are good at one language tend to be good at another, while people who are good at one science are good at another. There are six school subjects, but only two underlying abilities.

Table 2.2   (Fictitious) correlations between school subject marks.

	Maths	Physics	Chemistry	English	French
Maths					
Physics	0.67				
Chemistry	0.76	0.55			
English	0.33	0.23	0.25		
French	0.23	0.31	0.30	0.77	
German	0.11	0.21	0.22	0.80	0.67

top performers were higher on emotional intelligence (EI); subsequently this study has been widely quoted as showing the value of EI. However 'careful reading of the original shows this is pure conjecture – Bell Laboratory engineers were never actually tested with any instrument designed to assess EI' – a classic example of mythical validity.

META-ANALYSIS

For some selection methods, hundreds of validity studies had accumulated by the 1960s. This created problems in summarizing and interpreting research, especially when studies gave inconsistent results. It proved difficult at first to answer the apparently simple question: does it work?

Narrative reviews

Earlier reviews of selection research did not use any quantitative means of summarizing research. They often failed to enlighten because they first listed 10 studies that find that interviews do predict job performance, then listed 10 studies that find they do not, and finished by listing 20 studies that are inconclusive. Readers typically react by exclaiming 'Do interviews work or

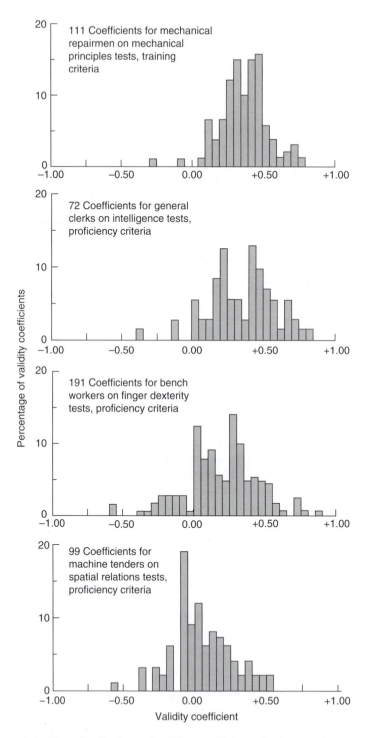

Figure 2.4 Four distributions of validity coefficients, for four combinations of test and criterion (Ghiselli, 1966b). Reproduced with permission of John Wiley & Sons, Inc.

not? The psychologists don't seem able to make up their minds!' At their worst narrative reviews can be exercises in preconception: reviewers read into the research whatever conclusions they want to find.

Meta-analysis

Meta-analysis pools the results of many different researches, and generates a single numerical estimate of link between selection test and work performance, usually average correlation, weighted by sample size (because research based on 1,000 persons carries more weight than research based on 50 persons). Ghiselli (1966b, 1973) collated hundreds of validity coefficients for mental ability tests, classified by test type, job type, and measure of work performance; Figure 2.4 presents his distributions of validities for four test–job combinations. These days meta-analyses are usually presented as tables, as in Table 2.3, where k is the number of correlations, and r is the average correlation. Current meta-analyses also give N, the total pooled sample size, but Ghiselli's pioneering meta-analysis did not include this information.

Meta-analysis proved a very useful development in selection research. Large bodies of research could be summarized in a single overall validity. Meta-analysis sometimes found fairly encouraging results; average validity for some selection methods turned out to be greater than zero, despite the many 'negative' results. Meta-analysis could generate 'league tables' of selection validity. One of the first, by Hunter and Hunter (1984), concluded that mental ability tests achieved good validity, whereas the conventional unstructured interview achieved very poor validity.

Moderator variables

Suppose a test had good validity for men, but poor validity for women, i.e. differential validity. Pooling data from men and women might conceal this important fact. Meta-analysis can code every correlation for any variable that might be relevant, and for which there are enough studies to allow a comparison. So if gender is important, moderator variable analysis could discover this.

Table 2.3 Ghiselli's (1973) meta-analysis of ability test validity.

Job	Mechanical repair worker	Bench worker	Clerk	Machine tender
Test	Mechanical principles	Finger dexterity	General mental ability	Spatial relations
1. k – number of validities	114	191	72	99
2. N – total sample size	Not reported	Not reported	Not reported	Not reported
3. r – average validity	0.39	0.25	0.36	0.11

PROBLEMS WITH META-ANALYSIS

Meta-analysis first appeared, in as many as four places more or less simultaneously, in the 1970s. The idea of averaging across different researches had occurred to people before then, but had been dismissed on the 'chalk and cheese' argument: that pooling results from different tests, or different workforces, or different work performance measures was wrong. Critics still argue that combining different measures can be a mistake: Hogan and Holland (2003) argue that meta-analysis pools good personality measures with poor, which may obscure the former's contribution. Hogan also notes that different measures of conscientiousness are based on different concepts of conscientiousness, so it is misleading to pool them.

Quality not quantity?

Early critics of meta-analysis argued it would be better to base conclusions on a smaller number of high-quality researches, not on averaging a larger number of poorly conducted studies. A first problem is that ratings of research quality are very unreliable, so identifying the high-quality studies might be difficult. A second problem might be that setting very high standards for selection research could leave too few studies to conduct a meta-analysis, given the practical difficulties and consequent necessary compromises.

Disagreement

Table 2.4 summarizes four meta-analyses of the same relationship, between mental ability and interview ratings. The four analyses reach four different conclusions:

- The more structured the interview, the less it correlates with mental ability (Huffcutt, Roth & McDaniel, 1996).
- The more structured the interview, the more it correlates with mental ability (Cortina *et al.*, 2000).
- There is not much difference between structured and unstructured interviews, in terms of correlation with mental ability (Salgado & Moscoso, 2002).
- The correlation between MA and interview rating is much higher for medium-structure interviews than for high- or low-structure interviews (Berry, Sackett, & Landers, 2007).

How can four analyses of the same data reach four different conclusions? Inspection of the k values in Table 2.4 reveals that the first three analyses did not in fact analyse the same data. The three earlier analyses collectively find 102 relevant studies, but two-thirds of these included in only one meta-analysis, while only 10% are included in all three. The three earlier analyses are effectively of three largely different sets of research data. Why? Seventeen studies were not published until after Huffcutt *et al.*'s analysis. Salgado and Moscoso appear to have found more researches on unstructured interviews partly by including European studies the other reviews

Table 2.4 Summary of four meta-analyses of the correlation between interview and mental ability.

Interview structure						
Huffcutt	Low		Medium		High	
Salgado	Conventional		Level 2		Behaviour	
Cortina	Level 1		Medium		Levels 3 & 4	
Berry	Low				High	
	k	r	k	r	k	r
Huffcutt	8	0.30	19	0.25	22	0.23
Salgado	53	0.20			22	0.14
Cortina	3	0.04	8	0.20	10	0.22
Berry	3	0.14	6	0.38	27	0.16

Data from Huffcutt et al. (1996), Salgado & Moscoso (2002), Cortina et al. (2000), and Berry et al. (2007). k = number of correlations; r = average correlation.

overlooked, partly by including research on student admissions the others did not consider relevant. Otherwise the reason for the differences in coverage and conclusions is unclear. The fourth and most recent analysis (Berry et al.) was intentionally much more selective: they excluded any research where interviewers had, or might have had, access to the MA test data, so might have allowed it to influence their rating, which would make a correlation fairly uninteresting. Note that this exclusion greatly reduced the number of studies of unstructured interviews that could be included in the meta-analysis.

Reporting bias

Do meta-analyses of selection research overestimate average validity by leaving out studies that find selection methods do not work? Reporting bias covers a range of possibilities, from researchers losing interest in a project that is not coming up with 'good' results, through the notorious difficulty of getting journals to publish 'negative' results, to the deliberate suppression of inconvenient findings. This issue seems to interest academics more than practitioners, but a few findings are worth a mention.

- Russell et al. (1994) showed that researches reported by academics find lower average validity than researches reported by authors employed in private industry, possibly because academics have less vested interest in showing that tests 'work'.
- Ferguson and Brannick (2012) note that many meta-analyses say that enquiries were made to identify unpublished studies, but also note that meta-analyses often do not seem to find very many, although a higher than expected proportion were very easy to find because they were written by the author of the meta-analysis. Ferguson and Brannick suggest the search

for unpublished research seems something of a ritual, and possibly not very effective.

- Some research is very easy to find: it is published in academic journals like *Personnel Psychology* and instantly available, fully indexed, in databases like *Psychinfo*. Other research is called the *grey literature*: journals in other languages, chapters in edited books, doctoral and master's theses, US government and military research reports, other employers' reports, conference papers, test publishers' research data, and unpublished research reports. The meta-analyst must learn of the research's existence, then secure a copy, and finally perhaps get it translated.
- One final hurdle has recently become apparent. The meta-analyst who has a physical copy of the research report in his/her hands may find lawyers for the publishers of the test telling them they do not have permission to include it in the meta-analysis (van Iddekinge *et al.*, 2012b).
- Kepes, Banks and Oh (2014) examine four meta-analyses, and find evidence of publication bias in three, including one on assessment centre validity, and one on the role of experience in predicting work performance.

Identifying reporting bias

Checks on reporting bias have been devised, based on plotting correlation against sample size in a *funnel plot*. The smaller the sample, the more the correlation will vary by chance, so the wider the spread of correlation size. Figure 2.5 shows three funnel plots. The area of interest is correlation based on smaller samples, where more sampling error is found, and where a lot of selection research is also to be found. Correlations based on smaller samples should be found evenly spaced about the funnel plot, as in the lower part of Figure 2.5a. Sometimes however, these correlations are not evenly spaced, but bunched to one side, as in Figure 2.5b, where there are more correlations in the 0.20 plus region, and fewer in the zero region. This suggests some correlations below 0.20 have somehow been overlooked. Duval's (2005) *trim and fill* procedure first estimates how many correlations are 'missing', and then calculates what the overall validity for the meta-analysis would be if the missing correlations existed to be included. Figure 2.5c shows presumed missing values that have been added. Trim and fill has found some evidence of reporting bias in selection research, for personality questionnaires and mental ability tests (McDaniel, Rothstein & Whetzel, 2006a; Pollack & McDaniel, 2008), structured interviews (Duval, 2005), and ethnicity differences in work performance (McDaniel, McKay & Rothstein, 2006b). McDaniel *et al.* (2006a) note that most earlier meta-analyses of selection research did not check for reporting bias, and suggest they should all be re-analysed. Reporting bias was previously assessed by the *File Drawer* statistic, which calculated how many unknown researches with negative results would need to be reposing in researchers' file drawers to reduce a given meta-analytic correlation to insignificance: the answer typically being in the order of hundreds or thousands convinced everyone that reporting bias was *not a problem*.

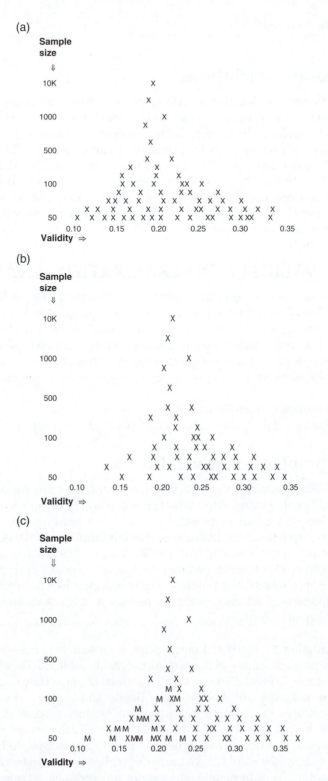

Figure 2.5 Three funnel plots, of sample size and correlation. The Xs show the actual distribution of correlations in the meta-analysis. In Figure 2.5c the Ms show the presumed missing values, according to trim and fill analysis.

Premature conclusions

McDaniel (McDaniel *et al.*, 2006a) suggests that publication of a major meta-analysis, for example his own on interview research in 1994 (McDaniel *et al.*, 1994), tends to discourage further research in the area. If 140 researches on interview validity show that structured interviews work better than unstructured interviews, what is the point of carrying out a 141st study and how will it advance the career of the researcher who does it? If the meta-analysis reached sound conclusions, further research may not be needed. But if the meta-analysis is vitiated by reporting bias, or some other deficiency, then its conclusions may be premature.

VALIDITY GENERALIZATION ANALYSIS

Ghiselli (1966b) found the results of his 1966 meta-analysis disappointing: 'A confirmed pessimist at best, even I was surprised at the variation in findings concerning a particular test applied to workers on a particular job. We certainly never expected the repetition of an investigation to give the same results as the original. But we never anticipated them to be worlds apart.' Ghiselli identified two problems, both very worrying from the selector's point of view:

* Problem 1 – validity was low.
* Problem 2 – validity varied a lot from study to study.

First problem – low validity

Ghiselli's distributions of validity had averages of around 0.30 at best, which made people start asking whether it was worth using tests that contributed so little information, especially when they were getting very unpopular, and starting to meet difficulties with fair employment laws. Like other early meta-analyses, Ghiselli had analysed raw correlations, between test and outcome. Raw correlations may be low because test and work performance are not closely related, but they may only appear low through two well-known limitations of selection research: restricted range, and unreliability of work performance measures.

Limitation 1 – restricted range Suppose researchers examine running speed and physical fitness in a group of university athletes. They might get results like those in Figure 2.6a – a very weak relationship. They might then conclude there is hardly any link between fitness and running speed, so that using fitness tests to select athletes would not be very successful. This would be a mistake, because it overlooks the fact that all athletes are physically fit and most can run fast. If researchers widened their sample to include all 18–22-year-olds, they would find a much clearer link, shown in Figure 2.6b. Including lots of not very fit people who cannot run very fast reveals the true relationship. In technical terms, in Figure 2.6a *range* of fitness is *restricted*. Restricted

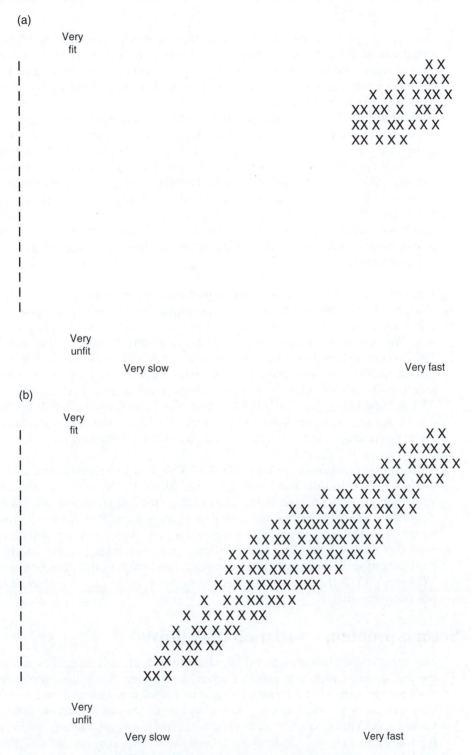

Figure 2.6 Fictitious data illustrating restriction of range, in data on the correlation between fitness and running speed.

range greatly reduces the correlation, and may conceal it altogether. Restricted range almost always happens in personnel selection, because only successful As can contribute work performance data. The researcher never knows what the work performance of unsuccessful As would be like, because they never get the chance to try the job.

There are two ways of dealing with the restricted range problem. The first is *assess all and employ all*, so as to get work performance data from everyone. This is very expensive, and can be very risky, so is rarely used. During the Second World War, the US Air Force did send a large unselected sample through pilot training, enabling Flanagan (1946) to calculate validity without restriction of range. The failure rate was high, at 77%, but so was the correlation between test scores and success, at 0.64. The other solution is easier, safer, and very widely used: *statistical correction*. A simple formula allows the researcher to 'correct' the raw correlation for restriction of range, which usually increases it.

Limitation 2 – unreliability of work performance measure Every validity study needs an index of successful work performance (discussed in Chapter 12). Whatever is used will be less than perfectly reliable. The most widely used measure – supervisor rating – has fairly poor reliability: Schmidt and Hunter's (1977) estimate was 0.60. Two or more supervisors will not agree all that well in their rating of an employee's work performance. The next most widely used measure – training grades – is more reliable; Schmidt and Hunter's estimate is 0.80. An unreliable outcome is difficult to predict, and necessarily reduces the correlation between predictor and outcome. The usual solution is statistical correction, using a simple formula based on outcome reliability.

Validity generalization analysis (VGA) This is a development of meta-analysis, by Schmidt and Hunter, (1977, 2004). VGA routinely corrects validity for both restricted range and outcome reliability, which can nearly double the validity correlation. Comparing rows 3 and 8 in Table 2.5 illustrates this. The corrections for restricted range and outcome reliability were devised long ago, and had been used in research long before validity generalization. It was not usual, however, to make both corrections, as VGA does. VGA therefore generates a very much more positive account of selection validity.

Second problem – variation in validity

The correlation between general mental ability and clerical proficiency in Figure 2.4 varies from –0.45 to 0.75. Such wide variation means that employers can never be sure whether a selection test will work (moderately) well, or not very well, or not at all. Work psychologists initially hoped to find moderator variables (v.i.) to explain the wide variation: type of job, type of organization, type of applicant, etc. Moderator variables were found for some selection methods, but not sufficient to explain all the variation in validity. Work

Table 2.5   Validity generalization analysis of the data of Figure 2.4, based on data given by Schmidt & Hunter (1977).

Job	Mechanical repair worker	Bench worker	Clerk	Machine tender
Test	Mechanical principles	Finger dexterity	General intelligence	Spatial relations
1. k – number of validities	114	191	72	99
2. N – total sample size	nr	nr	nr	nr
3. r – average validity (raw)	0.39	0.25	0.36	0.11
4. Observed variance of validity	0.21	0.26	0.26	0.22
5. Estimated variance of validity	0.19	0.14	0.17	0.12
6. Observed minus estimated	0.02	0.12	0.09	0.10
7. Observed variance accounted for	90%	54%	65%	54%
8. ρ – average validity (corrected)	0.78	0.39	0.67	0.05

ρ, in line 8, is operational validity, corrected for restricted range and reliability of work performance measure.

psychologists next turned to the very pessimistic *situational specificity hypothesis*: so many factors affect test validity, so complexly, that it is impossible to construct a model that predicts validity in any particular setting. Employers must rely on *local validation studies* to check whether their particular tests work for their particular workforce. However, there is a third possible explanation for variation in validity – sampling error.

Sampling error   The *law of large numbers* states that *large* random samples will be highly representative of the population from which they are drawn. The *fallacy of small numbers* is to suppose that *small* random samples are also representative; they are not. Correlations calculated from small samples vary a lot, and most validity research has used fairly small samples. Schmidt *et al.* (1985b) suggest that one 'rogue' observation in a sample of 40 to 50 can change the correlation considerably; this can easily happen, if for example the best worker happens to be absent when the testing is done.

US Postal Service data demonstrated conclusively how small sample correlations vary a lot, in the absence of any possible real cause (Figure 2.7). Schmidt *et al.* (1985a) randomly divided a large sample of 1,455 letter sorters into 63 smaller groups of 68 each (68 because Lent, Aurbach & Levin (1971) had shown this was the average sample size in validation research at that time). Validity of a clerical test for the whole sample was 0.22; Figure 2.7 shows the distribution of validity coefficients for the 63 mini-samples, which can only vary through sampling error. Validity ranges from –0.03 to 0.48; most were statistically insignificant, so researchers using such small samples are more likely than not to 'miss' the link between test and work performance. Figure 2.7 shows that correlations calculated on small samples are misleading, and that 68 is a small sample, too small. If the 63 correlations in Figure 2.7 vary so much just by chance, perhaps the 72 correlations for Ghiselli's clerical workers in

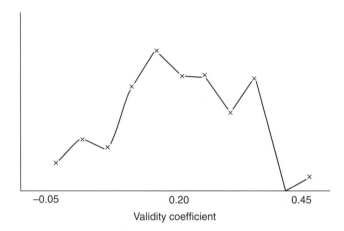

Figure 2.7 Distribution of validity coefficients for 63 sub-samples, each of 68, drawn randomly from a larger sample of 1455 US postal workers. Data from Schmidt *et al.* (1985a).

Figure 2.4 vary as much by chance too. The other limitations of selection research – unreliability of outcome measure and range restriction – also add some more error, because they vary from study to study.

Observed and expected variation in validity Validity generalization analysis (VGA) asks: 'Can all the variation in validity be explained as error? Or is there some real variation? Even after making allowance for the known limitations of selection research?' VGA compares *observed variance* with *estimated variance*. Observed variance is how much validity actually varies; estimated variance is how much one would expect validity to vary given what is known – or can be estimated – about sources of error. Hunter and Schmidt (2004) give computational details. *Zero residual variance* means there is no variance left when estimated variance has been subtracted from observed variance, which suggests there is no true variation in validity.

Table 2.5 applies VGA to the four sets of Ghiselli's data in Figure 2.4 and Table 2.3. Line 7 of Table 2.5 shows that between 54% and 90% of the observed variance in validity can be accounted for by error. For testing repair workers with tests of mechanical principles, 90% of the variation in validity can be explained, suggesting validity does not 'really' vary much. However, for testing bench workers with finger dexterity tests, only half the variation in validity can be explained, which suggests validity does 'really' vary. The reader may wonder why it seems to matter so much whether validity of selection methods does or does not 'really' vary. There are three reasons.

- One is practical. If the correlation between mental ability and work performance is always 0.50, then HR can use MA tests 'off the shelf', in the knowledge they will work.
- The second reason has more do with the standing of psychology as a science. A true science states laws; for example 'every schoolboy knows' Boyle's law

in physics, that the pressure of a gas varies inversely with its volume. Psychology has always seemed short of such general laws with which to impress the public. Perhaps the Schmidt–Hunter Law, that mental ability and work performance always correlate 0.50, would fill this gap. (But given the general unpopularity of mental ability tests, perhaps it would not.)

• A third reason is identifying research needs. If VGA finds substantial unexplained variation in validity, it is worth looking for moderator variables. Newman, Jacobs and Bartram (2007) list four areas where VGA finds unexplained variation: mental ability tests for clerical workers, conscientiousness tests for managers, assessment centres, and interviews, especially structured interviews. By contrast VGA of work sample tests and biodata find no evidence of any true variation in validity still needing to be explained.

Schmidt *et al.* (1985b) suggested researchers could – and perhaps should – have concluded as long ago as the 1920s that tests have generalized validity, and that validity only appears to vary from study to study through sampling error. Why did work psychologists cling to the doctrine of situational specificity for so long? Perhaps they did not read their statistics books carefully enough and overlooked sampling error. Perhaps they were reluctant to admit that researches on samples of 50 or 60 were not very useful, especially as it can be very difficult to find larger numbers. Perhaps they just wanted to carry on selling employers local validity studies.

Correcting for test reliability Some VGAs make a third correction, for the (un) reliability of the selection test. From the selector's perspective, it is pointless estimating how much more accurate selection would be if tests were perfectly reliable, because no test is perfectly reliable. Validity is necessarily limited by test reliability. However, researchers devising a theory of, for example, numerical ability and work performance may find it useful to regard both as things that could ideally be measured perfectly reliably, so could legitimately correct for reliability of both before calculating their true correlation. Many analyses distinguish between estimated *true validity* which is corrected for range restriction and unreliability of both test and criterion, and *operational validity* which is corrected for range restriction and criterion reliability only. This book will quote operational validity rather than true validity wherever possible.

VGA extends the contribution of meta-analysis, showing that selection tests work more consistently, and work much better than people thought in the 1960s and 1970s.

CRITICISMS OF VALIDITY GENERALIZATION

Landy (2003) describes VGA as the 'psychometric equivalent of alchemy. Lead was turned into gold – a collection of disappointing and contradictory validity studies were unravelled to show that we had been doing the right thing all along'. However, VGA has attracted its share of critics. Critics dismiss it as the 'hydraulic' model of test validity; if your validity is not large enough, simply inflate it to the desired size by making corrections.

Correcting for restricted range

How much allowance for restricted range should be made? The bigger the allowance made, the bigger the consequent increase in corrected validity. Correcting for restricted range uses a formula based on the ratio of sample standard deviation (SD) to population SD. *Sample* means successful As, where researchers have the data to compute SD. *Population* might mean all As, where researchers also have the data to calculate SD. But often population is taken to mean everyone who *might have applied* or *who ought to have applied*, which makes it harder to find a value for their SD.

One approach is using normative data from the test's manual. Sackett and Ostgaard (1994) presented estimates of range restriction in the Wonderlic Personnel Test, comparing SD of scores for each of 80 jobs with the overall SD of the whole database. On average, SDs for particular jobs are 8.3% smaller than the overall SD. For 90% of jobs, restriction is less than 20%. For more complex jobs, range restriction is greater, whereas for simple jobs it is much less.

Hunter and Hunter's (1984) VGA of the General Aptitude Test Battery GATB database (see Chapter 6, p. 115) used a similar strategy, and also produced a fairly low estimate of range restriction, but has nevertheless proved controversial. Hunter used the SD of the whole GATB database, i.e. of everyone who got a job in all 515 studies, as his estimate of population SD, which generates an estimate of restriction of 20%. Critics, such as Hartigan and Wigdor (1989), objected to this. They argued that doctors and lawyers, at the 'top' of the GATB database, are not likely to apply for the minimum wage jobs at the 'bottom', while the people in minimum wage jobs could not apply for 'top' jobs because they lacked the necessary qualifications. Hartigan and Wigdor argued that the purpose of correcting validity coefficients should not be to produce the largest possible correlation, but to give the test's user a realistic estimate of how well it will work in practice, avoiding underestimates that do not allow for known methodological limitations, and avoiding overestimates based on showing how efficiently the test could reject people who would never actually apply for the job. Schmitt (2007) points out that range restriction is often much less in reality, because the best scorers often do not accept the job offer, so less high-scoring persons are appointed instead, which reduces range restriction in the selection process. Hartigan and Wigdor also noted that GATB validity seemed to have fallen over time; they found 240 newer GATB validity studies, which reduced their average for raw validity to 0.19, and their estimate for corrected validity to 0.22.

Correcting for outcome reliability

How much allowance for unreliability of work performance measures should be made? Again the bigger the allowance, the bigger the resulting increase in corrected validity, which creates the worrying paradox that the less reliable the performance measure, the higher validity becomes. Assuming reliability of supervisor rating is 0.60 increases corrected validity by 29%. Hartigan and

Wigdor preferred a more conservative assumption, that supervisor rating reliability averages 0.80, which increases raw-to-true validity by only 12%. The most recent meta-analysis of supervisor reliability (Viswesvaran, Ones & Schmidt, 1996) favours Hunter, reporting a value of only 0.52. LeBreton *et al.* (2003) remark that 'Nowhere else in the organizational sciences do we routinely accept and use measurement procedures yielding reliabilities of .52.' How high should reliability be? LeBreton *et al.* note that 0.70 is widely accepted as a lower limit for reliability of measures in research work, and suggest that measures used to make decisions about individuals – i.e. anything used in personnel selection – should aim for 0.95. Mental ability tests sometimes do as well as this, but most selection tests fall well below.

An interesting aside is that other lines of research that correlate tests with 'real-life' behaviour, for example Funder's (2007) research on personality, report raw correlations, and make no corrections at all. Uncorrected correlations will allow researchers to compare validities of different measures, and to test theories of personnel selection. Correlations of 0.20 or so have the disadvantage of looking very small, and looking even smaller when converted into estimates of variance accounted for.

LATEST DEVELOPMENT IN VGA

Presently VGA corrects for restriction of range using the formula for direct restriction of range (DRR), which compares the average score of successful applicants with the average score of all applicants. This is not actually the right formula to use, because DRR does not happen all that often in selection research. Applicants are not usually selected by the test being researched, either because the scores are not used to make selection decisions, or because 'applicants' are not applicants at all but present employees, selected some time previously by whatever test the employer was then using. This previous test will have restricted the range of ability in the 'applicant' sample, creating *indirect restriction of range* (IRR).

A more complex correction formula for indirect range restriction was devised by Thorndike 60 years ago, but requires data about scores on the previous test that are rarely available. It also requires the variable(s) indirectly restricting range to be clearly identified, which they are often are not. Applicants may have been sifted by education, or by vague concepts of the 'right background', which can restrict range of mental ability through links to social class.

The new development in VGA (Schmidt Oh & Le, 2006) depends on the distinction between true general mental ability (GMA), and GMA test score. *Classical test theory* says scores on a GMA test contain two elements: true GMA and error. Error is everything that makes the test less than perfectly reliable: items that do not work very well, poor test administration, person tested having an 'off day' etc. Therefore GMA score is always imperfectly correlated with true GMA. Note that true GMA is a hypothetical entity that can never be observed. It could be approximated if the person took the test many times

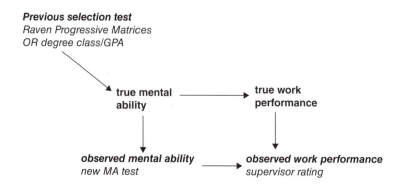

Figure 2.8   Indirect restriction of range. Observable variables are in *italic*. True variables are in **bold**. The lines show paths between the variables.

over, on the analogy of an athlete running a 100 metre race every day for a year (but doing the same MA test 365 times is only a theoretical possibility).

Figure 2.8 shows five elements in the link between mental ability and work performance, according to classical test theory. The observable elements are supervisor rating of work performance and score on the new test of mental ability. Both are less than perfectly accurate measures of hypothetical true mental ability, and true work performance. In classical test theory they are a mixture of true mental ability/work performance *and* measurement error. The reliability of the MA test, and of supervisor rating, is always less than perfect, and indicates how much measurement error there is. The fifth box in the diagram is the previously used selection test which has restricted range of mental ability. This is observable in theory but probably not in practice. This may have been a different mental ability test used when the present employees were originally selected. Or it may be something linked to mental ability such as education or social background.

The previous selection test will have restricted range of MA, *but* it will have restricted range of true mental ability, which in turn will restrict range of scores on the new MA test. The previous selection cannot directly affect the scores on the new test. However, the link between previous test and true MA will always be greater than the link between the previous test and the new test, because the new test is always an imperfect measure of true ability. The IRR correction uses the reliability of the new test to estimate how much bigger the link between the previous test and true ability is, and how much more it has restricted range. Reliability information is always available, so the correction can be applied to any set of data.

Table 2.6 shows how the revised procedure compares with conventional VGA, for Ghiselli's (1973) data. True validities are 20–30% higher, reaching 0.73 for work of high complexity, and breaking a new barrier – accounting for half the variance in work performance. Beatty *et al.* (2014) identify some limiting conditions; for example the model will not work if the 'previous test' was actually a set of tests, which included the new test.

Table 2.6 VGA of Ghiselli's (1973) data on correlation between GMA and work performance, for five levels of job complexity, using 'conventional' VGA, and VGA correcting for indirect range restriction.

Job complexity	Conventional VGA	VGA correcting for indirect range restriction
1 (high)	0.58	0.73
2	0.58	0.74
3	0.49	0.66
4	0.40	0.56
5 (low)	0.25	0.39

Data from Schmidt, Oh & Le (2006).

What does this new correction mean? It seems to indicate how well GMA would correlate with performance as, for example, a doctor in a truly unselected sample. Not merely unselected for GMA score, but unselected for anything linked to GMA, such as education or social background. The resulting 0.70+ true correlations show how important individual differences in mental ability really are for success in high-level jobs. This is a challenging conclusion, if not one likely to be warmly welcomed by – to suggest a few possibilities – the educational establishment, the media, politicians, anyone scoring below the 95th percentile on general intelligence tests. But from the narrower perspective of the American or European HR manager using GMA tests to select doctors (or any other professional), how relevant is it? Preselection by education and social background is a fact of life; knowing how well GMA tests would work if it did not happen may not be very useful.

KEY POINTS

In Chapter 2 you have learned the following:

- Selection methods should be reliable and valid.
- Validation is necessary to ensure that the test is selecting good applicants and rejecting poor applicants.
- There are various ways to validate selection methods, some of which are more useful than others.
- Criterion validation correlates test scores with work performance scores. This is the most convincing approach since it relies on empirical evidence, but requires large numbers.
- Predictive validation is preferable to concurrent validation.
- Content validation focuses on what people need to know to do the job, and does not require large numbers, but is only suitable for assessing fairly specific skills and knowledge.
- Meta-analysis pools the results of many separate researches to generate a single overall estimate of validity.

- Meta-analysis has proved very useful but has some problems, and may have led to premature conclusions in some areas. Publication bias has been shown to be a problem.
- Validation research has methodological limits, including small samples, unreliable work performance measures, and restricted range, that create the impression of low validity; research needs therefore to be analysed carefully.
- Validity generalization analysis (VGA) is intended to generate an accurate estimate of test validity. VGA suggests that validity of mental ability tests may be fairly constant.
- VGA suggests that some selection tests' true relationships with work performance are higher than they appear.
- VGA makes assumptions about reliability of performance measures, and restriction of range in applicants that have been questioned.
- Correcting for indirect restriction of range, using Schmidt and Hunter's new procedure, find the true correlation of selection test (especially mental ability) and work performance to be even higher.

KEY REFERENCES

Duval (2005) describes the 'trim and fill' method of testing for publication bias in meta-analysis.

Hunter & Hunter (1984) describe the first application of VGA to selection data, and present the first 'league table' of selection and promotion methods.

Hunter & Schmidt (2004) describe in detail methods of meta-analysis and VGA.

Landy (2003) describes the development of meta-analysis and validity generalization.

Schmidt et al. (1985b) answer 40 questions about validity generalization analysis.

Schmidt and Hunter (1998) present an analysis of incremental validity in selection.

Schmidt, Shaffer & Oh (2008) describe the latest development in meta-analysis, correcting for indirect range restriction.

Super & Crites (1962) review early research on selection testing.

CHAPTER 3

Job description, work analysis and competences

If you don't know where you're going, you'll end up somewhere else

Selectors should always start by deciding what they are looking for. In Britain, this is often done very inefficiently (but not necessarily very quickly; I once sat through a three-hour discussion of what or who we wanted in a new head of department, which succeeded only in concluding that we did not really want a psychoanalyst but would otherwise like the 'best' candidate. I did not feel my time had been usefully spent.)

JOB DESCRIPTION AND PERSON SPECIFICATION

Traditional British HR practice recommends selectors to write a job description and a person specification. Job descriptions start with the job's official title – 'Head of Contracts Compliance Unit' – then say how the job fits into the organization – 'organizing and leading a team of seven implementing [a London borough] Council's contracts compliance policy' – before listing the job's main duties:

1. devise and implement management control systems and procedures
2. introduce new technology to the Unit
3. develop strategies for fighting discrimination, poverty, apartheid, and privatization.

Job descriptions commonly fall into one of two traps. They list every task – important or unimportant, frequent or infrequent, routinely easy or very difficult – without indicating which is which. Secondly, they lapse into a vague, sub-literate 'managementspeak' of 'liaising', 'resourcing', and 'monitoring', instead of explaining precisely what successful applicants will find themselves doing. Many job descriptions aim to list everything employees might ever be asked to do, so no one can subsequently say 'That's not part of my job'. Person specifications also suffer from vagueness and vacuity. Having dealt with specifics – must have HRM qualifications, must speak Mandarin

Personnel Selection: Adding Value Through People – A Changing Picture,
Sixth Edition. Mark Cook.
© 2016 John Wiley & Sons, Ltd. Published 2016 by John Wiley & Sons, Ltd.

Chinese – many British person specifications waste time saying applicants must be keen, well motivated and energetic, as if any employer were likely to want idle, unmotivated employees. American job descriptions usually focus much more sharply on KSAs – *knowledge, skills, aptitudes*. Ideally the person specification indicates which selection tests to use.

WORK ANALYSIS METHODS

Job descriptions and person specifications can be drawn up by a committee in half a day. Work analysis (formerly called job analysis) is much more ambitious, much more detailed, and has many more uses. Some methods require complex statistical analysis.

Source of information

Information about a job can be obtained from employees doing the job, from supervisors or managers, or by expert job analysts. Employees are a good source because asking them makes the system acceptable and plausible, but are less suitable in other ways: they may not understand the paperwork, and may not be motivated to give accurate information. Traditional work analysis, with repeated meetings of large panels of employees or supervisors, takes up a lot of staff time, which employers are increasingly reluctant to pay for.

Analysing information

Having collected information about the work being done, the researcher faces the task of making sense of it; this can be done subjectively, by a committee, or by statistical analysis.

Subjective After spending a month, or a week, or an afternoon watching people doing the job, or talking to them, the analyst writes down his/her impressions. This is often good enough as the basis for writing a job description but does not really merit the title 'analysis'.

Rational Jobs are described and grouped by rational methods, i.e. by committee and consultation. This helps ensure the analysis makes sense to the organization, and will be accepted by it.

Statistical analysis Some time ago Krzystofiak, Newman and Anderson (1979) wrote a 754-item Job Analysis Questionnaire for use in a power utility (power station) employing nearly 1,900 individuals in 814 different jobs. Employees rated how often they performed nearly 600 tasks. This creates a dataset far too large to be able to make sense of by eye. Krzystofiak and Newman factor-analysed (Box 2.7, page 37) their data, and extracted 60 factors representing 60 themes in the work of the 1,900 employees. The profile for the company's Administrator of Equal Employment Opportunity showed his/her work had six themes (in order of importance): personnel administration, legal/commissions/agencies and hearings, staff management, training, managerial supervision and decision-making, and non-line management. Knowing that a particular job has six main themes gives HR a much clearer idea how to recruit and select for it. If HR could find a test for each of the 60 factors, they would have an all-purpose test battery for every one of the 800+ jobs in the plant.

SELECTED WORK ANALYSIS TECHNIQUES – AN OVERVIEW

Over the last 30 years work analysis techniques have multiplied almost as prolifically as personality questionnaires. This chapter has space to describe only a few of the most widely used.

O*NET / Dictionary of Occupational Titles

O*NET is an electronic replacement for the former (US) Dictionary of Occupational Titles (DOT). O*NET (Converse *et al.*, 2004) includes for each job details of:

- Experience requirements.
- Worker requirements.
- Worker characteristics.
- Occupational requirements, including 42 generalized work activities (GWAs), for example *inspecting equipment, structures or materials*, and *electronic and electrical repair*.
- Occupation-specific requirements.
- Occupation characteristics.

DOT also included ratings of the complexity of each job, which have been widely used in research on mental ability.

O*NET's list of skills is necessarily fairly general, for example *instructing* – teaching others how to do something, or *installation* – installing equipment, machines, wiring, or programmes to meet specifications. The lay person tends to think of a skill as something more specific, for example bricklaying or pipefitting. O*NET's list also includes six social skills, such as *persuasion* – persuading others to change their minds or behaviour – and management skills – *motivating, developing and directing people* as they work, which seems to cover most of HR and quite a bit of general management. It would be difficult to devise a single test of such broad skills, which may limit O*NET's usefulness in selection. O*NET is being updated with information on new and emerging occupations – 102 so far (Morgeson & Dierdorff, 2011), including fuel cell engineers, non-destructive testing specialists, spa managers, and homeland security intelligence analysts. O*NET differs from DOT by collecting information from people doing the job, rather than from work analysts; Dierdorff and Morgeson (2009) have shown present employees seem able to provide reliable data about most aspects of work, with the possible exception of what traits people need to do the job.

Critical incident technique (CIT)

CIT is the oldest work analysis technique, devised by Flanagan (1954) to analyse failure in military pilot training during the Second World War. Flanagan found the reasons given for failure too vague to be helpful – 'poor judgement' – or completely circular – 'lack of inherent flying ability'. Flanagan identified flying's critical requirements by collecting accounts of critical incidents which caused recruits to be rejected. Typical incidents included trying to land on the wrong runway or coming in to land too high. CIT is open-ended and flexible but can be time-consuming. In modern CIT hundreds, or even thousands, of accounts are collected, then sorted by similarity to identify the main themes in effective and ineffective performance. CIT is the basis of behaviourally anchored rating scales (BARS) (Chapter 5), and of some structured interviewing systems (Chapter 4). Lievens and Patterson (2011) describe a job analysis for general practitioners/family physicians in Britain, based in critical incidents. Information is collected from three sources: critical incident focus groups with experienced GPs, behavioural observation and coding of GP–patient consultations, and critical incident interviews with patients. The data are analysed to generate six performance dimensions: empathy, communication, problem-solving, professional integrity, coping with pressure, and clinical expertise. The assessment centre set up to assess these is described in Chapter 10.

Future-oriented work analysis (aka strategic work analysis)

Ford *et al.* (1999) described a project to decide what would be needed in the US soldier over the next 10 to 25 years, based on information from senior NCOs and psychologists. It listed four main attributes: cognitive aptitude (highest priority), conscientiousness/dependability, selfless service orientation, and good working memory capacity.

Position analysis questionnaire (PAQ)

Despite its title, PAQ is not a questionnaire, but a structured interview schedule (McCormick, Jeanneret & Mecham, 1972). PAQ is completed by a trained job analyst who collects information from workers and supervisors; however, analysts do not simply record what informants say but form their own judgements about the job. The information PAQ collects covers nearly 200 elements, divided into six main areas (Table 3.1). Elements are rated for importance to the job, and for time spent doing each, amount of training required, etc. The completed PAQ is analysed by comparing it with a very large American database. The analysis proceeds by a series of linked stages:

1. Profile of 32 *job elements*. The original factor analysis of PAQ items identified 32 dimensions which underlie all forms of work, for example watching things from a distance, being aware of bodily movement and balance, making decisions, dealing with the public.

Table 3.1 Position Analysis Questionnaire's (PAQ) six main divisions, and illustrative job elements.

PAQ division	Illustrative job elements
1. Information input	Use of written materials Near visual differentiation (i.e. good visual acuity, at short range)
2. Mental processes	Level of reasoning in problem-solving Coding/decoding
3. Work output	Use of keyboard devices Assembling/disassembling
4. Relationships with other people	Instructing Contacts with public or customers
5. Job context	High temperature Interpersonal conflict
6. Other	Specified work space Amount of job structure

2. Profile of 76 *attributes:* aptitudes, interests or temperament the person needs to perform the job elements. Aptitudes include movement detection – being able to detect the physical movement of objects and to judge their direction – and selective attention – being able to perform a task in the presence of distracting stimuli. Temperament includes empathy and influencing people. The attribute profile provides a detailed person specification.
3. *Recommended tests*. The attribute profile leads naturally on to suggestions for tests to assess the attributes. If the job needs manual dexterity, the PAQ output suggests using General Aptitude Test Battery's pegboard test of gross dexterity.
4. *Job component validity (JCV) data*. Based on the job's component elements, estimates are generated of the likely validity of the nine abilities (verbal, numerical, spatial, dexterity, etc.), assessed by GATB, as well as estimates of likely average scores (Jeanneret, 1992). This forms part of synthetic validity, described in a later section.
5. *Comparable jobs and remuneration*. The job element profile is compared with PAQ's extensive database, to identify other jobs with similar requirements, and to estimate the appropriate salary in US$. An early study by Arvey and Begalla (1975) obtained PAQ ratings for 48 home-makers (house-wives), and found the most similar other job in PAQ's database was police officer, followed by home economist, airport maintenance chief, kitchen helper, and firefighter – all trouble-shooting, emergency-handling jobs. Arvey and Begalla also calculated the average salary paid for the 10 jobs most like housewife – $740 a month, at 1968 prices.

Fleishman job analysis survey (FJAS)

This lists 73 abilities, some general and intellectual, for example problem-solving, others more specific and physical e.g. gross body co-ordination (Buffardi *et al.*, 2000). The FJAS also covers social and interpersonal abilities. The emphasis on abilities makes the FJAS more useful in selection, especially as the package includes tests matched to the listed abilities.

A possible problem with work analysis systems that list large numbers of abilities is (lack of) differentiation. Rotundo and Sackett (2004) factor analyse three large datasets including O*NET's 46 skills, and DOT's 11 aptitudes, to find one or two large general factors in every dataset. One factor is general mental ability, the other a motor or technical factor. Note that the data being analysed here are not test scores, but experts' ratings of what they think 400 to 500 different jobs need in way of skills, abilities, etc. Rotundo and Sackett consider the possibility that the high intercorrelations reflect the job analyst's conceptual system, not reality, but dismiss it because the three datasets were collected in different ways. The high intercorrelations are surprising in places, given that some abilities look very specific, for example glare sensitivity, night vision, or arm–hand steadiness. Bartram (2005) describes the 'Great Eight' framework of themes running through work, such as leading/deciding, supporting/co-operating, derived from self- and supervisor ratings of various lists of competences. Bartram's analysis reveals that the 'great eight' are themselves quite highly correlated (average correlation 0.45), suggesting again that job or competence analysis may not always succeed in differentiating work as finely as it seeks to.

WORK ANALYSIS AND PERSONALITY

Traditional work analysis systems tended to emphasize abilities needed for the job; with the growing popularity of personality testing in selection, new systems are emerging that focus more on personality requirements.

Personality-related Position Requirement Form (PPRF)

Raymark, Schmit and Guion's (1997) PPRF contains items in the format:

> *Effective performance in this position requires the person to take control in group situations — not required / helpful / essential*

Preliminary results indicated that leadership is needed in management but not in cashiers, while a friendly disposition is needed in sales assistants but not in caretakers. Conscientiousness by contrast seems needed in every job. PPRF enables selectors to use personality measures in a more focused way, and to be able to justify assessing aspects of personality if challenged. Aguinis, Mazukiewicz and Heggestad (2009) found that PPRF ratings were linked to the rater's own personality to some extent (ca 0.30), but that this could be reduced by suitable training.

Personality-oriented job analysis (POJA)

Goffin *et al.* (2011) offer another work analysis system that incorporates personality as well as skills and abilities: personality-oriented job analysis (POJA). Unlike PPRF, POJA allows for possible negative trait by work performance links: that people with trait X will be unsuited to job A, something job analysis does not normally offer. POJA is linked to specific personality questionnaires, including NEO (see Chapter 7). Data are collected from medical students doing on the job training in six medical specialities – an interesting cross between being students and being 'real workers'. Goffin *et al.* conclude there is a different personality profile for each speciality: if POJA says family medicine needs Agreeableness, while surgery needs Endurance, then the validity of the PQ data is higher for these combinations.

RELIABILITY AND VALIDITY OF WORK ANALYSIS

Reliability

Two meta-analyses of work analysis reliability have been reported. Dierdorff and Wilson (2003) find inter-rater reliability higher for rating specific tasks than for rating more generalized work activities. Dierdorff and Morgeson (2009), analysing O*NET data for 309 occupations, confirm that agreement on the traits needed for a job is far lower than agreement about the job's tasks, responsibilities, knowledge or skills. Lievens *et al.* (2010) argue that inter-informant disagreement in job analysis should not necessarily be regarded as error, but might be genuine differences in how people see the job. They show that type of job is linked to agreement, so that disagreement between job-analysis ratings is not just 'noise'. Reliability is lower for complex jobs, and for managerial jobs, but higher for jobs involving handling equipment, and contact with the public.

Validity

Research on validity of work analysis faces a dilemma familiar to psychologists. If results agree with 'common sense' they are dismissed as redundant – 'telling us what we already know'; if results do not agree with common sense they are simply dismissed as wrong. Evidence for the validity of work analysis derives from showing its results make sense, and from showing that work analysis leads to more accurate selection.

Is there such a thing as a 'true' account of what a particular job involves, and what it needs in the way of worker qualities? Or is it more useful to regard work as a 'social construct', defined by the views of the various parties involved: workers, management, experts, government? Morgeson and Dierdorff (2011) note that it is possible to identify sources of inaccuracy in WA, such as people reporting doing non-existent tasks (inserted in the list to catch people out), or treating rating scales as meaning the same when they do not. It is also clear that different parties have different agendas when describing work. Those doing it tend to see it as more complex and difficult partly because it is 'their' job, and partly to justify higher pay, something management will wish to avoid. Morgeson and Dierdorff (2011) note the possible advantages of collecting WA information from workers who are more intelligent so they can understand difficult questions, or more conscientious so they will not lose interest in a long questionnaire, or more experienced so they know the job better, or who are better workers so they will describe how to do the job properly. This suggests work analysis may not be something to be too democratic or inclusive about.

BIAS IN WORK ANALYSIS

Morgeson and Campion (2012) point out that work analysis relies heavily on subjective judgement, so is open to the many – they list 16 – types of bias documented for such judgements. For example judgements may be subject to conformity pressures, if management has definite views about the nature of the job. This could create ratings that are very reliable, because everyone agrees with everyone else, but which may not be valid. Recent research has identified several biasing factors.

Gender

Dick and Nadin (2006) argue that gender discrimination in employment often starts with job analyses or descriptions, which incorporate gender-biased assumptions. They give a 'blue collar' example, of apparently objective analysis for lathe operator being written around lathes, which were designed for use by men, who tend to have bigger hands and longer arms. They give a 'white collar' example, for managers, where analysis identifies *commitment*, meaning being available at all times (because someone else looks after the children).

Work attitudes

Conte *et al.* (2005) examined the role of involvement in work analysis ratings in a sample of travel agents: the more involved people are with their work, the more often they see themselves meeting its more difficult tasks, and the more important they see everything to be. The differences were quite large, up to $d = 0.49$.

Wording

Morgeson *et al.* (2004) find choice of wording in work analysis makes a big difference. Describing the job in terms of abilities, as opposed to tasks, creates considerable inflation in frequency and importance ratings, even though the two sets of wording were nearly identical: *record phone messages* / *ability to record phone messages*. When ability wording was used, people were much more likely to claim non-existent activities, such as *checking against MLA standards*. Grouping a set of tasks into a competency inflated ratings even further.

USES OF WORK ANALYSIS

Work analysis has a variety of uses in selection in particular, and HR work in general – so many uses in fact that one wonders how HR ever managed without it. Some uses are directly connected with selection:

- *Write accurate, comprehensive job descriptions* which help recruit the right applicants.
- *Select for, or train for?* Some competences can be acquired by most people but others are difficult to train so must be selected for. Jones *et al.* (2001) show that experts achieve a high degree of consensus on the trainability of the competences needed for school teaching. Van Iddekinge, Raymark and Eidson (2011) found work analysis experts more likely than psychologists to rate attributes as 'needed-at-entry'.
- *Choose selection tests.* A good work analysis identifies the knowledge, skills, and abilities needed, allowing HR to choose the right tests.
- *Defend selection tests.* Work analysis is legally required by the Equal Employment Opportunities Commission in the USA if the employer wants to use selection methods that create adverse impact.
- Work analysis also allows more elaborate selection methods to be devised.
- *Devise structured interview systems.* Structured interviews (Chapter 4) may be more accurate than conventional interviews, but most systems require a detailed work analysis.
- *Write selection tests by content validation.* Work analysis allows selectors to write a selection test whose content so closely matches the content of the job that it is content-valid (Chapter 2), which means it can be used, legally in the USA, without further demonstration of its validity.

USING WORK ANALYSIS TO SELECT WORKERS

Analysis by PAQ of the job of plastics injection-moulding setter in a British plant identified seven attributes needed in workers (Table 3.2), then recommended a suitable test for each attribute: Raven Progressive Matrices (RPM) for intelligence, an optician's eye chart for visual acuity, etc. (Sparrow *et al.*, 1982). Sparrow's research illustrates the use of work analysis first to generate a person specification, then to choose appropriate selection tests. This may seem obvious, but it is surprising how many employers even now fail to do this, which places them in a very dangerous position if someone complains about their selection methods. If the employer is unable to say why they are using RPM, they will find it extremely difficult to justify themselves if RPM creates adverse impact on e.g. minorities.

More ambitiously, work analysis systems can be linked to aptitude batteries. Jeanneret (1992) analysed 460 jobs for which both general aptitude test battery (GATB) and PAQ data were available, and then asked two questions:

1. Does the PAQ profile for a job correlate with the GATB profile for the same job? If PAQ says the job needs spatial ability, do people doing the job tend to have high spatial ability scores on GATB?

Table 3.2 Work analysis by Position Analysis Questionnaire, showing choice of tests for plastic injection-moulding setters (Sparrow *et al.*, 1982).

Attribute	Test
Long-term memory	Wechsler Memory Scale
Intelligence	Standard Progressive Matrices
Short term memory	Wechsler Memory Scale
Near visual acuity	Eye chart at 30cm
Perceptual speed	Thurstone Perceptual Speed Test
Convergent thinking	Raven Progressive Matrices
Mechanical ability	Birkbeck Mechanical Comprehension Test

2. Does the PAQ profile for a job correlate with GATB profile validity for the same job? If PAQ says the job needs spatial ability, do people with high spatial ability scores on GATB perform the job better?

The answer to both questions was Yes. The correlation between PAQ profile and GATB profile across jobs was 0.69. The correlation between PAQ profile and GATB validity across jobs was lower but still positive, at 0.26. This research implies each job needs a particular set of attributes that can be identified by PAQ, and then assessed by GATB. Jeanneret and Strong (2003) report a similar analysis for generalized work activities (GWA) ratings of O*NET, and GATB scores. For example, people doing jobs that included GWAs of operating vehicles, repairing electronic equipment, using computers, etc. tended to have higher scores on GATB finger dexterity.

Improving selection validity

From the selector's viewpoint, work analysis has validity if it results in more accurate selection decisions. Three meta-analyses have shown that personality testing (Tett, Jackson and Rothstein, 1991), structured interviewing (Wiesner & Cronshaw, 1988), and situational judgement tests (McDaniel *et al.*, 2007) achieve higher validity when based on work analysis.

SYNTHETIC VALIDATION

Synthetic validation uses work analysis to identify underlying themes in diverse jobs and select appropriate tests. Synthetic validation works on the principle that validity, once demonstrated for a combination of theme–test across the workforce as a whole, can be inferred for subsets of workers, *including sets too small for a conventional validation exercise*. The idea was first proposed, and named, in 1952 by Lawshe, and is currently advocated by Johnson *et al.* (2010). Table 3.3 illustrates the principle with fictional data. A city employs 1,500 persons in 300 different jobs. Some jobs, for example local tax clerk, have enough people to calculate a conventional validity. Other jobs, for example

Table 3.3   Illustration of synthetic validation in a local authority (city) workforce of 1,500.

Attribute ⟹		Ability to influence	Attention to detail	Numeracy
TEST ⟹		PQ dominance	PQ detail	Numeracy test
JOB ↓	N			
1 – Local tax clerk	200	–	XX	XX
2 – Refuse collection supervisor	25	XX	XX	XX
3 – Crematorium receptionist	1	XX	XX	–
Total N involved		430	520	350
Validity		0.30	0.25	0.27
Diversity facilitator	10	XX	–	XX

refuse collection supervisor, have too few to make a conventional local validity study worth undertaking. Some jobs are done by only one person, rendering any statistical analysis impossible. Work analysis identifies a number of themes underlying all 300 jobs; suitable tests for each theme are selected. Validity of PQ dominance score for the 25 refuse collection supervisors is inferred from its validity for all 430 persons throughout the workforce whose work requires *ability to influence others*. It even becomes possible to prove the validity of PQ *detail-consciousness* scale for the one and only crematorium receptionist by pooling that individual's predictor and criterion data with the 520 others for whom detail is important. Synthetic validity also makes it possible to plan selection for new jobs: when the city takes on 10 diversity facilitators, work analysis identifies the themes in their work, and the tests to use.

The combination of PAQ and GATB is well suited to synthetic validation, because Jeanneret (1992) has shown that PAQ scores correlate with GATB scores very well, and with GATB validity fairly well. This implies PAQ work analysis can predict what profile of GATB scores will be found in people doing a job successfully. PAQ can generate job component validity (JCV) coefficients which represent a different approach to synthetic validity. Rather than identify a single test for each competency, as in Table 3.3, JCV uses the PAQ database to generate a regression equation (Box 3.1) that indicates which tests to use for a job and what weight to give each, based on the competences PAQ lists for that job. Hoffman, Holden and Gale (2000) use JCV estimates to create test batteries for the many jobs in the gas industry that have too few incumbents to allow conventional validation. Some work analysis systems use expert panels to match test to job theme. Johnson *et al.* (2010) argue for a national database of job information that can be used to plan tailored selection batteries. In a sense these already exist, in the O*NET system, and in several commercial work analysis systems, such as PAQ, or Fleishman's JAS. Combining these all into a single database might be useful, but seems unlikely to happen.

Schmidt and Oh (2010) see fundamental problems with synthetic validation, on both the test side and the work performance side. On the test side, the problem is that all ability tests are positively correlated, often quite highly, so the plan to find a specific set of ability tests for every job proves an unnecessary complication because a standard all-purpose set will do as well. Murphy, Dzieweczynski and Zhang (2009) take this argument a step further with the *positive manifold* hypothesis, that most selection tests are positively correlated, so the plan to find a selection battery specific to every job will prove unsuccessful, and unnecessary (see also Chapter 6). Schmidt and Oh also note that work performance is usually defined by supervisor ratings, and that these are notoriously global (see Chapter 12), so the strategy of showing test 1 will predict aspect A of work performance, while test 2 predicts aspect B, etc. will fail on both sides of the test–work performance relationship. Viswesvaran and Ones (2005) propose the *monolithic hypothesis*, that sees all aspects of work performance as positively correlated (Chapter 12), which could leave little room for job analysis to play a useful role in deciding who can do job A better, and who will be better suited to jobs B, C or D.

Box 3.1   Regression equation

GATB generates 10 separate scores. Research could correlate all 10 in turn with e.g. work performance. However, this would be misleading in the sense that GATB's 10 scores are all quite highly intercorrelated. Instead researchers correlate a regression, which calculates the multiple correlation between all 10 GATB scores and work performance. Regression also reveals which GATB scales are most closely related to the outcome, and which are redundant because they do not improve the multiple correlation.

THE FUTURE OF WORK ANALYSIS

Is work analysis always essential?

Pearlman, Schmidt and Hunter (1980) used validity generalization analysis to show that tests of mental ability predict performance equally well throughout a large and varied set of clerical jobs. They argue there is therefore no need for detailed analysis of clerical work. However, it would be difficult to act on Pearlman *et al.*'s conclusions in the USA at present. Deciding a job is clerical, and using a clerical test for selection, may satisfy common sense, and may be good enough for Pearlman *et al.*, but it probably will fail to satisfy the (US) Equal Employment Opportunities Commission, if there are complaints about the composition of the workforce. The full detail and complexity of PAQ may be needed to prove a clerical job really is clerical.

Is work analysis becoming obsolete?

Latham and Wexley (1981) described a very long rating schedule for janitors, in which item 132 read

> *Places a deodorant block in urinal*
> *almost never – almost always*

The rest of the janitor's day was specified in similarly exhaustive, almost oppressive, detail. Management and the HR professionals have begun to question this type of approach. Rapid change implies less need for task-specific skills and more need for general abilities, to adapt, solve problems, define one's own direction, and work in teams. Work analysis is backward-looking and encourages cloning, whereas organizations need to be forward-looking. Work analysis assumes the job exists apart from the employee who holds it, whereas organizations are being 'de-jobbed', meaning employees work on a fluid set of activities that change rapidly so no job descriptions exist. Current management trends also suggest a shift to broad personal characteristics, rather than long lists of very specific skills or competences.

COMPETENCES/COMPETENCY MODELLING

Over the last 25 years, the HR world has adopted with great enthusiasm the competence (or competency) modelling approach. A competence has been defined as: 'an observable skill or ability to complete a managerial task successfully'. From the selector's point of view, competences are often a very mixed bag:

- Very specific skills or knowledge that workers will acquire as part of their training but would not possess beforehand, for example knowing how to serve meals and drinks on an aircraft.
- More generalized skills or knowledge that organizations might wish to select for, for example communicating well in writing.
- Aptitudes that would make it easier for a person to acquire more specific competences, for example flexibility, or ability to learn quickly.
- Personality characteristics, for example resilience, tolerance.

Campion *et al.* (2011) list 10 differences between traditional WA and newer competency modelling (CM) approaches, including:

- CM is intended to distinguish top performers from average (whereas WA can point HR towards tests that might achieve this).
- CM is linked to the organization's business objectives and strategy, such as sales growth, or identifying innovative new products, so CM can provide more direction.

- CM has a common set of competences for all staff from the top to the bottom (but can describe how competences will change as salary/grade increases).
- Traditional WA is geared to defensibility of selection in event of legal challenge.
- CM can 'align' main HR systems: selection, training, evaluation, remuneration, promotion.
- CM is intended to create change, not simply to describe. This could get slightly sinister, with elements of pressure to conform, seeking out 'wrong attitudes', or detecting 'thought crime'.

One could add that CM might prove a rather more subjective procedure that traditional WA: it is easier to determine whether Smith has assembled a component correctly than to decide if Jones has demonstrated strategic vision or diversity awareness. Pearlman and Sanchez (2010) note that some competence systems seem to be work analysis accounts, presented in competence terms to gain acceptance. Others they dismiss as 'little more than a "wish list" of desired worker attributes or purported organizational values along with brainstormed (and typically unvetted and unvalidated) examples (behavioural indicators)'. Lievens and Sanchez (2007) note that some 'competency modelling' systems achieve very poor levels of inter-rater reliability, unless users are trained properly.

Big five competences grid

Consiglio *et al.* (2013) suggest a work analysis/competency model based on the Five Factor Model of personality (Chapter 7). They propose five very broad personality-based themes underlying work, and corresponding to the five themes in human personality (Table 3.4).

Table 3.4 A personality-based work competency model proposed by Consiglio *et al.* (2013).

Personality factor	Competency	Typical items
(low) Neuroticism	Emotion management	I keep calm even in the presence of a negative work climate
Extraversion	Proactivity	At work I initiate rather wait for instructions
Openness	Innovation	I adopt innovative approaches when faced with problems
Agreeableness	Teamwork	I help colleagues who are in trouble
Conscientiousness	Accomplishment	I guarantee the accomplishment of the goals assigned to me

KEY POINTS

In Chapter 3 you have learned the following:

- It is absolutely vital to decide what you are looking for before starting any selection programme.
- If you fail to do this, you will be unlikely to make good selection decisions, and you will be unable to justify your selection methods if they are questioned or become the subject of legal dispute.
- Conventional job descriptions and person specifications are better than nothing. Competence frameworks are also useful, although often conceptually rather confused.
- Quantitative or statistical analysis is usually essential to make sense of large sets of job-descriptive data.
- Work analysis can identify the main themes in a specific job, or whole sets of jobs, or in work in general.
- Work analysis methods include some that are fairly open-ended such as critical incident technique, and some that are more structured such as the Position Analysis Questionnaire.
- Work analysis uses subjective judgements which opens the way to some biases.
- Work analysis can improve selection systems.
- Work analysis has other uses besides guiding selection.
- Work analysis can be used to validate tests for small samples within a larger workforce.
- Work analysis needs to look forwards as well as backwards.

KEY REFERENCES

Campion *et al.* (2011) compare competency modelling and work analysis.

Converse *et al.* (2004) describe some applications of the O*NET system.

Dick & Nadin (2006) argue that work analysis may be affected by implicit gender bias.

Dierdorff & Morgeson (2009) describe a meta-analysis of work analysis reliability.

Jeanneret & Strong (2003) describe how GATB scales can be linked to O*NET's generalized work activities.

Johnson *et al.* (2010) make the case for synthetic validity

McCormick *et al.* (1972) describe the original research on the PAQ.

Raymark *et al.* (1997) describe a work-analysis system specifically geared to personality requirements and assessment.

Rotundo & Sackett (2004) show how skills and competences in work-analysis systems are highly intercorrelated.

USEFUL WEBSITES

onetcenter.org. O*NET site.
occupationalinfo.org. Dictionary of Occupational Titles.
paq.com. PAQ Services Inc.
job-analysis.net. US work analysis site.

CHAPTER 4

The interview

'I know one when I see one'

Interviews have been used for a long time. The examination for promotion to lieutenant in the Royal Navy at the beginning of the nineteenth century was an interview with three captains. Interviews are used very widely today; the Cranfield Price Waterhouse survey (Dany & Torchy, 1994) confirmed that 80% to 100% of European employers interview prospective staff, the exception being Turkey, where only 64% of employers interview. Interviews are similarly popular in North America. Lievens, Highhouse and DeCorte (2005) find that managers place more weight on interview information than on psychological test results. Interviews vary widely. They can be as short as three minutes or as long as two hours. There may be one interviewer or several, in a panel or board. In France it is apparently quite common for As to be interviewed by everyone who will work with them. Phone interviews are increasingly widely used, as a preliminary screen, or when a face-to- face interview is difficult e.g. overseas As.

The interview is a selection *method*, that can be used to assess a wide range of different *constructs*. Reviewing 47 studies, mostly in the USA, Huffcutt *et al.* (2001) find personality dimensions, especially conscientiousness, most frequently assessed (35%), followed by applied social skills (28%) and mental ability (16%); interviews are less often used to assess knowledge and skills (10%), interests and preferences (4%), organizational fit (3%), or physical attributes (4%). Interviewers are given between three and 18 dimensions to assess, with an average of seven. As Huffcutt *et al.* note, it is odd that interviews are so widely used to assess personality and mental ability, given that tests of both are widely available, possibly more accurate, and certainly more economical to use. On the other hand, the interview may be particularly well suited to assess social skills, since it is itself a social encounter.

The interview is primarily a *self-report*, in which As tell interviewers about their abilities, achievements, potential, etc. However the interview also gives As the opportunity to *demonstrate* specialized knowledge, or the ability to be fluent, friendly, persuasive etc. It is much easier to circle *true* against *I am*

Personnel Selection: Adding Value Through People – A Changing Picture,
Sixth Edition. Mark Cook.
© 2016 John Wiley & Sons, Ltd. Published 2016 by John Wiley & Sons, Ltd.

forceful with others on a personality questionnaire than to create an effective impression of forcefulness on an interviewer, or to describe convincing examples of past forcefulness.

RELIABILITY AND VALIDITY

Reliability

Conway, Jako and Goodman (1995) analysed 160 researches and concluded interviewers agree well if they see the same interview, but less well if they see different interviews with the same A. The difference arises because As do not perform consistently at different interviews. Conway *et al.* argue that 0.53 is the better estimate of interview reliability in practice, because inconsistency of applicant behaviour is an inherent limitation of the interview. Conway *et al.* also find that interviews are more reliable if based on a work analysis, and if the interviewers are trained. Schleicher *et al.* (2010) report data on As who experienced the same interview, for promotion in the US public sector, twice, at a one-year interval. Performance in the two interviews correlated poorly, indicating poor retest reliability. Macan (2009) notes that interviews often do not seem to include enough questions per construct assessed to have much chance of achieving acceptable internal consistency reliability.

Validity

As Arthur and Villado (2008) have noted, reviewers sometimes confuse *method* and *construct* by talking about 'the validity of the interview', when perhaps they should really talk about validity of interviews for *assessing sales potential*, or for *assessing intellectual ability*. Huffcutt *et al.*'s survey has shown the interview can be used to assess a wide variety of skills, abilities, and traits; the very popularity of the interview may derive from its versatility. In practice, selection interviews are usually used to make a simple decision – to hire or not – and are often validated against a global assessment of how well the person does the job. In this context, perhaps it is possible to talk about 'the validity of the interview'.

Research on interview validity has been reviewed frequently, from Wagner (1949) to Macan (2009). Most earlier reviews concluded interviews did not seem to be a very good way of choosing productive workers and rejecting unproductive ones, a fact which took a long time to begin to penetrate the consciousness of line managers or HR departments. Dunnette (1972) reported the first meta-analysis of interview validity; 30 validity coefficients in the American petroleum industry had a very low average of 0.13. Hunter and Hunter (1984) obtained a similarly low average validity (0.11), rising to 0.14 when corrected for unreliability of the work performance measure, and to 0.22 when also corrected for restricted range (see Chapter 2 for more detail of these corrections).

Table 4.1 Summary of three meta-analyses of interview validity, by Wiesner & Cronshaw (1988), Huffcutt & Arthur (1994) and McDaniel *et al.* (1994).

	Wiesner & Cronshaw		Huffcutt & Arthur		McDaniel *et al.*	
	k	ρ	k	ρ	k	ρ
All interviews	150	0.47	114	0.37	160	0.37
All unstructured	39	0.31	15	0.20	39	0.33
one-to-one	19	0.20			19	0.34
board	19	0.37			15	0.33

Three subsequent much larger meta-analyses presented a more complex, and in places more favourable, picture. Wiesner and Cronshaw (1988) analysed 160 validities from research in Germany, France, and Israel, as well as the USA. Huffcutt and Arthur (1994) set out to replicate Hunter and Hunter's earlier analysis of the interview as a selection test for entry-level jobs, based on 114 samples. McDaniel *et al.*'s (1994) review covers 245 correlations from a total of 86,000 persons. Table 4.1 gives operational validities, for all interviews, ranging from 0.37 to 0.47. As Wiesner and Cronshaw remarked, the interview may not be quite such a poor predictor as many work psychologists have assumed. However the first row of Table 4.1 is probably an overestimate of the validity of the typical interview, because it includes research using structured interview systems, which differ radically from the traditional or unstructured interview. The second row shows unstructured interviews achieve lower operational validity, from 0.20 to 0.33.

Validity for different characteristics

Attempts to identify which characteristics interviews can assess accurately are limited by the point already noted, that the outcome measure is usually a global rating of work performance. Huffcutt *et al.*'s (2001) meta-analysis showed that interview ratings of some attributes, for example creativity, correlate better with supervisor ratings of overall job performance. However, this does not show that interviews are better at assessing creativity than persuasiveness, because creativity and persuasiveness in the workplace have not been assessed, only overall performance. McDaniel *et al.*'s meta-analysis reported that *psychological interviews* that try to assess personality were less successful than *situational interviews* that ask hypothetical questions such as 'What would you do if ...?', or *job-related interviews* that assess training, experience, and interests.

REASONS FOR POOR VALIDITY

Why is the conventional unstructured interview apparently such a poor predictor of work performance?

Interviewer motivation

Anyone who has spent a day interviewing knows how one's attention can start to wander by the late afternoon. Brtek and Motowidlo (2002) show that college students watching videotaped interviews can be more accurate if they try; being told they would have to explain their ratings to the researchers makes them pay more attention to the interview.

Applicant anxiety

McCarthy and Goffin (2004) found a correlation of –0.34 between applicant anxiety and interview rating, implying interviews may 'miss' some good As whose high anxiety prevents them performing well.

Interview-specific self-efficacy

The notion of interview-specific *self-efficacy* has been floated recently: the belief that one can do well in interviews. Tross and Maurer (2008) show interview self-efficacy can be increased by interview training, but does not necessarily reduce interview anxiety. From the selectors' point of view interview self-efficacy is probably a source of 'noise': something unrelated to work performance, which may affect how people perform in interviews, and something which ideally either everyone, or no one, will exhibit.

Office politics

Bozionelos (2005) describes how a UK business school used an interview to appoint four favoured As, even though they lacked published work or PhDs (usually essential qualifications for an academic). Bozionelos suggests the interview is particularly easy to 'fix'. During the interview, the interviewers can encourage favoured As by smiling and eye contact, while provoking unfavoured As by aggressive or offensive comments. In the post-interview discussion, interviewers can get away with vague assertions that favoured As 'performed well at interview', and accept their promises to start work on a PhD. Above all, the process leaves no record, either of the interview or of the post-interview discussion, so no one can find out what out happened, or challenge it. Other methods, such as psychological tests, leave a paper record.

IMPROVING THE INTERVIEW

Assuming the interview is here to stay, what can be done to improve it?

Select interviewers

Some time ago Ghiselli (1966a) found one interviewer – himself – whose accuracy in selecting stockbrokers over 17 years yielded a personal validity coefficient of 0.51. It is easy to calculate personal validities of this type, and tempting to use them to select the selectors. Recall, however, that validity data contain a lot of error (discussed in detail in Chapter 2), so it would be easy to reach the false conclusion that Smith is a better interviewer than Jones. (If they each do another 10 interviews, the difference might vanish.) Van Iddekinge *et al.* (2006) analyse data from 64 US Army interviewers, who had given an average of 30 interviews each, and were able to conclude real differences in 'personal validity' existed. Van Iddekinge *et al.* found that nearly a quarter of their interviewers had personal validities lower than zero, which implies weeding them out of the interview system (or giving them more training) would definitely be worth considering. However, an organization that wants to select good interviewers will need good records of a very large sample of comparable interviews to base its decisions on. 'Political' problems may also arise: telling senior managers they will not be allowed to do interviews because they are not very good at it may cause considerable friction.

The good judge of others

People often flatter themselves they are good judges of character. If there is such a class of person, they might be also make successful interviewers. If research could find a way to identify 'good judges of others', HR could select the selectors in advance, rather than by track record. O'Brien and Rothstein (2008) review the extensive literature and conclude the good judge of others cannot be identified, at least not with any certainty.

Use more than one interviewer

Two meta-analyses (Wiesner & Cronshaw, 1988; McDaniel *et al.*, 1994) compared one-to-one with panel or board interviews, with conflicting results; Table 4.1 shows Wiesner and Cronshaw found board interviews get better results, but McDaniel *et al.* found no difference. Conway *et al.* (1995) found that panel interviews are more reliable than one-to-one interviews. Many employers insist on panel interviews, and equal opportunities agencies also recommend their use.

Use the same interviewers throughout

Sharing out interviewing often means different As, even for the same job, are interviewed by different interviewers. Huffcutt and Woehr (1999) compared 23 studies where the same interviewers interviewed all As with 100 studies where different interviewers interviewed different As, and found using the same interviewers throughout significantly improves interview validity.

Train interviewers

Conway *et al.* (1995) analyse 160 studies, and find training makes interviewing more reliable. Huffcutt and Woehr (1999) compare 52 studies where interviewers were trained with 71 studies where they were not, and find training significantly improves interview validity. Using untrained interviewers makes it difficult to defend selection decisions if they are challenged.

Take notes

Some interviewers refrain from taking notes on the argument that it distracts the applicant. Huffcutt and Woehr (1999) compare 55 studies where interviewers did not take notes with 68 studies where they did, and find taking notes significantly improves interview validity.

Transparency

Klehe *et al.* (2008) study the effect of telling interviewees what is being assessed, which has proved useful in assessment centres (Chapter 10). In Klehe *et al.*'s research it improved construct validity but not predictive validity; different things being assessed were more clearly differentiated, which is useful, but overall prediction of work performance was not increased.

RESEARCH AGENDA

- Continue the search for the 'good judge of others'.
- More research on what interviewees think about interviewer note-taking.
- Whether note-taking improves interview validity.
- Whether note-taking interferes with the conduct of the interview.

STRUCTURED INTERVIEWS

Structured interview systems change every part of the interview.

- Interviewers' questions are structured, often to the point of being completely scripted.
- Interviewers' judgements are structured by rating scales, checklists etc.
- Some systems – but not all – do not allow the interviewer to ask any follow-up, probing or clarifying questions.
- The traditional last phase of the interview – asking As if they have any questions – is sometimes dropped, on the grounds that As could bias the interviewers by asking foolish questions.

Most structured interviewing systems start with a detailed job analysis, which ensures the questions and judgements are job-related. Structured interviews are seen as legally safer, being closely job-related, and not allowing the interviewer to wander off into irrelevant and possibly dangerous areas.

Some structured interview systems also ensure every interview is the same, which avoids one source of possible complaint. Structured interviews are beginning to be used in Britain, in local government, the financial sector, for sales, manufacturing, and the hotel industry. There are several structured interview systems in current use, devised in the USA, Canada, and Germany:

- Situational Interviews (Latham *et al.*, 1980).
- Patterned behaviour description interview (Janz, 1982).
- Multimodal interview (Schuler & Moser, 1995).
- Empirical interview (Schmidt & Rader, 1999).

Situational Interviews

Situational Interviews are developed from critical incidents (Chapter 3) of particularly effective or ineffective behaviour:

The employee was devoted to his family. He had only been married for 18 months. He used whatever excuse he could to stay at home. One day the fellow's baby got a cold. His wife had a hangnail or something on her toe. He didn't come to work. He didn't even phone in.

The incidents are rewritten as questions:

Your spouse and two teenage children are sick in bed with a cold. There are no friends or relatives available to look in on them. Your shift starts in three hours. What would you do in this situation?

The company supervisors who generate the incidents also agree benchmark answers for good, average and poor workers:

– I'd stay home – my spouse and family come first (poor)
– I'd phone my supervisor and explain my situation (average)
– Since they only have colds, I'd come to work (good)

At the interview, the questions are read out, the applicant replies, and is rated against the benchmarks. The questions are said to be phrased to avoid suggesting socially desirable answers. The situational interview looks *forward*, asking As what they would do on some future occasion.

Patterned behaviour description interview (PBD)

PBD interviews also start by analysing the job with critical incidents, but differ from the situational interview in two ways. The PBD interviewer plays a more active role than the situational interviewer, being 'trained to redirect [As] when their responses strayed from or evaded the question'.

The PBD interview looks *back*, focusing on actual behaviour that occurred in the past. A typical question reads:

> *Balancing the cash bag [day's accounts] is always the bottom line for a cashier position, but bags can't always balance. Tell me about the time your experience helped you discover why your bag didn't balance.*

Taylor and Small (2002) report a meta-analysis comparing forward-oriented or hypothetical questions with past-oriented or experience-based questions, and find the two do not differ significantly in validity. They suggest the two types of questions may assess different things. Situational questions – they argue – assess what people know, i.e. ability, whereas behaviour description questions describe what people have done, so also reflect typical performance, i.e. personality. Questions about past work behaviour cannot be used for people with no employment experience such as school leavers or new graduates.

Multimodal interview

Devised in Germany, this has eight sections, including an informal rapport-building conversation at the beginning, self-presentation by A, standardized questions on choice of career and organization, behaviour description questions, situational questions, and realistic job preview.

Empirical interview

Present good performers are interviewed to identify themes in effective performance, for example teamwork (Schmidt & Rader, 1999). Next an expert panel develops around 120 possible interview questions, which are tested in interviews with 30 outstanding and 30 unsatisfactory present employees. Questions that best distinguish good from poor employees are retained. The empirical interview does not favour any particular type of question – past behaviour, future behaviour, etc.; any question that works is used, even apparently vague ones like *How competitive are you?* The same empirical approach is used to develop biodata (Chapter 9) and some personality questionnaires (Chapter 7). The empirical interview has some other novel features. Applicants are interviewed by telephone, the interview is recorded and scored later by someone else. (It is strange how seldom interviews are recorded, given how difficult it is to remember everything As say, or to take accurate and detailed notes.)

Validity of structured interviews

Two analyses (Wiesner & Cronshaw, 1988; Huffcutt & Arthur, 1994) find validity for structured interviews is twice that for unstructured (Tables 4.1 and 4.2). A third (McDaniel *et al.*, 1994) finds a smaller difference, possibly because they defined structure differently. Wiesner and Cronshaw found structured interviews work equally well whether there is one interviewer or several, but McDaniel *et al.* – analysing a larger number of studies – found one to one structured interviews achieved slightly higher validity.

Table 4.2 Summary of three meta-analyses of structured interview validity by Wiesner & Cronshaw (1988), Huffcutt & Arthur (1994) and McDaniel *et al.* (1994).

	Wiesner & Cronshaw		Huffcutt & Arthur		McDaniel *et al.*	
	k	ρ	k	ρ	k	ρ
All interviews	150	0.47	114	0.37	160	0.37
All structured	48	0.62	33	0.57	106	0.44
						0.37[a]
one-to-one	32	0.63			61	0.46
board	15	0.60			35	0.38

[a] Re-analysed by Oh *et al.* (2007) to take account of publication bias.

After 1994 it was generally accepted that structured interviews are superior to unstructured. However two re-analyses of McDaniel's data by Duval (2005) and Oh *et al.* (2007) throw doubt on this. Trim-and-fill technique (described in Chapter 2), indicates 'substantial publication bias' towards 'good' results for structured interviews, suggesting the possible existence of an estimated 19 studies with poorer results that have been somehow overlooked. By contrast trim and fill finds no evidence of 'missing' studies of the unstructured interview. Duval's revised validity estimates find no difference between structured and unstructured interview validity. Oh *et al.* further re-analyse the data correcting for both publication bias and indirect range restriction (described in Chapter 2), and find structured interview validity lower, at 0.45, than unstructured, at 0.56. McDaniel, Rothstein and Whetzel (2006) appear to apologize for having persuaded many practitioners to 'create fairly laborious structured interview systems', and for discouraging further research comparing structured and unstructured interviews. Huffcutt, Culbertson and Weyhrauch (2014) report a new meta-analysis using indirect range restriction correction, and report structured interviews achieve a true validity of 0.70.

Schmidt & Rader (1999) report an analysis of 107 researches on the empirical interview, which showed they achieve good validity ($\rho = 0.40$) for the conventional supervisor rating criterion. Empirical interviews can also predict other aspects of work performance: output, sales, and tenure – staying with the organization. Only absence was less well predicted ($\rho = 0.19$). As Schmidt & Rader note, no other previous research had shown the interview able to predict sales, output or absence.

The re-analysis of McDaniel *et al.*'s 1994 data creates great uncertainty in one of the most important areas of selection research. It might be difficult to resolve the issue. A further meta-analysis that tries to collate every study in the three original meta-analyses, and to include research since 1994, would be worth doing. Note, however, that the number of unstructured interview validities in Table 4.1 is not that great, and if McDaniel *et al.*'s (2006) point about premature meta-analytic conclusions is correct, it may not have increased much. If most employers have gone over to structured interviewing, partly to avoid fair employment problems, it may be difficult to obtain further data on unstructured interviews.

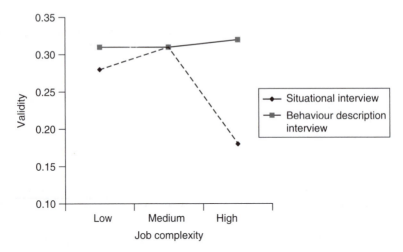

Figure 4.1   Validity of situational and behaviour description interviews for jobs of high, medium and low complexity. Data from Huffcutt *et al.* (2004).

Huffcutt *et al.* (2004) compare 31 studies of the situational interview with 20 studies of the behaviour description interview and find overall relatively little difference, corrected validities being 0.44 and 0.50 respectively. However, Figure 4.1 suggests that the situational interview may be less suitable for highly complex jobs.

Schmidt and Zimmerman (2004) argue that structured interviews achieve good validity simply because they are much more reliable, and note that correcting unstructured interview validity for its very low reliability increases it to almost the same level as structured interview validity. This has an important practical implication: pooling three or four unstructured interviews might achieve acceptable reliability, and match the structured interview's validity. This could be useful for the smaller employer who cannot afford to devise a structured interview system, or who has too few employees.

Interview or spoken questionnaire?

Very structured interviews, such as Latham's situational interview, blur the distinction between interview and paper-and-pencil test. If interviewers read from a script and do not interact with As, are they really needed? Why not print the questions in a question book, and have As answer them in writing? This would be much quicker and cheaper. Schmidt and Rader give one answer – interview format ensures people do not have time to prepare a carefully thought-out answer, which might not be entirely frank.

Resistance

The structured interview deprives interviewers of most of their traditional autonomy. They have to follow a script, have to use rating scales, and are not allowed to chat with As or tell them about the organization. Sometimes they are virtually reduced to being a substitute for a written test. This may mean interviewers will start to deviate from their prescribed role, unless they are closely monitored. In many organizations the managers who give the interviews are more powerful than HR, who bring in structured interviewing and try to maintain its quality. This suggests structured interviewing systems may not always achieve such good results in practice. Harris (2000) reports that structured interviews in a large UK city council proved very unpopular with recruiters, being seen as inflexible, mechanical, and over-structured. Lievens and De Paepe (2004) list three reasons why structured interviews seem relatively unpopular in Europe: interviewers want discretion in how interviews are conducted, interviewers do not want to lose informal personal contact with As, and they think too much time is needed to develop structured interview systems.

'Cribbable'?

Structured interviews have set lists of questions, and set marking schemes, which creates the risk of 'cribs' being generated – guides to what to expect and what to say, especially when the interview is used for promotion. Devising new questions requires elaborate data collection and analysis, so will not be easy.

RESEARCH AGENDA

- Re-compare structured and unstructured interview validity by (1) re-analysing all available data on validity of structured and unstructured interviews, (2) reopening research on 'traditional' interviews.
- Whether structured interviews work well in practice or whether validity decays through misuse.
- Whether structured interviews achieve higher validity simply through greater reliability.
- Which features of structured interviews need to be retained, and which could be dispensed with.
- Whether asking every A exactly same questions increases reliability and validity.
- Whether excluding interviewee questions improves reliability and validity.

CONSTRUCT VALIDITY OF THE INTERVIEW

Convergent validity

Several studies, most recently van Iddekinge et al. (2004) and Mussel, Berhmann, and Schuler (2008), have found that interviews seem to have poor convergent/divergent validity. Assessments of the same dimension in different interviews agree poorly, while assessments of different dimensions within the same interview agree too well. This suggests that interviews may be assessing 'interview performance' rather than the set of dimensions their users think they are assessing. A similar problem arises with assessment centres (Chapter 10). To the extent that interviews 'work' – are able to predict work performance – it could be argued this lack of convergent validity does not matter.

Construct validity

Research comparing interview ratings with other assessments, usually psychological tests, gives some indication what the interview is actually assessing (which may not be the same as what it is intended to assess).

Mental ability

Two earlier meta-analyses (Huffcutt, Roth & McDaniel, 1996; Salgado and Moscoso, 2002) had reported the 'true' correlation between interview rating and tested mental ability is around 0.40, suggesting that the interview makes a moderately good disguised mental ability test. This is quite surprising; most applicants, interviewers, HR managers and lay people do not see interviews as mental ability tests. However, Berry, Sackett and Landers (2007) argued that 0.40 is an overestimate, based on correcting for restricted range, where range has not in fact been restricted. Their re-analysis finds a lower true correlation of 0.27. Roth and Huffcutt (2013) make a fourth contribution to the discussion of mental ability and the interview, taking issue with Berry et al.'s (2007) conclusions. They note that Berry et al. include studies of interviews for educational selection, and suggest these differ from job-selection interviews in two important ways. Firstly, selection for higher education in the USA always uses mental ability tests, so the interview is likely to focus on other aspects of the applicant, such as personality or motivation. Interviewers do not need to try to assess mental ability if they have recent highly accurate test data. Secondly, interviews for admission to higher education in the USA are often used to look for reasons to admit As with lower test scores, to achieve targets for more representative admission: these too will focus on personality and motivation. The rest of the paper contains a detailed review, study by study, of Berry et al., questioning some of their coding decisions. Roth and Huffcutt (2013) conclude the correlation between interview rating and mental ability is 0.42, as they had found in their first (1996) meta-analysis. The ongoing discussion of mental ability and interview data shows clearly that meta-analysis is not an entirely mechanistic and objective process that is guaranteed to find the single right answer to a question. Chapter 2 noted that four meta-analyses of mental ability and interview structure (Huffcutt et al., 1996; Salgado and Moscoso, 2002; Cortina et al., 2000; Berry et al., 2007) find differing results, so it is not clear whether the link with mental ability is stronger for structured interviews, or for unstructured.

Table 4.3 Meta-analysis of construct validity of unstructured and structured interviews.

Type of interview	Unstructured		Structured	
	k	ρ	k	ρ
Job knowledge	*		8	0.53
Situational judgement	*		6	0.46
Grade point average	28	0.13	5	0.17
Social skill	6	0.46	5	0.65
Neuroticism	16	0.38	10	0.08
Extraversion	19	0.34	7	0.21
Openness	16	0.30	6	0.09
Agreeableness	18	0.26	6	0.12
Conscientiousness	18	0.28	13	0.17

Data from Salgado & Moscoso (2002).
ρ – true correlation, corrected for restricted range and reliability of both measures.
* insufficient data.

Personality

Salgado and Moscoso's (2002) meta-analysis also reports data for personality. Table 4.3 shows that ratings in unstructured interviews correlate with the five main factors in personality to some extent. Interview ratings reflect As' extraversion, neuroticism, etc., whether or not the interview is intended to assess these attributes. Table 4.3 shows structured interview ratings are less affected by personality. Subsequently Roth *et al.* (2005) report two further studies correlating personality with structured interview rating in 500 persons, and conclude there is a weak relationship with extraversion and conscientiousness, but none with agreeableness, neuroticism or openness.

Social skill and situational judgement

Structured interviews correlate surprisingly highly with the applicant's social skill and situational judgement, which suggests structured interviews may not entirely succeed in excluding irrelevant considerations from the interviewers' decisions.

Job knowledge

Structured interviews correlate quite well with paper-and-pencil job knowledge tests. Critics might say this is not surprising because some structured interviews could be viewed as little more than oral job knowledge tests.

Incremental validity

Can the interview improve on predictions made by other methods? Schmidt and Hunter (1998) argue that unstructured interviews will give little or no incremental validity over mental ability tests, because unstructured interviews are highly correlated with mental ability (although Berry *et al.*'s re-analysis suggests the correlation is not so high). Cortina *et al.* (2000) provide empirical confirmation; they find that an unstructured interview adds little to tests of conscientiousness and mental ability. Schmidt and Hunter conclude that structured interviews by contrast will have some incremental validity over mental ability tests, because both have good predictive validity but are not so highly correlated. Cortina *et al.* (2000) confirm that a structured interview has considerable incremental validity over tests of mental ability and conscientiousness.

TRUTHFULNESS OF INTERVIEW INFORMATION

Interviews are mostly self-reports, where interviewees describe their achievements, their abilities, their strengths, and their weaknesses. The question therefore arises: Do interviewees always tell the truth about themselves? Several lines of research are relevant.

Impression management (IM)

There is a growing body of research on ploys that As might use in the interview to try to create a better impression (Table 4.4). Ellis *et al.* (2002) analysed promotion interviews for firefighters, and found virtually everyone used IM tactics. The most commonly used are self-promotion and opinion conformity; excuses and flattery, on the other hand, were hardly ever used. Lievens and Peeters (2008) study interviewers' sensitivity to interviewee impression management in a highly controlled way, using filmed staged interviews with known levels of interviewee impression management. They find IM does affect interview rating, but the effect is relatively small. Barrick, Shaffer and DeGrassi (2009) report a meta-analysis showing that people who seek to ingratiate and self-promote in the interview do succeed in getting much better ratings. This may be a source of error, but not necessarily; ingratiators and self-promoters may at some level be better performers in the workplace. Silvester *et al.* (2002) show that the type of explanation people offer for past failures affects the impression they create. Admitting the failure was the candidate's fault – *I failed the exam because I didn't revise hard enough* – was better received than blaming other people. Schmid Mast, Frauendorfer and Popovic (2011) report a strong cultural effect in reactions to self-promotion in two French-speaking samples, in Canada and Switzerland. They prepared two versions of a staged interview, one self-promoting, the other modest in tone. In Canada recruiters much preferred the self-promoting performance, but in Switzerland it got the same rating as the modest version.

Table 4.4 Some impression management (IM) tactics used in interviews, with examples.

Assertive IM

Self-promotion	Positive descriptions of oneself.
	People look to me for leadership.
Entitlements	Claiming responsibility for success, even when it was really someone else's work.
	I helped make the reorganization a great success.
Enhancements	Saying an achievement was bigger than it appears
	The increase in sales I achieved was one of the biggest for some years.
Overcoming obstacles	How A got round barriers to success.
	I realised that we weren't getting bids out quickly enough, and reorganized the system to use e-mail.

Defensive IM

Excuses	Claiming to have no responsibility for failures.
	We lost that bid because the IT system let us down.
Apologies	Admitting being responsible for a failure.
	I got the projections for that scheme wrong which is why it didn't make a profit.
Justification	Accepting responsibility for failure but trying to minimize it.
	We lost the XYZ bid, but it wasn't a particularly large project and wouldn't have made much money.

Ingratiation

Flattery	*I have always greatly admired your work on …*
Opinion conformity	Saying things the interviewer will agree with.
	I think it's very important to keep oneself in good shape.

Non-verbal behaviour

Smiling, eye-contact, nodding, hand gestures, etc.

It could be argued that at least some IM techniques in Table 4.4 come under the heading of what interviewees are expected to do. One sometimes hears interviewers complaining an applicant 'didn't make an effort' – to describe his/her achievements at sufficient length and with sufficient enthusiasm. However, 'making an effort' can shade imperceptibly into untruth, from genuinely thinking one did more than one really did, through claiming most or all responsibility for something that others did some or most of, to describing entirely fictitious achievements. It has been suggested structured interviews may make IM more difficult, because all applicants are asked same questions, and have less opportunity to control the interview's agenda. Barrick *et al.*'s (2009) meta-analysis confirms this, although even structured interview ratings correlate 0.30 with interviewees' IM use.

Faking good

Levashina and Campion (2006) note that there has been little research on faking good in the selection interview (in sharp contrast to the flood of research on faking PQs, described in Chapter 7). They suggest some features of interviews will make them harder to fake, but others may make faking easier. The longer the interview, the more difficult it might be to avoid contradicting oneself, especially if the interviewer presses hard for examples of claimed abilities or achievements. The more interviewers there are, the more time they may have to detect inconsistencies, think of probing questions, and notice hesitation or non-verbal 'give-aways'. On the other hand features of the structured interview, designed to ensure consistency and prevent bias, may make faking easier, especially the absence of follow-up or probing questions, and not being allowed to see A's CV or application form. Van Iddekinge, Raymark and Roth (2005) found a structured interview assessing vulnerability, altruism, and self-discipline could be faked to some extent, but the change in scores was much less than for a PQ. Allen, Facteau & Facteau (2004) found students unable to fake good in a structured interview assessing organisational citizenship (Box 4.1), even if they are helped by being told what is being assessed.

Box 4.1   Organizational citizenship

Organizational citizenship means volunteering to do things not in the job description, helping others, following rules willingly, and publicly supporting the organization. Generally assessed by supervisor's rating, but can be assessed by self-report.

Interviewee lying

One step on from faking good or impression management is outright lying. One of the supposed traditional virtues of the 'good interviewer' was his/her ability to detect lies. Ekman's research casts some doubt on this; of five sets of experts who ought to be good at detecting lies – Secret Service, CIA, FBI, National Security Agency, Drug Enforcement Agency – only one did better

---

RESEARCH AGENDA

- How truthful As are in selection interviews.
- How good interviewers are at detecting untruths.
- How far untruthful As can improve their ratings, and whether this affects interview validity.
- More data on the frequency of different types of IM, in different types of interview, in different sectors, and different cultures.
- More data on how interviewers and interviewees view IM tactics, and how they affect interviewers' judgements.

---

than chance (Ekman & O'Sullivan, 1991). Weiss and Feldman (2006) describe an ingenious experiment, where students attend for research on personality and are unexpectedly offered an interview for a tutoring job. After the interview they are told the job does not exist, and asked to watch a recording of the interview, and pick out anything they said that was not true. Most (81%) admitted to telling at least one lie, with an average of just over two per person, in a 10–15-minute interview. The examples given suggest most 'lies' were exaggerations rather than outright untruths.

Interview coaching

Students at British universities are often offered 'how to be interviewed' courses; books offering the same proliferate. There is not much research on the effectiveness of interview coaching. Maurer *et al.* (2001) find coaching gets people better ratings in interviews for US fire and police services. Coaching seems to work by teaching people to be more organized, thinking about their answers, even making notes, before answering. Note, however, that Maurer *et al.*'s research describes a highly structured interview which asks only factual questions. Taking a long time to answer and making notes might not secure a good rating in more traditional interviews.

RESEARCH AGENDA

- How many interviewees are coached.
- How far coaching can improve interview ratings.
- Whether coaching affects validity.
- What effect coaching has in unstructured interviews.

HOW THE INTERVIEWER REACHES A DECISION

Ideally the interviewer will listen carefully to everything A says, and reach a wise decision based on all the information available. Research has documented a number of ways in which interviewers depart from this ideal.

Interviewers make their minds up before the interview

Barrick, Shaffer and DeGrassi's (2008) meta-analysis of 45 studies finds application form and CV/résumé have a big effect on interview rating. Some structured interview systems do not allow interviewers to see any other information about As.

Interviewers make up their minds quickly

A frequently cited study by Springbett (1958) showed that interviewers make up their minds after only four minutes of a 15-minute interview, although his methodology was not very subtle, and his sample very small. Frieder,

Van Iddekinge and Raymark (2015) analysed a considerably larger sample of interviewers, and found only a quarter said they had reached a decision within the first five minutes. Assessing personality and ability took longer than assessing physical attributes or social skills, which are more 'visible' so perhaps easier to assess. Applicants who tried to ingratiate themselves were judged more quickly.

The interviewer looks for novel information

Roulin, Bangerter and Yerly (2011) identify a new form of interview error: the uniqueness effect. The applicant who gives a unique answer to the question *What is your main weakness?* – i.e. an answer no one else gives – gets a better rating and is more likely to get the job.

The interviewer simplifies the task

Defenders of the interview argue a good interviewer can see complex patterns in the information that mechanistic methods, like checklists and weighted application blanks, miss. However research casts some doubt on interviewers' claim to be doing something so complex that no other method can replace them. Research suggests:

1. Human experts do not perform better than a system,
2. Human experts do not use information as complexly as they claim.

1. *Expert vs. System.* Over 60 years ago Meehl (1954) reviewed 20 studies comparing mechanistic systems against human experts, and concluded system always predicted as well as expert, often better. Research since 1954 has not disproved Meehl's conclusion; a meta-analysis of nine researches predicting work performance found mechanistic systems much superior to human experts when analysing complex data (Kuncel *et al.*, 2013).

2. *Does the expert use information complexly?* Research on how experts make decisions mostly uses the *policy capturing* paradigm. The researcher constructs sets of cases in which information is systematically varied, asks experts to assess each case, then deduces how the experts reached their decisions. If the expert accepts one set and rejects another, and the only feature distinguishing the two sets is exam results, it follows that the expert's decisions are based on exam grades. Experts claim they do not think as simplistically as this; they say they use configurations, for example exam grades are important in young candidates but not for people over 30 – an interaction of age and grades. Policy capturing finds experts rarely use configurations, even simple ones. Hitt and Barr (1989) found HR managers using cues complexly, but not wisely, making 'different attributions when comparing a Black, 45-year-old woman with 10 years of experience and a master's degree with a White, 35-year-old man with 10 years of experience and a master's degree'. (Not wise because fair employment law frowns on basing decisions on gender, age or ethnicity.)

BIAS IN THE INTERVIEW

The interview provides an ideal opportunity for the exercise of whatever bias(es) interviewers have, because they cannot avoid knowing every A's gender, ethnicity, age, social background, and physical attractiveness, and because they are rarely required to justify their decisions. (Whereas selectors can use psychological tests or biographical methods, without seeing As or knowing their gender etc.)

Are interviewers biased against women?

Huffcutt *et al.* (2001) find unstructured interviews do create some adverse impact on females, whereas structured interviews do not. The research reviewed is nearly all North American, so one cannot safely assume similar results will be found in other countries, given that attitudes to gender vary widely.

Are interviewers biased by race?

Huffcutt *et al.*'s (2001) meta-analysis shows that unstructured interviews do create some adverse impact on non-white Americans, especially interviews that assess intellectual ability and experience. Huffcutt *et al.* also concluded that structured interviews do not create an adverse impact on minorities, which is one reason why they are popular in the USA. However, there are two reasons for being less optimistic. Firstly, Bobko and Roth (1999) note that structured interviews do create some adverse impact on African Americans ($d = 0.23$). Secondly this may be an example of the Bobko–Roth fallacy. Roth *et al.* (2002) point out that adverse impact computations for interviews are often made in organizations where the interview is used after As have been screened already, for example by tests. Pre-screening by tests will tend to restrict the range of ability of those interviewed, and possibly lead to an underestimate of the adverse impact of the structured interview. Roth *et al.* corrected for this restriction of range and found structured interviews created fairly large adverse impact, d ranging from 0.36 to 0.56. Prewett-Livingston *et al.* (1996) found interviews show own-race bias, where whites favour whites, blacks favour blacks, Hispanic Americans favour other Hispanic Americans, etc. McCarthy, van Iddekinge and Campion (2010) note that same-ethnicity and same-gender bias in interview ratings, documented in several previous studies, was found to be absent from a large-scale program of US government interviews, and suggests careful practice can prevent the problem. This includes giving all interviewers two full days' training, and, perhaps most important, using three successive structured interviews of different types to ensure enough 'individuating information' is obtained, i.e. information about the candidate as an individual, not as e.g. an Asian American. Nearly 20,000 applicants were studied, which allowed every combination of interviewer–interviewee ethnicity to be analysed separately.

Audit studies

There is an extensive literature on discrimination using the audit method. White and e.g. Asian persons apply for a real job, and attend a real interview. White and Asian are matched exactly in age, experience, qualifications, etc., so the conclusion can be drawn that lower hiring rates for Asian As indicate deliberate discrimination. Such discrimination is usually found. Psychologists see fatal flaws in these studies. How can one be sure that white and Asian people behave comparably at interview? The 'applicants' are carefully trained, sometimes professional actors, but interviews are inherently unpredictable, so it is impossible to be completely prepared. Moreover audit 'applicants' may have expectations that minority As will be discriminated against, which may subtly affect their behaviour. Medical research has shown how pervasively expectations affect people, so great care is taken that no one knows who gets the active drug and who gets the placebo. This 'double blind' precaution is not possible when audit studies of ethnicity go as far as a face-to-face interview.

Are interviewers biased against older applicants?

Morgeson, Reider, Campion and Bull (2008) review 16 laboratory studies of age discrimination in employment interviews, and five field studies, and find age discrimination in real interviews much less than in simulated interviews. They suggest laboratory studies make age more salient, and provide less other relevant information.

Are interviewers biased by accent?

George Bernard Shaw once remarked that no Englishman can open his mouth without making other Englishmen despise him. Hosoda, Nguyen and Stone-Romero (2012) showed a Hispanic accent in the USA reduces one's chances of promotion. Huang, Frideger and Pearce (2013) conclude the effect of a non-native accent is mediated by perceived (lower) ability to influence others (not by racism or poorer ability to communicate). Shaw was probably thinking of social class rather than nationality or ethnicity, in which case his hypothesis has yet to be tested in the area of selection.

Are interviewers biased by appearance?

Most people can agree whether someone is conventionally 'good-looking' or not. Barrick et al.'s (2008) meta-analysis of 17 studies finds a large (0.52) correlation between attractiveness and interview rating. The effect is very strong (0.81) in unstructured interviews, but almost absent (0.17) from highly structured interviews.

Are interviewers biased by weight?

Fikkan and Rothblum (2005) review extensive evidence of consistent negative stereotypes of overweight people as lacking in self-discipline, lazy, having emotional problems, or being less able to get on with others, and find overweight people discriminated against in every aspect of employment, including selection. Kutcher and Bragger (2004) found interviewers biased against overweight applicants; they used actors, whose apparent body weight in the overweight condition was increased by make-up and padding. However the bias was only found in unstructured interviews, not in structured ones. Hebl and Mannix (2003) report the extraordinary finding that merely sitting next to an overweight person reduces an applicant's chance of getting the job. Rudolph *et al.* (2008) provide an estimate of effect size of being overweight on hiring decisions across 25 studies of $d = 0.52$, which does not seem to vary much for different types of job.

Are interviewers biased by height?

Height was formerly sometimes an explicit consideration in hiring decisions; Judge and Cable (2004) suggest that 'What was once explicit may now be implicit.' They review four longitudinal researches on height and earning power, including one in the UK, and find a correlation of 0.31–0.35 (the issue of correction does not arise with income or height because both can be measured with near-perfect reliability). The link is found in both men and women despite the average difference in height. The link is slightly stronger in sales and management, but present in all types of work: blue-collar, clerical, craft, service, professional/technical. Height might be genuinely useful in sales and management if it helps people persuade and influence others, but its relevance to clerical work is harder to discern. Judge and Cable offer a model: height leads to increased self-esteem and social esteem, which contributes to success. It remains unclear whether the link is a positive preference for taller people, or a bias against shorter people.

Are interviewers biased against gay applicants?

Hebl *et al.* (2002) sent people to apply for jobs at local stores in the USA, some identifying themselves as gay. The 'gay' As got a more negative reception – shorter interview or less friendly interviewer – but were not actually discriminated against in terms of getting job offers. Hebl *et al.* avoided creating expectations in 'applicants', with an ingenious way of identifying some 'As' as gay without their knowing; 'As' were given a hat to wear, which either said 'Proud to be Gay' or 'XYZ University', but they did not know which.

RESEARCH AGENDA

- Gender, ethnicity or age bias in interviews in countries outside North America.
- Whether structured interviews reduce interviewer bias.
- Whether interviews create adverse impact, correcting for indirect range restriction.

LAW AND FAIRNESS

Terpstra, Mohamed and Kethley (1999) noted that unstructured interviews are the most frequent source of dispute in the USA. They estimated how many complaints one would expect for any selection method, given its frequency of use. Unstructured interviews are complained about twice as often as would be expected, whereas structured interviews are only complained about half as often as would be expected. Terpstra *et al.* found another even more compelling reason to commend structured interviews to employers. When structured interviews were the subject of complaint, the employer always won the case, whereas with unstructured interviews 40% of employers lost their case. Williamson *et al.* (1997) analysed 130 American court cases, and found two interview features that helped employers defend themselves against claims of unfairness. The first was structure: the use of standard sets of questions, limiting interviewer discretion, and ensuring all interviews are the same. The second was the use of objective, specific, behavioural criteria, as opposed to vague, global, subjective criteria, also an interviewer who is trained and who is familiar with the job's requirements. Use of multiple interviewers, or panel interviews, however, made no difference to whether employers won their cases. Clearly, structured interviewing is much better in terms of achieving fairness, and avoiding losing fair employment claims.

KEY POINTS

In Chapter 4 you have learned the following:

- Interviews vary in form, and in what they seek to assess.
- Conventional unstructured interviews have poor reliability, and may have poor validity.
- Interviewees try to present themselves in a good light, and may sometimes even fail to tell the truth about themselves.
- Interviews can be improved by selecting interviewers, training interviewers, and using multiple interviewers.
- Structured interviews are based on job analysis, and control interview format and questions, while providing detailed rating systems.
- Research indicates structured interviews are highly reliable.
- Earlier research suggested structured interviews achieve better validity than unstructured, but re-analysis has thrown some doubt on this.
- Research suggests question format in structured interviews is not critical.
- Interview ratings correlate with mental ability, personality and social skill.
- Interviewers do not always reach decisions very efficiently or rationally.
- Interviewers' thought processes may be less complex than interviewers suppose.
- Interviewers may be biased by many factors including gender, ethnicity, age, appearance, weight, or accent.

- Unstructured interviews have been the subject of many fair employment claims, many of which have been successful; structured interviews have been the subject of fewer claims, fewer of which proved successful.

KEY REFERENCES

Bozionelos (2005) describes a case study of interview 'fixing' in a British university.

Fikkan & Rothblum (2005) review research on weight bias in selection.

Huffcutt *et al.* (2014) report a new meta-analysis of interview validity using the new indirect range restriction methodology.

Klehe *et al.* (2008) examine the role of transparency, knowing what is being assessed, in the interview.

Latham *et al.* (1980) describe the first structured interview technique, the situation interview.

Levashina & Campion (2006) discuss the fakability of the interview.

McCarthy *et al.* (2010) describe a programme of structured interviews in the US public sector that succeed in avoiding own-race bias.

Morgeson *et al.* (2008) review research on age discrimination in the employment interview.

Roth & Huffcutt (2013) make a very detailed reinterpretation of the research on the correlation between mental ability and interview success.

Salgado & Moscoso (2002) analyse research on the interview's construct validity.

USEFUL WEBSITES

bdt.net. Devoted to Janz's behaviour description interviewing.
best-job-interview.com; job-interview-wisdom.com. Typical how-to-be-interviewed advice, with examples of different types of question.

CHAPTER 5

References and ratings

The eye of the beholder

References and ratings work on the principle that the best way of finding out about applicants is to ask someone who knows them well – former employers, school teachers, or colleagues. They have seen A all day every day, perhaps for years, and can report how A usually behaves, and what A is like on 'off days'. The traditional way of doing this is the reference request; more recent developments include various types of ratings by other people.

REFERENCES

The Cranfield Price Waterhouse survey (Table 1.5, p. 19) finds references widely used throughout western Europe. Similarly most American employers take up references on new employees. References are cheap, and universally accepted, because everyone has always used them. References may be structured – checklists, ratings – or unstructured.

Uses of the reference

The reference is a *method* that can collect information on most of the headings (constructs) listed in Table 1.2 (page 12): mental ability, other abilities, personality, knowledge, skill, etc. References also have the unusual, and potentially valuable, feature of being able to get straight to the point. They can ask directly about work performance: Was Smith a good worker? Was Smith punctual? Most other selection tests can only infer from As' abilities or personality what their work performance is likely to be. Table 5.1 summarizes a survey of American HR professionals which showed references used for fact-checking, direct enquiry about work performance (with an emphasis on attendance), and for personal qualities, but not for ability, general or specific (Bureau of National Affairs, 1995). Taylor *et al.* (2004) suggest references may be particularly suitable for getting information on organizational citizenship (Box 4.1, page 86). Some employers use references at the sifting or shortlisting stage;

Personnel Selection: Adding Value Through People – A Changing Picture,
Sixth Edition. Mark Cook.
© 2016 John Wiley & Sons, Ltd. Published 2016 by John Wiley & Sons, Ltd.

Table 5.1 Survey of 1,331 US HR professionals about information sought in reference requests.

Dates of employment	96%
Salary history	45%
Qualifications for a particular job	56%
Eligibility for rehire	65%
Overall impression of employability	49%
Work habits (absence, punctuality)	41%
Human relations skills	37%
Personality	24%
Driving record	42%
Credit history	25%

Data from Bureau of National Affairs (1995).

others wait until they have chosen someone to appoint, and use the reference as a final check on qualifications, honesty, etc.

Telephone references

A 1998 SHRM survey of American employers (SHRM, 1998) found over 80% used telephone referencing. Telephone referencing has several possible advantages, apart from speed; referees can be asked for examples or for clarification. Hesitation or tone of voice may be informative. One apparent advantage may really be a major snag. Some people prefer phone referencing because they think it leaves nothing for lawyers to 'discover' later, but lack of written trace is actually risky, making it very difficult to prove what was or was not said. Also phone conversations can be recorded. Many organizations' rules forbid either giving or seeking phone references, but Andler and Herbst (2002) suggest these rules are often broken. They present quite detailed scripts for getting information, including the distinctly unethical ploy of telling the referee the applicant will not get the job unless the referee gives the information requested.

Reliability

American research suggests references lack reliability. Referees agree among themselves very poorly about applicants for (US) civil service jobs, with 80% of correlations lower than 0.40 (Mosel & Goheen, 1959). More recent research (Taylor et al., 2004) has confirmed that references have very poor inter-referee reliability, generally less than 0.25. Some very early British research looked at reliability from a different slant. The Civil Service Selection Board (CSSB) in the 1940s collected references from school, university, the armed services, and former employers (Wilson, 1948); CSSB staff achieved reasonably good inter-rater reliability (0.73) in assessments of As based on references alone. CSSB used five or six references, which will tend to increase reliability. Note that Wilson is addressing a different issue: whether the panel agree about what the five or six referees collectively are saying about A, not whether the five or six agree with each other.

VALIDITY

American research

Mosel and Goheen (1959) reported research on the Employment Recommendation Questionnaire (ERQ), a structured reference developed by the US Civil Service, which covered ability, character and reputation, skill, knowledge, and human relations. For some jobs in the civil service and armed forces ERQ had zero validity, while for other jobs ERQ achieved limited validity (r = 0.20 to 0.30). Note that these are uncorrected correlations, from generally small samples, so will tend to be low, and variable. Goheen and Mosel (1959) also compared 109 ERQs with a more searching field investigation which 'interrogated' up to six people who knew A well (but were not necessarily nominated by A). In seven cases, the investigation uncovered serious disqualifying facts, such as gross incompetence or alcoholism, none of which had been mentioned in the written reference. The low validity of the reference, documented by the ERQ research, implies such problems will arise.

Two early meta-analyses of US research (Reilly & Chao, 1982; Hunter & Hunter, 1984) concluded reference checks give fairly poor predictions of four outcomes, but – being very early – made few corrections for unreliable outcome or restricted range (Table 5.2). Hunter and Hunter do not list the studies included, so one does not know how much their analysis overlaps with Reilly and Chao's. (The data for tenure/turnover look rather similar, except for the validity!)

There is a remarkable dearth of research on references since the 1980s (compared with the vast quantity on personality questionnaires, or interviews, or assessment centres). Kuncel, Kochevar and Ones (2014) report a meta-analysis of references for US undergraduate and postgraduate admissions, which finds predictive validities ranging from 0.10 to 0.28. The analysis probably underestimates validity, because it is not possible to correct for either reliability or range restriction as there is insufficient information about either.

Table 5.2 Two early meta-analyses of reference check validity by Hunter & Hunter (1984) and Reilly & Chao (1982).

Outcome ⇓	k	N	r	
Supervisor rating	10	5,389	0.26*	Hunter & Hunter
	8	3,696	0.18	Reilly & Chao
Promotion	3	415	0.16	Hunter & Hunter
Training success	1	1,553	0.23	Hunter & Hunter
Tenure	2	2,018	0.27	Hunter & Hunter
Turnover	2	2,022	0.08	Reilly & Chao

Correlations are uncorrected, except for *, which is corrected for reliability of supervisor rating.

European research

References for UK naval officer training by head teachers correlate moderately well (0.36, corrected for restricted range) with training grade in naval college (Jones & Harrison, 1982). Jones and Harrison argued that head teachers are more likely (than, say, former employers) to write careful and critical references, because they know they will be writing Naval College references for future pupils, and because their own credibility is at stake. Outside North America, Moser and Rhyssen (2001) report a low validity (0.20 uncorrected) for telephone references for German sales staff and supervisors.

Construct and incremental validity

There are also few data on how references relate to other tests or what they can add to them. Taylor *et al.* (2004) find assessments of conceptually distinct attributes – conscientiousness, agreeableness and customer focus – are highly correlated (0.68–0.77), suggesting references may lack divergent validity. Taylor *et al.* suggest references cover typical behaviour, not best behaviour, so might have incremental validity on tests of skill and ability. Zimmerman, Triana and Barrick (2010) find a structured reference had near-zero correlation with GMA, and consequently achieved incremental validity over a GMA test. Kuncel *et al.*'s meta-analysis of references for college admissions in the USA found low (but uncorrected) correlations with mental ability (0.08–0.14) and interview (0.18).

Reasons for poor validity

Referees may lack the time or motivation to write careful references. Some referees may follow a hidden agenda to retain good staff and 'release' poor staff, by writing deliberately untrue references.

Leniency Numerous researches report that most references are positive, called the 'Pollyanna effect' after the little girl who wanted to be nice to everyone. Early research by Mosel and Goheen found ERQ ratings highly skewed; hardly anyone was rated poor. Grote, Robiner and Haut (2001) presented two parallel surveys of US psychologists: the first set of psychologists say they disclose negative information in references they write, but the second set complain they are rarely given any negative information in references they receive. Nicklin and Roch (2009) report a survey of HR professionals which also identified leniency as a major problem. It is not hard to see why this happens. Referees are usually nominated by applicants, who will obviously choose someone likely to give them a good reference. These days many employers fear an unfavourable reference may result in a libel suit. But if referees are reluctant to say anything negative, references will remain a poor source of information. Murphy and Cleveland (1995) noted that performance appraisal has a similar problem – pervasive leniency – and suggest some reasons why. Managers can observe employees' shortcomings but have no incentive to communicate them to others, and many reasons not to, including fear of creating ill feeling, and not wanting to describe any of their staff as poor performers because this reflects on their own management ability. Murphy's argument implies references could be an excellent source of information, if only referees could be persuaded to communicate it.

IMPROVING THE REFERENCE

Various attempts have been made to improve the reference, with mixed results.

Forced-choice format

Carroll and Nash (1972) used pairs of statements equated for social desirability; the referee must choose one of each pair as describing the applicant.

- *has many worthwhile ideas / completes all assignments*
- *always works fast / requires little supervision*

This format is intended to limit leniency. Scores predicted performance ratings four months after hire quite well in university clerical workers.

Competence-based

References can use the organization's competence framework, and ask for behavioural evidence of, for example, resilience or time management; Figure 5.1 shows part of a typical request of this type. There seems to be no research on whether competence-based references achieve higher reliability or validity.

For each heading, give your overall assessment of A on the scale: 5) very good ...1) very poor. Then give examples of A's behaviour or achievements which form the basis of your assessment.

Interpersonal sensitivity. *Listens well, encourages contributions from others and responds constructively. Can establish co-operative relationships with others and defuse potential conflicts. Can build useful relationships and alliances with others. Shows awareness of diversity and is sensitive to issues of gender, ethnicity, disability, and social exclusion.*

Rating:
Evidence:

Drive. *Able to set well-defined and challenging goals for his/her work. Shows unflagging energy and enthusiasm across a wide range of varied employment or extracurricular activities. Shows determination in overcoming obstacles. Always meets deadlines.*

Figure 5.1   Extract from a competence-based reference request.

Relative Percentile Method

McCarthy and Goffin (2001) describe the Relative Percentile Method, a 100-point scale where the referee says what percentage of persons score lower than the applicant on, for example, responsibility. McCarthy and Goffin estimate the method's validity at 0.42. The technique may work by allowing referees to be lenient – the mean percentile given was 80 – but also to differentiate at the top end of the scale, giving someone they consider really responsible 95 rather than 85.

Personality-based structured references

Taylor *et al.* (2004) describe a telephone reference covering conscientiousness, agreeableness, and customer focus. The reference is structured using items taken from Goldberg's bank (Chapter 7), and a comparison format similar to McCarthy and Goffin (2001): How organized is (A) compared to others you have known? Pooled referees' rating predicted work performance rating 0.25, rising to 0.36 when corrected for reliability of work performance measure. The reference check is the final stage of selection, after two interviews, so restriction of range is likely, but could not be calculated or corrected for. The reference also predicted turnover to a more limited extent (0.16). Zimmerman *et al.* (2010) report a similar study, achieving an operational validity of 0.37. Both researches averaged across three referees, which would increase validity through better reliability; Zimmerman *et al.* argue that even allowing for this the structured reference achieves better validity than the traditional unstructured one. Note that both Taylor *et al.* and Zimmerman *et al.* use items from personality questionnaires, so may achieve their better results by using questions selected – by the PQ development – to be relevant to the traits assessed. Both Taylor *et al.* and Zimmerman *et al.* are describing references that are in effect others' report form personality questionnaires, i.e. PQs completed by the referee to describe the applicant. Self-report personality questionnaires are reviewed in Chapter 7, and others' report PQs in Chapter 8.

UNSTRUCTURED REFERENCES

The traditional reference in the UK was, and often still is, unstructured or free-form, effectively saying *Tell me what you think of John/Jill Smith in your own words*. Research is more difficult because unstructured references contain no numbers to put into statistical analysis. Early researches, for example Wiens, Jackson and Manaugh (1976), showed that more favourable reference letters tended to be longer, which might not be very useful in practice, because one needs to know how long a reference each referee usually writes.

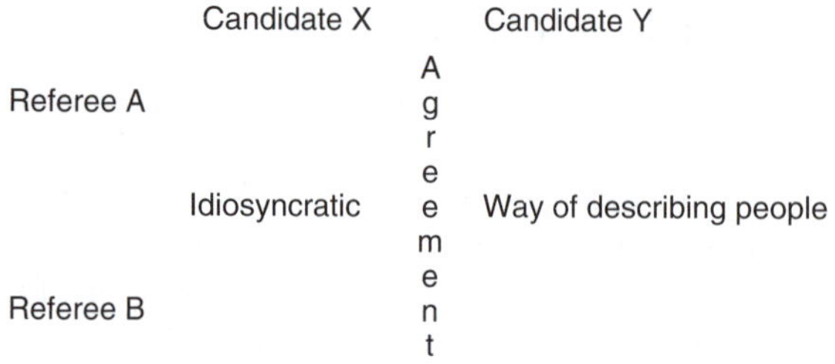

Candidate X   Candidate Y

Referee A

Idiosyncratic   A g r e e m e n t   Way of describing people

Referee B

Figure 5.2   Schematic representation of the study by Baxter *et al.* (1981) of letters of reference.

Idiosyncrasy

Baxter *et al.* (1981) searched medical school files to find 20 cases where the same two referees had written references for the same two candidates (Figure 5.2). If references are useful, what referee A says about candidate X ought to resemble what referee B says about applicant X (i.e. show good inter-rater reliability). Analysis of the qualities listed in the letters revealed a different, and much less encouraging, pattern. What referee A said about candidate X did not resemble what referee B said about candidate X, but did resemble what referee A said about candidate Y. Each referee had his/her own idiosyncratic way of describing people, which came through no matter whom he/she was describing. The free-form reference appears to say more about its author than about its subject. Differences in reference writing may reflect personality (of author not applicant); Judge and Higgins (1998) showed that happier people write more favourable references.

Content analysis

Colarelli, Hechanova-Alampay and Canali (2002) collected 532 letters describing 169 As for psychologist posts at a US university, and made global ratings of the favourability of each letter. These proved to have near-zero (0.19) inter-referee reliability, and zero validity when correlated with number of publications (a key index of work performance in academics). Loher *et al.* (1997) attempted a content analysis of reference letters, but could find no relationship between types of words used, or types of evidence given, and overall impact of the reference. Most HR managers are familiar with the complexities of hinting at weaknesses in an ostensibly favourable reference, for example 'perfectionist' means 'never gets anything finished'. Private languages of this type are easily misunderstood.

Keyword counting

Peres and Garcia (1962) factor-analysed data from 625 reference letters, and found five factors distinguishing good from poor As (Table 5.3). Many years later, Aamodt, Bryan and Whitcomb (1993) used Peres and Garcia's lists in

Table 5.3   Examples of words relating to five factors in letters of reference.

Co-operation	Mental agility	Urbanity	Vigour	Dependability
Good-natured	Imaginative	Talkative	Hustling	Precise
Accommodating	Ingenious	Chatty	Active	Persistent
Congenial	Insightful	Forward	Energetic	Methodical
Likeable	Knowledgeable	Bold	Self-driving	Tenacious
Co-operative	Intelligent	Sparkling	Vigorous	Determined

Data from Peres & Garcia (1962).

selecting trainee teachers; they found counting mental agility keywords predicts mental ability, while counting urbanity key words predicts teaching performance ratings. The keyword method may partially solve the leniency problem, by allowing a referee who wants to be really positive to say someone is intelligent not just once, but several times. Keyword counting needs free-form references; the documented idiosyncrasy of reference writers means HR will need a baseline for each referee. However, text-scanning software makes keyword-counting techniques much more feasible. Note that Peres and Garcia's list bears a partial, but not exact, resemblance to the five-factor model of personality described in Chapter 7.

Computerized linguistic analysis may help understanding free-form references. Madera, Hebl and Martin (2009) have used the Linguistic Inquiry and Word Count (LIWC) program to analyse reference letters for psychology faculty posts in the USA. Women tended to be described in *communal* terms (agreeable, tactful, warm, etc.), whereas men were more likely to be described in *agentic* terms (confident, aggressive, ambitious, etc.). A second paper applicant study showed applicants described by more *communal* words were less likely to get the job (but found no effect of *agentic* words). In other words, *communal* descriptions may mediate sex bias in hiring. Stedman, Hatch and Schoenfeld (2009) use LIWC to analyse references for medical training posts in the USA, and confirm a very large leniency effect in unstructured references. *Positive emotion/attribution* words – alert, brilliant, pleasant – outnumber negative words – loser, messy, obnoxious – 10 to one, and are present in exactly the same proportion in references for As who are shortlisted, and As who are rejected. Positive words tend to be used in patterns – warm, genuine, and empathic – but 'lose any power to discriminate between applicants due to their frequent use'. The reference begins to sound almost like a ritual. Stedman *et al.* found the average length of references was 520 words, which makes it a time-consuming and expensive ritual.

The unstructured reference lends itself to being analysed in terms of the Brunswik lens. Figure 5.3 shows three components: the reference writer's intention, the text of the reference, and the recipient's interpretation.

In a structured reference, there should be little scope for misunderstanding. If the referee gives a rating of 'very unpunctual', the recipient cannot suppose this is meant to be favourable. In an unstructured reference, by contrast, things

REFEREE		REFERENCE		RECIPIENT
intention	>>>>	**text**	>>>>	**interpretation**
write Smith good reference		*'sound chap'*		Smith sounds good A
write Jones subtly poor reference		*'novel ideas'*		Jones sounds OK

Figure 5.3   A Brunswik lens model of the unstructured reference letter.

can go wrong in either of two places (or even both). The referee means to say Jones is not entirely suitable because he has some peculiar ideas about managing staff, but the recipient interprets 'novel ideas' as meaning Jones is very creative. References could fail to work because the writer does not express him/herself clearly *or* because the recipient habitually misunderstands things. The key to deciding which is the text. If 18 of 20 people who read it think it means creativity, then the fault lies with the referee. But if 18 of 20 think it means Jones has peculiar ideas about managing people, then the fault lies with the recipient.

LAW AND FAIRNESS

In the USA employers find the law seems to have placed them in a very difficult position with references. Little and Sipes (2000) note that more and more Americans are suing employers over unfavourable references, which has resulted in more and more employers providing only *minimal* references. These give dates of employment, job title, possibly salary, but refuse to express any opinion about performance at work. This greatly reduces the value of the reference as a selection assessment tool. People dismissed for sexual abuse of children or violent behaviour at work can get another job, and do the same again, because the next employer is not warned about them. American courts have also introduced the concept of *negligent referral* – failing to disclose information to another employer about serious misconduct at work. This means employers risk being sued by the employee if they write a bad reference, and being sued by the next employer if they do not! To try to preserve the reference system, most states in the USA have passed immunity laws that restore 'privilege' to reference letters, meaning that employees cannot sue if the information is given in good faith, even if it proves not entirely correct. These laws require employers to show references to employees so they can make corrections or include their version of events.

In Britain the 1994 case of *Spring v Guardian Assurance* (Parry, 1999) made it possible to sue if a reference was inaccurate, whereas previously one had to prove also *malice*: that the referee knew the reference was inaccurate – a virtually impossible task. A number of libel cases involving references have been tried since. People have right of access to references held by their present employer, but not to those held by past employers. This could make it difficult for Smith to find out if he/she is not getting jobs because a past employer is giving him/her an undeserved bad reference. These days referees generally assume that what they say can be seen by the applicant, which may imply that American-style minimal references will be increasingly used in Britain.

Discussion of references so far has assumed that employers use them to evaluate potential employees, but references may have another purpose. The employer can refuse a reference or give a bad one, and so block the employee's chance of getting another job. To be certain of getting a good reference, the employee must avoid doing anything that might offend the employer. On this argument, the reference system is used by employers to control present staff, not to assess new staff.

RESEARCH AGENDA

The reference is one of the most under-researched areas in personnel selection. There is barely enough research to justify a meta-analysis of validity. Little research has been attempted on the widely used free-form reference. Promising leads, such as forced-choice format, are not followed up. Sample sizes are often barely adequate. This generates a lengthy research agenda. As time passes, and successive editions of this volume appear, the list of research questions about references gets longer, but the list of answers does not.

- More current information on what references actually ask about.
- More data on validity of references, including validity for a wider range of outcomes: task performance, organizational citizenship, counter-productive behaviour.
- More data on construct validity, including correlation with other selection tests.
- More data on incremental validity of references over other selection tests.
- Some data on reliability, acceptability or validity of competence-based references.
- More research on improvements to the reference, including forced-choice format, relative percentile format.
- Reasons for pervasive leniency, and how to persuade referees to be more frank.
- More research on free-form references, including keyword counting, and use of private languages.
- How many unstructured references convey a clear meaning to most others.
- Data on the frequency of use of phone references.
- Whether telephone references are lenient, reliable, and valid.
- Whether referees allow bias – gender, ethnicity, liking, etc. – to affect what they write.

- Whether references create adverse impact on protected minorities.
- More research on structured references, clarifying whether better validity is achieved by pooling across referees.
- Whether referees chosen by A give more favourable or less valid references than referees chosen by the employer.
- What purpose(s) references serve, and why so many employers use them.

RATINGS

In personnel selection, ratings can be used both as the *predictor* and as the outcome or *criterion* measure. This chapter will cover research on ratings by others as a predictor of work performance; the more extensive body of research on ratings as the criterion of work performance is covered in Chapter 12. It is clearly completely circular to use the same set of ratings as both predictor and criterion, but this is not too difficult a trap to fall into if one does not think carefully enough about who is rating whom, on what, and for what purpose. Chapter 8 covers the use of ratings of personality as predictor.

Ratings used as predictor, in selection, are usually made by external referees, or by A's peers. Criterion or outcome ratings, of work performance, were traditionally made by supervisor or manager. From the 1990s ratings by co-workers, aka peers, subordinates or customers, have been used as well, originally called 360-degree feedback, now known as multi-source performance ratings (MSPR).

Rating systems usually contain half a dozen scales, often many more. However, it can be a mistake to multiply rating scales, because factor analysis (Box 2.7, on page 37) usually shows a large number of ratings reduce to a much smaller number of factors. Ratings can take various forms. Figure 5.4a shows the conventional graphic rating scale; different formats vary the number of scale points, or supply anchors for each point – very, fairly, slightly etc. Figure 5.4b also shows behaviourally anchored rating scale (BARS) format, which aims to make each point of the scale more meaningful to the rater, and the ratings less arbitrary. BARS aims to reduce leniency and to increase inter-rater agreement. BARS require a lot of research, and tend to be job-specific, which makes them expensive.

PEER OR CO-WORKER ASSESSMENTS

Conway and Huffcutt (1997) meta-analysed research on inter-rater reliability of ratings of targets by peers and subordinates at work, made as part of '360 feedback' or multi-source performance rating. Some ratings are *cognitive* – job knowledge, diagnosing problems, etc.; some are *interpersonal* – human relations skill, communication; some are a mix of work performance and personality – drive and effort. One person's view of the target agrees fairly poorly with

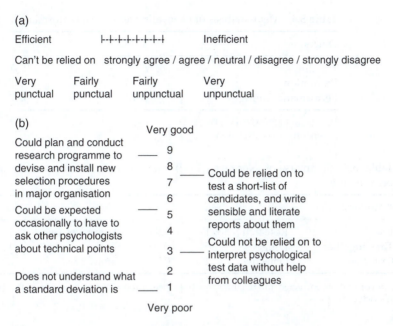

Figure 5.4   Rating formats. (a) graphic rating scales; (b) (invented) example of behaviourally anchored rating scale (BARS), for rating occupational psychologists.

another's: an average uncorrected correlation of 0.37 for peers and 0.30 for subordinates. However, the consensus of four peers can achieve a reliability of 0.70, and the consensus of seven 0.80. Peers, subordinates and supervisors all agree moderately well (0.57 to 0.79, corrected), suggesting the ratings do contain some useful information (but note the reputation issue).

Reputation

When psychologists talk about inter-observer reliability, they assume the observations are independent. But this may not be the case when people rate colleagues at work. A person's virtues and shortcomings may have been discussed at length, so a shared view of Smith's merits may have emerged, or may even have been constructed, by Smith's friends or enemies. Chapter 12 outlines some ways in which the targets themselves can try to shape a shared consensus of their merits. In this context high levels of agreement may cease to be impressive.

VALIDITY OF PEER RATINGS

An early meta-analysis by Reilly and Chao (1982) calculated average validities for three outcomes (Table 5.4), finding fairly large correlations, especially for promotion.

A later meta-analysis of peer rating and work performance by Norton (1992) covered 56 validities and 11,000 people. The results were at first sight impressive: an uncorrected average validity of 0.48, rising to 0.58 when corrected for

Table 5.4   Meta-analysis of peer rating and work performance.

Outcome	k	r
Training	10	0.31
Promotion	5	0.51
Performance ratings	18	0.37

Data from Reilly & Chao (1982).
r = uncorrected correlation.

Table 5.5   Summary of Norton's (1992) meta-analysis of peer rating and work performance.

⇓ Moderator ⇓		k	ρ		k	ρ
Use	Research	17	0.56	Administrative	10	0.37
Time together	Long	54	0.69	Short	11	0.20
Criterion	Objective	43	0.73	Subjective	22	0.39

ρ = correlation corrected for reliability of both peer rating and outcome measure but not for restricted range.

reliability of work performance measure. However, all the samples were present employees (and mostly military, but results for military and non-military do not differ). Norton also reported some powerful moderator variables (Table 5.5), which clearly imply peer rating will not be very useful in selection.

- Ratings made for research only were far more accurate than ratings used to make decisions about people.
- Ratings made after long acquaintance were far more accurate, whereas ratings made after short acquaintance correlated with work performance fairly poorly.

Norton's third moderator showed peer ratings predicted objective indices of work outcome better than subjective ones. Perhaps outcomes like sales figures or training grades are clearly visible to the rest of the group, which tends to make the high correlation trivial; peers may not be predicting the target's work performance, but may simply be reporting known facts.

Conway, Lombardo and Sanders (2001) report a meta-analysis of nine studies comparing peer rating and objective measures of work performance (production, profit, absence of demerits). They find much lower validity than Norton, a correlation of only 0.28, barely increased to 0.29 by correcting for reliability of work performance measure. The difference may arise because Conway *et al.* only include correlations between peer rating and actual work outcomes, whereas Norton includes correlations between peer rating and measures of skill, ability and personal characteristics. Conway *et al.* also found 14 studies comparing subordinates' rating with objective work performance measures, and found another fairly weak relationship.

Multi-source performance rating (MSPR)

This has become very popular in HR and management, and several commercial systems are very big business, especially in the USA. MSPR is mostly used for training and development, but has from time to time struck people as potentially useful in selection. Hoffman *et al.* (2012) researched an MSPR that assessed seven performance dimensions, some of which sound potentially very useful as predictors in selection: problem-solving, motivating followers, participative leadership, stress tolerance, conflict management, interpersonal sensitivity, and being able to manage others' performance. Fleenor and Brutus (2001) note that MSPR is sometimes used for internal promotions; there seems, however, to be no research on validity. MSPR might be very useful for external selection but for a major practical problem. MSPR is usually conducted within a single organization, for that organization's purposes, which are unlikely to include helping other employers to poach their best employees. Hoffman *et al.* (2012) note some other problems with MSPR, which could tend to make it less useful as a selection measure:

- MSPR is mostly generic, not job-specific. MSPR is usually based on broader competence models. Some MSPR systems are all-purpose competence frameworks intended to apply to virtually any employer. In the USA especially, selection tests should ideally be clearly related to specific jobs.
- MSPR systems typically contain a very large number of ratings, which purport to measure numerous aspects of work performance, but which often prove to be very highly correlated.
- MSPR data may be 'characterized by diverse sets of raters with limited experience evaluating others, lack of familiarity of the demands associated with the job being rated, and different perspectives on the nature of effective performance', which sounds like a polite way of saying they may be largely useless.

Peer rating and promotion

Peer rating seems promising for promotion decisions; Hunter and Hunter (1984) place it at the top of their promotion 'league table'. There are, however, two problems. Table 5.5 shows that peer ratings collected for *administrative* purposes, i.e. used to make decisions about people, have considerably lower validity than ratings collected for research only. Secondly, peer rating is unpopular, especially if used to promote people rather than to 'develop' them (McEvoy & Buller, 1987). It may be significant that so much research is done in a military setting, where people are more accustomed to obeying instructions without question. In some workforces, especially ones that are strongly unionized, peer rating might be rejected altogether.

Peer rating in selection

Is there any way of using peer rating in selection? One in five assessment centres included it, according to Spychalski *et al.*'s (1997) survey, although no data on its separate contribution to validity seem to exist. Even the longest ACs only last three days, which falls within the short duration of acquaintance in Norton's meta-analysis, where peer ratings achieve very poor validity. Employers will find it difficult to gain access to an applicant's former colleagues in another organization, a problem which will be considered further in Chapter 8.

Construct and incremental validity

There is not much research. Mount, Barrick and Strauss (1994) found ratings by co-workers and customers have incremental validity on self-report by personality questionnaire.

Convergent/divergent validity

Peer ratings of a target's conscientiousness should agree with conscientiousness in a PQ completed by the target (convergent validity), but not with other ratings of the target for, for example, extraversion, agreeableness, etc. (divergent validity). Early research (Becker, 1960) based on Cattell's 16PF did not find this, indicating poor convergent and divergent validity.

RESEARCH AGENDA

- Data on construct validity of peer ratings.
- Data on incremental validity over other selection methods.
- Data on convergent/divergent validity of peer ratings.
- Whether peer ratings are used in promotion, and whether they predict work performance.

KEY POINTS

In Chapter 5 you have learned the following:

- References can be free-form or structured.
- References are rarely a very useful source of information, generally lacking reliability or validity.
- References may be improved by forced-choice format or keyword counting, but there is not yet sufficient research to be certain.
- American research shows references rarely contain any negative information.

- The traditional free-form reference is difficult to analyse quantitatively.
- Telephone references seem a grey area; it remains unclear how widely they are used.
- The nature or purpose of the reference seems unclear.
- Law in US and UK seems to have placed employers in a difficult position, which may mean the future of the reference is in doubt.
- References may have the potential to communicate valuable information if the right format can be identified. Some variations on the reference request may have promise.
- Peer ratings agree with work performance very well.
- Ratings by peers seem unlikely to be useful in selection, and to have limited practical value in promotion.

KEY REFERENCES

Conway *et al.* (2001) report a meta-analysis of peer rating and work performance.

Grote *et al.* (2001) describe American research on the consistent favourability of references.

Little & Sipes (2000) describe the dilemma the law seems to have placed American employers in with regard to references.

Madera, Hebl & Martin (2009) use the Linguistic Inquiry and Word Count program to analyse differences in how males and females are described in references.

McCarthy & Goffin (2001) describe research on the relative percentile method which appears to get better results with references.

Mosel & Goheen (1959) described early US public sector on the validity of structured references.

Murphy & Cleveland (1995) review research on performance appraisal which has much in common with reference research.

Taylor *et al.* (2004) describe a successful structured reference system.

CHAPTER 6

Tests of mental ability

'a … man of paralysing stupidity'

In Orwell's *Nineteen Eighty-Four* the main character, Winston Smith, has a neighbour, dismissively characterized as 'A fattish man of paralysing stupidity, a mass of imbecile enthusiasms'. Orwell clearly thinks that some jobs need intelligent people (while other jobs do not). Tests of mental ability are widely used in personnel selection. They also have a multifaceted history of controversy and unpopularity going back to the 1960s.

- In 1969 Arthur Jensen published an article on *How Much Can We Boost IQ and Scholastic Achievement*, which stated the evidence on heritability of mental ability more forcefully than people in the USA were used to, or cared for. The original researches were then reread more carefully, and their limitations noted.
- Jensen also raised the issue of ethnicity differences in mental ability, a subject notorious for its ability to 'generate more heat than light'.
- Jensen argued that remedial education, on which the American government was spending very large sums, was achieving little or nothing.
- The Civil Rights Act of 1964 led within a few years to many American employers abandoning mental ability testing because of adverse impact problems that have still not been resolved.

In the 1990s controversy about mental ability tests was revived by Herrnstein and Murray's (1994) *The Bell Curve*, which covered much the same ground as Jensen a quarter of a century earlier – heritability, ethnic differences, remedial education – and which has been at least as widely publicized. *The Bell Curve* added one new controversial element: the possible existence of an 'underclass' of persons whose employment prospects are limited by low mental ability.

OVERVIEW OF MENTAL ABILITY TESTS

General mental ability, aptitude, achievement

An *achievement test* or *job knowledge test* assesses how much someone knows about a particular body of knowledge, for example gasfitting or Microsoft EXCEL. An *aptitude test* assesses how easy it would be for someone to acquire knowledge they do not presently possess, for example of computer programming. A test of *general mental ability* (GMA) or general intelligence seeks to assess how good the individual is at understanding and using information of all types. (American psychologists seem to prefer to avoid the word *intelligence*, and mostly refer to it as *general mental ability*, so this book will do the same.)

Tests of general mental ability (GMA)

GMA tests are the most controversial level of ability testing, for a variety of reasons, some outlined at the beginning of the chapter. Mental ability test questions, always called *items* in the trade, vary in content: verbal, numerical, abstract. Items vary in difficulty. Items vary in universality; few people in Britain, however bright or dull, know the distance from Denver to Dallas, whereas adding 5 to 6 should be possible for anyone whose culture uses numbers.

Because the items in Table 6.1 vary so much, 'common sense' would expect ability to answer one to have little to do with ability to answer another. For example knowing what a word means (item 1) depends on education and home background, whereas complex reasoning and mental arithmetic (item 6) require mental speed. The items in Table 6.1 are fictitious, but results with similar items in real tests show fairly high positive correlations. This reflects what Spearman discovered 100 years ago and from which he developed the theory of general intelligence, or g: people who are good at one intellectual task tend to be good at others. Spearman's model is convenient and very simple, which makes it attractive to HR, who only need assess one thing. More elaborate accounts of mental ability are discussed in the section on specific abilities.

Table 6.1 Six varied items typical of mental ability tests.

1. What does the word 'impeach' mean?
   - preserve   accuse   propose   give a sermon
2. How far is it from Dallas to Denver in miles?
   - 50   300   600   2,000
3. How much is 5 plus 6?
   - 11   12   56   1
4. How many players are there in a football team?
   - 16   15   11   5   7
5. Who wrote *The Pickwick Papers*?
6. Divide the largest number by the next-to-smallest number, then multiply the result by the next-to-largest number:
   - 20   15   11   14   5   2

Practice effects

Hausknecht *et al.* (2007) meta-analyse a large number of studies where people have done the same test twice, or even three times, and find quite large practice gains ($d = 0.24$ for the first retest, and 0.51 for the second). Repeated testing with the same test, or an alternative form, gives people a considerable advantage and could distort results where some As have done the test before and some have not. Organizations like the US Army that have their own tests can prohibit retesting, but most employers cannot prevent it. Lievens, Reeve and Heggestad (2007) analyse large-scale testing for entry to medical school in Belgium, and suggest that retests predict performance poorly, and that retest gain is largely a memory effect. This implies that retests should be discouraged.

Bias in testing

Problems arise when one identifiable section of the people tested does worse than another, and it is claimed that items were selected that favour one group. For example item 4 in Table 6.1 might be easier for men, assuming women on average have less interest in football. Most tests are checked for *differential item functioning*, based on gender and ethnicity, and offending items discarded.

Equivalence of paper and electronic versions of ability tests has been researched. Stone *et al.* (2013) note two major problems: speeded tests do not seem to achieve acceptable equivalence when computerized, and there is some reason to suppose that computerization adds extra difficulty, in needing to manage the computer system. Since some people will be used to this, while others will not, and since the two groups may differ in age and education level, this creates both a source of error and a source of potential discrimination.

Internet testing

Tests can be completed over the Internet, and many electronic recruiting systems include on line assessment of ability. Quite often this is done from the A's home, called *unproctored* (unsupervised) *Internet testing*, so popular that it has acquired acronym status – UIT. Wunder, Thomas and Luo (2010) comment that in the days before the Internet no work psychologist would contemplate sending a test to an applicant's home by post, and wonder why now people contemplate such an obviously dubious process as UIT. One answer is to save time and money. It is easy to list potential problems. Is the person doing the test really John Smith or someone else? How can HR stop people applying several times under different names and so giving themselves unfair practice on the test? How can they prevent people using calculators or reference books? How can they stop people copying the test and producing 'cribs'? How can they prevent unauthorized use of the test by unqualified users? Lievens and Burke (2011) report data comparing UIT on 72,000 job applicants, against supervised tests on the 8% shortlisted. They found no evidence of significantly lower scores on the supervised tests, which suggested this system might prevent or deter cheating. Landers and Sackett (2012) note that Internet testing allows far more As to be tested, which means the cut-off score can be raised. They suggest this may offset the loss of validity created by those who cheat. It is frequently said that only a minority of applicants cheat in UIT, which may seem reassuring until one reflects that only a minority of applicants get job offers, and wonders to what extent the two minorities will comprise the same people. Wunder *et al.* suggest many managers do not care about data quality because they do not think tests useful or important.

RESEARCH AGENDA

• Frequency of impersonation and other cheating in Internet testing.

INTERPRETING TEST SCORES

Ability tests produce raw scores, which mean very little in themselves. The raw score must be interpreted by comparing it with *normative data*, for example scores for 1,000 apprentices, which tells the tester whether the score is above average or below, and how far above or below average. Lay people often make the mistake of asking how many or what percentage of right answers someone gave; this depends largely on how easy the test is, and tells you very little. Several systems are used to interpret raw scores.

Box 6.1   Percentiles

For a sample of 466 British health service managers, a raw score of 7 on the Graduate and Managerial Assessment – Numerical translates to a percentile of 30, meaning that someone who scores 7 gets a better score than 30% of health service managers.

---

1. *Mental age and intelligence quotient (IQ)* were used for early tests; a person with a mental age of 5 does as well on the test as the average 5-year-old. IQ was originally calculated by dividing mental age by actual (chronological) age, and multiplying by 100. This system is no longer used.
2. *Percentiles* (Box 6.1) indicate what percentage of the norm group scores lower than the candidate. Percentiles are easy for the lay person to understand.
3. *Standard scores* are based on standard deviations and the normal distribution. In Figure 6.1, candidate A's raw score is 1.6 SDs above average, while candidate B's is 0.4 SDs below average. The simplest standard score system is the z score (Box 6.2), in which A's z score is +1.6 and B's is –0.4.

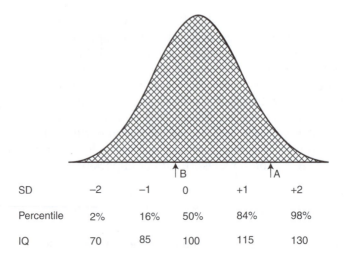

SD	−2	−1	0	+1	+2
Percentile	2%	16%	50%	84%	98%
IQ	70	85	100	115	130

Figure 6.1 Distribution of mental ability scores, showing mean, standard deviations, percentiles, and IQs.

Box 6.2   *z* Scores

Raw score is converted to *z* score using the formula *z* = (raw score − sample mean) / sample SD. On the AH4 test candidate Smith's raw score is 98, while the normative sample's mean and SD are 75.2 and 14.6. Calculating *z* gives a value of +1.6 which shows that Smith scores 1.6 SDs above the norm group mean. Jones's raw score is 66, which gives a *z* of −0.40 which means Jones scores 0.4 SDs below the norm group mean.

Norms

The normative sample should ideally be large, relevant, and recent. Comparing applicants with 2,000 people who have applied for the same job within the last three years is clearly better than comparing them with 50 people doing a roughly similar job in Czechoslovakia in the 1930s. Normative data, even for long-established and widely used tests, tend to be far from ideal. Most normative data are occupational – bank managers, mechanics, etc. – but a few tests have norms based on a representative sample of the general population.

THE VALIDITY OF MENTAL ABILITY TESTS

Early validation research was described in a narrative review by Super and Crites (1962). Ghiselli (1966b, 1973) reported the first meta-analysis of GMA and work performance; his distributions of validity had generally rather low averages – around 0.30 (Figure 2.2 on page 39). Hunter and Hunter (1984) re-analysed Ghiselli's data, correcting for unreliability and range restriction, as described in Chapter 2. They concluded that general mental ability achieved corrected, or operational, validities higher than 0.40 for work performance (Table 6.2).

Table 6.2 Correlation between general mental ability and work performance, for nine general types of work.

	N	r	ρ
Manager	10K+	0.29	0.53
Salesperson	1–5K	0.34	0.61
Clerk	10K+	0.30	0.54
Protective (police and fire)	1–5K	0.23	0.42
Skilled trades and crafts	10K+	0.25	0.46
Vehicle operator	1–5K	0.15	0.28
Service (hotel and catering)	1–5K	0.26	0.48
Sales assistants	1–5K	−0.06	0.27
Unskilled and semi-skilled	10K+	0.20	0.37

r = uncorrected average, from Ghiselli (1973).
ρ = operational validity, corrected for restricted range and reliability of work performance measure, from Hunter & Hunter (1984).
Ghiselli gave no information on number of validities in the meta-analysis, or of exact pooled sample size.

General aptitude test battery (GATB)

The next major meta-analysis of GMA data used the very large GATB database. GATB is a test used by the US Employment Service since 1947, which had accumulated 515 validation researches by the early 1980s. The GATB database includes mostly 'ordinary' jobs rather than higher-level ones. Hunter and Hunter (1984) showed that an uncorrected average validity of 0.25 for GMA rose to 0.47 when corrected for unreliability and range restriction, confirming their re-analysis of Ghiselli's data. VGA also shows that validity of ability tests does not vary as much as Ghiselli thought his distributions showed. Schmidt and Hunter (2004) argue that validity of ability tests does not 'really' vary at all; the apparent variation is noise or error produced by the known limitations of validation research (Chapter 2).

Validity for different types of work

Hunter and Hunter's re-analysis of Ghiselli's data showed operational validity higher than 0.40 for most types of work, except semi-skilled and unskilled workers, vehicle operation, and sales assistants (Table 6.2). Table 6.3 summarizes 14 subsequent meta-analyses for specific types of work. For most, operational validity is around 0.40 to 0.60, which tends to confirm Schmidt and Hunter's (2004) argument that GMA correlates well with performance in all types of work. There are, however, some exceptions:

- Funke *et al.* (1987) found GMA tests one of the poorest predictors of achievement in science and technology, lagging behind creativity tests and biographical measures.
- Hirsh, Northrop and Schmidt (1986) found low correlations with performance in police work.

Table 6.3 Summary of 14 meta-analyses of general mental ability and work performance, for 12 types of work.

Type of work	k	N	ρ	Source
Science and technology	11	949	0.16	Funke *et al.* (1987)
Pilots	26	15,403	0.16[u]	Martinussen (1996)
Sales (rated)	22	1,231	0.40	Vinchur *et al.* (1998)
Sales (objective)	12	1,310	0.04	Vinchur *et al.* (1998)
First line supervisor	75	5,143	0.64	Schmidt *et al.* (1979)
Clerical	194	17,539	0.52	Pearlman *et al.* (1980)
Computing/accounts	58	5,433	0.49	Schmidt *et al.* (1979)
Shorthand/typing/filing	65	3,986	0.61	Schmidt *et al.* (1979)
Police officers	7	828	0.25[2]	Hirsh *et al.* (1986)
Firefighters	24	2,791	0.42	Barrett *et al.* (1999)
Skilled crafts (utility)	149	12,504	0.38[1]	Levine *et al.* (1996)
Skilled crafts (electricity utilities)	37	2,274	0.33	Jones & Gottschalk (1988)
Skilled crafts (oil refinery)	37	3,219	0.32	Callender & Osburn (1981)
Soldiers (noncommissioned/enlisted)	9	4,039	0.65	McHenry *et al.* (1990)[3]

[1] Calculated from true validity using test reliability of 0.80.
[2] Calculated from true validity using test reliability of 0.88.
[3] General soldiering proficiency.
nr = not reported; [u] = uncorrected correlation; ρ = operational validity.

- Vinchur *et al.* (1998) found that GMA correlates with rated sales ability but not with actual sales figures.
- Martinussen (1996) found GMA tests fairly poor predictors of performance as a pilot.

The poor results for science/research and pilots could be a 'pre-screening' effect, if earlier stages in selection for these types of work had excluded low GMA scorers. The poor results for sales and police may indicate supervisor rating is a poor criterion, a point developed in the section in different outcomes, and in Chapter 12. Muchinsky and Raines (2013) point out that research (in North America) is concentrated in certain types of work, management, business and finance, military, and production, but largely lacking in others, art and design, community and social science, entertainment and sports, healthcare, and personal care and service. They suggest some of these might not show such a strong link between performance and GMA. Lyons, Hoffman and Michel (2009) confirm this for professional football (American football, not soccer). In a sample of 762 players, there was no correlation between GMA and various objective indices of proficiency, such as touchdowns, interceptions, or 'fumbles'.

Validity in different countries

People sometimes ask if it is safe to extrapolate from American research to other countries, which may have different ideas about work and selection. Salgado *et al.* (2003) report a VGA across the European Community which finds an operational validity for job performance of 0.62, a little higher than in the USA. Coverage of individual European countries was, however, uneven. The UK, France, the Netherlands, Germany and Spain contributed a lot of data, Belgium, Ireland, Portugal and Scandinavia a handful of studies, Austria, Italy, Greece, and Luxembourg none. Salgado and Anderson (2003) compare the UK, France, the Netherlands plus Belgium, Germany, and Spain and find no difference in GMA test validity. Salgado *et al.* (2003) then analysed the European data by 10 types of work, and found validity higher for managerial, engineering and sales jobs, but very low for police work (confirming Hirsh *et al.*'s earlier American analysis). Kramer (2009) reports a new meta-analysis of German researches, using correction for indirect range restriction, and reporting operational validities of 0.66 for supervisor rating, 0.35 for income, and 0.33 for 'advancement'. There are as yet few data on GMA and work performance from remoter, possibly more culturally different, parts of the world.

Validity for different outcomes

Most research uses supervisor rating to define success at work. Chapter 12 will note that supervisor ratings correlate poorly with measures of actual output where these exist. It is fairly easy to make a plausible case that supervisor rating might correlate with GMA through paths other than good work. One could argue that brighter people will be less trouble to supervise, or be more interesting and agreeable company, or be better at seeming to do good work without actually doing so. Judge, Ilies and Dimotakis (2010) note Deary *et al.*'s (2004) Scottish data on the link between tested intelligence in childhood and health in adult life, and suggest this indicates an overlooked path from GMA to work performance, through health. They suggest that employers could reduce rates of ill-health-related absence by selecting more intelligent employees; they also note that this would be 'unlikely to pass legal muster' in the USA. Vinchur *et al.*'s meta-analysis showed that GMA correlates with supervisor rating but not with sales figures, which is consistent with the hypothesis that some salespersons are good at creating a favourable impression on their supervisor, but not so good at actual selling. Hirsh *et al.* suggest the supervisor rating criterion does not work well for police work, because supervisors rarely see officers 'in action'. This makes it important to find, or do, research showing how well GMA predicts other aspects of work performance.

Self-rated work performance This criterion is rarely used. Joseph *et al.* (2015) find four researches, with a total sample of 3,298, in which there is almost zero correlation between GMA and self-rated work performance.

Work samples Schmitt *et al.*'s (1984) review located three researches using work samples, in which the worker performs key tasks and is observed by an expert; GMA test validity was as high as for supervisor rating.

Output There was an important gap in Schmitt *et al.*'s review: there were not enough studies correlating mental ability with countable output to calculate a correlation. Nathan and Alexander's (1988) meta-analysis of clerical work located 22 validities for production quantity, which gave an overall validity only slightly lower than for supervisor rating.

Work quality Nathan and Alexander's (1988) meta-analysis of clerical work found only six studies of production quality, which achieved zero validity. Hoffman, Nathan and Holden (1991) assessed quality in gas appliance repair work, using an inspector's error count done 'blind'; quality did not correlate at all with mental ability, which did however predict the more usual output and supervisor rating criteria. DuBois *et al.* (1993) obtained similar results for supermarket checkout operators; mental ability tests are not related to accuracy, but do predict speed. GMA seems unrelated to work quality, in the limited range of jobs studied.

Training success Hunter (1986) analysed an enormous set of US military data, for nearly half a million persons, and found a high correlation between GMA and training performance. Note however that training success in the USA military is generally defined by scores in timed multiple choice exams, which are very similar in form to GMA tests, so issues of common method variance may arise. Other US research summarized by Ones *et al.* (2010) finds generally high correlations between GMA and training success. Analysis of European data (Salgado *et al.*, 2003) confirm a strong link between GMA and training success. Kramer (2009) analyses a substantial amount of German data, and confirms Hunter's result, with a correlation, corrected for indirect range restriction, of 0.62.

Leadership Research has also examined links between GMA and less task oriented aspects of work performance. Judge, Colbert and Ilies (2004) report a meta-analysis of GMA and leadership in 151 samples with a total of 40,000 people, and report a corrected correlation of 0.27. Just over half the samples were students, the rest business and military, but results were much the same for both. In 14 studies where leadership was defined by objective effectiveness rather than perceived effectiveness, the link was higher: a corrected correlation of 0.33. Judge *et al.* remark that the link between GMA and leadership is weaker than the link with personality, and perhaps weaker than many expect.

Counterproductive behaviour and organizational citizenship One tends to suppose that 'bad behaviour' at work – breaking the rules or being unco-operative – will have more to do with personality than mental ability. Gonzalez-Mulé, Mount and Oh (2014) report a meta-analysis of GMA tests, organizational citizenship (OCB), and counterproductive work behaviour (CWB). They find a zero correlation overall between mental ability and CWB, but a very weak negative relationship between GMA and CWB which is not self-reported. This seems to consist in large part of a rather narrow set of studies of US police officers and their disciplinary problems. There is a modest correlation (0.23) overall between mental ability and OCB. The analysis compares the relative importance of GMA and personality, and finds mental ability accounts for most of the differences between people in task performance, while personality accounts for most in CWB. Mental ability and personality account for roughly equal amounts of the variance in OCB.

Adaptability Adaptability has been proposed as an important aspect of work performance (see also Chapter 12). Pulakos *et al.* (2002) report low correlations between overall adaptability and mental ability in the US military. Adaptability can also be studied by laboratory experiment. Although this book has generally, as a matter of policy, not described research that does not derive from 'real' work, one recent study is worth a mention. Lang and Bliese (2009) use a complex computer war game to search for correlates of adaptability. In the first phase, performance did correlate moderately well with tested intelligence. After a while the rules of the game suddenly changed, causing performance to get drastically poorer, then recover as people adapted to the changes. Contrary to Pulakos *et al.*'s findings, and contrary to one's expectations, more intelligent people were *less* well able to cope with sudden change: they showed a greater fall off in performance, and did not fully recover their previous lead over average and lower GMA scorers in 300 post-change trials. This seems to indicate high GMA scorers may be less well able to adapt to change, in the short term. Lang and Bliese suggest high GMA scorers may become more automatic more quickly, so find it more difficult to revert to a step-by-step approach. The study covers a very short time span compared with 'real' work.

ORGANIZATIONAL PERFORMANCE

Gottfredson (1997) and Schmidt (2002) argued that organizations that employ large numbers of low GMA people will suffer 'dramatic declines in quantity and quality of work performed', placing US international competitiveness in danger. Numerous studies show that people with lower GMA get poorer supervisor ratings or poorer training grades, which implies that organizations that employ many low scorers may tend to perform poorly. However, there is no empirical demonstration of this at the organizational level. Gottfredson cites the Washington DC police, described in the press as having very lax selection standards and as being very inefficient. Press reports are a useful starting point, but detailed study of the functioning of organizations that employ large numbers of less able people is needed. Within a given sector, organizations with lower levels of GMA in their workforce should, on Schmidt and Hunter's hypothesis, prove less successful. Commercial organizations may be expected to be less profitable, and more likely to go out of business. Non-commercial organizations may make more mistakes, attract more complaints, or work very slowly. The hypothesis may be easier to confirm in the commercial sector.

Research might also usefully analyse work histories of able and less able persons in similar jobs. If less able employees on average get poorer ratings from supervisors, they will presumably be less likely to be promoted, may tend to become dissatisfied, and to leave, willingly or unwillingly. Research is also needed on the way less able employees do their work, perhaps making more mistakes, perhaps being slower to complete a given task, etc. Hunter and Schmidt (1996) speculate that the survival of low-ability workers will depend on their level of organizational citizenship. Less able workers who are, however, good citizens will be tolerated by supervisors because they are obviously trying hard, and may be moved to easier work. The less able worker who is also a poor citizen is – they suggest – more likely to have their employment terminated.

Career success

Career success research has in common with validation research a correlation between a test, such as GMA, and a work-related outcome. The main difference is focusing on a set of people, typically assessed at school or college, and following them through a number of years and a number of jobs. Success is defined from their point of view, rather than the employer's perspective. Success is cumulative, rather than at one single point in time, as in most validation research. Career success has been researched for managers, defining success by salary or promotion achieved by middle age. Eight studies find a 'moderate' correlation of 0.27 between GMA and salary (Ng *et al.*, 2005). Judge, Klinger and Simon (2010) also report a long-term follow-up, through about three-quarters of an average career span. The cohort were assessed as part of the National Longitudinal Study of Youth in 1979, and their career traced every year or two years until 2006. Judge *et al.*'s analysis focused on high GMA scorers in 1979 (1 SD above average) compared with low scorers (1 SD below). The two groups start off in 1979 about equal in income and occupational prestige, then diverge over time; the high-scoring group's income and occupational prestige rise steadily, whereas the low-scoring group stay largely where they were in 1979.

Job complexity

Hunter concluded the validity of GMA tests is not moderated by anything except job complexity. Figure 6.2 shows Hunter's (1983) data on the correlation between GMA and work performance in the US Employment Service (USES) database, for five levels of job complexity. It is said to show that the correlation is higher in complex jobs, but lower in less complex jobs. Complexity was defined by three ratings in the (US) Dictionary of Occupational Titles (DOT; see Chapter 3). Hunter's 1983 complexity analysis has been quoted very widely, including in previous editions of this book. It makes intuitive sense: more complex work might be expected to require more intelligence than low-level 'fetching and carrying' work, and so demonstrate a closer link between intelligence and performance. Complexity could almost be a respectable code-word for social class, white/blue-collar, 'them and us'. Recently, however, the link has been questioned.

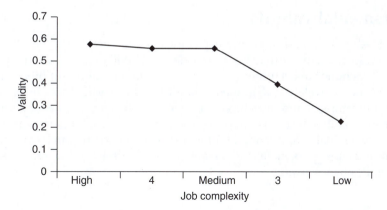

Figure 6.2   Corrected validity of GATB General + Verbal + Numerical composite with work performance, for five levels of job complexity. Data from Hunter & Hunter, 1984.

- An alternative view of Figure 6.2 says it shows that jobs at the lowest level of complexity differ from the rest.
- There is not all that much data for either the most complex jobs, or the least complex. What one might call really low-level jobs have not been researched much, despite the number of people doing them.
- Johnson *et al.* (2010) suggest Hunter reordered the DOT complexity classification to suit the validity data.

Accounts of the complexity analysis in Hunter and Hunter (1984) and Hunter (1986) are rather vague; the 1983 reference is a US government report, which is unobtainable in Britain. Hartigan and Wigdor (1989) give some information about the jobs in Hunter's complexity analysis. The four examples for the highest complexity level are: machinist, cabinet maker, metal fabricator and loom fixer. These are skilled jobs, but not what one thinks of as the highest level of complexity. Perhaps managerial and professional jobs in the USA are not generally filled through the USES.

Some European data are available, in Salgado *et al.* (2003) and Hülsheger, Maier and Stump (2007). Hülsheger *et al.*'s German data appear to contradict Hunter: validity for the highest level of complexity is lower (0.30) than for medium and low (0.45 and 0.52). There are, however, only six studies of high-complexity jobs. Schmidt and Oh (2010) argue this result is an artefact of the German education system, which they describe as highly stratified, so applicant pools tend to score equally on selection tests, which reduces range, and hence lowers correlations. The Hülsheger database appears to differ from the USES database in being at a generally higher level of job complexity. The low-complexity jobs mentioned include office clerk, mechanic and police officer, which are certainly not unskilled low-level work. It might be useful to pool the European datasets with the USES database, recode all the jobs for complexity on a common system, and conduct a new test of Hunter's job complexity hypothesis.

Incremental validity

GMA tests by and large predict work performance fairly well. What other assessments are worth using alongside them? Will that give a better prediction still? Schmidt and Hunter (1998) review data on validity of other predictors, and their correlation with mental ability, and conclude that personality tests, work samples, and structured interviews will offer incremental validity on mental ability tests, whereas assessment centres or biodata will not. Note, however, that Schmidt and Hunter are not reviewing research that shows that, for example, personality tests *do* offer incremental validity, but research that implies they *should*.

RESEARCH AGENDA

- The role of GMA in types of work that have been neglected by research so far, including health care, entertainment and sport, and creative work.
- GMA and work performance outside North America and Western Europe.
- GMA and other aspects of work performance, including output and work quality.
- Mediation of the link between GMA and supervisor rating by irrelevant factors such as liking or ability to present oneself well.
- GMA and work performance link, at the organizational level.
- Work careers of persons of low GMA.
- Replication of Lang and Bliese's research on intelligence and adaptability, with other work-like tasks, and with real work, and over a longer time scale.
- Re-analysis of the data on job complexity used by Hunter (1983): pool and re-analyse existing data, for US and Europe, using a common definition of complexity, then collect further data, focusing on the top and bottom of the job complexity distribution.

---

g OR SPECIFIC COGNITIVE ABILITIES?

Spearman had noted that a general factor of intellectual ability seemed to underlie most tests with any intellectual content. An alternative approach has proved influential, especially in the USA. Thurstone described seven Primary Mental Abilities, or specific cognitive abilities (SCAs): verbal, verbal fluency, numerical, spatial, perceptual, inductive reasoning and memory. These, however, proved to be correlated, so did not directly contradict Spearman's hypothesis of general mental ability. Multiple aptitude batteries, like PMA or GATB, form a hierarchical model (Figure 6.3) in which a set of tests measure from five to 10 different aspects of ability or SCAs, and can be scored as well for general intelligence. There has been a long history of debate as to which level of the hierarchy gives a better account.

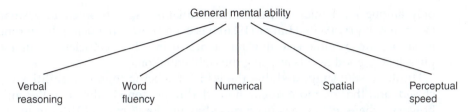

Figure 6.3   Hierarchy of general mental ability, and specific cognitive abilities.

As far back as 1928, Hull had argued that profiles of specific abilities will predict work performance better than tests of general mental ability, or g, on the assumption that each job requires a different profile of abilities: accountants need to be numerate, whereas architects need good spatial ability, etc. The US military has used a succession of aptitude batteries, the latest being Armed Services Vocational Aptitude Battery (ASVAB); they calculate regression equations (Box 3.1, page 66) for different jobs, in which each aptitude score is given a different weight according to how well it predicts performance. Aptitude batteries are especially useful for attempts to devise synthetic validation: job analysis lists the main aspects of the work, while aptitude batteries measure the corresponding abilities. Aptitude batteries and SCAs have also become a focus of interest recently because some hope they might solve the 'diversity-validity dilemma', meaning the fact that tests that best predict work performance also tend to create the most adverse impact on minority groups in the USA.

However, during the 1980s some American psychologists rediscovered g, and started asking themselves whether the extra time needed to administer the whole of GATB or ASVAB adds much. Ree and Earles (1991) analysed ASVAB data for nearly 80,000 USAF personnel doing 82 different jobs and concluded that, while ASVAB's 10 tests include

> some seemingly specific measures of automotive knowledge, shop information, word knowledge, reading, mathematics, mechanical principles, electronic and scientific facts, as well as clerical speed … its predictive power was derived from psychometric g. The training courses prepared students for seemingly different job performance, such as handling police dogs, clerical filing, jet engine repair, administering injections, and fire fighting, yet a universal set of weights across all jobs was as good as a unique set of weights for each job.

Schmidt-Atzert and Deter (1993) reported similar data for the German chemical industry. Interestingly British military research in the Second World War had earlier made the same discovery: 'We would naturally have expected the verbal and educational tests to show relatively low validities in mechanical and spatial occupations, and the mechanical spatial tests to be of value only among mechanics. But such differentiation was conspicuously small' (Vernon & Parry, 1949). Hunter (1986) has even shown that using the 'wrong' equation, for example selecting mechanics using the electricians' equation, gives just as good results as using the right equation.

Hunter (1986) suggested that the issue of specific cognitive abilities was closed, and that no more research needed to be done in the area. Recently, however, the question has been raised again. Lang *et al.* (2010) argue that the customary analysis of incremental validity by stepwise regression 'cheats' by first analysing the contribution of g or general mental ability/ intelligence, then assessing the contribution of more specific abilities. This allows g to take variance from specific abilities, so giving g an unfair 'advantage'. There is considerable overlap, or shared variance, between for example g and numerical reasoning ability (N). Does this shared variance 'belong to' g or to N? Allocating it to g necessarily increases the importance of g. Hence the type of analysis reported by Ree, where g explains 20%+ of WP variance, whereas specifics only explain 2%. Lang *et al.* (2010) use a new statistical analysis called *relative importance analysis*, which they argue is more suitable for looking at incremental validity issues in aptitude batteries, and conclude that g is not necessarily the most important predictor of work performance, when using multiple aptitude batteries. They suggest verbal comprehension may be the best predictor of job performance, doing slightly better than GMA, in explaining 19.5% of the variance in work performance, compared with GMA's 18.1%. Three other SCAs did nearly as well: numerical ability, reasoning, and word fluency. A verbal comprehension test will be much shorter than an entire aptitude battery like GATB (but not shorter than a single test of GMA, such as the Wonderlic, or the British AH4). Using SCAs rather than g has several possible advantages.

Advantage 1 *Differentiation.* Goertz, Hülsheger and Maier (2014) meta-analyse German data and find different SCAs predicting success in different types of training, which previous researches had generally failed to find. For example, verbal comprehension predicted for professionals, craftsmen, and technicians, but not for clerical work, while memory was the only SCA that predicted training performance in clerical jobs.

Advantage 2 *Reducing adverse impact.* Wee, Newman and Joseph (2014) suggest specific abilities may help solve the adverse impact problem, which tests of general mental ability tend to exacerbate. Wee *et al.* suggest selection might usefully seek a trade-off between higher validity and lower adverse impact, by using subsets of specific abilities that will maximize the latter, while not lowering too much the former.

Advantage 3 *Acceptability.* Goertz *et al.* (2014) suggest that tests of SCAs may be more acceptable to applicants, and to workers' councils, whose views must be taken into account in Germany.

RESEARCH AGENDA

- Replication of Goertz *et al.*'s finding that specific abilities predict training success better than general ability, in other countries.
- Extension of Goertz *et al.*'s finding for work performance.

MENTAL ABILITY AND THE SUCCESS OF TEAMS

Selection persists in assessing the individual's character, and trying to relate it to the individual's success at work. Yet a lot of work is done by teams of people. So should selection consider the team as a whole? Does a successful team consist of people who are all able, or will a mixture of ability be sufficient, or even better? Can one person of low ability hold everyone back? Will one very able person be able to get the group moving forwards, or will he/she be submerged and frustrated? Bell (2007) reports a meta-analysis summarizing eight studies of work team mental ability and team performance, which finds a fairly weak link between average ability and performance (0.26 corrected). Little evidence of more complex effects emerged; neither variability nor presence of extremes made much difference. However, seven of the eight researches studied 'physical' teams such as soldiers or assembly workers; a stronger link was found in the solitary study of 'intellectual' teams (HR staff). Research on teams is much more difficult because testing an entire team of 5–15 persons yields only data point, yet the correlation still needs a large number of observations to give a meaningful result.

RESEARCH AGENDA

- Research link between average and distribution of GMA and team performance, in a wider range of work.

WHY MENTAL ABILITY TESTS PREDICT PRODUCTIVITY

Mental ability testing has never pretended to much in the way of systematic theory. Binet's first test was written to identify slow learners in French schools, and derived its items from the convenient fact that older children can solve problems younger ones cannot.

Occupational differences in mental ability level

Gottfredson (1997) reviewed the Wonderlic database, which gives averages for 72 varied occupations. The highest-scoring occupations are lawyer, research analyst, editor, and advertising manager; the most average are cashier, clerical worker, sales assistant, and meter reader; the lowest-scoring are packer, material handler, caretaker (janitor), and warehouse worker. However, these data merely show that people in different jobs have different average ability levels, and do not prove they *need* particular levels of GMA to perform successfully.

Threshold hypothesis

A widely held 'common sense' view claims that, above a certain minimum level, most people are capable of most jobs. All that ability tests can accomplish is to screen out the unfortunate minority of incompetents. This view implies a threshold or step in the relation between test scores and work performance. Mls (1935) found a clear break in truck-driving proficiency at approximately IQ 80; any Czech soldier with an IQ over 80 was equally competent to drive a truck, while all those whose IQ fell below 80 were equally unfit to be trusted with an army vehicle. Wai, Lubinski and Benbow (2005) report an interesting long-term follow-up of a group at the very high end on the ability distribution. The starting point was a cohort of US 13-year-olds with mathematical ability scores in the top 1%, which was used to predict their accomplishments at age 33. The top quarter of the group did better than the bottom quarter on income, having achieved tenure (a permanent job) at a top US university, having obtained a PhD, and having taken out patents, i.e. invented something. Wai *et al.* argue patents are a sign of real creativity, so this finding refutes the 'swot' or 'book-learning' type of criticism of ability tests. It is also remarkable to be able to find differences within the top 1% of the distribution, which represents an extreme of range restriction.

Linearity hypothesis

Linearity means work performance improves as test score increases, throughout the entire range of test scores, with no step or threshold (Figure 6.4). Several large analyses, for example Coward and Sackett (1990), have shown test–performance relationships are generally linear, aka 'more is better', which implies Mls's results with the Czech army were atypical. The threshold vs. linearity issue has important fair employment implications. Linearity implies As should be placed in a strict rank order on the test, and selected in that order, because the higher the test score, the better their job performance. If the threshold hypothesis is true, all As in a broad band of scores will be equally suitable. The employer can then select to ensure a suitably diverse workforce without reducing overall efficiency.

Arneson, Sackett and Beatty (2011) note that the threshold hypothesis has been proposed again recently, now called the 'good enough' hypothesis, based on the argument that there are not many people at the top end of the distribution, so it is hard to test conclusively the hypothesis that very high scores are really linked to very high performance. Arneson *et al.* retest the linearity hypothesis with four large datasets, and confirm it. In fact they find some evidence that

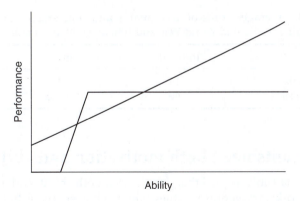

Figure 6.4 Linear vs. threshold models of the relationship between mental ability and work performance.

ability–performance relations are stronger at the high end than at the low end. If we wanted a snappy – but unkind – name for this, we could call it the 'they'll do' effect, when filling lower-level jobs. Note, however, that Arneson *et al.*'s data are all from educational or military testing, so replication with civilian employment is a priority.

Setting cut-off scores

Selectors are often asked: Is this applicant appointable? In other words, what is the minimum level of mental ability necessary to function in this job? Questioners sometimes seem to assume a book of minimum scores for different occupations exists, which it does not. The commonest approach to setting cut-offs is distribution-based: do not appoint anyone who falls in the bottom one-third of existing post-holders, or more than 1 SD below the mean. Strictly speaking the idea of a fixed cut-off is simplistic. The relationship between test score and performance is linear and probabilistic; the lower the score, the poorer the person's performance is likely to be. This implies any cut-off must be arbitrary.

Necessary but not sufficient

Table 6.4 shows few accountants had IQs more than 15 points below the accountant average, whereas quite a few lumberjacks had IQs well over their average of 85. Assuming the latter had not always wanted to be lumberjacks, the data imply they either could not or did not use their high GMA to find more prestigious work. Perhaps they lacked some other important quality: energy, social skill, good adjustment, or luck. Chapter 7 shows that personality tests have incremental validity over GMA, which confirms Herrnstein's (1973) hypothesis that GMA alone is not always sufficient for success.

Table 6.4   Average scores of accountants and lumberjacks conscripted into US Army during the Second World War, and 10th and 90th percentiles.

	10th %ile	median	90th %ile
Accountants	114	129	143
Lumberjacks	60	85	116

Do applicants need both motivation and ability?

It can be plausibly argued that people need both ability and motivation to succeed in work; lazy geniuses achieve little, while energetic but dim people only succeed in making a nuisance of themselves. Sackett, Gruys and Ellingson (1998) tested this with four separate sets of data, covering 22 different jobs, and found no evidence for it; ability and motivation do not interact. Hunter *et al.* (2008), however, argue that tenure – time in the job – may moderate the link. They find a multiplicative interaction between conscientiousness and GMA in law enforcement personnel who been in the job for more than four years.

Class and education

Some sociologists argue that any apparent link between occupation and GMA is created by the class system. Children from better-off homes get better education, so do better on GMA tests, which are in any case heavily biased towards the middle classes; better-off children go on to get better-paid jobs. On this argument there is no true link between GMA and work performance; psychological tests are merely class-laden rationing mechanisms. The social class argument is countered to some extent by data from the (US) National Longitudinal Study of Youth (Wilk & Sackett, 1996). ASVAB score in 1980 predicted whether people would move up or down the occupational ladder between 1982 and 1987; higher scorers tended to move up into work of greater complexity, while lower scorers tended to move down into work of less complexity. This implies lower scorers have more difficulty coping with complex work, so gravitate to work more within their intellectual grasp – which would not happen if testing is just an arbitrary class-based way of keeping some people out of better jobs.

Box 6.3   Path analysis

This is essentially a correlational analysis in which the researcher is prepared to make some assumptions about direction of cause. To take an obvious example, height might affect success as a police officer, but it is very hard to think of any possible way is which being successful as a police officer would make someone taller. Path analysis is generally calculated by structural equation modelling.

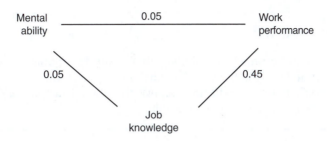

Figure 6.5   Schematic path diagram showing the paths from mental ability to work performance.

Mental ability, job knowledge and work performance

Some research has used path analysis (Box 6.3) to explore why GMA tests predict work performance. Hunter (1983) found GMA did not correlate directly with supervisor ratings, but did correlate with job knowledge and work sample performance, which in turn correlated with supervisor ratings. Figure 6.5 shows that more able people are better workers primarily because they learn more quickly what the job is about. In high-level work, this may mean learning scientific method, scientific techniques, and a large body of knowledge. In low-level work it may mean only learning where to find the broom, and where to put the rubbish when you have swept it up. In Hunter's model there is no direct path from GMA to work performance.

An unemployable minority?

Eighty years ago Cattell (1936) made some pessimistic comments about employment prospects for people with limited mental ability in a complex industrial society: 'the person of limited intelligence is not so cheap an employee as he at first appears. His accident prone-ness is high and he cannot adapt himself to changes in method.' Gottfredson (1997) has raised the same issue, arguing that the American armed services have three times employed low GMA recruits, once when short of recruits during the Second World War, once as an idealistic experiment during the 1960s, and then by mistake in the 1970s when they miscalculated their norms for ASVAB. Gottfredson says of the third occasion: 'these men were very difficult and costly to train, could not learn certain specialities, and performed at a lower average level once on a job'. What is the threshold of unemployability? Cattell estimated it at IQ 85, while Gottfredson mentioned a figure of IQ 80. Hunter and Schmidt (1996) suggest America should consider a two-tier economy in ability and fair employment law. The first tier is international, where the country must be competitive, so employers must be free to select the most able. The second tier is the domestic economy, which is not subject to foreign competition, and where reduced efficiency caused by employing the less able will cause less harm. What sectors fall into this second tier? Hunter and Schmidt mention only catering, insurance, and hairdressing.

RESEARCH AGENDA

- Replicate Arneson *et al.*'s finding that ability–performance relations are stronger at the high-ability end, in civilian employment.
- Test the Cattell–Gottfredson hypothesis that there is a level of GMA below which people become unemployable.

LAW, FAIRNESS, AND MINORITIES

As noted in Chapter 1, tests used in selection should ideally never generate any age, sex, or race differences in people tested; such differences can constitute adverse impact, which can cause difficulties with fair employment laws and agencies. Ideally GMA tests will only 'discriminate' between the bright and the less bright. GMA tests do not always meet this ideal.

Sex differences

Hyde (2005) summarizes five meta-analyses of gender differences, which find no difference in GMA. There are, however, differences in spatial perception and mental rotation tests, favouring males, and in some verbal tests, favouring females.

Age differences

Avolio and Waldman (1994) analyse age differences in a large set of GATB data, covering verbal, numerical, spatial and clerical abilities, and form perception, as well as GMA. All GATB abilities decline with age, the effect being least for verbal ability, and greatest for form perception (rapid comparison of shapes or pictures). General intelligence falls by not far off a whole standard deviation, by the 55–65 age band. The decline is progressive from age 20–35 onwards, not a sudden fall near retirement. Note these are cross-sectional data, i.e. from people of different ages tested at the same time, not from repeated tests of the same people at different ages. Age may be become more of a concern in employment testing in Britain as the retirement age is raised, eventually to 70.

Race/ethnicity differences

GMA tests create adverse impact on some sections of the American population. Roth *et al.* (2001b) reported a meta-analysis which found quite large differences between white and African Americans ($d = 0.99$), and between white and Hispanic Americans ($d = 0.72$). Berry, Clark and McClure (2011) and Berry, Cullen and Meyer (2014) use 113 new GATB validity studies reported during the 1980s to generate similar estimates, for white/African American comparisons

(d = 1.14), and white/Hispanic American comparisons (d = 0.76). Roth *et al.*'s and Berry *et al.*'s analyses do not appear to overlap. Berry *et al.* find the difference is greater in people doing work of low complexity.

Outside the USA

Adverse impact of mental ability tests has been documented in Israel, on Israelis of non-European origin (Zeidner, 1988), and in the Netherlands, where de Meijer *et al.* (2006) find large (ca d = 1.00) differences between native Dutch applicants for police work and immigrants from Caribbean, North Africa, Surinam and Turkey. However, the differences are much smaller in the second generation, and are linked to proficiency in Dutch, which suggests a short-term acculturation effect. Information about ethnicity differences in test scores in Britain is conspicuous by its absence.

Age and sex differences in mental ability scores have not generally created many fair employment problems as yet, but the ethnicity differences have, in the USA in particular. More detail is given in Chapter 13.

RESEARCH AGENDA

- Research on work performance and test scores in the 65–75 age group.
- Collect data on average scores for GMA and SCAs for persons of different ethnic origins in Britain.

DEALING WITH ADVERSE IMPACT IN MENTAL ABILITY SCORES

Dealing with adverse impact 1. Altering the way scores are used

In the 1980s the USES used a separate norms system, which eliminated differences between means for ethnic groups, but this has been prohibited since the Civil Rights Act of 1991. Since then score banding has been suggested. Score banding means raw scores between, for example, 25 and 30 are regarded as equivalent. The principle will be most familiar to American readers in the shape of college grades, and to British readers in the shape of degree classes. Banding makes scores easier to describe, at the expense of losing some information. The main problem with score bands will also be familiar to American and British readers: the difference between grade B and grade A, or a lower second and an upper second is one mark, which is bad luck for those who are short of that one mark.

Degree class bands are arbitrary, whereas test score banding systems are based on error of measurement, which can define a range of scores that would not be considered reliably different if one were deciding who to appoint. Suppose the highest-scoring applicant scores 55, and error of measurement covers 11 raw score points, then the band starts at 55 and extends down to include 45. Within this band all As are regarded as equal in ability. If everyone within the band is defined as having an equal score, the employer can then give preference to minority persons, without engaging in reverse discrimination. This is called *diversity-based referral*. A number of criticisms of banding have been made (Schmidt & Hunter, 1995).

- Banding fails to distinguish individual scores and average scores. It is true that two As scoring 55 and 54 are interchangeable in the sense that if they do the test again in a week's time, they might score 52 and 56. However, it is also true that research with vast numbers would show that people who score 55 perform better on average than people who score 54. This follows necessarily from the fact that test and work performance are linearly related.
- The error of measurement criterion used creates a fairly broad band. The broader the band, the less selective selection becomes.
- If the test is not very reliable, the size of the band can extend to cover most of the range of scores, meaning the test's scores would convey very little information.
- Banding will not look very fair to an unsuccessful applicant who scores one point outside the band, with a score of 44, and who does not differ significantly from most of those appointed, using exactly the same reasoning and calculation as are used to define the band.

Score bands have been criticized as a 'fudge', complicated and ingenious but a fudge none the less. They are one way to try to solve the *diversity/validity dilemma*: how to appoint the best, while also creating a suitably diverse workforce. However, the legal position is uncertain (Henle, 2004); score banding is accepted by American courts, but giving preference to minority persons within bands may not be legal.

Dealing with adverse impact 2. Altering the tests

The 'holy grail' of American selection psychologists is an assessment of GMA that does not cause adverse impact. Many modifications to traditional tests have been tried in the hope of achieving this: computer rather than paper administration, video presentation, open-ended response rather than multiple choice (item 5 in Table 6.1), giving people more time to complete the test. Long established 'culture-free' tests such as Raven's Progressive Matrices do not reduce adverse impact. Sackett's papers on 'high stakes' testing give more detail (Sackett *et al.*, 2001; Sackett, Bornemann & Connelly, 2008). From time to time new tests appear that their authors hope will solve the problem; none has been convincingly shown to achieve this yet.

McDaniel and Kepes (2012) complain that it often difficult to obtain definite information about such tests, or to find any published research. Ones *et al.* (2010) are rather dismissive of research on ways to reduce adverse impact in GMA tests: 'structural and procedural proposals to reduce adverse impact are stopgap measures that are too little and too late to deal with profound group differences observed in occupational settings'. They do not offer any suggestions about what to do.

Dealing with adverse impact 3. Altering the way applicants perceive tests

Stereotype threat (ST) refers to the hypothesis that African Americans feel threatened by GMA tests, because they know people expect them to score lower. Research with student samples has reported that the gap between white and African American applicants can be narrowed by telling them the test assesses problem-solving, not intelligence, or widened by asking people about race before starting the test. Nguyen and Ryan (2008) report a meta-analysis of ST research, which confirms that issuing any sort of stereotype threat decreases African Americans' scores. However, both the type of threat and the difficulty of the test are important moderator variables. More difficult tests increase the effect considerably, which could imply ST will be more of a problem in selection for higher-level jobs. Three types of ST are distinguished. 'Blatant' means telling people the test finds differences between white and non-white Americans. 'Moderately explicit' means saying that 'some groups' perform 'differently' (but not which, nor in what direction). 'Subtle' means asking people to state their race, to make this salient in their minds. (Some views of ST seem to see it as partly unconscious, and as more easily evoked by subtle hints than by overt statements.) Blatant threat shifted African Americans' scores downward to the extent of d of 0.44. Moderately explicit threat had the biggest effect, a d of 0.70. Subtle threats had the least effect, a d of only 0.24. Subtle threats are the only sort likely to arise in real selection testing. However, as Nguyen and Ryan point out, this small difference is still sufficient – if it happens in real selection – to exclude quite of lot of African Americans who 'should have' been selected. In selection testing As will always be asked at some point to state gender and ethnicity for equal opportunities monitoring, although not necessarily at the same time as they complete GMA tests. Research has also investigated two strategies for preventing ST, neither of which looks remotely suitable for use in selection. Both involve telling people things that are not true: either that the test does not measure anything important, which is clearly untrue in selection testing, and unlikely to be believed by applicants, or that there are no group differences in test scores. Employment testing is 'for real', not a laboratory experiment where you can say things that are not true, and take them back later. There seem to be no studies of ST in 'real' selection for anything, or where the test has any real or important consequences for the people doing it.

Differential validity

Adverse impact means one group of persons has on average a higher or lower score on a test. Differential validity means the correlation between the test and work performance is higher or lower for one group of people compared with another (usually the white majority). The existence of adverse impact does not imply the existence of differential validity. Differential validity will be discussed in Chapter 13.

RESEARCH AGENDA

- Use of modified format GMA tests with real applicants.
- Research on stereotype threat in testing which has important consequences for those tested.

OTHER WAYS OF ASSESSING MENTAL ABILTY

Mental ability tests have advantages of economy, reliability, and validity. However, they also have problems of adverse impact and considerable unpopularity. Are there any other ways of assessing mental ability?

Self-report

Assessing GMA by direct self-reports has rarely been suggested, which makes an interesting contrast with personality, where self-report is the method of choice. Newman and Lyon (2009) report data comparing actual test scores (on the American Scholastic Aptitude Test, used for admission to higher education) with students' estimates of their SAT score. Overall the two correlate very well, at 0.83, suggesting self-reports of GMA might form a quicker, and more palatable, way of assessing it. Note, however, that the SAT research was not done in a selection context, where people might not be unbiased or even honest. Newman and Lyon find a serious problem, a version of the Dunning–Kruger effect, described in Chapter 11. People whose SAT scores are actually low overestimate their ability considerably, implying that self-report will fail to give accurate results for precisely the people the employer is most likely to want not to employ. Chapter 4 noted that interviews assess intelligence to some extent, although not necessarily intending to.

Others' report

Conway, Lombardo and Sanders (2001) found 22 studies correlating peer ratings with GMA test scores, which achieved an average correlation of only 0.32 at best, i.e. correcting for reliability of both. Others' reports have been shown to correlate slightly better with tested intelligence, up to 0.40 where several observers' ratings are aggregated (Borkenau and Liebler, 1993). These researches were not done in an employment context.

Demonstration evidence

Schmidt and Hunter (1998) note that several types of demonstrated evidence, besides tests, may be useful measures of GMA: assessment centres, biodata, work samples, structured interviews and job knowledge tests.

Recorded evidence

Educational achievement is discussed in Chapter 11. In the USA *authentic assessment* is popular in education. People are assessed from portfolios of intellectual accomplishments, on the topic of their choice, in the form of their choice. This is promising because it is likely to prove acceptable, but could be very time-consuming, and possibly not very reliable.

DNA testing

Research has identified genes associated with high and low mental ability, so it may one day be possible to assess mental ability from a sliver of skin or drop of saliva. DNA testing would bypass entirely many problems of measurement, such as item bias, test anxiety, or motivation. However, DNA testing can only assess the genotype, the person's inborn potential, unaffected by culture, upbringing, education and training, or social disadvantage, which would limit its value in selection. DNA testing of mental ability is certain to be very controversial. If DNA testing is considered to be a 'medical examination', its use in selection may already be prohibited by disability discrimination laws in the UK and USA – even before it has been invented!

KEY POINTS

In Chapter 6 you have learned the following:

- Mental ability tests are the centre of considerable controversy.
- There are various ways of presenting and interpreting test scores.
- There are quite large practice and coaching effects.
- Mental ability tests can break the '0.30 barrier', and can achieve corrected correlations with performance around 0.50.
- The relationship between mental ability is continuous and linear: the brighter someone is, the more likely their work performance is to be good.
- There are some areas of work where the link between GMA and work performance is not so strong.
- The link between GMA and work performance is fairly simple. There are no known moderator variables, except job complexity.

- There are also links between GMA, and organizational citizenship and counterproductive work behaviour.
- VGA indicates there may not be much variation in validity left to explain, once error is allowed for.
- Research on mental ability in teams finds a correlation between team average and team performance.
- There is some dispute about whether multiple aptitude batteries achieve better validity than single tests of general mental ability.
- Research on why mental ability tests predict work performance is less well developed, but suggests that mental ability leads to improved job knowledge, which in turn leads to better work performance.
- Mental ability tests create large adverse impact on some ethnic minorities in the USA.
- Attempts to solve the adverse impact problem in the USA include trying to identify features of GMA tests that will reduce adverse impact.
- Attempts to deal with the adverse impact problem in the USA include score banding, which defines a range of scores as equivalent, thus allowing selection within the band to be based on achieving diversity.

KEY REFERENCES

Bell (2007) reviews evidence on mental ability and team performance.

de Meijer *et al.* (2006) present data on ethnicity differences in GMA test data in the Netherlands.

Goertz *et al.* (2014) describe German research on specific cognitive abilities and training success.

Gonzalez-Mulé, Mount & Oh (2014) present a meta-analysis of the links between GMA, organizational citizenship, and counterproductive work behaviour.

Hausknecht *et al.* (2007) review research on coaching and practice effects with mental ability tests.

Judge, Ilies & Dimotakis (2010) follow the careers of people scoring higher and lower on GMA across 25 years.

Newman & Lyon (2009) describe a specific form of inaccuracy in self-rating of mental ability.

Nguyen & Ryan (2008) present a meta-analysis of research on stereotype threat.

Ree & Earles (1991) present data suggesting that general mental ability predicts work performance as efficiently as differential aptitude batteries.

Salgado *et al.* (2003) present European data on validity of mental ability tests.

Schmidt (2002) argues forcefully for the predictive power of mental ability in the workplace.

Schmidt & Hunter (1998) analyse the likely incremental validity of various other selection tests over mental ability tests.

USEFUL WEBSITES

ptc.bps.org.uk. British Psychological Society's Psychological Testing Centre, which includes a list of UK test publishers.

apa.org/science/testing.html. American Psychological Association's site which has information about American test publishers.

buros.org Buros Institute, which reviews commercially available tests.

CHAPTER 7

Assessing personality by questionnaire

Do you worry about awful things that might happen?

Guilford (1959) defined personality as 'any distinguishable, relatively enduring way in which one person differs from another'. In practice most psychologists exclude mental abilities and physical attributes from the definition. There are up to eight different models of personality (Cook, 2013):

- *trait*   5 to 10 traits
- *factor*   16 statistical abstractions
- *social learning*   bundles of habits
- *motives*   profile of needs
- *phenomenological*   the way one sees the world
- *self*   the way one sees oneself
- *psycho-analytic*   system of defences
- *constitutional*   inherited neuropsychological differences

Most work psychologists adopt the trait or factor models. Traits are mechanisms within people that shape how they react to classes of event and occasion. On the traditional view, a trait summarizes past behaviour and predicts future behaviour. People who are assertive have asserted themselves often in the past, and can be expected to do the same in future. Factors are similar to traits, but are derived by statistical analysis. Both models offer a convenient view of personality, with 5, 10, or at most 20 broad characteristics common to everyone. Simplicity and universality make this an attractive model for selectors.

Mischel's criticisms

Some psychologists have questioned the trait and factor model; Mischel (1968) reviewed evidence, much of it by no means new even 50 years ago, that seemed to show that behaviour is not consistent enough to make general statements about personality meaningful. Consider the trait of honesty, which a whole industry in the USA undertakes to assess people for. In the 1920s the

Personnel Selection: Adding Value Through People – A Changing Picture, Sixth Edition. Mark Cook.

Character Education Inquiry (Hartshorne & May, 1928) found seven sets of measures of honesty correlated very poorly, which implies it may not be very informative to describe someone as 'honest' unless one specifies when, where, with what, and with whom. Mischel reviewed similar evidence for other traits that often feature in job descriptions: extraversion, punctuality, curiosity, persistence, attitude to authority. Mischel favoured a habit model of personality; habits are much more specific and idiosyncratic, so a habit model may not lend itself to convenient all-purpose assessments. Mischel also pointed to what has become known as 'the 0.30 barrier', the fact that personality tests rarely to seem to predict anything in the real world to an extent greater than a correlation of 0.30.

Measuring personality

There are many approaches to assessing personality, categorized here by the nature of the information used:

- *Self-report*   personality questionnaire
- *Other report*   peer rating, references
- *Demonstration*   assessment centre exercises
- *Recorded*   achievements, previous jobs held, qualifications and degrees
- *Involuntary*   graphology

PERSONALITY QUESTIONNAIRES

This chapter covers the most widely used method: the personality questionnaire (PQ). PQs are what most people think of as 'personality tests'. Table 7.1 shows some typical PQ items and formats. Some PQs use an *endorsement* (yes/no) format, which is quicker and easier; others use a *rating* format, which generates a wider range of scores. *Forced-choice* format equates the attractiveness of the alternatives, usually to try to limit faking.

PQs have a number of advantages for the selector:

- Like all self-reports, PQs are self-contained: all the information needed is provided by the applicant.
- PQs are very accessible: HR staff can use them after a few days' training.
- PQs are fairly cheap because As can be tested in groups, or over the Internet.
- PQs generate a lot of information, very quickly. Even a long PQ, with several hundred items, can be completed within an hour. Elliott, Lawty-Jones and Jackson (1996) timed people completing the Eysenck PQ, and found they answered on average 15–16 questions a minute, one every four seconds.
- Items 5 and 6 in Table 7.1 suggest PQs may tap thoughts and feelings, as well as behaviour.

Table 7.1   A selection of PQ items and formats.

Endorsement format items

1. I am always punctual.	true	false
2. I keep my office tidy at all times.	true	false
3. Do you enjoy meeting new people?	yes	no
4. I got on better with my mother than with my father.	true	false
5. Some minorities make too much fuss about their 'rights'	true	false
6. I believe there is a life after death.	true	false
7. I have a satisfying sex life.	true	false
8. I suffer a lot from indigestion.	true	false
9. Do you sometimes hear voices?	yes	no
10. I never use bad language	true	false
11. As a child I always did what I was told	true	false
12. Dogged	[tick if the word applies to you]	

Forced-choice format items

13. On your day off would you rather paint a picture OR paint your house?
14. Would you rather be Dr Crippen OR Jack the Ripper?
15. Which of these words do you prefer?   profit   prophet

Rating format

16. I wait to find out what important people think before offering an opinion.

never	5	4	3	2	1	always

17. I feel tired at the end of the day.

never	5	4	3	2	1	always

18. energetic

very	5	4	5	2	1	not at all

- PQs are thought not to create serious adverse impact on ethnic minorities, unlike mental ability tests. This has been a major factor in their recent popularity in HR work in the USA.

Keying and validation

There are four main ways of writing PQs (*construction*) and trying to show that they work (*validation*).

1. *Acceptance or face validity*. People accept the PQ's results as accurate. This is a very weak test of validity, because people are easily taken in by all-purpose personality profiles – the so-called *Barnum* or *horoscope* effect.
2. *Content*. The PQ looks plausible. The first ever PQ, Woodworth's Personal Data Sheet of 1917, intended to assess emotional fitness in US Army recruits, gathered its questions from lists of symptoms in psychiatric textbooks, to ensure item content was plausible and relevant.

3. *Empirical*. The questions are included because they predict. The PQ is *empirically keyed* using *criterion groups* of people of known characteristics. For example the California Psychological Inventory (CPI) developed its Dominance scale from answers that distinguished college students nominated as leaders from those seen as followers.

4. *Factorial*. The questions have a common theme. After choosing the questions, the author tests their fit by correlation and factor analysis (see Box 2.7 on page 37). Factor analysis estimates how many themes or factors the PQ covers: Cattell found 16 factors in his 187 questions. Some questions do not relate to any theme and are discarded. In practice, development of a new PQ almost always includes factor analysis, however the questions are chosen.

Interpreting PQ scores

A raw score on a PQ, like a raw score on a mental ability test, means little, until it is related to a population – people in general, bank managers, bus drivers, or students. Variations on the standard score theme (Chapter 6) are used to interpret raw scores, most commonly T scores (Box 7.1).

Reliability

Viswesvaran and Ones's (2000) meta-analysis found average re-test reliabilities for PQ scales between 0.73 and 0.78, less than for mental ability tests. This level of reliability is consistent with some scores changing considerably over fairly short periods of time. Changes exceeding 0.5 SD, i.e. five *T* points, may be expected to occur in one in three retests, and changes over one whole SD (10 *T* points) in 1 in 20.

Box 7.1   *T* scores

The *T* score is a form of standard score in which the mean is set at 50 and the SD at 10. A raw score is converted into a T score using the formula $T = 50 + (10 \times ((\text{raw score} - \text{mean}) / SD)$. *T* scores give the same information as z scores (page 114) but avoid decimal points and minus signs.

The five-factor model of personality

The first generation of PQs, such as 16PF, California Psychological Inventory, and Eysenck Personality Questionnaire, assessed from two to 20 traits, very varied in nature. Tupes and Christal (1961/1992) used factor analysis to suggest there were five basic factors in personality (listed in Table 7.2). Subsequently Costa and McCrae took up this idea, wrote the first of many five-factor PQs, called NEO, and soon persuaded most personality theorists and researchers to recognize the five-factor model (FFM). The 'big five' are

Table 7.2   The big five personality factors.

Big five factor	Alternative titles	Alternative titles (reversed)
Neuroticism	Anxiety	Emotional stability
	Emotionality	Emotional control
		Resilience
		Adjustment
Extraversion	Surgency	Introversion
	Assertiveness	
	Ascendancy	
Openness	Culture	Dogmatism
	Intellect	Closedness
	Flexibility	
Agreeableness	Likeability	Antagonism
	Friendly compliance	Psychoticism
Conscientiousness	Will to achieve	Negligence
	Dependability	
	Prudence	
	Ego control	
	Super ego strength	

said to emerge reliably in many different cultures , including North America, Europe, Israel, Russia, Japan and China, so may represent a truly global model of personality. Most recent analyses of personality and work behaviour have used the FFM.

USING PQs IN SELECTION

Opinion on the value of PQs in selection has shifted over time. In the 1960s and 1970s they were widely dismissed as useless. Since 1990 they have grown steadily more popular, and new PQs have proliferated. But does validation research justify this new optimism? PQs try to answer five main questions:

1. Has A got the right personality for the job?
2. Will A do the job well?
3. Does A have a good 'attitude' (aka organizational citizenship behaviour; OCB)?
4. Will A behave badly in the workplace (aka counterproductive work behaviour; CWB)?
5. Will the team work well?

Questions 1 and 2 look similar, but differ subtly: question 1 is answered by comparing bank managers with people in general, while question 2 is answered by comparing successful and less successful bank managers.

QUESTION 1: THE RIGHT PERSONALITY?

The A-S-A model argues that certain personalities are attracted to psychology (*Attraction*), that certain personalities are selected to become psychologists (*Selection*), and that certain personalities find psychology does not suit them (*Attrition*). Some employers seem to want a book of perfect personality profiles for manager, salesperson, engineer, etc. PQ manuals meet this demand to some extent, by giving norms for different occupations. The perfect profile approach has several limitations.

- Sample sizes are often too small, and cross-validation information is rarely available. Ideally a perfect profile for a cost accountant will be based on two or more large, separate, samples.
- Most perfect profiles derive from people doing the job, taking no account of how well they do it.
- A perfect profile may show how people have changed to fit the job's demands, not how well people with that profile will do the job.
- Using perfect profiles encourages *cloning*, i.e. selecting as managers only people who resemble as closely as possible existing managers. This may create great harmony and satisfaction within the organization, but may make it difficult for the organization to cope with change.
- Success in some jobs, for example management, may be achieved by two, or more, different personality profiles.

QUESTION 2: WILL HE/SHE DO THE JOB WELL?

The second, more important, question is whether PQs can select people who will do their job well, defined by supervisor rating, sales figures or training grades. Two important reviews appeared in the 1960s and 1970s: Lent, Aurbach and Levin (1971) found only 12% of validity coefficients were significant, while Guion and Gottier (1965) found only 10%. These reviews, and Mischel's 1968 criticism of the trait model, led to the general feeling that PQs had no useful place in selection. Guion and Gottier concluded 'it is difficult to advocate, with a clear conscience. the use of personality measures in most situations as a basis for making employment decisions'.

Since 1990 numerous meta-analyses have been calculated, most also using validity generalization analysis, and most fitting PQs into the FFM (Hough, 1992, 1998; Barrick & Mount, 1991; Tett, Jackson & Rothstein, 1991; Salgado, 1998; Hurtz & Donovan, 2000; Vinchur *et al.*, 1998).

Barrick, Mount and Judge (2001) summarized all these various meta-analyses in a 'meta-meta-analysis' (Table 7.3). Conscientiousness has the largest correlation with work performance, followed by (low) neuroticism and extraversion; values for openness and agreeableness do not differ significantly from zero. Critics (Morgeson *et al.*, 2007) note that even making corrections for outcome reliability and restricted range, PQs do not correlate with work performance better than 0.20; they cannot even reach the 0.30 barrier, let alone break it.

Table 7.3   Meta-meta-analysis of the big five and job performance.

	k	N	r	ρ
Neuroticism	224	39K	−0.06	−0.11
Extraversion	222	39K	0.06	0.11
Openness	143	23K	0.03	0.04
Agreeableness	206	36K	0.06	0.09
Conscientiousness	239	48K	0.12	0.20

r = raw correlation; ρ = operational validity, estimated from true validity on the basis of correction for test reliability of 0.80.
Data from Barrick *et al.* (2001).

Schmidt, Shaffer and Oh (2008) apply the indirect range restriction correction (see Chapter 2) to meta-analyses of PQ validity, and find it makes little difference, because there is less restriction of range on PQ scores than for tests of mental ability.

Different occupations

Barrick *et al.*'s meta-meta-analysis finds some small differences between five broad classes of work. Low neuroticism correlates better with success in police work and skilled and semi-skilled work. Extraversion correlates better with success in management. Some individual meta-analyses have also reported occupational differences.

- Hough (1998) and Vinchur *et al.* (1998) both found extraversion correlates with sales performance.
- Two meta-analyses suggested a role for agreeableness in some types of work. Hurtz and Donovan's analysis found agreeableness and openness correlate with performance more strongly for customer service work. Mount, Barrick and Stewart (1998) found that agreeableness correlates better with performance in work where co-operation and teamwork are important (as opposed to work which simply involves interacting with clients, for example hotel work).
- Some jobs involve *emotional labour,* meaning having to control one's emotions, or having to be nice to people. The person who repairs your car expends only physical labour: the person who tells you it has failed the official road-worthiness test and will cost £1,000 to repair may have to expend some emotional labour. Joseph and Newman (2010) test the plausible hypothesis that *emotional labour* will be a moderator variable for PQ validity, but do not confirm it.

Themes in work performance

Table 7.4 summarizes research on personality and leadership, expatriate work, and success as an entrepreneur.

Table 7.4 Personality and specialized work performance.

	N	E	O	A	C
Leadership – business	−0.14	0.23	0.21	−0.04	0.05
Leadership – government & military	−0.22	0.15	0.05	−0.04	0.16
Expatriate performance	−0.09	0.15	0.05	0.10	0.15
Entrepreneurship	−0.14	0.10	0.15	−0.07	0.19

Data on leadership from Judge *et al.* (2002).
Data on expatriate performance from Mol *et al.* (2005).
Data for entrepreneurship from Zhao & Seibert (2006).
r calculated from uncorrected *d* values.

Leadership For some jobs, ability to lead others is critical. Judge *et al.* (2002) meta-analysed leadership and the FFM, and found modest correlations for (low) neuroticism and extraversion. In civilian management, openness correlated positively, while in the military and government, conscientiousness correlated positively (Table 7.4). Hoffman *et al.*'s (2011) meta-analysis of leadership compares *distal* factors such as personality that can be selected for, with *proximal* factors such as interpersonal skills that can be developed, and finds the two equally strongly linked to leadership. This confirms both the 'Great Man' theory (leaders are rare, are born not made, and are male), and the 'leadership as role (that anyone can take on)' theory. Hoffman *et al.* also find links with personality stronger in lower-level managers than in top managers, and suggest this may be because success in top leadership depends more on events outside the organization, and beyond the leader's control.

Expatriate work Mol *et al.* (2005) meta-analyse 12 studies linking expatriate performance to the FFM, and find modest correlations with extraversion and conscientiousness, even more modest correlations with agreeableness and (low) neuroticism, but – perhaps surprisingly – none with openness.

Entrepreneurship Entrepreneurs found, own and run their businesses (whereas managers work for someone else). Zhao and Seibert (2006) meta-analyse 23 studies comparing the two, and find entrepreneurs higher on extraversion, openness, and conscientiousness, but lower on neuroticism and agreeableness. More detailed analysis finds the difference in conscientiousness is for achievement, not dependability. The multiple correlation between all five factors and entrepreneurial status is fairly high at 0.37.

Combat effectiveness Hough (1998) found (low) neuroticism correlated with combat effectiveness in US military samples. Salgado (1998) confirmed this in European military samples. Meta-analyses of conscientiousness and combat effectiveness disagree; Mount and Barrick (1995) reported 0.47 in 10 studies, whereas Hough reported much lower correlations between achievement and dependability and combat effectiveness.

Table 7.5   Meta-meta-analysis of the big five and three measures of work performance.

	N	E	O	A	C
Supervisor rating	−0.10	0.10	0.04	0.09	0.23
Objective measures of performance	−0.08	0.10	0.02	0.11	0.17
Training grade	−0.07	0.20	0.21	0.10	0.20

Operational validity, estimated from true validity, on the basis of correction for test reliability of 0.80. Data from Barrick *et al.* (2001).

Different measures of work performance

Barrick *et al.* (2001) distinguished supervisor rating, training grades, and objective performance such as sales (Table 7.5). Extraversion did not relate much to overall work performance, but did relate to training performance. Perhaps extraverts like new experiences, or meeting new people, (or getting away from work for a day or two). Openness correlated with training performance; perhaps open-minded people like gaining new knowledge and skills. Conscientiousness correlates with all three performance measures, leading Barrick *et al.* to suggest it may be 'the trait-oriented motivation variable that industrial-organizational psychologists have long searched for'. (But they will need to keep searching if they want correlations larger than 0.20.)

Vocational interest questionnaires (VIQs)   VIQs, aka career interest tests, have been around as long as PQs, and are similar in format. VIQs are intended more to help people choose the right work than to help employers choose the right applicants. Early reviews, for example Hunter and Hunter (1984), concluded VIQs were not useful in selection. VIQs, it was generally supposed, assessed whether people were interested in a job, but not whether they could do it well. Van Iddekinge *et al.* (2011) report a meta-analysis of VIQs and work performance, training performance, and turnover. The results tend to confirm earlier conclusions that VIQs are not very useful in selection, with a correlations of only 0.14 with work performance; training performance was predicted rather better, at 0.26. VIQs are also fairly poor at predicting turnover. Van Iddekinge *et al.* analyse what one might call 'uninterests' – whether going in for a job the VIQ specifically said would *not* suit would be linked to (poorer) performance or (higher) turnover. The correlations are reversed in sign, but no different in size. Two issues remain largely unexplored. Will VIQs achieve incremental validity on other measures, particularly PQs which are very similar in format? Will VIQs prove easy to fake?

Incremental validity

Both conscientiousness and mental ability correlate with work performance, but not with each other, so it follows logically that conscientiousness will have incremental validity on mental ability (and vice versa). Schmidt and Hunter

(1998) estimate the incremental validity of conscientiousness on mental ability at 18%, and list the combination as one of the four most useful. Salgado (1998), reviewing European data, confirmed this, and concluded that neuroticism too will have incremental validity.

Direction of cause

Much has been made in some quarters of the concept of self-efficacy as a predictor of work success. People who are confident they can do a job, or master its skills and challenges, are more likely to perform well. Various self-efficacy questionnaires have been developed, and have generated correlations with work performance. Sceptics see direction of cause issues with the self-efficacy concept. Do people who think they can do the job succeed because they have a positive attitude? Or do they have a positive attitude because they have done the job successfully? Sitzmann and Yeo (2013) have data on both past and present performance, so can show that controlling for past performance reduces the 0.23 validity for self-efficacy to insignificance, implying that self-efficacy describes past performance rather than predicting future performance.

Conclusion

PQs seem generally fairly poor at answering the question, 'Will he/she do this job well?' Possibly questions about ability are better answered by ability tests. Some 15 years of intense interest and research activity do not generally seem to have produced results that are very much more impressive than those reported in the 1960s and 1970s, and which led many to dismiss PQs as not helpful in selection. Defenders of personality tests argue that even low validities can secure a worthwhile increase in performance when cumulated across a large workforce, especially when the assessment is quick and cheap to make.

RESEARCH AGENDA

- More research on which aspects of personality might be changed by doing what sorts of work, over what time span.

QUESTION 3: HAS HE/SHE GOT A GOOD ATTITUDE TO WORK? ORGANIZATIONAL CITIZENSHIP

Interest in personality and work has shifted somewhat since 1990, from performance, defined by output or supervisor rating of proficiency, to a broader set of outcomes, best summarized by 'attitude', as in 'you have a bad attitude' or 'he has an attitude problem'. Employers usually prefer employees who

Table 7.6   Meta-analyses of FFM and 'attitude' aspects of work performance.

	N	E	O	A	C
Commendable behaviour	−0.15[u]	0.08[eu]	nd	0.08[u]	0.23[u]
Job dedication	−0.13	0.05	0.01	0.08	0.18
Interpersonal facilitation	−0.16	0.10	0.05	0.17	0.16
Getting along	−0.31	0.01[a]	0.03[b]	0.19	0.21
		0.15[c]	0.12[d]		
Organizational citizenship	−0.12	0.09	0.14	0.14	0.18

Operational validity except [u] where uncorrected validity; nr – not reported.
Data for *commendable behaviour* from Hough, Barge & Kamp (2001); [e] potency facet of extraversion.
Data for *job dedication* and *interpersonal facilitation* from Hurtz & Donovan (2000).
Data for *getting along* from Hogan & Holland (2003). Extraversion split into sociability[a]/ambition[b]; openness split into intellectance[c]/school success[d].
Data for *organizational citizenship* from Chiaburu et al. (2011), excludes studies which used self-reports of OCB.

are keen, co-operative, and helpful. This is also referred to as organizational citizenship behaviour (OCB), or contextual performance. In the USA broadening the concept of work performance is also motivated by equal opportunities concerns. Emphasizing ability, assessed by written tests and defined by training grades and supervisor ratings, creates large adverse impact problems. Emphasizing 'attitude' or OCB, and measures that assess it, such as PQs, may reduce adverse impact. Ability and proficiency are sometimes called 'can do' aspects, while motivation and attitude are called 'will do'.

Table 7.6 shows 'attitude' aspects of work performance are linked to conscientiousness, like task aspects. Links to neuroticism and agreeableness may be stronger for attitude than task. Results for extraversion seem more variable: Table 7.6 may show that extraversion is linked to attitude to co-workers (citizenship, getting along, interpersonal facilitation) but not to attitude to the job itself (dedication). Validation of the US military's PQ, called Assessment of Background and Life Experiences (ABLE), showed ABLE correlated with three *will do* criteria – *effort and leadership*, *personal discipline*, and *physical fitness and military bearing* – better (0.16, uncorrected) than two *can-do* criteria – *technical proficiency* or *general soldiering proficiency* (Hough et al., 1990; McHenry et al., 1990). Mount and Barrick (1995) reported a meta-analysis for conscientiousness and various *will do* criteria: reliability, effort (defined as hard work, initiative, motivation, energy and persistence), and quality, finding fully corrected or 'true' correlations of 0.40 to 0.50. They pooled all the *will do* criteria and found an overall true validity of 0.45, against 0.22 for pooled *can do* criteria.

RESEARCH AGENDA

• More longitudinal research in which personality is assessed when people start a new job and linked to later OCB.

QUESTION 4: WILL HE/ SHE BEHAVE BADLY AT WORK? COUNTERPRODUCTIVE WORK BEHAVIOUR

PQs can be used like the driving test: not to select the best, but to exclude the unacceptable. Using personality measures to screen As has a long history. Anderson's (1929) survey of staff at Macy's department store in New York found 20% of employees fell into the 'problem' category: they suffered chronic ill health, were in constant trouble with fellow-employees, could not adjust satisfactorily to their work, etc. Some research has looked at fairly specific forms of misbehaviour, absence, theft, or violence; other research groups diverse behaviours together as *counterproductive work behaviours* (CWBs), which include breaking rules, illegal activities, theft, drug use, lateness, and violence. A series of meta-analyses have covered various aspects of CWB (Table 7.7).

Violence and aggression

In 1979 the Avis car-rental company was sued when an employee raped a customer and was found to have a record of similar offences. Avis should, it was claimed, have discovered the man was dangerous. *Negligent hiring* claims have become common in the USA. Hershcovis *et al.* (2007) report a meta-analysis of

Table 7.7 Summary of meta-analyses of correlations between FFM PQs and counterproductive work behaviours.

	N	E	O	A	C
Aggression to co-workers	−0.25				
Aggression to organization	−0.26				
Absence	−0.04	0.08	0.00	0.04	−0.06
Accidents	0.06	−0.11	0.05	0.07	−0.12
Unsafe behaviour	0.13	0.10	0.02	−0.26	−0.25
Substance abuse	0.07	0.06[uP]		−0.04	−0.28
Turnover	0.20	−0.04	0.10	−0.27	−0.22
Law-abiding behaviour	0.41[u]	0.29[uP]			0.58[u]
Deviant behaviour	0.06	0.01	0.11	−0.20	−0.26
Interpersonal deviance	0.24	0.02	−0.09	−0.46	−0.23
Organizational deviance	0.23	−0.09	−0.04	−0.32	−0.42

[P] potency aspect of extraversion only.
[u] uncorrected correlation.
Data on *aggression* from Hershcovis *et al.* (2007).
Data on *substance abuse* from Hough *et al.* (1990).
Data on *law abiding behaviour* from Hough *et al.* (2001).
Data on *absence* and *deviant behaviour* from Salgado (2002).
Data for *accidents and safety* from Beus *et al.* (2015).
Data on *interpersonal and organizational deviance* from Berry, Ones & Sackett (2007).
Data on *turnover* from Zimmerman (2008).

workplace aggression and personality, restricting itself to trait anger and negative affectivity. Trait anger correlates well with aggression, especially aggression directed at people rather than the organization (0.43 true validity). Negative affectivity, which has some overlap with FFM neuroticism, correlates less strongly with aggression; Hershcovis *et al.*'s analysis suggests it may overlap with trait anger. Note that their definition of aggression appears to be fairly broad, extending to rudeness and 'retaliation'.

Accidents and safety

Beus, Dhahani and McCord (2015) summarize research on personality and safety at work. Conscientiousness is linked to safer behaviour and having fewer accidents. So is agreeableness. There is a weaker relationship with extraversion, and neuroticism, both of which accompany less safe behaviour and more accidents. Beus *et al.*'s results confirm the value of conscientiousness in employees.

Absence

Absence is a major problem for many employers, so the possibility of selecting people less likely to be absent is attractive. Salgado (2002) summarized 8–10 studies and found virtually no correlation with any of the big five. However Salgado was unable to distinguish voluntary from involuntary absence, a notorious problem with absence research.

Turnover

Employers often view staff leaving their employment as counter-productive behaviour, if only because it costs them time and money. Reasons people leave also include furthering their career, or to escape a boring and unpleasant job. Zimmerman's (2008) meta-analysis suggests poor adjustment and impulsivity also play a part.

The very high (and uncorrected) correlations for law-abiding behaviour reported by Hough (1992) may be slightly misleading. Some studies compared criminals with non-criminals, and calculated correlations from the difference between them. Finding personality differences between delinquents and non-delinquents may have problems of direction of cause. Convicted criminals might experience some difficulty plausibly presenting themselves as honest, and the fact of having been convicted might remove any incentive to do so. However, some studies were more convincing, for example quite large correlations between PQ scores when joining the army, and subsequent absence without leave. The high correlations reported by Berry *et al.* (2007) may result in part from common method variance, because both personality and deviance are for the most part self-reports.

PQs seem more strongly linked to tendencies to misbehave at work, with a pattern of high neuroticism, low agreeableness and low conscientiousness.

However, these stronger links will not necessarily translate into better predictions of work behaviour, given that a lot of research has used concurrent validation and self-reported misbehaviour.

More research showing that PQs can predict today who will misbehave in future is still needed.

RESEARCH AGENDA

- More longitudinal research in which personality is assessed when people start a new job and linked to later CWB.

THE SAGA OF HONESTY TESTS

Numerous surveys have concluded that employee theft is a widespread problem in the USA, and may contribute to 30% of company failures. Honesty tests (HTs), aka integrity tests, are a form of PQ that became popular in the USA, after use of the polygraph (or lie-detector test) was restricted in 1988. They do not seem to have been used much in Europe. Table 7.8 shows some typical HT questions, some tapping attitudes related to honesty, others seeking admissions of past dishonesty. HTs have been validated against polygraph assessments, or till shortages, or even low takings (on the assumption low takings mean the person is stealing). Ones, Viswesvaran and Schmidt (1993) reported a meta-analysis of 665 HT validities, covering no fewer than 576,460 persons, which produced some surprising results:

- HTs predict CWBs very well, achieving an operational validity of 0.47. Validity for self-reported CWBs is higher than for recorded CWBs.
- HTs are surprisingly versatile; they can predict accidents at work, and property damage, as well as training performance and output.
- Perhaps the most surprising result was that HTs also predict work performance very well, achieving an operational validity of 0.34, which is better than FFM PQs.

Table 7.8   Some questions of the type found in honesty tests.

Attitudes and beliefs
Employees who take things from work are criminals who should be punished.
Employers who don't treat their staff right deserve to get ripped off by them.

Admissions
Have you taken anything from your place of work over the last five years?
I have never sold things to my friends or family for less than the right price.
How much money do you spend on alcohol in a typical week?
I bet on horse racing or sporting events quite frequently.

Critics (Berry, Sackett & Wiemann, 2007) have expressed some cautions about the validity of HTs. Many are validated by including questions asking people to admit past dishonesty, and using these questions as a criterion for the rest of the measure. This is obviously a very weak form of validation, in effect asking people twice if they will admit to dishonesty. Perhaps the correlation should be a lot higher than 0.30 to 0.40. The number of studies that use behavioural measures of dishonesty is considerably smaller than 665, and the number that use actual theft as the outcome smaller still. Only seven studies, with a total of 2,500 persons, used actual theft, and these achieved much poorer results, a corrected validity of only 0.13.

McDaniel, Rothstein and Whetzel (2006) report trim-and-fill analyses (Chapter 2, p. 42) for reporting bias in four sets of validity data presented by four unnamed American test vendors. Two of the four datasets appear to report less evidence of limited validity than trim and fill indicates might be expected; McDaniel *et al.* suggest this 'calls into question past meta-analyses that have relied primarily on test vendor data', specifically mentioning Ones *et al.*'s (1993) meta-analysis of HTs. Campion (Morgeson *et al.*, 2007) states that some HT publishers exhibited gross publication bias, not wanting even to hear about studies that found negative results.

Twenty years after Ones *et al.*, Van Iddekinge *et al.* (2012a) set out to perform a new meta-analysis of HTs, with some interesting results.

1. The re-analysis concludes HTs predict CWB (0.26) better than work performance (0.16).
2. Research done by test publishers gets better results than research from other researchers for work performance, but poorer results for CWB, showing no overall pattern of effect.
3. One might suppose that van Iddekinge *et al.* would find more research to include in their meta-analysis, compared with Ones *et al.*, given that nearly 20 years have passed during which research on personality and work behaviour has flourished. However, they did not. Van Iddekinge *et al.* report they wrote to 30 test publishers. Two co-operated fully and gave van Iddekinge *et al.* access to their research data. Other test publishers variously did not respond, declined to participate, or wanted to impose conditions on use of their data. One test publisher 'informed us that [its] corporate attorneys wanted us to know that we did not have permission to use several technical reports we had obtained from another researcher because the reports had not been released into the public domain (yet apparently were provided to Ones *et al.*, 1993, and other researchers' (van Iddekinge *et al.*, 2012b). Van Iddekinge *et al.* were unable to include in their re-analysis much of the data Ones *et al.* had used in 1993, so were unable to achieve the intended replication.

Sackett and Schmitt (2012) compare the two analyses' conclusions about HTs predicting work performance in general, one of the more surprising results of Ones *et al.*'s 1993 analysis. They restrict their analysis to methodologically superior studies that use a predictive design, with real applicants, and do not rely on self-report outcome measures. Using these fairly strict criteria for inclusion, Sackett and Schmitt found that Ones *et al.* reported a corrected validity of 0.35, larger than conventional PQs, whereas van Iddekinge *et al.* reported validity of only 0.11, smaller than conventional PQs. Note that both estimates are based on just 20 samples (not the same 20) with a total sample size of 7,000–8,000. The enormous total sample in Ones *et al.*'s meta-analysis seemed to consist mostly of less useful studies. Sackett and Schmitt (2012) wonder what to do with research that has 'important flaws (small sample sizes, inadequate criteria, questionable methods of data collection, inadequate reporting) that really call into question their value for any purpose'. Their answer is essentially to start all over again: 'There is a need for a large scale, multi-test, multi-organization, multi-investigator study of the validity of integrity tests. Such a study may be much more credible than the data base that is now being a meta-analysed.' They note that they are not criticizing meta-analysis as such, but the inclusion of poor quality research.

RESEARCH AGENDA

- Large scale research testing 'real' applicants and linking personality to 'real' CWB.
- More research on source of research as a moderator variable for validity.

QUESTION 5: WILL THE TEAM WORK WELL?

Chapter 6 noted that selection research remains focused on the individual employee, even though a lot of work is done by teams, where personality could be especially important. Bell's (2007) meta-analysis finds 11 studies of work team performance and FFM; Bell analyses average personality, variation in personality within the team, and extremes. Table 7.9 shows team performance linked to team's average PQ score for all five factors. In particular higher levels of conscientiousness and agreeableness are linked to better performance. Earlier analyses, for example Table 7.3, showed agreeableness does not correlate with performance at the individual level, but Bell's findings show it becomes important in team work. Bell finds weaker effects for variability, where more variation in conscientiousness and openness is linked to poorer performance. Perhaps the most striking results are for extremes – what one might call the 'bad apple' effect. The higher the minimum score for conscientiousness and agreeableness, the better the group works. This suggests one single low-scoring person, on either conscientiousness or agreeableness, can hold back the entire group.

RESEARCH AGENDA

* More research on team personality and performance, with wider range of jobs.
* Links between team personality and other aspects of work performance, including attitude and CWBs.
* Exploration of how low scorers affect team functioning.

Table 7.9   Meta-analysis of links between team personality and team performance.

	N	E	O	A	C
k	4–5	5–7	4–5	7–9	8–10
N teams	207–354	227–492	176–323	301–495	301–525
Team average	−0.21	0.18	0.25	0.34	0.33
Team variability	0.05	0.06	−0.13	−0.08	−0.16
Extreme – max	−0.13	0.13	0.17	0.14	0.14
Extreme – min	0.00	0.04	0.09	0.37	0.27

Correlations corrected for reliability of both PQ and performance measure, but not restricted range. Data from Bell (2007).

COMPLEXITIES OF PQ VALIDITY

People commonly react to research on personality and performance by say-ing 'It's much more complicated than that', and can readily list half a dozen possible complexities that the researcher has overlooked, or which might explain their negative results. Unfortunately it is far easier to propose com-plexities than to resolve them. Three examples have been chosen for discussion.

Linearity

Le *et al.* (2011) make a plausible case for non-linear relationships between two personality factors and work performance. Too much conscientiousness can be 'a bad thing', because highly conscientious people are more prone to rigidity: in the low to average range conscientiousness will correlate with better work performance, but in the average to high range, work performance may flatten off, or even decrease. Le *et al.* also argue that high conscientiousness may be more of a problem in low-complexity jobs, which often require speed but not accuracy, whereas high-complexity jobs require accuracy but less speed, and so may require higher persistence. For neuroticism, a good applicant needs just enough emotional stability to avoid being distracted by emotion at work, but beyond this point there is no extra advantage. Both hypotheses are very plausible, and both are confirmed by Le *et al.* in two large samples, but only for extraversion in one sample, and neuroticism in the other. Non-linear effects are likely to depend on the type of work, and the type of applicant, so will require a large volume of research to document, and replicate.

Quadrant analysis

Some American employers used to consider joining a trade (labour) union as evidence of maladjustment, and tried to use PQs to avoid employing such 'misfits' (Zickar, 2001). Parkes and Razavi (2004) report personality data on union membership, using the Eysenck PQ. Neither extraversion nor neuroticism alone has a good prediction of joining a union, but the combination of low extraversion and low neuroticism predicted *not* joining; perhaps stable introverts need neither the reassurance nor the social opportunities union membership can bring. This is an example of a *quadrant analysis* (Figure 7.1), dividing people into four boxes, based on scores on two personality dimensions. Putting people into sets of boxes seems to be a favourite pastime of managers, or people who would like to be managers, judging from popular management books. Quadrant analysis has a basic problem: it is incompatible with a normal distribution. On Eysenck's personality dimensions, like almost all others, most people are in the middle, so do not fall neatly into either the extravert or the introvert box. If tested a second time, many will 'change sides' from extravert to introvert or neurotic to stable.

Situational strength

Situational strength is an idea originally proposed by Mischel (1968) to explain why personality is often less important than people suppose. Some situations create such powerful demands that individual differences have little or no scope to affect how people behave. A university lecture is an example: the students sit, listen, and take notes; only the lecturer stands up, and speaks. Standing and speaking reveal nothing of his/her personality, but reflect his/her role in a well-defined situation. In a weak situation by contrast there are no clear rules or expectations, so personality can influence who speaks first, and what they say. Is work a strong situation, where personality will not have much effect, so need not be selected for? Or is it a weak one? Meyer, Dalal and Bonaccio (2009) use 14 items from the O*NET work analysis system (Chapter 3) to estimate situational strength in different jobs, for example *responsible for*

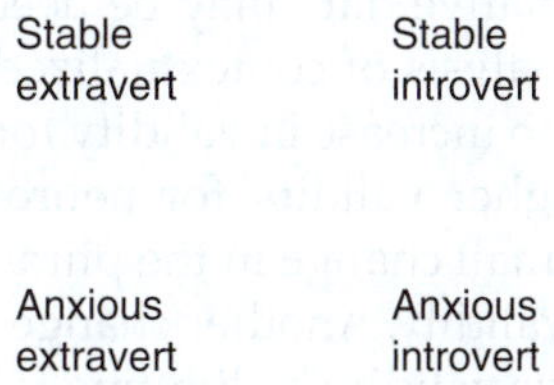

Stable extravert	Stable introvert
Anxious extravert	Anxious introvert

Figure 7.1 Quadrant model of extraversion and neuroticism.

others' health and safety or *(not)* *making decisions and solving problems*. High situational strength jobs include airline pilot, nuclear equipment operation technician, and subway and streetcar operator. Low situational strength jobs include hairdresser, lyricist or creative writer, and personnel recruiter (despite all the fair employment law they must know and conform to). Results confirm their hypothesis. The link between conscientiousness and work performance is lower in situationally strong jobs (0.09), but higher (0.23) in situationally weak jobs.

RESEARCH AGENDA

- More research on moderator variables, both other aspects of personality and external factors.
- Whether mental ability moderates link between personality and work performance.
- More research on non-linear relationships between personality and work behaviour.
- More research on the feasibility and usefulness of quadrant models.

IMPROVING PQ VALIDITY

PQs seem to give generally fairly poor predictions of how people will behave at work, especially compared with tests of mental ability. Attempts to improve validity have centred on changing the format of the items, and changing the number of aspects of personality measured.

Contextualization, or frame of reference

Most PQs assess personality in general, but selectors do not need to know what someone is like at home, and probably should not ask. A PQ may give misleading results in selection if people describe how they behave outside work. Robie *et al.* (2000) describe a contextualized PQ which inserts *at work* into every question: *I take great care with detail at work*. Robie *et al.* found contextualization raised scores – perhaps because people really are more careful at work – so new normative data may be needed. Shaffer and Postlethwaite (2012) report a meta-analysis of contextualized PQs which specify behaviour *at work*. These achieve an increase in validity for conscientiousness of 33%, and achieve very much higher validity for neuroticism, extraversion, openness and agreeableness. A small change in the phrasing of PQs seems to generate a large increase in their validity. Another change in format is forced choice, usually intended to improve validity by limiting faking, and discussed later under that heading.

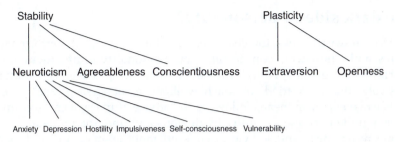

Figure 7.2   (Partial) hierarchical model of personality, at three levels, of two factors, five factors, and 30 facets. Only the neuroticism facets are listed.

More than five scales – FFM facets

Previous analyses, for example Hough (1992), have sometimes split FFM factors into two, arguing that conscientiousness conflates two aspects of personality, for example achievement and carefulness, with opposing implications for work performance, and may therefore miss important trends. Some versions of the FFM contain facets nested within the factors, giving a more elaborated account of personality (Figure 7.2). Judge *et al.* (2013) report a meta-analysis of FFM facets, and find the six-facet-per-factor model generates a range of validities within factor differing by 15 correlation points (0.15) on average, confirming that the facets do indeed have different relationships with work performance, i.e. that the facets may contain more information than the factors. For example the *positive emotion* facet of extraversion correlates 0.20 with work performance, whereas the *excitement-seeking* facet does not correlate at all. Judge *et al.*'s results open up the possibility of generating a work performance version of the FFM, that includes only the most relevant facets, or even of selecting from the full 30-facet model the 'right' subset of facets for different types of work.

Less than five? The FFM as a whole

Multiple correlation assesses the power of all five FFM factors collectively to predict work performance. If the five were as uncorrelated as originally supposed, the multiple correlation would be higher than any single correlation. Most researchers have not reported multiple correlation, but Ones *et al.* (2007) generate estimates for previous MAs, from factor validities, and estimates of FFM intercorrelations. This gives a value of 0.27 for overall job performance for Barrick *et al.*'s meta-meta-analysis, which still fails to break the 0.30 barrier. Research has also found some evidence for a two-factor model: *plasticity*, comprising openness and extraversion, and *stability*, comprising agreeableness, conscientiousness and (low) neuroticism (Figure 7.2).

The dark side of personality?

Most research looks for characteristics linked to good performance; some research, however, concentrates on personality traits to avoid (Spain, Harms & Lebreton, 2014). Three traits in particular have been studied extensively: the 'dark triad' of Machiavellianism, narcissism, and psychopathy. Machiavellianism means following the advice of the sixteenth-century author of a guide to ruling a country by devious and underhand means. Narcissism means having an inflated view of oneself, fantasies of control and success, and the desire to have one's self-love reinforced by others; it is assessed by items such as *I am going to be great person*, or *I insist on getting the respect that is due to me*. Psychopathic personality has been very extensively researched: its key features include impulsivity and thrill-seeking combined with low empathy and anxiety. O'Boyle *et al.* (2012) report a meta-analysis of dark triad PQs in selection; they find the dark triad generally unrelated to work performance, except that people in positions of authority (which includes managers) who are high in narcissism show much poorer performance. O'Boyle *et al.* find a link with CWB, especially for narcissism, but not for psychopathic personality. All the data in O'Boyle *et al.*'s analysis came from self-report PQs. One could argue that PQs are particularly ill suited to assess the dark triad, since narcissism is partly defined by lack of self-insight, and Machiavellianism and psychopathy by willingness to lie to achieve one's ends. (Lie for different reasons: Machiavellians know they are lying but consider it justified, while psychopaths have no concept of truth so do not know they are lying.) Kish-Gephart, Harrison and Treviño's (2010) meta-analysis of unethical decision-making in the workplace finds a 0.27 correlation with Machiavellianism. There is a much larger body of research on 'the dark side', including specifically narcissism and psychopathy, conducted under the heading of 'personality disorder', which – in the USA – forms part of the official psychiatric diagnostic system, which brings it within the scope of disability discrimination laws (see Chapter 13). Spain *et al.* note that some approaches use less medical, but less colourful, names for the dark triad: sceptical, bold and mischievous. O'Boyle *et al.* (2012) note a problem others often overlook: *circularity*, in the shape of questions in PQs that link directly to the outcome being predicted. Questions about arrest or getting into trouble appear in some dark triad PQs, which tends to guarantee a link with measures of CWB. One could speculate that items tend to be selected for inclusion in PQs on the basis of item statistics, as much as by content, and that once included, their content tends to be forgotten about.

RESEARCH AGENDA

• More research on relative success of two, five or 30 scale models in predicting work behaviour.

THE PROBLEM OF FAKING

Personality questionnaires are not *tests* but *self-reports*; a test has right and wrong answers but a self-report does not. Many PQs look fairly transparent to critics and lay people, who argue no one applying for a job as a manager is likely to say *true* to *I am poor at organizing myself*. PQs, argue the critics, are easily faked. For many uses of PQs this does not matter; the tester can rely on the principle of *rational self-disclosure*: a person seeking career advice will see it as in his/her own interests to answer honestly when completing a PQ. It might be unwise to rely on the same assumption when people complete PQs to get a job they really want, or really need. This implies PQs may be less useful in selection. Some experts, however, disagree, and make three assertions:

1. Most people tell the truth when completing PQs in job applications.
2. It does not matter if they do not tell the truth, because 'faking' does not reduce PQ validity.
3. Faking is not a problem.

Assertion 1 – people tell the truth on PQs when applying for jobs

Can people fake? In directed faking studies, people complete the PQ with instructions to give answers that will create a good impression, or secure a job they really want. A meta-analysis (Viswesvaran & Ones, 1999) showed that people find these directions easy to follow, and can achieve large increases in scores (Figure 7.3). Conscientiousness, which predicts work performance best of the big five, can be improved by nearly one whole SD. Directed faking research shows people *can* fake PQs, but does not prove they actually do fake when applying for jobs.

Do people fake? There are several lines of evidence on 'real-life' frequency of faking in selection. Surveys, for example McDaniel, Douglas and Snell (1997), reported that some people say they would fake good on a PQ, or have faked good, but more say they would not, or have not. But do people tell the truth about the telling the truth?

Applicant/present employee (PE) comparisons PEs – it is argued – have got the job so have less need to fake the PQ. Birkeland *et al.* (2006) meta-analyse 33 studies comparing As and PEs, and find As score higher on conscientiousness, and lower on neuroticism (Figure 7.3). This strongly suggests some As fake good, but suggests also that directed faking research overestimates faking good in job applications. (One could question the argument that PEs have no motivation to fake; it may depend whether the results remain anonymous, or whether they could affect career or reputation, a point not addressed in Birkeland *et al.*'s meta-analysis.)

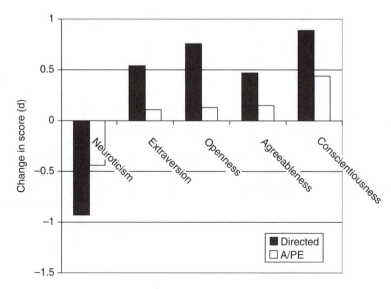

Figure 7.3   Effect of directed faking, and applicant status on PQ measures of the big five. Baseline represents averages for unfaked big five, or present employees. Data for directed faking from Viswesvaran & Ones (1999). Data for applicant/present employee comparison from Birkeland *et al.* (2006).

Applicant/research comparison   The ideal research sees the same set of people complete the PQ twice, once for research or their own enlightenment, and once in a real application for a real job. Two studies have achieved this in slightly different ways, and both suggest that some applicants do fake. Griffith, Chmielowski and Yoshita (2007) contacted people who had completed a conscientiousness scale when applying for temp work, and asked them to complete it again, this time 'as honestly as possible'. Faking is defined as a change in score greater than error of measurement. Griffith *et al.* found 31% had faked in selection. Stewart *et al.* (2008) use a slightly unethical 'bogus job' method. Students who had completed a PQ for research were later contacted, ostensibly by someone else, and told they had been identified as possible candidates for corporate recruiting and asked to complete the same PQ. Changes larger than error of measurement defined those who faked; 14% increased their conscientiousness score.

RESEARCH AGENDA

- Replication of Griffith *et al.* and Stewart *et al.*, with larger samples and higher return rate.
- Replication, or re-analysis, of Birkeland *et al.*'s meta-analysis of faking by applicants and present employees, distinguishing whether the assessment has any implications for present employees.

Why people fake good (or do not) Kuncel and Tellegen (2009) explore peoples' thinking when answering PQs. In their first research they ask people which answers are the 'best' to give. Consider the item *not easily upset*: how desirable is it to be in the top 1%, above-average meaning in the top 30%, average, below average, or in the bottom 1%? Many PQ items get a skewed distribution, where it is less desirable to be in the top 1% than in the top 30%. Some items have their desirability peak at average, for example *talkative*. Next Kuncel and Tellegen asked people to fake good on a PQ, then asked them to explain their answers, especially when they had not chosen the (apparently) 'best' answer. Kuncel and Tellegen detected three main themes in the explanations: making a good impression, being credible, and being true to oneself. It is reassuring that some people are apparently unwilling to give an answer they feel 'isn't really them'. Unfortunately, from the selectors' point of view, only some people think this way, and it only takes some people faking to create problems in selection. The third aim – being true to oneself – is interesting and worth exploring further. Is it simply being realistic? *If I claim to be in the top 1% for forcefulness (which I'm not really), I might find I can't cope with the job.* Or is it more core true self image: *I really don't see myself as a forceful person* or *I don't like pushy people and don't want to be seen as one.*

Assertion 2 – faking does not reduce PQ validity

Available evidence strongly suggests some applicants fake good on PQs. Lay people tend to see this as a serious problem: it seems intuitively obvious that untrue answers will not predict work performance. Some researchers, for example Ones and Viswesvaran (1998), asserted however that faking does not reduce PQs' validity, so does not present a problem. Four lines of research are relevant.

1. *Faking and factor structure.* Some research has suggested faking may change the factor structure of PQs, i.e. may change what the PQ is measuring, which could invalidate it altogether. Schmit and Ryan (1993) found faked NEOs acquired a sixth 'ideal employee' factor, while Ellingson, Sackett and Hough (1999) found faking weakened the factor structure of ABLE. However, these were directed faking studies which generate larger effects.
   Two lines of research depend on *lie scales*, which seek to detect people who are faking good, and which are discussed further on page 165.
2. *Comparing fakers and non-fakers.* With very large samples, researchers can divide fakers from non-fakers, using the lie scale, and compute separate validities for each. Hough *et al.* (1990) concluded that validity coefficients in US Army recruits who faked ABLE were no lower than in those who did not; Burns and Christiansen (2006), however, suggest that validity was in fact slightly reduced. Note also that later research has shown lie scales are very poor at detecting faking.
3. *Correcting for faking.* Some research has 'corrected' PQs for faking good, usually by partialling out lie scale scores, and concluded that this does not

affect validity (Christiansen *et al.*, 1994). Like line 2 above, this again suffers from the problem that lie scores do not seem to be good indicators of actual faking.

4. *Applicant/present employee comparisons.* If PEs do not need to fake because they have already got the job, whereas As do fake because they want to get the job, validity of PQs may differ for the two populations. If As' PQ data are less trustworthy, validity may be lower in As. Three meta-analyses have compared As and PEs (Hough, 1998; Ones *et al.*, 1993; Tett *et al.*, 1999), with conflicting results. Ones *et al.* and Tett *et al.* found validity is higher in As than in PEs, implying faking good does not reduce validity. Tett *et al.* assembled 83 studies of present employees, but could find only 12 of applicants. Hough found no difference between concurrent and predictive validity, for job performance (but found concurrent validity much higher for counterproductive behaviour). Concurrent validation usually means testing PEs, whereas predictive validation includes research with As.

Does faking matter in selection? Some research casts doubt on the comforting conclusion that faking does not matter. Ellingson *et al.*'s (1999) sample completed ABLE twice, once honestly, once faking good. Ellingson used the unfaked ABLEs to decide who *ought* to get the job, and the faked ABLEs to see who *actually* would get the job. Where one in three fake and one in three are appointed, 40% of those who 'ought to have' got the job did not, seeing it go to someone who faked good. Stewart *et al.* (2008) report a similar analysis with similar results; they note the interesting point that people whose scores improve when completing the PQ for selection do not always maximize their score; some people whose conscientiousness is 'really' low fake an increase that still leaves them below average, and far below the point of getting a job offer. Campion (Morgeson *et al.*, 2007) offers another argument why faking does matter: 'The fact that some candidates fake means that other candidates are denied jobs' – honest applicants should not be penalized.

Assertion 3 – faking is not a real issue

'Faking' covers a range of possibilities, from having a positive self-image to deliberate lying. Dipboye (Morgeson *et al.*, 2007) describes some PQ answers as aspirational: *I am a good leader* may really mean *I would like to be a good leader*. Is this faking? Zickar and Robie's (1999) analysis of faking rating format PQs suggested people use the extreme answers more: *I am polite to others – always*, rather than *usually*. Is this faking, or just being a bit more emphatic?

Several authors have argued that PQs are not intended to be a literal description of real behaviour. They are, rather, a way of 'negotiating an identity' (Hogan, Barrett & Hogan, 2007). Most people have a favourable self-image so will present a generally favourable view of themselves. Civilized life – it is argued – requires a degree of dissimulation; only criminals and small children make no attempt to conceal negative feelings or unacceptable urges. It has even been suggested that faking good is an aspect of emotional intelligence:

knowing what people want to hear and being prepared to say it. There are several snags with this argument. There are jobs where saying what people want to hear is sometimes necessary or useful, but there are lots more where it is not remotely appropriate: accountant, doctor, surveyor, engineer. Research has found no correlation at all between faking good scores and work performance (Ones, Viswesvaran & Reiss, 1996). A PQ is an unnecessarily long and complicated way of determining if someone is a good liar. The whole argument has an air of desperation about it.

Ambiguity of PQs Several features of PQs strongly suggest they probably do not generate accurate accounts of real behaviour. They are full of vague adverbs of frequency: *sometimes, usually, generally*, etc. If PQ writers wanted to know how often As lose their temper or run out of energy, they could at least specify *once a month, once a week*, or *several times a day*. The speed with which people complete PQs also suggests answers are not literal descriptions of behaviour. If people can find an answer to *I generally complete tasks on time* in four seconds, they cannot be reviewing all the tasks they have completed in the last year, and calculating what proportion were finished on time. They must be answering at some more generalized level, along the lines of *I see myself as someone who* finishes tasks on time. Actually a big problem with PQs is that we do not really know quite what people are telling us when they answer them.

Unverifiability of PQs Faking is not a real issue for very many PQ items, in the sense that it is often very hard to prove someone's answer is not true. Some PQ items can be confirmed by observation, such as items 1 and 2 in Table 7.1. Some could be verified in theory but probably not in practice, such as item 4: the person's parents could tell you, if you can find them, if they are willing to discuss intimate family matters with a stranger, if they can remember events and feelings from many years ago. Many PQ items *appear* verifiable but are not, such as item 3: it is easy to see if Smith meets a lot of people but only Smith knows if he/she enjoys it or not. A quick check of the 60 items of the shorter version of the NEO PQ finds only one question where one could definitely prove an answer was untrue. In this respect faking a PQ is not 'as bad as' someone claiming to have a medical degree when they do not.

Act Frequency Buss and Craik (1983) suggested assessing personality by visible, verifiable behaviours, not thoughts and feelings. The more often someone gives orders to others, the more dominant they are. The more often they apologize, the more submissive they are. So far act frequency data has mostly been collected by self-report, which turns act frequency into a variant of the PQ. It may, however, lend itself well to 'at work' forms of PQs, and may make warnings of verification (v.i.) more plausible. It would also work well for reports by others: what Smith does is more visible than what he/she thinks and feels.

RESEARCH AGENDA

- Whether different item types in PQs, for example actions versus thoughts and feelings, are more or less fakable, or more or less valid predictors of work performance.

DEALING WITH FAKING

There are many lines of defence against faking good. Some modify the way the test is administered. Some add questions to check on faking. Some alter the PQ's entire format. Some try to find ways of reversing the effects of faking. Some alter the way the PQ is used in selection.

Changing how the PQ is administered

Warnings Dwight and Donovan's (2003) meta-analysis distinguished warnings that faking can be detected, which have little or no effect, from warnings that faking will have consequences, for example not getting the job, which reduce faking somewhat ($d = 0.30$). Warning is potentially a quick and easy solution to faking, but creates some problems. It might not survive against well-informed coaching. Zickar and Gibby (2006) think people will soon realize warnings are empty threats. Vasilopoulos, Cucina and McElreath (2005) identify another possible problem: their warning said friends, family, teachers and past employers would be used to verify PQ responses, which reduced faking more in less intelligent As. Perhaps brighter As could work out which PQ items are verifiable, or realize how implausible the idea of getting information from others really is. A PQ that incidentally assesses GMA could start creating adverse impact on some minorities – the very problem selectors in the USA hope to avoid by using PQs.

Elaboration Schmitt and Kunce (2002) found that asking As to give examples reduces faking good (of biodata) considerably. Someone who claims to have led work groups is asked to describe the groups and the projects they worked on. Elaboration will lose the speed and convenience of the PQ, but could be done as part of an interview.

Administer by computer It has been claimed people are more honest about themselves when giving information to a computer. Feigelson and Dwight's meta-analysis (2000) found people slightly more willing to reveal sensitive or embarrassing information to a computer than on paper, but none of the research derives from applicants or employees.

Response speed It can be argued that faking good will take longer than honest completion: A must first retrieve the 'real' answer, then decide it is not the right one to give, then choose a different, 'better' one. However, Elliott *et al.*

(1996) reported that faking the Eysenck PQ, to look like either a librarian or a stockbroker, took no longer than normal completion, suggesting people completing PQs can access a stereotype – 'the best answer for a managerial job' – as quickly as an accurate self-description. Also response speed depends on item length, item format (true/false or rating), and reading speed, so using it to detect faking will prove complex. Robie *et al.* (2000) reported that people can be coached to avoid taking longer.

Adding items to the PQ that detect faking

Faking good scale, aka good impression scale, aka lie scale Most PQs contain one of these: a list of common faults to deny possessing, and rare virtues to claim to have (items 10 and 11 in Table 7.1). A high score is taken to indicate likelihood of faking, although test manuals do not always commit themselves to an actual value of 'high'. However, most lie scales turn out to be more complex. Typically lie scores correlate with other scores on the PQ; Ones *et al.*'s (1996) meta-analysis found correlations of –0.37 with neuroticism, and 0.20 with conscientiousness. This suggests lie scales measure real aspects of personality as well as faking good. Ones *et al.* found a few researches that compared Smith's self-reported lie score with others' ratings of Smith's neuroticism and conscientiousness – which are independent of Smith's faking good – and still found correlations with social desirability scores on the PQ. Zickar and Drasgow (1996) used large military samples to show that lie scales were not very good at detecting directed faking; a cut-off score on the lie scale that made 5% false positives (saying an honest completion was faked) detected only 28% of directed fakings. Two studies (Stewart *et al.*, 2008; Quist, Arora & Griffith, 2007) identify 'real fakers' – people whose scores rose by more than error of measurement when completing the PQ for selection – and find that lie scales generally missed them.

Bimodal items Kuncel and Borneman (2007) note that some rating format PQ items show a bimodal distribution when people fake. An example is *imperturbable* where fakers check either 1 or 5, whereas 'honest' answers are centred around 3. A set of items like this could be used to construct a faking good scale, which Kuncel and Borneman note would not be related either to GMA or to 'real' personality.

Covariance of items Another subtle faking scale relies on the fact that faking usually increases correlations between scales, in extreme cases collapsing the usual factor structure to a single good applicant factor. This could be detected by including pairs of items that are normally completely uncorrelated, but which will become correlated when people fake good (Burns & Christiansen, 2011).

Changing the PQ's format – forced choice

Making As choose between statements equated for desirability, like items 13 to 15 in Table 7.1, is intended to prevent them giving inflated estimates of how 'good' their personality is. However, Putka and McCloy (2004) sound a note of caution. The US Army's new forced-choice PQ – Assessment of Individual Motivation (AIM) – resisted faking successfully until it was used with real recruits, when scores rose considerably ($d = 0.85$), and no longer predicted success so well. This suggests that techniques that deal with faking in laboratory tests, or with students or present employees, may not survive when used 'for real', with real applicants. The US Army developed AIM after it abandoned its earlier PQ – ABLE – because of faking good. AIM seems to be in use still, judging by the number of websites advising people how to fake it.

Forced-choice format usually creates a subtle problem – interdependence between scales. On the Allport–Vernon–Lindzey Study of Values (AVL), the six scores must total 180; the test's instructions advise using this as a check on accuracy of scoring. This happens because within each forced choice, one answer scores for, for example, social interest, while the other scores for, for example, aesthetic interest. However, if all six scores must total 180, the person who wants to express a strong preference for one value must express less interest in one or more others; it is impossible to get six very high (or six very low) scores on AVL (whereas this is entirely possible on conventional PQs like NEO). This type of scoring is called *fully ipsative*. It means the PQ cannot conclude that Smith is more interested in dominating others than is Jones – a *normative* comparison, the one selectors usually want to make. *Quasi-ipsative* tests try to avoid this feature by including some choices which are not scored, or giving different scores to different answers, or having different numbers of items in different scales.

Salgado, Anderson and Tauriz (2015) report a meta-analysis of forced-choice PQs, distinguishing between fully ipsative and quasi-ipsative tests (v.s.). Fully ipsative tests do less well than conventional PQs in predicting work performance. Quasi-ipsative tests on the other hand do very much better than conventional PQs, achieving 0.38 validity for conscientiousness, and finding higher correlations for the other factors. However, most of the data for quasi-ipsative tests come from one measure, and most of these data come from that test's manual. The notion of quasi-ipsative test seems rather unsatisfactory, in that it is defined primarily by what it is *not*: the scores do not add up to constant.

Reversing the effects of faking

A high lie score implies the applicant's personality data are suspect, so cannot be used at face value. That A could simply be rejected, if there are enough good As. Alternatively the applicant can be told his/her data are suspect, and asked to complete the PQ again, answering more 'carefully'. Ellingson, Heggestad and Makarius (2012) looked at the effects of this on NEO scores, and found the retest was more accurate, but that the faker's second completion was still much 'better' than his/her true personality. The measure of true personality was Goldberg's IPIP, completed previously, and with no reason for people to fake. (People were not applying for real jobs, but trying to win a $50 prize, arguably a less powerful incentive to fake.)

Correcting for faking Some PQs use the lie scale to 'correct' other scores. MMPI's K key assesses defensiveness, then adds varying proportions of K to other scores to estimate the shortcomings people would have admitted if they had been more frank. Long ago Cronbach (1970) expressed scepticism: 'if the subject lies to the tester there is no way to convert the lies into truth'. Authors of PQs have nevertheless continued trying. Ellingson *et al.* (1999) compared faked and unfaked ABLEs from the same sample, so could answer the question: Do correction scales succeed in turning lies back into truth? At the average level the answer was 'Yes'. Faked ABLEs were 'better' than unfaked on average, but the corrected faked ones were no 'better' than the unfaked. At the individual level however the answer was 'no'. Faking changed the rank order of As (compared with a rank order based on unfaked completion), and so changed who 'got the job'. Correcting for faking did not change the rank order back, so did not ensure the 'right' people were appointed after all.

Faking and coaching Sliter and Christiansen (2012) demonstrate that reading Hoffman's self-coaching book *Ace the Corporate Personality Test* enables people to increase their conscientiousness score by 2.6 SDs. A d value of 2.6 indicates a very large difference, indicating the lowest faked good score is not much lower than the highest 'real' score. Coaching also enabled people to avoid increasing their lie scale scores. Hoffman's book seems to achieve its stated aim very successfully.

Faking and retests Three studies have managed to find data from people who have completed a PQ twice, once for selection, and once for some other reason, where they may have less reason to fake good. Hausknecht (2010) reported data on 357 hotel chain employees who completed the Gordon PPI twice, seeking promotion. The organization allowed employees to keep trying for promotion, and required them to complete the GPPI again if more than 12 months had elapsed since the first completion, apparently supposing someone's personality might change over a longer time span. Of the 357 retested persons, 56 had succeeded in getting promotion, and were retaking the GPPI for their own development; the other 312 were still trying to get promoted. Hausknecht suggests the majority who missed promotion may have been thinking that they must have given the wrong answers the first time, whereas the lucky 56 will have been confident they gave the right answers. Hausknecht's hypothesis proved correct: there was no difference at all on average between first and second completions for the 56 promoted, but quite large differences for six out eight scales for those who were not. On second completion, they scored higher

(d = 0.40 to 0.60) on responsibility, sociability, original thinking, personal relations and vigour, but lower on cautiousness. Landers, Sackett and Tuzinski (2011) found 488 people who had completed an unidentified PQ twice. The test was being used to make promotion decisions within the organization, but these 488 said they had not realized this when they first completed it, and thought it was for 'developmental' reasons, i.e. for their own enlightenment and self-improvement. The second time they completed the PQ they definitely knew it was for promotion. Their second scores were on average much higher (d of 1.40).

The third study, however, found a different result. Ellingson, Sackett and Connelly (2007) have data from 713 people, in a range of jobs and organizations, who had completed the California Psychological Inventory twice, some for 'development' then for selection or vice versa, others for selection both times or development both times. The development then selection group showed increases in 16 out of 20 CPI scales, but only relatively small ones, averaging d = 0.26, suggesting faking good is not necessarily always a big problem. Allowing for the tendency of scores to increase slightly on second test, regardless of purpose, the change from development to selection shrinks to a very small d = 0.12. The three studies give very different estimates of changes in score on retest, depending on precisely why the second test was being made, but do seem to confirm that doing a test to get a job or promotion may give different results from a test done to find out about oneself.

Changing the way PQs are used in selection

Sackett (2011) argues that faking will not have as much effect on validity as is often supposed, focusing on fears that faking will mean honest As are displaced by fakers in rank-ordered applicant lists: 'my impression is that rank-order selection is rare in the personality domain'. Sackett suggests that PQs are generally used more to exclude the unacceptable by setting relatively low cut-offs. This is a very plausible hypothesis, which needs testing by more surveys of how PQs are used in practice in selection. Berry and Sackett (2009) suggest this custom might be made more systematic by excluding the bottom third of As on the PQ. This will not exclude any 'deserving applicants', who will get their chance to show their strengths on the rest of the selection system, where hopefully those who faked their way through the PQ will be found out. The 'bottom third' should be defined by sound normative data, of present employees, or general population samples, but not by applicant data which will be contaminated by fakers. In practice the cut-off might also take account of how many people HR want to test at next stage. Sackett's suggestion implies PQs should be used for all As, not just the shortlist, which is easier to achieve with Internet testing. It would be advisable to check the PQ for gender or ethnicity differences.

Faking good is not a new problem: Zickar and Gibby (2006) note that the first directed faking study was published in 1934, the first forced-choice PQ in 1939, and the first lie scale in 1942.

RESEARCH AGENDA

- Whether idiosyncratic or bimodal items in PQs will detect faking in PQS, in 'real-life' selection.
- Validity of forced-choice format, using a wider range of PQs.
- Whether PQs achieve validity by excluding low scorers, i.e. those who lack that trait, and cannot or will not fake it.
- What happens if fakers are excluded, in terms of validity, and subsequent work performance.
- Replication of Griffith *et al.* with larger sample, and higher 'return rate', and in range of different jobs.
- Further exploration of what answers to PQ questions really mean.
- Testing Sackett's hypothesis that PQs are used to screen out unsuitable applicants.

PQS, LAW AND FAIRNESS

PQs have encountered surprisingly little trouble with the law, especially compared with mental ability tests. In fact part of their recent popularity reflects the view that they create little adverse impact, unlike ability tests.

Gender differences

There are gender differences in many PQ scores (Hough, Oswald, & Ployhart, 2001); men tend to report being more forceful and competitive while women tend to report being more caring, as well as more anxious. (Note the important distinction between 'report being' and 'are'; it can be argued that men experience as much anxiety as women but are more reluctant to admit it.) Gender differences create a dilemma for HR. Using separate norm tables for men and women is prohibited in the USA by the Civil Rights Act of 1991, and may be frowned on elsewhere. On the other hand, using pooled gender norms may create adverse impact. Using a cut-off score of $T = 60$ on dominance to select managers might exclude more women than men.

Ethnicity

Foldes, Duehr and Ones (2008) present a meta-analysis of ethnicity differences in the USA, covering white, African, Asian, Hispanic and Native Americans. They conclude that 'most group comparisons and personality scales yielded negligible differences and are not likely to cause adverse impact in selection'. 'Most', however, is not the same as all: the finding that white Americans score higher than African Americans on sociability ($d = 0.39$) suggests problems could arise in some types of work. Some European data are available. Ones and Anderson's (2002) analysis of college students in Britain finds few white/Afro differences, while white/Asian and white/Chinese differences 'favoured' minorities, showing them to be more conscientious. In the Netherlands, te Nijenhuis, van der Flier and van Leeuwen (1997) find some immigrant groups score higher on neuroticism and lower on extraversion.

Age

Large age differences are found in some PQ scales; extraversion, measured by the Eysenck PQ, falls steadily and considerably ($d = 0.88$) between ages 18 and 65 (Cook *et al.*, 2007).

Disability

The Americans with Disabilities Act (ADA) prohibits health-related enquiries before a job offer is made, which has two implications for PQs. Firstly, questions that could be seen as health-related enquiries, such as items 8 and 9 in Table 7.1, have been deleted from some scales. Secondly, health includes mental health, so scales with psychiatric-sounding names, such as neuroticism, may become suspect for selection use (whereas reversed neuroticism, called *emotional stability* or *resilience*, is more acceptable).

Starting afresh

Attempts to edit unwanted group differences out of existing tests frequently fail. Gill and Hodgkinson (2007) try a more radical approach. They check all 533 possible items for their new Five Factor Model PQ for gender, ethnicity, age and education differences as the first stage of generating the PQ, and retain only items that show no such differences. The full text is given in their article, and the measure is described as 'freely available for research purposes and selected commercial applications'.

Privacy

Items 5, 6, and 7 in Table 7.1 may be too intrusive to use in selection. In the *Soroka vs. Dayton-Hudson* case an applicant claimed PQ items about politics and religion were contrary to the Constitution of the State of California (Merenda, 1995); the case was settled out of court, so no definitive ruling emerged.

The potential danger of multi-score PQs

Most PQs come as fixed packages. The 16PF assesses all 16 factors every time it is used. One cannot decide to use only dominance, ego strength, and shrewdness, or to leave out suspicion and guilt-proneness. This is just an inconvenience to researchers, but a serious problem for selectors. Suppose work analysis has identified dominance, ego strength, and shrewdness as the (only) personality characteristics needed for the job. The other 13 scores are not job-related, and so should not be used in making the decision. If selectors do use them, the employer could have serious problems defending the selection system in the event of complaints. PQs that assess weakness and poor adjustment can be particularly dangerous: someone applying for a clerical job will be justifiably annoyed to find their psychopathic deviance or level of fantasy aggression have been assessed. Lewis Goldberg offers an extensive bank of scales from which a job specific PQ can be generated, based on work analysis, to avoid assessing anything irrelevant. Goldberg's bank, which contains analogues to many popular PQs, has another unusual feature: it is in the public domain, and can be used by everyone without restriction or payment, through his IPIP website (address at end of chapter). Users will have to generate their own normative data.

RESEARCH AGENDA

- Survey of which types of PQ items are seen as intrusive in selection.

KEY POINTS

In Chapter 7 you have learned the following:

- Personality is a vaguer and more diffuse concept than ability, and there are many models of personality.
- Personality is most conveniently assessed by personality questionnaire.
- PQs are written by a variety of methods which generally overlap to some extent, including internal analysis by statistics, and external analysis comparing groups of people of known characteristics (empirical keying).
- The big five factor model is widely accepted, but may not give the best prediction of work behaviour; other models, with more than five or fewer than five, exist.
- PQs have limited value in predicting how well people can do a job.
- PQs may prove slightly more successful predicting 'attitude' aspects of work behaviour, although most correlations are still lower than 0.30.
- PQs may also be more successful at predicting avoidance of deviant or problematic behaviour at work.
- Preliminary results suggest the relationship between team personality and team performance may be complex, and that low scorers may be able to hold back the entire group.
- PQs are self reports, not tests, and can be faked.
- Directed faking research shows that most people can fake; the proportion who actually do fake in selection is less clearly documented.
- Faking may affect the outcome of selection.

- Faking can be limited but not eliminated by warnings and forced choice format.
- Gender differences are often found with PQs but ethnicity differences do not seem to be a major problem.
- PQs have been criticized as unduly intrusive in some of their questions.

KEY REFERENCES

Barrick *et al.* (2001) present a meta-meta-analysis of PQ validity.

Bell (2007) presents a meta-analysis of personality and team performance.

Cook (2013) gives a general introduction to personality theory and research.

Foldes *et al.* (2008) present a meta-analysis of ethnicity differences in personality in the USA.

Guion & Gottier (1965) present an early, and not very optimistic, review of personality tests validity.

McDaniel *et al.* (2006) describe the application of trim-and-fill technique to detecting selective reporting of PQ validity data.

Morgeson *et al.* (2007) discuss the issues of validity and fakability of PQs. The same issue also contains articles by Ones *et al.* and Tett & Christiansen offering counter-arguments.

Spain *et al.* (2014) describe the 'dark side' of personality, and its links with work.

Van Iddekinge *et al.* (2012a, 2012b) describe their attempts to re-analyse honesty test data.

Zickar (2001) describes the use of PQs to try to screen out 'thugs and agitators'.

Zickar & Gibby (2006) give an interesting historical account of the faking issue.

USEFUL WEBSITES

ipip.ori.org/ipip. Goldberg's bank of PQ scales.

CHAPTER 8

Alternative ways of assessing personality

What year was the Bataan death march?

Murphy (Morgeson *et al.*, 2007) thinks the PQ 'not salvageable' as a selection method, which creates an urgent need for a replacement. This chapter will consider possible alternatives, using the five headings of types of information outlined in Chapter 1.

SELF-REPORT

Chapter 1 considered the application form and CV, which raise the same issue as PQs: can the selector believe the information the applicant supplies? Applicants who claim qualifications or experience they do not possess can be found out if the employer checks up, whereas PQs can be very hard to verify.

Chapter 4 examined the interview, which is a mixed method, largely self-report but with elements of demonstration evidence when used to assess knowledge or social skill. Chapter 4 showed one in three selection interviews are used to assess personality, especially conscientiousness, and that they are moderately successful, to the extent that they correlate with PQs (Table 4.3, page 83). Some structured interview systems have been written specifically to assess personality; Trull *et al.* (1998) describe a 120-question system for assessing the five-factor model.

Chapter 9 will consider biodata and weighted application blanks, which can be faked, but also tend to collect more readily verifiable information.

PROJECTIVE TESTS

Projective tests assume that people project their personality into what they see in drawings or patterns, or how they complete sentences or stories. Projective tests are *self-reports* because they use what A says, but have elements of *involuntary assessment*, because they may discover things A does not mean to reveal.

Personnel Selection: Adding Value Through People – A Changing Picture,
Sixth Edition. Mark Cook.
© 2016 John Wiley & Sons, Ltd. Published 2016 by John Wiley & Sons, Ltd.

Figure 8.1   A picture similar to those used in the Thematic Apperception Test.

Thematic Apperception Test (TAT)

This uses pictures chosen for their vagueness and suggestive content (Figure 8.1). People describe 'what led up to the event shown in the picture, what is happening, what the characters are thinking and feeling, and what the outcome will be', and are supposed to project into the story their own 'dominant drives, emotions, sentiments, complexes and conflicts'. The TAT is most often used to assess need for achievement, or ambition. McClelland (1971) argued that need for achievement is unconscious, and cannot be assessed by PQ.

Defence Mechanism Test (DMT)

This is a variant on the TAT, using a picture showing a hero figure and a hideous face. The picture is made more ambiguous by being shown at first for only a small fraction of second. Various defence mechanisms can be inferred from responses to the DMT; for example seeing the hideous face as an inanimate object is coded as repression, because the person is pushing emotion out of the picture.

Rorschach test

People are asked what they see in 12 ink blots (Figure 8.2). Various scoring systems are used, for example inanimate movement (seeing objects, rather than people or animals, moving) indicates inner tension and feelings of helplessness, and may be a sign of poor response to stress.

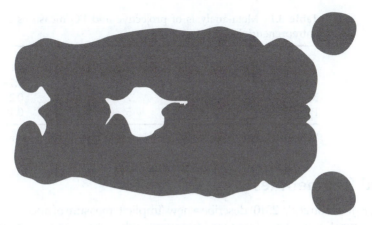

Figure 8.2   An ink blot similar to those used in Rorschach test.

Sentence completion

The Miner Sentence Completion Scale is written for selecting managers, and assesses attitude to authority, competitive motivation, etc. by how people complete *My last boss was …* or *I don't like people who …*

Validity

Kinslinger (1966) reviewed early US personnel research, using Rorschach, TAT, and sentence-completion tests, and found fairly limited predictive validity. Four small-scale meta-analyses have since found generally more promising results.

1. Reilly and Chao (1982) found an average uncorrected validity of 0.28 in six studies published since Kinslinger's review; removing an *outlier* (an unusually high value) of 0.68 reduced average validity to 0.18.
2. Martinussen and Torjussen (1993) meta-analysed 15 studies of the DMT in mostly military pilot selection, and reported an uncorrected validity of 0.20. The rationale of using the test for selecting pilots is that defence mechanisms bind psychic energy, so it is not available for coping with reality in an emergency. However, Martinussen and Torjussen did discover one worrying moderator variable: the DMT works in Scandinavia but not in Britain or the Netherlands. Martinussen and Torjussen think the test may be administered or scored differently in different countries. A test becomes very much less useful if one is unsure how to use it.
3. Collins, Hanges and Locke (2004) report a meta-analysis of measures of need for achievement and entrepreneurial performance. Table 8.1 shows two projective tests achieve validity as good as a PQ.
4. Hoffman, Woehr *et al.*'s (2011) meta-analysis found projective tests the least successful predictor of leadership, doing less well ($p = 0.19$) than PQs, but better than zero.

Table 8.1   Meta-analysis of projective and PQ measures of entrepreneurial performance.

	k	N	r
TAT	8	915	0.16
Miner Sentence Completion	7	463	0.20
PQ	5	803	0.19

Data from Collins *et al.* (2004). Correlations not corrected in any way.

Word fragment test

R. E. Johnson *et al.* (2010) describe a new 'implicit' measure of affectivity (an aspect of neuroticism), based on word fragments which the applicant completes into words. Given FEXX applicants can generate a neutral word – FEED – or an affective word – FEAR. Johnson *et al.* collected data on work performance, organizational citizenship, and counterproductive work behaviour, and showed the word fragment test correlated with all three (0.48 to 0.55) better than a PQ. The technique will need to be adapted to assess conscientiousness, which research finds more closely linked to work performance than affectivity. Will conscientiousness have the necessary emotional basis to make the method work?

Projective tests seem to work at least as well as PQs. A key issue therefore is whether they are as easily faked, There is extensive research in the clinical field, which seems to produce mixed results, but little or none for selection. Carter, Daniels and Zickar (2013) review half a dozen projective tests and suggest some reasons why they may not be ideal for personnel selection. One is disability discrimination: any assessment that 'looks' medical is suspect, and many projective tests have psychiatric origins, or use psychiatric terminology. A related problem is that projective tests seem to focus on what is 'wrong with' people, whereas Americans especially prefer to focus on more positive features. Both these problems are likely to make projective tests less acceptable to applicants.

RESEARCH AGENDA

- More research on projective test validity.
- Fakability of projective tests used for selection.

OTHERS' REPORTS

Others' reports (ORs) describing a target person (T) can be collected in various formats including ratings, other form PQs, and Q sorts. A great potential advantage is that more than one other can describe the target, which gives higher reliability, and possibly greater validity. A fundamental limitation of self–report data is there can only be one source. Others' report data may give better results than self-report (SR) because ORs avoid two sources of error: inflation by self-deception, and inflation by deliberate faking. Hogan and Holland (2003) suggest that SR assesses the internal dynamics of personality, whereas OR assesses reputation, based on past behaviour, which they suggest will give a better prediction of behaviour at work.

Other form PQs

PQs can be reworded to describe other people rather than oneself. *I enjoy meeting new people* becomes [*Smith*] *enjoys meeting new people*. However, Hogan's dynamics versus reputation hypothesis implies other form PQs should not be generated by simply rewording conventional PQs, but should use different types of items.

Q sort technique

This uses statements similar to PQ items, which are sorted into nine categories according to how well they describe the target. The nine categories must form a rough normal distribution, forcing the completer to differentiate and preventing undue leniency. The California Q Sort asks for interpretations of behaviour, for example *target habitually tests the limits, to see how much he/she can get away with*, whereas the Riverside Q Sort is more descriptive and verifiable: for example *verbally fluent*. Q sorts do not appear to have been used in selection.

There are other possibilities, which have not been researched much, if at all. Chapter 5 noted that research has not made much progress with free-form references, where sources describe targets in their own words. Research could also analyse behavioural or emotional reactions to others. It might be instructive to know that everyone always stands up when Smith enters the room, or that many people experience fear at the sight of Jones.

Two meta-analyses of others' reports have been reported, by Connelly and Ones (2010) and Oh, Wang and Mount (2011). Oh *et al.*'s analysis is more recent and contains more studies than that of Connelly and Ones, but it is not clear how much the two overlap. Three comparisons can be made:

1. Other's report–other's report, showing whether different others agree about the target, i.e. inter-observer reliability.
2. Other's report–self-report (SR), showing whether what others say about Smith's personality agrees with what Smith says.
3. Others' report–work performance.

Other–other

Line 1 of Table 8.2 shows that observers agree moderately well, confirming that ORs do contain some reliable information. Line 2 shows that agreement among work colleagues is slightly lower.

Table 8.2 Summary of two meta-analyses of others' reports of personality and work performance.

FFM factor	N	E	O	A	C	Source	k	N
Reliability								
Agreement between others								
1. OR × OR (all)	0.40	0.51	0.39	0.40	0.44	C&O	53–83	8–13.5K
2. OR × OR (work)	0.34	0.44	0.36	0.37	0.40	C&O	5–18	0.7–2.4K
Agreement between self and others								
3. SR × 1 OR (all)	0.43	0.51	0.39	0.39	0.50	C&O	105–186	20–29K
4. SR × 1 OR (work)	0.18	0.30	0.27	0.31	0.24	C&O	6–11	981–1647
Validity								
Personality questionnaire								
5. PQ × work performance	−0.11	0.11	0.04	0.09	0.20	BMJ	143–239	23–42K
Others' rating and work performance								
6. OR × WP	−0.17	0.11	0.22	0.17	0.29	C&O	6/7	1.1–1.2K
7. OR × WP	−0.21	0.27	0.26	0.31	0.37	OWM	14-17	1.7K–2.2K
Others' rating and work performance: number of others								
8. 1.7 others	−0.21	0.27	0.26	0.31	0.37	OWM		
9. 1 other	−0.18	0.24	0.22	0.26	0.32	OWM		
10. 3 others	−0.24	0.29	0.29	0.34	0.41	OWM		
11. 'large number' others	−0.37	nr	0.45	0.31	0.55	C&O		
Self + others' rating and work performance								
12. SR+1.7 ORs × WP	−0.20	0.24	0.22	0.26	0.34	OWM		

Data from Barrick, Mount & Judge (2001) [BMJ], Connelly & Ones (2010) [C&O] and Oh, Wang & Mount (2011) [OWM].

Self–other

Line 3 of Table 8.2 compares self-ratings and others' ratings, and finds overall correlations ranging from 0.39 to 0.50 for all others. These correlations are corrected for the reliability of both measures so estimate the 'true' relationship. Line 5 makes the same comparison for workplace others, and shows self–other agreement much lower.

Others' report–work performance

Line 5 of Table 8.2 shows correlations between FFM self-report PQ scores and work performance from Barrick and Mount's (1991) meta-meta-analysis, described in Chapter 7. Lines 6 and 7 give meta-analytic estimates for others' reports. The difference between self-report and others' report is striking; in Barrick and Mount's PQ data, only conscientiousness generates even a very moderate correlation, but in the OR data, especially Oh *et al.*'s, all five personality factors correlate as well as PQ conscientiousness.

However, the OR correlations in line 7 are slightly misleading, because some of the studies in Oh *et al.*'s meta-analysis collected data from more than one other, with an average of 1.7 others per target. Line 9 estimates what the OR–work performance relationship would be for one other, while line 10 estimates what it would be for three others. Line 11 gives Connelly and Ones's estimate of the validity achievable by 'large numbers' of others. As Connelly and Ones note, these estimates take the value for conscientiousness across a magic line in selection: 0.50, the operational validity of GMA tests.

Self *and* other rating–work performance

Oh *et al.* make an estimate of the validity achievable by the combination of SR and OR, where the person describes him/herself, and is described by one or more observers. Line 12 shows this achieves no increase on the validity of the one or more observers. This has two implications, one practical, and one more theoretical. The practical implication is that self-report may have no incremental validity on others' reports. The theoretical implication is that people may not possess any special insight into themselves that is denied to others.

Others' reports of personality clearly contain some accurate information, and could represent a potentially powerful development in selection. There are, however, two doubts, one statistical and one practical.

Neither meta-analysis gives any information about the intercorrelation of FFM scores in the observer data. If the observers saw the five factors as highly correlated, that might account for all five being correlated with the work performance. Peoples' ratings of other people often show 'halo' where targets get consistently high ratings across a number of logically or empirically unrelated dimensions (see Chapter 12).

A more serious doubt concerns the practicalities of others' reports in personnel selection. Who will provide ORs? How will these people be located? Will they agree to participate? Will they say what they really think about the target person? As noted before, the beauty of self-reports is their practicality: the applicant is there, his/her time belongs to the selectors, return rate is 100%. Research on references, reviewed in Chapter 5, identified likely problems with relying on others' reports: low return rate, and pervasive leniency. What works in a research project, where it has no consequences for any of the people involved, will not necessarily work in 'real life'.

ORs may be possible to use in promotion, where the target's colleagues are accessible, and may be willing to make ORs. Using ORs for selecting As from outside the organization looks much more difficult. Family and friends are probably not even worth thinking about trying to use. Andler and Herbst (2002) suggest a 'snowball' technique, asking each A for the names and phone numbers of two peers and two subordinates at work, then asking these in turn for more names. Some As do not want to have it known they are looking for a new job, so will not welcome enquiries among their present colleagues.

Important classes of As do not have any present work colleagues: school leavers, new graduates, unemployed people, recent immigrants. Perhaps the Internet could be used: some people might welcome the chance to say what they think of X who is applying for a job at ABC. Ways of filtering out malicious or uninformed or wonderful (but false) reports could possibly be devised. Connelly and Ones suggest the target's last two supervisors might be used. (If they can be identified. If they can be contacted. If they are willing to give the information. If they are allowed to.) There is a worrying element of circularity in using the previous supervisor's opinion (test) to predict the new supervisor's opinion (criterion).

Using ORs to select does not seem to break any of Gilliland's nine rules of procedural fairness in selection, listed in Chapter 14 (p. 301), except possibly 'not asking improper questions' (if that covers *who* is being asked as well as *what*), but one has a strong feeling that it might prove very unpopular. It might attract bad publicity for the organization. There could be legal problems: data protection, libel, even human rights.

Others' reports can be useful where the target person is too important or too distant to be asked to complete a PQ. Research has assessed the personality of US presidents, all the way back to Washington in 1776, by asking historians to complete other form assessments. Rubenzer, Faschingbauer and Ones (2000) correlated other form FFM PQs with ratings of presidential 'greatness', which can be seen as an index of job performance: 'greater' presidents were more open, more extravert, but less agreeable. Conscientiousness showed how correlation based on small samples can fluctuate: including an unnamed recent president changed an insignificant 0.06 to a definitely positive 0.17.

Expert opinion

The limited amount of research on 'expert opinion' reviewed by Reilly and Chao (1982) did not yield a very high validity. Judge *et al.* (1999) used three California cohort studies to study career success longitudinally. Personality in childhood and adolescence was assessed retrospectively using ratings made by experts from detailed case histories, then related to occupational status and income when the cohort had reached their fifties. The five personality factors combined correlated 0.54 with career success. Studies using conventional PQs, meta-analysed by Ng *et al.* (2005), found much weaker links between the big five and career success.

Background checks

Some types of background check are said to include trying to find out what applicants' friends and neighbours think about them, but there seems to be no research on how often this is done, or whether it contributes any useful information.

RESEARCH AGENDA

- How accurate reference checks are as assessments of personality.
- Whether others' descriptions of a target's personality show 'halo', or can differentiate the five factors.
- Whether use of others' reports in selection would be seen as acceptable by applicants, or by those asked to provide the information, or by other employers.
- Whether others' reports would continue to correlate with work performance, when used for actual selection decisions.
- Whether using others' reports will prove feasible as a working selection system.
- Extent of use, and validity, of background checks of 'lifestyle'.

DEMONSTRATION EVIDENCE

Demonstration by paper-and-pencil test

Cattell devised two personality measures that are paper-and-pencil, but not (entirely) self-report. The Motivation Analysis Test (MAT) (Bernard, Walsh & Mills, 2005) uses some novel item formats (items 1 and 2 in Table 8.3), based on the assumption that people's motives shape the information they acquire, or the estimates they make. An aggressive person knows about machine guns, while a fearful person overestimates the risk of rabies, or knows the date of the Bataan death march. No data on the use of the MAT in selection have been reported. MAT would need extensive modification to be used today in the USA, and even more change to be used elsewhere (e.g. the probability of catching rabies in Britain is actually zero). The Objective-Analytic Battery is more ambitious, assessing 10 factors, using seven or eight tests for each. The O-AB is only half objective, for many components are actually self-reports. Kline and Cooper (1984) concluded that many O-AB sub-tests measure ability rather than personality. The O-AB is very time-consuming, taking an estimated seven times longer to complete than the self-report 16PF.

Conditional reasoning (CR)

James (Bing et al., 2007) describes a conditional reasoning test of aggression, intended for use in selection. James argues that aggressive people have justification mechanisms which cause them to draw different conclusions, in a test that resembles a verbal reasoning measure (item 3 in Table 8.3): answer (b) reveals a degree of paranoia and hostility, whereas answer (a) is sensible, and answer (c) is simply wrong. James's research showed scores predict deviant behaviour in the workplace very well, uncorrected correlations averaging 0.42. However subsequent meta-analysis of a larger database (Berry, Sackett & Tobares, 2010) found

Table 8.3   Four sample items from personality tests.

1. Which of the following is not a type of machine gun?
    uzi   sterling   sten   gresley
2. What is the probability of catching rabies in Britain?
    1 in 100   1 in 1,000   1 in 10,000   1 in a million
3. Far Eastern cars are cheaper than British cars because
    a – labour costs in the Far East are lower
    b – British car manufacturers like overcharging people
    c – it costs more to ship cars to Britain
4. You are given a task you do not feel trained or qualified to do. What do you do?
    a – complete the task as best you can
    b – complain
    c – ask colleagues for help
    d – ask for the task to be given to someone else

much poorer results for CWB and work performance, no better than conventional PQs. Banks, Kepes and McDaniel (2012) re-analysed Berry *et al.*'s (2010) meta-analysis and found definite evidence of publication bias. Trim-and-fill analysis (see Chapter 2, p. 42) suggested seven 'missing' small sample studies with low to zero correlations, which would reduce the overall correlation for CWB even further, to 0.08.

Situational judgement

Lahuis, Martin and Avis (2005) describe a situational judgement test written specifically to assess conscientiousness, using questions like item 4 in Table 8.3, but have no data on its validity or relationship to other measures of conscientiousness. Further research, described in Chapter 11, shows SJTs in general, not written specially to assess personality, have low correlations with agreeableness, conscientiousness and neuroticism.

RESEARCH AGENDA

• Revise Motivation Analysis Test, and assess its potential as a selection test, in terms of reliability, validity and acceptability.
• Devise SJTs for all five personality factors, and collect data on reliability, validity and fakability.

Behavioural demonstration

Lievens *et al.* (2006) use expert panels to assess the suitability of various assessment centre exercises for revealing personality. Figure 8.3 shows that written exercises may have limited scope for assessing personality, but group

AC exercise ⇓ Personality ⇒	N	E	O	A	C
Competitive group	√	√	√	√	√
Co-operative group	–	√	√	√	√
Oral presentation	√	–	–	–	√
Role-play	–	√	–	√	–
Case analysis	–	–	–	–	√
In tray	–	–	–	–	√

Figure 8.3   Links between six generic assessment centre exercises, and FFM, according to experts. √ indicates experts rated that exercise likely to reflect that personality factor. Data from Lievens *et al.* (2006).

discussions, especially competitive ones, may prove very versatile. Gosling *et al.* (1998) found that people in a group discussion did not do anything 'prototypical' of neuroticism or openness, whereas extraversion, conscientiousness and agreeableness could be coded from behaviour such 'laughs out loud' or 'yelling at someone'. Hoffman *et al.*'s (2015) meta-analysis of five AC exercises finds modest correlations with extraversion, smaller correlations with openness, and none with agreeableness, conscientiousness or neuroticism. There is little evidence of different types of AC exercise assessing different aspects of personality.

Numerous other behavioural assessments of personality have been proposed (Cattell & Warburton, 1967; Borkenau *et al.*, 2001). Many of these pre-date the FFM, but can be fitted into it.

Neuroticism The Office of Strategic Services (OSS Assessment Staff, 1948) used deliberately stressful exercises to assess ability to remain calm under pressure, for selecting secret agents during the Second World War. For example As try to explain to hostile and bullying interrogators their unauthorized presence late at night in a government office. Clinical psychology provides behavioural tests of fear of snakes or of public speaking.

Extraversion Tell a joke to the group, or sing a song to them. Be persuasive, fluent and forceful in a group discussion.

Open-mindedness Evaluate three ways of spending a budget to reduce drug use in young people, and generate a fourth one. Tell the group a dramatic story about each one of three TAT cards.

Agreeableness The OSS used a construction task, in which A supervises two 'assistants' who are deliberately obstructive in contrasting ways. This checks whether A remains agreeable even when others behave in a way that might reasonably elicit less agreeable behaviour.

Conscientiousness Hartshorne and May's (1928) Character Education Inquiry (CEI) included some very ingenious behavioural tests of honesty, giving people opportunities to lie, steal or cheat. Their battery was intended for children, but could be adapted to adults. However, the CEI tests concealed their purpose, and their very existence, in a way that would not be possible in selection (nor ethical).

There is no shortage of ideas for demonstrated assessments of the five-factor model, but there are some major practical problems.

The 'personality sphere' Behavioural assessment of extraversion should cover the whole concept of extraversion, which requires demarcation of the relevant personality sphere. McFall and Marston (1970) developed a set of 16 representative examples of assertive behaviour.

Reliability Mischel (1968) noted that CEI's honesty tests intercorrelated so poorly as to cast doubt on the existence of a trait, but they were mostly one-item tests, which are inherently very unreliable. Choosing a representative set of behaviours, as in the McFall and Marston study, serves the two purposes: covering the whole concept of assertiveness, and generating a reliable score.

Length McFall and Marston listed 16 aspects of assertiveness. Assertiveness is one of six facets of extraversion, so 96 behavioural tests might be needed to assess extraversion, and no fewer than 480 to cover the entire FFM. How long will this take? Problems of applicant motivation and fatigue are likely to arise. Note also that McFall and Marston's behavioural tests are shorter than many: the assessee hears a brief description of a situation and line of dialogue, for example someone attempting to jump the queue in front of the assessee, then speaks his/her reply. A 480-item test is by no means a preposterous idea; the original MMPI PQ asked 550 questions.

Missing the point? Assertiveness is highly visible behaviour, by its very nature: assertion that is not noticed is not assertion. The same tends to be true of much of extraversion, which is all about how people behave with other people. The same, however, is not true for much of the neuroticism factor. Five of the six NEO neuroticism facets are primarily emotions: anxiety, hostility, depression, self-consciousness, and vulnerability. What does a behavioural test of vulnerability look like? Vulnerability is defined by the NEO Manual – in part – as 'feel(ing) unable to cope with stress, becoming dependent, hopeless, or panicked when facing emergency situations'. The OSS behavioural tests covered this; so to some extent does the pressure of competitive group discussions in assessment centres. But what about the rest of the definition of vulnerability: 'low scorers perceive themselves as capable of handling themselves in difficult situations'. Logically the fact that someone performs badly in an exercise says nothing about what they see or feel, and vice versa. The only source of information about how people feel – anxious, depressed, vulnerable, hostile – is what they say, which 'takes us back to where we came in', the self-report or PQ. In the short NEO PQ, six of the 12 neuroticism items start *I feel*. HR's problem is that people may not readily admit feelings of inadequacy, self-doubt, resentment, or hopelessness when applying for jobs.

A related issue arises with agreeableness and conscientiousness. Agreeable persons are nice to others because they like people and want to be nice to them. There are individuals who are nice to people because it suits their purposes, but they are not truly agreeable. It would be very difficult to tell the two apart by behavioural tests. Similarly part of conscientiousness is having principles and standards, and feeling that one must adhere to them, which could be difficult to distinguish by behavioural tests from conforming through fear or expedience.

Ethics and acceptability The OSS tests probably pushed As further and harder than many employers would want to do today, for fear of complaints or damaging the organization's reputation (problems that tend not to arise in wartime). However, if a job does involve a lot of stress and conflict, the employer should avoid taking on people who will not be able to cope. Demanding behavioural tests could be justified by careful work analysis, and warning As what to expect.

Rating Behavioural demonstrations usually need raters, to say how calm, or persuasive, or friendly the person was. Assessment centre research (Chapter 10) finds trained raters can achieve reasonable reliability, but also suggests assessors may have some difficulty differentiating different aspects of personality.

Can vs. will Behavioural demonstrations show what people *can* do, but not necessarily what they *will* do. People who can, for example, control their temper under provocation in a role play may not be able or willing to make the effort, day in day out, when actually 'on the job'. Only reports from others who have worked with, or lived with, applicants can tell HR how well As customarily do control themselves. (It is of course worth knowing which As can control themselves, and worth recalling that PQs may not tell HR even that much.)

Comprehensive assessment of the whole of personality by behavioural demonstration begins to look a very large undertaking. However, more focused behavioural assessments of relevant aspects of personality are more feasible. Careful work analysis can narrow down the requirement from emotional stability to resilience, and then from resilience to dealing with difficult customers, at which point a behavioural test begins to look manageable.

Validity Hoffman *et al.*'s (2011) meta-analysis finds performance tests, including AC exercises, correlate better with leadership (0.30) than PQs or projective tests.

RESEARCH AGENDA

A behavioural test of personality will need to establish construct validity by showing it can both relate to other measures of personality – self-report, including PQ, and other report – as well as correlating with outcomes, such as work performance. It is probably better to start with tests of fairly specific aspects of personality, and work up to a more general assessment, such as the FFM.

RECORDED EVIDENCE

Barthell and Holmes (1968) used American high school yearbooks to show that poorly adjusted persons had done less at school, in sport, drama, organizing societies etc. Similar information is often used in selection, but is obtained from self-reports – application form, interview, etc. Job applicants usually know that it is 'better' to have participated in many extracurricular activities at school and college. The high school yearbook provides the employer with recorded information on who actually did participate. In some countries military records might be useful; military service often subjects people to very testing experiences, and allows constant scrutiny by peers and authority.

A wealth of potentially useful information exists in computerized credit systems; personality may be revealed by how well people regulate their finances, and how they choose to spend their money. Surveys indicate that many American employers use credit records to assess job applicants. Bernerth *et al.* (2012) report one of the very few empirical researches on credit rating as a selection test. They correlated supervisor rating of work performance, employee's FFM PQ, and objective credit score, with remarkable results. PQ conscientiousness correlated with rated work performance 0.26, which is the usual result, but credit rating had a raw, uncorrected-for-anything correlation of 0.57, which is far higher than selection tests normally achieve. Bernerth *et al.* note that their sample was not very large, and that credit rating was not linked to counterproductive work behaviour or aggression, so that replication with larger samples in a range of occupations is urgently needed. Nielsen and Kuhn (2005) note possible problems with using credit rating to assess applicant personality. It may create adverse impact on some minorities; credit records contain many errors; potential applicants may be put off by it.

Some more 'science fiction' possibilities exist. There are presently an estimated half a million CCTV cameras in public places in London. Face-recognition software may make it possible to identify everyone, especially if the UK government ever achieves its planned national ID database. Mobile phones allow their owners' movements to be plotted accurately and continuously. These systems could be developed into an unfakable continuous input to an assessment system, that could allow employers to find out how applicants spend their time, and who their friends and 'associates' are. As Cervantes (1615/1950) said: 'Tell me the company you keep and I'll tell you what you are.' Orwell (1949/1984) foresaw universal continuous surveillance, extending into people's homes, and predicted that it would change behaviour: 'You had to live – did live, from habit that became instinct – in the assumption that every sound you made was overheard, and, except in darkness, every movement scrutinised.' An 'expression of quiet optimism' was advisable at all times.

RESEARCH AGENDA

Some specific issues could be researched immediately:
- Replication of Bernerth *et al.*'s research on credit rating and work performance.
- Whether activities outside work or school, college and military records can be linked to work performance.
- How applicants will react to being assessed by credit record, outside work activities and past records.

INVOLUNTARY EVIDENCE

Some involuntary evidence relating to personality uses psychophysiological methods; another major theme is handwriting.

Absolute threshold

Eysenck (1967) suggested a biological basis for neuroticism and extraversion, in the brain and nervous system. The central nervous system and brain of the extravert react less strongly to sensory input, which is why the extravert tends to seek excitement and company, whereas the introvert is more likely to seek quiet and solitude. Because the introvert's nervous system reacts more strongly, the introvert's absolute sensory thresholds are lower: the introvert can hear sounds or see light too faint for the extravert to detect. Absolute thresholds are difficult to test so this is probably not usable in selection.

Box 8.1   Electro-dermal activity (EDA)

Changes in the skin, preparatory to sweating, increase its electrical conductivity. Increase in EDA may indicate fear (or, as part of the polygraph, lying). Also referred to as galvanic skin response (GSR).

Response to threat

Psychopaths react physically far less, on electro-dermal activity (Box 8.1), to the threat of an electric shock, so employers could in theory use this to screen out some potentially disruptive applicants. The obvious problem is that employers cannot inflict pain on applicants as part of the selection process. The less obvious problem is a high false positive rate, wrongly identifying 10% of the general population as psychopaths.

Implicit Association Tests (IAT)

These were first devised to assess racism. IAT starts by asking people to make very simple decisions: press the left key if the word is pleasant, and the right key if it is unpleasant, then press the left key if the name is Asian, and press the right key if the name is white. These simple decisions take about half a second to make. In the second phase of IAT, the person gets a mix of names to sort by race and words to sort by pleasantness. The person does this twice, first pressing left key for own race and pleasantness, and right key for other race and unpleasantness, then – and this is the crucial part of IAT – pressing left key for own race or unpleasantness, and right key for other race or pleasantness. Having to remember that the left key stands for Asian and nice slows some people down, so they take around a 1/10th second longer for each decision. The test detects their implicit association between white and nice. IAT can predict behaviour towards persons of other races, is reasonably reliable, and not readily faked. IAT could be used to select for (absence of) racist attitudes, but no reports of this being done have been published. It could prove controversial: suppose someone who insisted they were not in any way racist were refused a job because IAT indicated they were.

IAT can be adapted to assess aspects of personality (Steffens & König, 2006). The two interleaved lists are for self/other, and for example extravert/introvert. Siers and Christiansen (2013) report some preliminary workplace data for IAT measures of extraversion, conscientiousness and neuroticism. They conclude IAT needs a lot of research on reliability, convergent validity (link to PQ measures) and discriminant validity (can IAT distinguish extraversion from conscientiousness?) Their results indicate IAT measures of personality may also reflect self-esteem and mental ability, which could be a problem; they suggest IAT may prove coachable, which would limit its value in selection.

DNA

One involuntary method may have considerable potential, which probably will not be realized. Personality has a substantial heritable element, which implies research may eventually identify particular genes associated with the differences between people described as personality. This could bypass entirely the faking problem in personality assessment. DNA testing might be able to assess the basic dimensions of 'temperament'; it clearly could not possibly detect any effects of background and experience. It will be interesting to see whether a DNA account of personality bears any resemblance to the big five, or Cattell's 16 factors, or any other current model. Chapter 6 noted that DNA testing may already be illegal in selection.

Language

Fast and Funder (2008) describe some promising research on word choice and personality. They collected interview data from 200 students, along with self-report and reports by two 'knowledgeable' others. Fast and Funder used the Linguistic Inquiry and Word Count computer program (see also Chapter 5) to search the interview transcripts for possibly revealing patterns of word use. They report two. Students who used a lot of 'certainty' words – *guarantee, completely, definite(ly)*, etc. – were described by self and others as smart, thoughtful, confident, and well-liked. The second set of results, however, shows a possible limit to the technique. Students who used a lot of sexual words – *gay, nude, stud*, etc. – tended to be seen, by others especially, as extravert, neurotic, self-centred, self-dramatizing, and unconventional. However choice of word is not entirely 'involuntary', and most people would 'know better than' to use words like *boob* or *butt* in a job interview.

Graphology

'… a hail-fellow-well-met who liked to eat and drink; who might attract women of the class he preyed on by an overwhelming animal charm. I would say in fact he was a latent homosexual … and passed as a man's man … capable of conceiving any atrocity and carrying it out in an organized way' – a graphologist's assessment of Jack the Ripper based on what might be one of his letters (Figure 8.4). No one knows who wrote the letter or committed the murders, so no one knows if the graphologist is right.

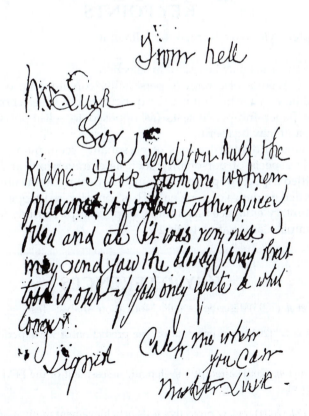

Figure 8.4   A letter attributed to Jack the Ripper.

If handwriting accurately reflects personality, it will make a very cost-effective selection method because As could be assessed from their application forms. Graphologists usually ask people to write pen pictures of themselves, so assessment is not solely based on handwriting. (The content of the letter in Figure 8.4 reveals quite a lot about the writer's mentality; the author enclosed half a human kidney and claimed to have eaten the other half.) Neter and Ben-Shakhar (1989) reviewed 17 studies comparing grapholo-gists and non-graphologists, rating neutral and *content-laden* scripts (such as pen pictures). With content-laden scripts, the non-graphologists, who know nothing about analysing handwriting, achieve better results than graphologists, suggesting they interpret *what* people write, not *how* they write it, and interpret it better than the graphologists. With neutral scripts, neither group achieves better than zero validity, suggesting either there is no useful information in handwriting, or that no one presently knows how to extract it. Bangerter *et al.* (2009) wonder why the myth that graphology is widely used in Europe persists; they show that fewer than 1% of job adverts in Switzerland require handwritten letters, and most of even these do not want to make graphological analyses.

KEY POINTS

In Chapter 8 you have learned the following:

- Projective tests may be useful in selection.
- Others' reports of a target's personality contain a lot of information, so could be very useful, but may be difficult to use in selection.
- Some paper-and-pencil tests (as opposed to self-reports) of personality exist, and may be useful.
- Behavioural demonstrations of personality seem more feasible for more visible aspects of personality such as extraversion, or for more closely specified aspects of personality, such as dealing with conflict.
- Recorded evidence of personality has some limited scope.
- Involuntary evidence has limited scope, except possibly for language use, and implicit association testing.

KEY REFERENCES

Bernard *et al.* (2005) describe Cattell's Motivation Analysis Test.

Bernerth *et al.* (2012) present data on the prediction of work performance by credit rating.

Borkenau *et al.* (2001) attempt a systematic assessment of the FFM by purely behav-ioural tests.

Collins *et al.* (2004) review projective tests of achievement motivation.

Connolly & Ones (2010) meta-analyse research on others' reports of personality and work performance.

Fast & Funder (2008) link language use to personality.

Johnson *et al.* (2010) describe a new word fragment test of personality.

Neter & Ben-Shakhar (1989) analyse research on the value of graphology as a selection method.

Oh, Wang & Mount (2011) describe a meta-analysis of others' ratings of personality.

Siers & Christiansen (2013) describe their research on assessing the FFM by implicit association test.

Biodata and weighted application blanks

How old were you when you learned to swim?

More than 90 years ago, Goldsmith (1922) devised an ingenious new solution to an old problem: selecting people who could endure selling life insurance. She took 50 good, 50 poor, and 50 middling salesmen from a larger sample of 502, and analysed their application forms. She identified factors that collectively distinguished good, average, and poor: age, marital status, education, (current) occupation, previous experience (of selling insurance), belonging to clubs, etc. Binary items – married/single – were scored +1/–1. Scoring age was more complicated: the best age was 30–40, with both younger and older age bands scoring less well. Non-linear scoring systems have remained a feature of some biographical measures. Low scorers in Goldsmith's sample almost all failed as insurance salespersons; the small minority of high scorers formed half of a slightly larger minority who were successful (Figure 9.1).

Goldsmith had turned the conventional application form into a *weighted application blank* (WAB). The principle is familiar to anyone with motor insurance. The insurance company analyses its records to find what sort of person makes more claims: people who drive sports cars, people who live in London, people who run bars, etc. Insurers do not rely on common sense, which might suggest that younger drivers, with faster reflexes, will be safer; they rely on their records, which show that young drivers on average are a poorer risk. If insurers can calculate premiums from occupation, age, and address, perhaps HR can use application forms as a convenient but powerful way of selecting employees.

There are two main forms of biographical predictor: the weighted application blank, and biodata. Both start by analysing past applicants to identify facts or items that are linked to an outcome. Both can be purely, even mindlessly, empirical. Items can be included if they predict the outcome, regardless of whether they 'make sense' or not. Both approaches need very large numbers, and both must be cross-validated before being used, i.e. items must be shown to work in both of two separate samples. As a consequence both are expensive to set up, but cheap to use thereafter. Both approaches

Personnel Selection: Adding Value Through People – A Changing Picture,
Sixth Edition. Mark Cook.

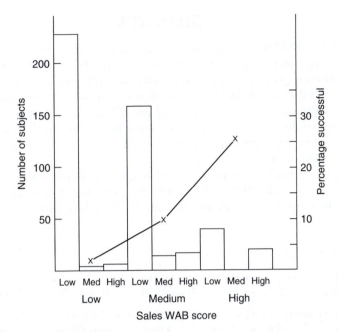

Figure 9.1 Results from the first published weighted application blank (WAB). Data from Goldsmith (1922).

are backward-looking; they will find 'more of the same', for example more managers like present successful managers. This may be a problem in times of rapid change. Both are *self-reports*.

WEIGHTED APPLICATION BLANKS

WABs were often used to select department store staff. Mosel (1952) found the ideal saleswoman was between 35 and 54 years old, had 13 to 16 years' formal education, had over five years' sales experience, weighed over 160 pounds, lived in a boarding house, was between 4'11'' and 5'2'' high, had between one and three dependants, was widowed, and had lost no time from work during the last two years. Harvey-Cook and Taffler (2000) used biographical methods to predict success in accountancy training in Britain, which had a very high drop-out rate. They found a surprisingly traditional set of predictors: school and university grades, being head boy/girl at school, and going to a public (i.e. private) school. Some WAB items are familiar to HR managers: (absence of) frequent job changes, being born locally, owning a home, being married, belonging to clubs and organizations, or sport. Some make sense when you know they work but need a very devious mind to predict – 'doesn't want a relative contacted in case of emergency', as a predictor of employee theft; some are bizarre – no middle initial given (employee theft again).

BIODATA

The classic WAB has tended to be supplanted since the 1960s by *biodata* or *biographical inventory*. Table 9.1 gives some typical biodata questions. Biodata uses questionnaire format with multiple-choice answers and loses the invisibility of the WAB because it becomes clear to applicants they are being assessed. Reynolds and Dickter (2010) suggest biodata are being replaced in their turn by applicant-screening 'tools' on the Internet, which are written by non-psychologists, and seem to have avoided being researched so far.

Biodata items divide into *hard*, which are verifiable but also often intrusive like item 6 in Table 9.1, and *soft* which cause less offence but are easier to fake like item 5. Some items are *controllable*, while others are not; people

Table 9.1   Some typical biodata items.

1. How old was your father when you were born?
   1] about 20   2] about 25   3] about 30   4] about 35   5] I don't know

2. How many hours in a typical week do you engage in physical exercise?
   1] none   2] up to 1 hour   3] 2–3 hours   4] 4–5 hours   5] over 5 hours

3. In your last year at school, how many hours in a typical week did you study outside class hours?
   1] none   2] up to 2 hours 3] 2–4 hours   4] 5–8 hours   5] over 8 hours

4. How old were you when you first kissed someone romantically?
   1] 12 or under   2] 13 or 14   3] 15 or 16   4] over 16   5] never kissed anyone romantically

5. How interested in current affairs are you?
   1] not at all   2] slightly   3] fairly   4] very   5] extremely

6. Which best describes your present height/weight ratio?
   1] definitely overweight   2] somewhat overweight   3] slightly overweight   4] just right   5] underweight

7. How often did you play truant from school?
   1] never   2] once or twice a year   3] 3 to 10 times a year   4] once a month   5] once a week or more

8. What do you think of children who play truant from school?
   1] very strongly disapprove   2] strongly disapprove   3] disapprove   4] unconcerned   5] can sympathize

9. My superiors at work would describe me as
   1] very lazy   2] fairly lazy   3] average   4] quite hard working   5] very hard working

10. How many times did you have to take your driving test?
    1] once   2] twice   3] three   4] four or more   5] never taken it

choose their exercise patterns but not their parents' ages. Some employers avoid non-controllable items, because they look unfair. Some biodata contain questions about attitudes (item 8), or about what (you think) other people think of you (item 9).

Biodata and personality questionnaire

Many biographical questions look very like PQ questions. What is the conceptual difference between PQ questions, like those listed in Table 7.1 (page 140), and biodata questions like those listed in Table 9.1?

1. The PQ infers from answers to trait, then from trait to work performance. Most biodata by contrast infer direct from answers to work performance, without any intervening variable such as dominance or conscientiousness. (Although some researchers use biographical factors, or even personality traits, as intervening variables in biodata.)
2. PQs have fixed keys, whereas biodata items are rekeyed for each selection task.
3. Overall, biodata questions are more likely to be factual than personality questions, although biodata measures include many non-factual questions.
4. PQ questions are phrased to elicit a rapid, unthinking reply, whereas biodata items often sound quite clumsy in their desire to specify precisely the information they want, for example:

With regard to personal appearance, as compared with the appearance of my friends, I think that:
(a) *Most of my friends make a better appearance*
(b) *I am equal to most of them in appearance*
(c) *I am better than most of them in appearance*
(d) *I don't feel strongly one way or the other*

In a PQ this would read more like: *I am fairly happy about the way I look – TRUE or FALSE*. Sometimes the distinction between PQ and biodata is so fine that one wonders if the choice of title reflects more the authors' perception of what will be acceptable in their organization.

Biodata keyed to personality dimensions

Mael and Hirsch (1993) described a biodata keyed to the US military's PQ, ABLE. More recently Cucina *et al.* (2013) have developed FFM keys to the US government's Individual Achievement Record biodata, and find these correlate with PQ scores 0.30–0.40, except for extraversion, which is only 0.17. The biodata, like the PQ, can be faked. Keying a biodata measure to known personality dimensions gives it psychological meaning, and may ensure more generalized validity.

CONSTRUCTING BIOGRAPHICAL MEASURES

Empirical keying

Traditional biographical methods were purely empirical. If inefficient clerical workers were underweight, or had no middle initial, or lived in Balham, those facts entered the scoring key. Purely empirical measures offend psychologists, who like to feel they have a theory. They are not happy knowing canary breeders make dishonest employees; they want to know *why*. Ideally they would like to have *predicted* from their theory of work behaviour that canary breeders will make dishonest employees. Critics of pure empiricism argue that a measure with a foundation of theory is more likely to hold up over time and across different employers, and may be easier to defend if challenged.

Factorial keying

The first attempt to give biodata a more theoretical basis relied on *factor analysis*, to identify themes in biographical information. If the no-middle-initial question proved to be linked to half a dozen other questions, all to do with, for example, sense of belonging, one has some idea why it relates to work performance, one can explain to critics why it is included, and one can perhaps search for better items to reflect the underlying theme.

Rational keying

Some approaches select questions to reflect particular themes. Miner (1971) stated specific hypotheses about eliteness motivation, for example that status-conscious Americans will serve (as officers of course) in the navy or air force, but not in the army. Some researchers use a *behavioural consistency* approach. If job analysis indicates the job needs good organizational skills, items are written that reflect this, either on the job – *How often do you complete projects on time?* – or off the job if the organization is recruiting new employees – *To what extent do you prepare when going off on holiday?* Recently researchers have increasingly used rational scales based on intervening constructs. Work analysis indicates that the job is stressful, so researchers seek biodata questions that tap stress tolerance. Factorial and empirical approaches can be used as well to check that the stress items do all reflect one single theme, and that they do predict work performance. This approach is easier to defend, and more versatile; a biodata for stress tolerance can be used for any job that creates stress. Barrick and Zimmerman (2005) describe a very short research-based biodata for predicting turnover. Less turnover should be predicted by longer tenure in previous jobs, being referred by a current employee, and by 'job embeddedness' – having family and friends in the organization. These three questions predicted 'avoidable' turnover quite well (0.30).

Reiter-Palmon and Connelly (2000) compare rational and empirical construction methods and find they work equally well, but empirical keys tend to contain more hard-to-explain items, for example, good grades predicted by admitting to often taking feelings out on parents. Graham *et al.* (2002) find that certain types of questions seem to predict work performance better: questions that are verifiable through records, such as lateness or work, or that reflect others' opinions, like item 9 in Table 9.1. Questions that record A's own opinion of him/herself and which are not verifiable, like item 5 in Table 9.1, were less successful. Cucina *et al.* (2012) compared empirical and rational biodata scoring in a large archival dataset for professional and technical jobs in the US government. They found rational keying markedly less successful than empirical in predicting work performance. They also compared various systems of empirical keying, and found keying made little or no difference to validity, so suggest using the simplest.

Option keying vs. linear rating

Biographical measures were traditionally scored by option keying, using tables drawn up by Strong in 1926 and revised by England in 1961. Table 9.2 illustrates the method for one of 88 WAB items from Mitchell and Klimoski's (1982) study of trainee realtors (estate agents), where the criterion of success was achieving licensed status. Columns 1 and 2 show successful realtors are more likely to own their own home, and less likely to rent a flat or live with relatives. Column 4 assigns a scoring weight from Strong's tables; larger percentage differences get higher weights. This technique allows for non-linear relationships.

Linear rating methods have become more popular. Linearity allows analysis by correlation and factor analysis. Mael and Hirsch (1993) argued that some apparently non-linear relations arise by chance. They cited the example of *How many years did you play chess in high school?* If the answer *three years* was less closely linked to work performance than the adjacent answers of *two* or *four years*, strict application of option keying would assign less weight to three than either two or four. 'The hand of reason', by contrast, suggests the relationship is more likely to be linear, and sets the scoring accordingly.

Table 9.2   A sample WAB item, and its scoring, from Mitchell & Klimoski (1982).

	Licensed	Unlicensed	Difference	Weight
Do you:				
– own your own home?	81	60	21	5
– rent home?	3	5	–2	–1
– rent apartment?	9	25	–16	–4
– live with relatives?	5	10	–5	–2

Reproduced with permission of APA.

Biographical classification

Owens and Schoenfeldt (1979) used biodata to classify people. Scores on the Biographical Questionnaire were factor-analysed, and the factor scores then used to group people with common patterns of prior experience. They showed successful salesmen came from only three (of nine) biodata groups (one-time college athletes, college politicians, and hard workers), and that biodata group membership predicted survival in selling very successfully.

RESEARCH AGENDA

• Further analysis comparing methods of writing and scoring biodata.

VALIDITY

Two reviews offer apparently very similar overall estimates of biodata validity.

• Bliesener (1996) reported a meta-analysis of 165 biodata validities, and found a mean validity of 0.30.
• Bobko and Roth (1999) also reported a meta-analysis, based in part on two earlier meta-analyses (but not Bliesener's) and in part on two large American studies; they reported a value of 0.28.

Neither analysis corrects for either restricted range or unreliability, so both represent conservative estimates of biodata validity. Biodata are evidently a fairly effective predictor. However, on closer inspection Bliesener's value is not after all the same as Bobko and Roth's. Bliesener's overall uncorrected correlation is actually considerably higher than 0.30, at 0.39. He did something unusual in selection research: making corrections that *reduce* the size of the validity coefficient. Bliesener identified and corrected for five methodological shortcomings of biodata research which he thought could inflate validity. For example concurrent designs achieve higher validity than predictive, although predictive designs offer more conclusive proof. Pure biodata achieve lower validity than biodata that include a lot of attitude or personality items. Standard scoring keys, i.e. ones already written in some other research, achieve lower validity than ones written specially, which may capitalize on chance more.

Different outcomes

Biodata have been used to predict a very wide variety of work-related outcomes. Table 9.3 summarizes some of this research. (These analyses are not

Table 9.3   Summary of validity of biodata for nine work-related outcomes.

Review	R&C		H&H		S		B&H		B			G	
	k	r	k	r	k	r	k	r	k	r	r_{net}	k	r
Proficiency rating	15	0.36	12	0.37	29	0.32	26	0.32	16	0.32	0.23		
Production	6	0.46			19	0.21	10	0.31					
Objective performance									19	0.53	0.30		
Promotion			17	0.26									
Training success			11	0.30			18	0.25	49	0.36	0.22		
Absence/turnover					28	0.21	15	0.25					
Tenure	13	0.32	23	0.26			18	0.32	39	0.22	0.15		
Turnover												6	0.31
Creativity									19	0.43	0.32		

R&C: Reilly & Chao (1982); H&H: Hunter & Hunter (1984); S: Schmitt *et al.* (1984); B&H: Barge & Hough (1986); B: Bliesener (1996); G: Griffeth *et al.* (2000)
k = number of validities; r = uncorrected correlation; r_{net} = correlation corrected downwards for methodological shortcomings 'Objective performance' includes production figures, sales, and absence.

entirely independent because the same original researches may be included in more than one review.) Table 9.3 indicates that:

- Biodata can successfully predict a wide variety of work behaviour.
- Validity is higher for Bliesener's objective performance category, which covers sales, production and absence.
- Validity is generally lower for predicting tenure.

Different types of work

Biodata have also been used for a wide range of types of work. Three meta-analyses (Table 9.4) find biodata achieve good validity for most occupations, with the possible exception of the armed forces, where Bliesener finds validity only 0.19. Bliesener finds biodata validity highest for clerical work. Validity is pooled across different criteria including training, tenure, salary, as well as supervisor rating and conventional output measures.

Several reviews and meta-analyses have been reported for specific occupations:

- Funke *et al.* (1987) reported a meta-analysis of 13 studies using biographical measures to predict research achievement in science and technology, and found an overall corrected validity of 0.47.
- Two reviews of sales staff agree on validity of 0.28 for sales figures, but disagree on validity for rated sales ability. Vinchur *et al.* (1998) find it higher, at 0.52, whereas Farrell and Hakstian (2001) find it lower, at 0.33.

Table 9.4   Summary of validity of biodata for six areas of work.

Study	Mumford		Reilly		Bliesener		
	k	r	k	r	k	r	r_{net}
Managers	21	0.35	7	0.38	11	0.42	0.27
Sales	17	0.35	5	0.50	24	0.23	0.27
Factory/craftsperson	14	0.46					
Clerical	13	0.46	6	0.52	22	0.46	0.39
Armed forces	13	0.34	9	0.30	33	0.25	0.19
Science/engineering			15	0.41	16	0.41	0.33

Data from Reilly & Chao (1982), Mumford & Owens (1987), and Bliesener (1996).
k = number of validities; r = uncorrected correlation; r_{net} = correlation corrected downwards for methodological shortcomings.

- Hunter and Burke (1994) report an uncorrected validity of 0.27 in 21 studies predicting success in pilot training. They find an unexpected moderator variable in publication date; researches reported before 1961, including many large-scale Second World War studies, achieved good validity, whereas those reported after 1961 found poorer results (another example of validity appearing to decline during the twentieth century).

Bliesener's analysis finds a very large gender difference; biodata work far better for women (0.51) than for men (0.27). This may be mediated by occupation; biodata work better for occupations in which a lot of women work, such as clerical jobs, and less well for occupations in which fewer women work, such as the armed forces.

Construct validity

Little is known about how biodata relate to other selection measures, or about what they measure. Purely empirical measures, keyed to particular outcomes, may not be closely related to other measures. Mumford and Owens (1987) reviewed 21 factorial studies and listed the seven most commonly found factors: adjustment, academic achievement, intellectual/cultural pursuits, introversion/extraversion, social leadership, maturity, career development. Obviously biodata keyed to personality will be expected to correlate with personality tests. Rothstein et al. (1990) reported a substantial correlation with mental ability in a single large study, but no meta-analysis has been published.

Incremental validity

Schmidt and Hunter (1998) argue the high correlation between biodata and mental ability reported by Rothstein et al. (1990) means biodata will not achieve much incremental validity. However, some researches have reported incremental validity. Mael and Ashworth (1995) find biodata improve on MA tests in predicting attrition in army recruits. Mount, Witt and Barrick (2000) find biodata have incremental validity on mental ability and the big five personality factors for clerical work. McManus and Kelly (1999) find that the big five and biodata each achieve incremental validity in predicting organizational citizenship.

Validity generalization and transportability

Early research concluded WABs and biodata did not seem to 'travel well', and tended to be specific to the organizations they were developed in. The best data on transportability come from the biodata used by the North American insurance industry since the 1930s, and dating in part back to 1919, variously called Aptitude Index Battery (AIB), Career Profile System, and Initial Career Profile. Figure 9.2 shows success is closely related to AIB score, and also shows how few succeed in insurance, even from the highest score bands. Figure 9.3 shows schematically the distribution of AIB scores against survival and sales, and suggests AIB is essentially a screening test, that eliminates potential failures but does not necessarily identify successes. Brown (1981) analysed AIB data for over 12,000 sales staff from 12 large US companies. AIB was valid for all 12 companies, but proved more valid for larger, better-run companies that recruit through press adverts and agencies, than for smaller companies that recruit by personal contacts. AIB has been rewritten and rescored several times, but has retained some continuity.

Consortium measures

Organizations that do not employ enough people to generate their own biodata can join a consortium. Consortium measures also deal with the problem of specificity to particular jobs, outcomes, or organizations. Rothstein

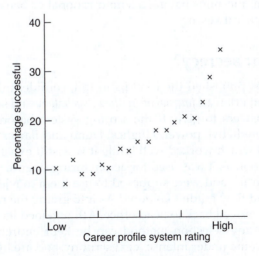

Figure 9.2   Predictive validity of the Career Profile System.

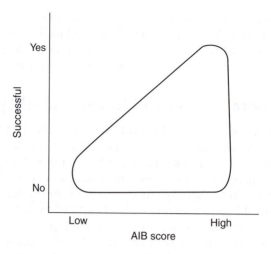

Figure 9.3 Schematic representation of the relationship between AIB score and success in selling insurance.

et al. (1990) suggested that biodata do not 'travel well' because they are usually keyed inside one single organization, which limits their generality. The Supervisory Profile Record (SPR) derived from 39 organizations, and proved to have highly generalizable validity, being unaffected by organization, sex, race, supervisory experience, social class or education. Schmidt and Rothstein (1994) analysed SPR data for 79 separate organizations and found relatively little variation in validity from one organization, or type of supervisor to another. Carlson *et al.* (1999) describe the Manager Profile Record, developed within one organization, but used successfully in 24 others to predict salary increase and promotion. Carlson *et al.* placed more emphasis on questions having a sound rational or behavioural justification than on empirical keying.

The need for secrecy?

Early studies published their WABs in full, confident that clerks and shop assistants did not read *Journal of Applied Psychology* and so could not discover the right answers to give. If the scoring system becomes known, biodata could lose predictive power. Hughes, Dunn and Baxter (1956) wrote a new form of AIB which worked well while it was still experimental, but lost its validity as soon as it was used for actual hiring (Figure 9.4). Field managers scored the forms and were supposed to use them to reject unsuitable applicants; instead they guided favoured As into giving the right answers. When scoring was moved back to head office, AIB regained its validity. It is doubtful whether any selection method can be kept entirely secret these days because all come under intense legal scrutiny, and are likely to be discussed on the Internet.

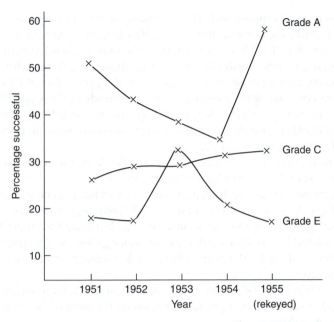

Figure 9.4   Results obtained with the Aptitude Index Battery (AIB) between 1951 and 1954. Data from Hughes *et al.* (1956).

FAKABILITY

Both WAB and biodata are self-reports. Some information is factual and could be independently verified. In practice this rarely happens, except for details of education and previous employment. Biodata often contain a lot of attitude and personality questions, which tend to be unverifiable. Research on biodata faking has some parallels with research on faking PQs, discussed in Chapter 7. People directed to fake good distort their answers far more than job applicants (Becker & Colquitt, 1992), so directed faking studies may be misleading. The extent of faking by real As is uncertain. Becker and Colquitt reported that only three items of 25 were answered differently by real As; these items were less historical, objective, and verifiable. On the other hand, Stokes, Hogan and Snell (1993) compare As with present employees (PEs), and find their answers much more 'socially desirable' in areas like preferred working climate, work style, or personal and social adjustment.

Research also suggests several possible ways of dealing with faking in biodata, again tending to repeat approaches tried with PQs.

- More objective and verifiable items create fewer differences between As and PEs (Stokes *et al.*, 1993).
- Harold, McFarland and Weekley (2006) describe a biodata for call centre workers, which has both verifiable and non-verifiable items, and is validated on both applicants and present employees. (Most biodata validation

uses present employees). The verifiable items were equally valid for applicants and PEs, whereas the non-verifiable items achieved lower validity for As than for PEs. This is consistent with As being less truthful or accurate in replying to non-verifiable items, and shows the desirability of validating biodata, and other selection tests, on 'real' applicants not PEs.

- More complex option-keying scoring methods are less fakable than simple linear scoring systems (Kluger, Reilly and Russell, 1991). However, Stokes *et al.* (1993) found that complex scoring does not seem to prevent As giving different responses to PEs.
- Warning people the biodata included a lie-detection scale (which it did not) reduced faking (Schrader & Osburn, 1977).
- Bogus items were first used in biodata, and have recently been resurrected in PQs. As who claimed to have used 'Sonntag connectors' (which do not exist) got better overall scores on the biodata, but their biodata score correlated less with a written job knowledge test, suggesting they were not better applicants (Pannone, 1984). Trick questions might not work for long in practice.
- Shermis *et al.* (1996) described a faking good scale, modelled on PQ faking good scales, consisting of 12 questions on the lines of *I have never violated the law while driving a car*.
- Schmitt and Kunce (2002) reported that elaboration reduces faking considerably: applicants who claim, for example, to have led several work teams are asked to give details. The reduction in faking generalizes to questions where elaboration is not asked for.

RESEARCH AGENDA

- New meta-analysis covering more recent validity researches.
- More research on fakability and ways of dealing with it.

BIOGRAPHICAL MEASURES, FAIRNESS AND THE LAW

For some years, biodata were included in the list of selection methods that were 'safe', because they found no gender or ethnicity differences. Reilly and Chao's (1984) review concluded that biodata did not by and large create adverse impact for minorities applying for work as bus drivers, clerical staff, army recruits, or supervisors. Subsequently Schmitt, Clause and Pulakos's (1996) meta-analysis found only fairly small Afro/white differences in biodata scores ($d = 0.20$). Later analyses were less optimistic. Bobko and Roth (1999) re-analysed Schmitt *et al.*, and concluded the Afro/white difference is larger, at 0.33. Roth *et al.* (2001a) described unpublished data with a white/African American d of 0.34, but noted that As had been pre-screened on mental ability tests, which also create AI. Correcting for pre-screening raised white/Afro biodata d to 0.73. Sharf (1994) noted that biodata had not been challenged directly under the Civil Rights Act. Perhaps everyone thought there was no adverse impact problem. One study reported that using biodata data can reduce adverse impact; the combination of Supervisory Profile Record and mental ability test, while predicting only slightly better than the MA tests alone, created less adverse impact (Rothstein *et al.*, 1990).

Item analysis

The differences discussed above are in total score, but it is possible also to analyse adverse impact at the question level. Biographical measures might discriminate against protected groups in subtle ways: having a city centre as opposed to suburban address in Detroit distinguished thieves from non-thieves but also tended to distinguish white from non-white. Questions about participation in sport could discriminate against disabled people. Sharf (1994) suggested it was unclear whether biodata could be challenged legally, question by question, so a few questions creating adverse impact may not matter. In fact it is extremely unlikely that no gender, age, ethnicity or disability differences would be found in any of 50 to 100 biographical questions. However, if many questions show, for example, ethnicity differences, it tends to follow that total scores will also differ. Whitney and Schmitt (1997) found significant black/white differences in a high proportion (25%) of biodata questions, and noted that explaining the differences in terms of, for example, different cultural values would lead to better understanding of which items to avoid in future. Unfortunately they were unable to identify any systematic trends in their sample.

Privacy

As Table 9.1 shows, some biodata questions can be very intrusive. Use of biodata in the USA is complicated by the fact that the 52 states all have their own, differing laws about privacy, so questions about, for example, credit rating are legal in some states but not in others. European employment law tends to emphasize the privacy and dignity of the applicant, which could make some biodata questions less acceptable.

Some psychologists have proposed the *Washington Post* test for biodata face validity. Imagine headlines in the *Washington Post* (or the *Guardian*). One headline reads *Psychologists reject people for officer training because they don't like the colour blue*, which sounds arbitrary and unfair. Another headline reads *Psychologists reject people for officer training because they weren't prefects at school*, which sounds much more reasonable.

RESEARCH AGENDA

• Research on acceptability of different types of biodata questions to applicants.

KEY POINTS

In Chapter 9 you have learned the following:

- There are two biographical approaches: weighted application blanks which are scored from the application form, and biodata which are separate questionnaires and so more visible to As.
- Biographical measures can predict work performance, and other related aspects of workplace behaviour such as tenure, training success, promotion, absence, or creativity.
- Biodata can be purely empirical, or can be guided by either a theory of, for example, eliteness motivation, or a relevant construct such as stress tolerance.
- Biodata face the usual problem of quality of information being compromised by faking.
- Biodata can be written that work across a number of different organizations.
- Biodata rarely seem to attract litigation, but can look unfair or arbitrary to candidates.
- Biodata do create some adverse impact on American minorities.

KEY REFERENCES

Barrick & Zimmerman (2005) describe a very short biodata for predicting turnover.

Bliesener (1996) presents a meta-analysis of biodata validity that makes some unusual corrections.

Cucina *et al.* (2012) describe personality-based keys for a US government biodata.

Harvey-Cook & Taffler (2000) describe a British biographical selection process for chartered accountants.

Hughes *et al.* (1956) describe how a biodata lost validity when its scoring was compromised.

Roth *et al.* (2001) argue that biodata do create adverse impact on minorities in the USA, when pre-selection is taken into account.

Rothstein *et al.* (1990) describe the development of a generic biodata, the Supervisory Profile Record.

CHAPTER 10

Assessment centres

Does your face fit?

The assessment centre was invented during the Second World War, on both sides of the Atlantic more or less simultaneously. The British Army expanded rapidly, and needed to recruit officers from unfamiliar backgrounds. A team of psychologists set up the War Office Selection Board (WOSB), a three-day program of tests, exercises and interviews. In the USA, psychologists led by Henry Murray were advising the Office of Strategic Services (OSS), forerunner of the CIA, how to select spies. Murray's team identified nine dimensions to effective spying, including practical intelligence, emotional stability, and maintenance of cover. Maintenance of cover required As to pretend to be someone else throughout the assessment; the OSS program must be unique in regarding systematic lying as a virtue.

THE PRESENT SHAPE OF ACs

ACs operate on the principle of *multi-dimension multi-exercise* assessment. The key feature of the AC is the *dimension × exercise matrix* (Figure 10.1). AC planners identify key dimensions of work performance by work analysis, then use at least two qualitatively different methods to assess each dimension. In Figure 10.1 ability to influence is assessed by group exercise and PQ, while numerical ability is assessed by financial case study and numerical reasoning test.

Dimensions – what the AC assesses

Arthur *et al.* (2003) listed 168 different dimension names in their review of AC research, and grouped them into six: *communication, consideration and awareness of others, drive, influencing others, organizing and planning,* and *problem-solving.* Meriac *et al.* (2014) point out that Arthur *et al.*'s account was qualitative, based on sorting by experts, and report a quantitative analysis using *confirmatory factor analysis,* which tests the fit of various models. A six-factor model fitted the 20 dimensions well, but contained two pairs of very similar factors: communication/consideration and awareness, and planning and organizing/problem-solving.

Personnel Selection: Adding Value Through People – A Changing Picture,
Sixth Edition. Mark Cook.
© 2016 John Wiley & Sons, Ltd. Published 2016 by John Wiley & Sons, Ltd.

	Influence	Numeracy	Delegation
Exercise A	XXX		XXX
Exercise B		XXX	
Test C	XXX	XXX	
Test D		XXX	XXX
In-tray			XXX

Figure 10.1   The dimension × exercise matrix underlying every assessment centre. XXX denotes influence is assessed by exercise A.

A three-factor model also fitted the data very well, whereas two-factor or single-factor models lost some information. The three factors are: relational skills, administrative skills and drive. All Meriac *et al.*'s sets of dimensions (1, 2, 3, 6) could be used in the sense that they all reflect how people perform in ACs. Meriac *et al.*'s analysis suggests performance in ACs has a hierarchical structure, similar to that of mental ability (Chapter 6) and personality (Chapter 7).

Exercises – how the AC assesses

Spychalski *et al.*'s (1997) survey distinguished six main types of exercise:

- Leaderless group discussions in which the group discuss a given topic and reach a consensus, but where no one is appointed as chair. Group discussions can be co-operative or competitive.
- Role play in which A handles, for example a dissatisfied customer, or an employee with a grievance.
- Presentation on either a specialist or a general knowledge topic. Used in about 50% of ACs.
- Interview. Included in about 50% of ACs.
- In-basket (or in-tray) exercise in which As deal with a set of letters, memos. etc. (Chapter 11). Used in most ACs.
- Case analysis, usually written, of a complex problem.

Krause and Thornton (2009) report a new survey of west European and North American practice which confirms the widespread impression that ACs have got shorter, lasting one or two days rather than the two or three of the 1980s. American practice seems to favour four to five exercises, typically role plays, presentation, and in-tray exercises, while European practice is more likely to include up to seven exercises, and favours group exercises, presentations, case studies, and interviews. Group exercises seem less widely used in North America than before 2000. Psychological tests are now included in only around 20% of ACs. Tests are useful because they provide normative data to what otherwise tends to be an *ipsative* assessment system (meaning As are compared with each other, not with an external standard).

Assessors may be line managers or psychologists. ACs use a bewildering array of *assessor/assessee designs*. Sometimes the assessor observes and rates the same As throughout the AC; sometimes they observe and rate different As in each succeeding exercise. The researcher would prefer either to have every assessor rate every A on everything, or to use each assessor only once, to rate only one A, on one dimension, in one exercise. Neither is feasible in practice. This makes AC data very messy, and may contribute to the dimension × exercise problem, discussed later. ACs are unsatisfactory in other ways, viewed as experimental designs for assessment. For example, most have a fixed sequence, so leaderless group discussion always precedes team negotiation. This is likely to create two types of order effect: assessor and applicant. If Applicant A does well in the leaderless group discussion, assessors may expect him/her to do well in the negotiation, while Applicant B who does poorly in the leaderless group may be demoralized and do poorly for the rest of the programme. Group exercises are particularly uncontrolled, since what one person does, or can do, depends on what the others are doing. Falk and Fox (2014) find evidence of group dynamic effects in ACs for educational management in Israel: a correlation of 0.30–0.40 between proportion of females in the group and average male scores, which they interpret as females expecting males to take the lead, which makes it easier for males to 'do well' in the group.

RESEARCH AGENDA

More 'analytical' research on ACs may be useful; issues such as order effects, cumulative effects, rating across and within exercises are difficult to address with real data from real ACs. Questions could be addressed by more controlled laboratory research, or by using filmed data from real ACs.

RELIABILITY OF ACs

Reliability is a complex issue; one can calculate – in descending order of generality – the reliability of the entire process, of its component parts, or of assessors' ratings. Connelly *et al.* (2008) find inter-rater reliability in ACs generally fairly good, at 0.80 for overall rating, and 0.73 for specific dimensions. Wilson (1948) reported a fairly good retest reliability for the UK Civil Service Selection Board (CSSB), based on As who exercised their right to try CSSB twice. Morris (1949) described two retest reliability studies with WOSB. In the first, two parallel WOSBs were set up specifically to test inter-WOSB agreement, and two batches of As attended both WOSBs. There were 'major disagreements' over 25% of As. In the second study two parallel boards simultaneously but independently observed and evaluated the same 200 As, and achieved good agreement.

VALIDITY OF ACs

Like the interview, the AC is a *method* of assessment, that can assess many different *constructs*. Hence one should, strictly speaking, ask about validity of the AC for assessing, for example, delegation. In practice the AC, like the interview, is often used to assess general suitability for the job, and its validity is computed against management's estimates, also of general suitability. When the AC tries to assess specific constructs or dimensions, there is some question whether it succeeds in doing so (see the section on 'Dimension × Exercise Problem' below).

AT&T's Management Progress Study (MPS)

The MPS was an early, and very influential, use of the AC in the USA, to promote people into middle management (Bray & Grant, 1966). People were originally assessed in 1957; on follow-up eight years later, as Table 10.1 shows, the MPS achieved very good predictive validity, an uncorrected correlation of 0.46.

Civil Service Selection Board (CSSB)

The most senior ranks of the UK Civil Service have been selected since 1945 by CSSB, whose elements include group discussions, written exercises, and interviews, preceded by biodata and mental ability tests. Vernon (1950) reported a follow-up study of CSSB's early years, which showed CSSB achieved good predictive validity (0.44 to 0.49), correcting for restricted range but not outcome reliability. Anstey (1977) continued to follow up Vernon's sample until the mid-1970s, when many were nearing retirement. Using achieved rank as criterion, Anstey reported an eventual predictive validity, after 30 years, that was very good (0.66, corrected for restricted range). All but 21 of 301 CSSB graduates in Anstey's analysis achieved Assistant Secretary rank, showing they made the grade as senior civil servants; only three left because of 'definite inefficiency'.

Table 10.1 Results of the AT&T Management Progress Study (Bray & Grant, 1966).

AC ratings	N	Achieved rank		
		1st line	2nd line	Middle
Potential middle manager	103	4%	53%	46%
Not potential middle manager	166	68%	86%	12%

Reproduced with permission of APA.

Politicians

Before the 2005 British General Election, the Conservative Party used an AC to select candidates to run for election as Member of Parliament (Silvester & Dykes, 2007). Applicants were assessed on communication skill, intellectual skill, relating to people, leading and motivating, resilience and drive, and political conviction, by group exercise, competency-based interview, public-speaking exercise, in-tray, and MA test. The AC achieved a modest correlation (0.25 corrected for restricted range) with the selected MPs' election success.

META-ANALYSES

Three meta-analyses (Arthur *et al.*, 2003; Gaugler *et al.*, 1987; Hardison & Sackett, 2007) of AC validity in North America have been published, and one (Becker *et al.*, 2011) for German-speaking countries (Table 10.2). Hardison and Sackett's analysis covers only research published since Gaugler *et al.*, so there is no overlap between the two. The two analyses both report operational validities around 0.30, which may seem rather low, compared with the 0.50 achieved by MA tests, which are so much quicker and cheaper. However, 0.30 may be an underestimate. Hardison and Sackett note that Gaugler *et al.*'s correction for restriction of range was very conservative. Where the original study gave insufficient information to allow any estimate of restriction, Gaugler *et al.* assumed there was none; most studies gave insufficient information, so most were not corrected. Hardison and Sackett's overall validity is lower than Gaugler *et al.*'s estimate; they suggest this is another effect of restricted range. Because ACs are expensive, employers increasingly use them only as the final stage of selection, after pre-screening As by biodata, tests, PQs, etc. This is likely to mean range is greatly restricted, but it is difficult to estimate exactly by how much, so no correction can be made.

Table 10.2 Summary of three analyses of assessment centre validity.

Reviewer	Gaugler *et al.*		Hardison & Sackett		Becker *et al.*	
Outcome	k	ρ	k	ρ	k	ρ
Performance	44	0.36	40	0.26	24	0.40
Supervisor rating					9	0.56
Potential	13	0.53				
Career advance	33	0.36				
Promotion			10	0.27[u]	7	0.39
Turnover			6	0.07[u]		
Training	8	0.35	10	0.35		
Sales			4	0.15	3	0.04

Data from Gaugler *et al.* (1987); Hardison & Sackett (2007); Becker *et al.* (2011).
ρ = operational validity, except [u] where uncorrected validity.

Gaugler *et al.*'s VGA uncovered several factors that moderated AC validity. AC validity was higher when:

- More assessments were included.
- Psychologists rather than managers were used as assessors.
- Peer evaluations were used.
- More As were female.

AC validity was not affected by:

- Ratio of As to assessors.
- Amount of assessor training.
- How long the assessors spent integrating the information.

Hardison and Sackett also found some moderators:

- Validity decreases, the longer the interval between AC and outcome, but remains usefully high ($\rho = 0.22$) even with a five-year interval.
- Simpler ACs, with fewer dimensions and fewer exercises, achieve better validity. (Note that Gaugler *et al.* had found the opposite: validity was higher the more assessments were included.)

Hardison and Sackett found two factors that had no effect on validity:

- Sector – business, military and police, or education.
- Discussion of AC ratings achieved no better validity than simply averaging across assessors, suggesting the assessors' conference – a defining feature of the AC – may not be absolutely necessary.

Becker *et al.*'s (2011) meta-analysis yields an operational validity of 0.40, with several moderator variables. Measure of work performance makes a big difference: supervisor rating achieves very high validity, promotion achieves average validity, while sales achieves near-zero validity. Validity for internal candidates is much higher than for external applicants. Published studies achieve slightly higher validity than unpublished. Becker *et al.* agree with Gaugler *et al.* that more exercises are linked to higher validity.

Arthur *et al.* (2003) prefer to analyse validity for each construct or dimension separately, using their six-way classification. Their meta-analysis finds validity divides into three bands: higher (0.30) for problem-solving, influence, organizing/planning, medium for communication, and lower (0.22) for drive and consideration/awareness. In a later analysis (Meriac *et al.*, 2008) they found stress tolerance falls in the low band. Note, however, that they are comparing AC rating of, for example, influence with a general performance outcome, not with a specific measure of workplace influence.

Both Thornton and Gibbons (2009) and Schuler (2008) note an apparent decline in AC validity over time from the 0.46 (uncorrected) of the AT&T study of the 1950s, through Gaugler et al.'s (1987) meta-analytic estimate of 0.37 (corrected), to Hardison and Sackett's (2007) 0.26 (corrected). Hardison and Sackett also found a –0.26 correlation between year of publication and validity: the more recent the date, the lower the validity. Thornton and Gibbons suggest a new form of publication bias: 'iconoclastic', meaning that studies that show ACs do *not* work are more 'news' than ones that show they do. Schuler attributes the decrease in validity to declining standards in AC design and practice.

No one seems to have used ACs to predict organizational citizenship, or counterproductive work behaviours. Perhaps ACs are too expensive, or perhaps it is a case of 'them and us'. ACs are for management, who do not have problems with OCB or CWB.

One could argue that research on 'the validity of the AC' is misguided in a second sense, because every AC is different, a unique combination of dimensions assessed and exercises used. Research should instead focus on the validity of each component of the AC, for each of Arthur et al.'s six dimensions. Given this information, and data on intercorrelation, planners could estimate the expected overall validity of any particular AC. There is plenty of research on validity of some more peripheral AC components, such as interviews, tests and PQs. Hoffman et al. (2015) report a meta-analysis of five 'core' AC exercises: in-basket, oral presentation, role play, leaderless group discussion, and case analysis. All five correlate with work performance, between 0.16 and 0.19 (true validity, i.e. corrected for range restriction, and reliability of both test and outcome). Hoffman et al. also report intercorrelations between the five AC components, which range from 0.16 to 0.38, with a median average of 0.30 (also true validity). Hoffman et al.'s analysis incidentally pointed to a worrying feature of ACs: replicability. They tried to characterize exercises for complexity, job-relatedness, extent of interpersonal interaction, etc., and found in many cases there was too little information provided. This suggests one could not re-use such exercises with any certainty that they were 'the same'. One advantage of psychological tests is knowing exactly how to use them.

RESEARCH AGENDA

- Whether shorter and simpler ACs, with fewer dimensions and exercises, are more or less valid.
- Further research on the contribution of different component exercises to AC validity, and development of models for predicting the overall effect.
- Devise ways of estimating restricted range in multi-stage selection systems.
- More validity research from more varied sectors of employment.

RESERVATIONS ABOUT AC VALIDITY

Criterion contamination

This can be a blatant self-fulfilling prophecy, which the uncritical observer might mistake for proof of validity: Smith returns from the AC with a good rating (predictor) and so gets promoted (criterion). A high correlation between AC rating and promotion is guaranteed, but proves little. Or criterion contamination can be subtler: people who have done well at the AC are deemed suitable for more challenging tasks, develop greater self-confidence, acquire more skills, and consequently get promoted. The AT&T Management Progress Study is one of the few studies that kept AC results secret until calculating the validity coefficient, thereby avoiding contamination.

'Face fits'

Some time ago Klimoski and Strickland (1977) commented on the 'curious homogeneity in the criteria used', namely 'salary growth or progress, promotions above first level, management level achieved and supervisor's ratings of potential'. These criteria 'may have less to do with managerial effectiveness than managerial adaptation and survival'. On this argument ACs answer the question 'Does his/her face fit?' but not the question 'Can he/she do the job well?' Criteria regarded as objective often involve, somewhere, management's opinion, for example promotion or training grade. Some research does use truly objective criteria.

- Seven studies used a sales criterion. Table 10.2 shows validity was much lower, which tends to confirm Klimoski's point.
- Silvester and Dykes (2007) use an objective criterion for politicians: 'swing', percentage change in vote for a given constituency compared with the previous election. Validity was lower than average, although not as low as that for sales.

RESEARCH AGENDA

- More research validating AC against objective criteria.

THE DIMENSION × EXERCISE PROBLEM

The dimension × exercise (D×E) question centres on ratings for dimension × exercise cells: how good Jones was for *influencing others* in the group exercise Doomsday, or how good Smith was at *communication* in the written case study

Armageddon. The D×E problem was first described by Sackett and Dreher (1982), who summarized data from three ACs, in the form of:

- Correlations for the same dimension assessed across different exercises (*convergent validity*).
- Correlation of different dimensions assessed in the same exercise (*divergent validity*). (Figure 2.2, page 33.)

In two sets of data, the convergent validity correlations were effectively zero. This means the assessment centre is not working as it is intended to: the same thing measured in two ways ought to show a positive correlation. Sackett and Dreher's data show ACs were not measuring decisiveness across a range of exercises; they were measuring general performance on each of a series of exercises. But if decisiveness in exercise A does not generalize to decisiveness in exercise B, how can one be sure it will generalize to decisiveness on the job? The fact that different dimensions measured in the same exercise correlated quite highly is less of a problem, because the different dimensions may 'really' correlate. In the 30-odd years since, a great deal of effort has gone into finding an explanation for the D×E problem, and finding a solution, or arguing that there is no problem.

LINE OF RESEARCH 1: TRYING TO FIND DIMENSIONS

Correlation

Woehr and Arthur's (2003) meta-analysis reports averages for convergent validity of 0.34 and for divergent validity of 0.55; convergent validity correlations ought to be higher than divergent, not lower.

Factor analysis

If an AC is intended to assess four main dimensions, then factor analysis of AC ratings 'ought' to find four corresponding factors. What frequently emerged from conventional or *exploratory factor analysis*, however, was a set of factors corresponding to the exercises, not the dimensions. Recent research uses *confirmatory factor analysis* (CFA), to test how well different models fit the data. For an AC with five dimensions and four exercises, five models can be compared:

1. Five dimension factors.
2. Four exercise factors.
3. Five dimension factors, and four exercise factors.
4. Five dimension factors, with 'correlated uniquenesses' corresponding to the four exercises.
5. Four exercise factors and a general factor (of overall performance).

Model 1 is what 'ought' to be found; the ratings ought to reflect dimensions. However, attempts to fit models that include only dimensions always fail completely. Model 2 is what actually happens in many sets of AC ratings from Sackett and Dreher onward: ratings reflect exercises rather than dimensions. Model 5 is a variant of model 2, which adds an overall performance factor to the exercise factors, but does not include any dimension factors. Models 3 and 4 include both dimensions and exercise, meaning ACs are at least partly successful in assessing dimensions. Several authors have tested the fit of these models to 30-plus sets of AC data, with varying results.

- Lievens and Conway (2001) concluded that model 4, including both dimensions and exercises, fits best. Dimensions and exercises each accounted for 34% of variance in rating.
- Lance *et al.* (2004) disagreed and argued that Lievens and Conway's modified dimensions and exercises model exaggerates dimension variance. They concluded that model 5 – exercises plus general factor – best fits 51% of the studies.
- Previous research tested model fit on each set of data in turn. Bowler and Woehr (2006) incorporate all 35 datasets into a single overall six dimensions × six exercises framework, and test model fit on the single meta-analytic dataset. They find a six dimensions and six exercises model fits best. Dimensions account for 22% of variance in ratings, while exercises account for 34%.

These complex analyses suggest AC ratings are dominated by exercise effects, and that ACs are struggling to distinguish separate dimensions of work performance. This is a serious problem. If the AC does not succeed in assessing the six dimensions its planners intend, what is it assessing? And how does it succeed in predicting overall work performance?

LINE OF RESEARCH 2: IMPROVING THE ANALYSIS

Recently three studies have suggested that better analysis of D×E data can find evidence of dimensions being important.

Hoffman, Melchers *et al.* (2011) suggested failure to find dimensions in analysis of ACs arises because dimensions are too similar to be distinguishable, so that fewer and broader dimensions should be used. They combined a larger number of narrow dimensions into a smaller number of broader ones, and found stronger evidence the existence of dimensions.

Monahan *et al.* (2013) proposed the dimension problem is partly caused by 'empirical under-identification', meaning, crudely speaking, not having enough numbers corresponding to dimensions to put into the analysis. They remedied this deficit by adding behavioural checklist data to the dimension ratings, and finding clear statistical evidence of the existence of dimensions. They note that the same effect could probably be achieved by using more exercises to assess each dimension.

Putka and Hoffman (2013) argue that many ACs cannot generate meaning-ful data for D×E cells, because there is only one rater per assessee. This means the rater's view of how Smith scores for persuasiveness in group discussion Armageddon cannot be distinguished from error variance. Only if Smith is rated by two raters can the analysis distinguish true variation in Smith's per-formance from rater error. Putka and Hoffman find data from ACs where each D×E cell is rated by two raters, so can they can capture that part of the persua-siveness variance.

LINE OF RESEARCH 3: IDENTIFYING DEFICIENCIES IN AC PRACTICE

There is a large body of research that sees the D×E problem as caused by poor AC practice, under four main headings: dimensions, exercises, raters and training, and AC design.

Dimensions

Arthur, Day and Woehr (2008) complain that many AC dimensions seem to be validated by 'self-proclamation': this exercise is intended to assess *blue sky thinking*, so that's what it assesses. Arthur *et al.* go on to note the 'Particularly esoteric nature of some of the construct labels, for example seasoned judge-ment, personal breadth', and argue that it is hardly surprising that such dimensions do not emerge clearly from the ratings.

ACs typically try to assess too many dimensions, an average of 11 in the 1980s. Why is 11 dimensions too many? Because the more dimensions are included, the more exercises are needed to assess them. Because the more dimensions, the more likely they are to be highly correlated and possibly redundant. Because theories of the structure of work performance (Chapter 12) tend to list far fewer than 11 dimensions (sometimes only one). ACs now use smaller sets of from three to seven dimensions, which may reduce the D×E problem.

Exercises

AC exercises are another possible source of the D×E problem. Brummel, Rupp and Spain (2009) have noted that AC exercises, like AC dimensions, typically come with little or no information about their reliability or validity. A group discussion about priorities is assumed to assess influence, but no proof is offered – validation by proclamation again. Lievens *et al.* (2006) introduce the concept of *trait activation potential*, and offer an example: a church service has little potential to activate the trait of aggression. Asking assessors to rate a dimension that is not manifest in observable behaviour encourages global rat-ings, i.e. an exercise effect. Lievens *et al.* (2006) match AC dimensions to the FFM model of personality, and then divide convergent validities into correla-tions based on pairs of exercises suited to assessing that dimension, and

Table 10.3   Convergent validity – assessing the same dimension in different exercises – for exercises of high and low relevance to that dimension.

Relevance or trait activation potential	Low		High	
	k	Mean r	k	Mean r
Extraversion	43	0.33	31	0.40
Conscientiousness	35	0.22	39	0.31
Openness	107	0.29	6	0.33
Agreeableness	41	0.27	20	0.30
Neuroticism	15	0.34	3	0.46
Overall	241	0.29	99	0.34

correlations based on pairs of exercises less well suited (having lower *trait activation potential*). Table 10.3 shows that where both exercises are well suited to revealing a factor, the correlation is higher for all five underlying personality factors, although the difference is not large.

Raters and training

Ratings by psychologists and HR specialists show more convergent validity than those from line managers or students (Gaugler *et al.*, 1987). Lievens (2001a) shows that frame of reference (FoR) training, which seeks to give all assessors the same view of what behaviour counts as, for example, decision-making, improves convergent validity.

Design

Some ACs, it has been suggested, require assessors to rate too many people on too many things – the cognitive (over)load hypothesis. Overload forces assessors to simplify the task by rating overall performance rather than aspects of it. Kuncel and Sackett (2014) estimate how variance accounted for by dimensions and exercises would change if the number of exercises per dimension were to increase. The 'good news' is that amount of variance accounted for by dimensions increases rapidly as the number of exercises is increased, reaching 40% for four exercises, and 50% for eight. However, the increase in dimension variance is for dimensions in *general*, not for *specific* dimensions. Increasing variance accounted for by a specific dimension, for example effective communication, is much more difficult, and Kuncel and Sackett's estimates show it does not get beyond 20%, however many exercises are used. This happens because dimensions as assessed by ACs prove to be very highly correlated, so adding more exercises improves prediction of general performance more than prediction of any specific aspect of performance. Kuncel and Sackett's analysis implies the 'average' AC plan of four to five exercises to assess six to seven dimensions is the wrong way round: there should be more exercises, and fewer dimensions.

ARGUMENT 1: 'NEVER MEANT TO BE'

The AC's D×E grid, summarizing *what* is being assessed, and *how*, seemed to many researchers a logical framework to use for analysis, especially as it slotted neatly into the Multi Trait Multi Method model, and the more recent construct/method distinction. However, several authors have argued that the D×E grid was never meant to used in quite this way. Gibbons and Rupp (2009) say that classic AC practice regarded D×E ratings as 'preliminary and tentative at best, to be discussed, reconciled, and modified if necessary when viewed in the light of all available information', *not* as the end product of the process. Instead the AC should generate an overall consensus rating for each dimension, at the key feature of the classic AC – the assessors' conference. The overall consensus was a single set of dimension ratings averaged over exercises, *not* a matrix of D×E ratings. A variant of this argument says that ACs were never meant even to collect ratings after each exercise. This is a puzzling idea for some, who are used to rating As immediately after each exercise, and cannot see how assessors could rate something that happened two days and eight exercises ago. Gibbons and Rupp describe the process: assessors make very detailed notes during each exercise but do not make any ratings until a rating session at the end of the AC. This generates a different sort of D×E matrix – one in which the assessor knows how each assessee has done in all the exercises, and possibly on any tests used.

A second related feature of the AC is the resolution of apparently inconsistent evidence. Gibbons and Rupp describe how D×E information was used in the original OSS assessment. The final OSS report had two parts: 'rating of several key abilities (such as practical intelligence, social relations, and emotional stability) and a narrative description of the person', which would try to resolve any apparent contradictions. If someone shows good leadership in part of the AC, but poorer leadership in others, the assessors' conference tried to make sense of this. The ratings made for dimensions within cells were seen as just the starting point of understanding the candidate as an individual. The idea of a panel of experts resolving apparent inconsistencies is appealing to some, but viewed with scepticism by others, who note that Meehl's (1954) analysis of expert interpretation of complex data found it did not seem all that sophisticated after all (Chapter 4, p. 88). These days ACs do not always include an assessors' conference: Hardison and Sackett's (2007) meta-analysis found it did not seem to make any difference to the AC's predictive validity. The assessors' conference sometimes seems to have an almost ceremonial role of making it evident to all concerned that the decision has been arrived at by careful consideration, involving the expenditure of a lot of time and effort. This is perhaps another example of 'them and us' in selection. Important people are selected by ACs; lesser mortals have to make do with group testing and fixed pass marks.

ARGUMENT 2: THE EXERCISE EFFECT IS NOT RATER ERROR

Lance (2008) notes that people tend to assume the exercise effect shows the AC is not working, and that assessors cannot accurately assess the all-important dimensions, because they are overwhelmed by the exercise effect, which is all error created by unclear dimensions, unsuitable exercises, or their own deficiencies as assessors. Lievens and Lance offer two different, but both quite compelling, reasons for arguing that assessor error is not necessarily the problem. Lievens (2001a) prepared recordings of staged AC performances. Three performers behaved consistently across the three exercises (group discussion, presentation, role play) but showed sharply contrasting levels of performance on the three different dimensions throughout, for example, average on problem-solving, high on interpersonal sensitivity, and low on planning and organizing, in all three exercises. Lievens found assessors were able to perceive these differences, and report them in their ratings. In other words, if there are dimension effects in assessees' performance, assessors will describe them. This tends to imply that in most assessment centres, where assessors apparently do not report dimension effects, it may be because there are none to report: candidates do well overall, or poorly overall.

Lance (2008) offers a statistical argument: that error by definition is random, so if exercise factors are simply measurement error, they cannot correlate with anything. However, exercise factors do correlate with an outcome, namely job performance, and with other predictors such as mental ability, showing exercises factors have both predictive and construct validity. Hence exercise factors cannot be dismissed as merely 'noise' or something that should not happen.

RESEARCH AGENDA

• Further replication of Lievens, with more variations in performance profile, for example six dimensions, including some that are not that clearly differentiated in terms of intercorrelation.

ARGUMENT 3: ACs ARE REALLY SETS OF KEY TASKS, OR WORK SAMPLES

Lance *et al.* (2000) offer a radical perspective on the D×E issue. They argue ACs have never worked as intended: 'assessors form overall judgements of performance in each exercise ... [then] produce separate post-exercise trait ratings because they are required to do so'. If assessors are 'working backwards' in this way, it is hardly surprising dimensions within exercises correlate highly. On Lance *et al.*'s hypothesis, ACs will work if the right exercises have been included, i.e. ones that 'replicate important job behaviors'. Lance argues that the AC is just a collection of tests, distinguished only by including a lot of behavioural demonstration evidence such as group discussions, role plays and simulations. AC planners should abandon the dimension/exercise framework, which just creates needless confusion for both assessor and researcher, and concentrate on choosing the right component exercises.

Several authors, going back to Sackett and Dreher (1982), have suggested that selectors could use a basic form of work analysis to devise ACs around key tasks or roles: chairing meetings, making a presentation, or talking to someone whose work is not satisfactory. One problem might be that jobs differ in the extent to which there are key tasks that can be simulated in the AC. Graduate-entry ACs could not expect As to have any particular skills, even ones as general as chairing meetings.

ARGUMENT 4: THE D×E PROBLEM IS NOT SPECIFIC TO ACs

All the very large volume of research on the D×E problem has focused on ACs. However, Chapter 7 noted that different scales on a questionnaire correlated highly, but that questionnaire measures and others' ratings measures of, for example, extraversion did not (Becker, 1960). Perhaps an 'exercise effect problem' would be found if HR used two different types of interview to assess the same four dimensions. There are several possible reasons why the D×E 'problem' has centred on assessment centres: because the AC approach makes a point of using qualitatively different methods, or because some of its methods are more difficult to use in a neat and precise manner, or perhaps just because it tends to be used for more 'important' selections. One occasionally gets the impression that the D×E problem presents an intellectual challenge to researchers, and that the volume of research may be greater than the issue merits.

Highly correlated dimensions

The D×E literature has incidentally highlighted another problem with ACs' dimensions: that they prove on average to be very highly correlated. Bowler and Woehr's (2006) meta-analysis found the average correlation between dimensions was 0.79, whereas the average correlation between AC exercises was only 0.10. Meriac et al.'s (2008) correlations between seven dimensions have an average of 0.49. Grouping dimensions does not entirely eliminate this: Meriac et al. (2014) found two of their three overall AC dimensions still 'overlapped substantially'. A well-documented rater bias is the 'halo effect': a tendency to form a favourable impression of someone, and then give them very favourable ratings on everything. The halo effect is extensively discussed in the performance appraisal literature (Murphy & Cleveland, 1995), but, curiously, not in that on ACs. Kuncel and Sackett (2014) suggest several other possible reasons for high correlations between dimensions: possible common performance determinants such as mental ability or personality, ability to identify what is being rated (and so consistently produce the 'right' behaviour), and the possibility of a true general factor in work performance (Chapter 12). If the hypothesis of a true general factor in AC performance were confirmed, it could imply that the whole AC enterprise is something of a waste of time, searching for complexities that do not exist, or which cannot be measured accurately.

CONSTRUCT VALIDITY

Lievens *et al.* (2006) take a list of seven generic AC dimensions (Arthur *et al.*'s six plus stress tolerance), and link them to the five-factor model of personality, using a panel of five experts (Figure 10.2). Three FFM factors correspond to one, and only one, AC dimension, while the remaining two correspond to two generic AC dimensions. Figure 10.2 suggests AC research can be linked quite closely to the broader field of personality. Note that the data of Figure 10.2 are expert opinion, not results of actual empirical research.

Three meta-analyses (Scholz & Schuler, 1993; Collins *et al.*, 2003; Meriac *et al.*, 2014) compare AC overall assessment ratings with ability and personality tests, with interesting results (Table 10.4).

- All three find a correlation with mental ability.
- In many ACs assessors can be biased by knowing test scores before rating applicants. However, Scholz and Schuler found four studies where assessors rated without knowing the test scores. Correlation between AC rating and GMA score was not lower, suggesting an absence of bias.
- Better AC overall ratings tend to be linked to extraversion, and (low) neuroticism, but not to conscientiousness, which is surprising as conscientiousness is the personality factor most closely associated with work performance. Few studies have assessed conscientiousness, however.
- Scholz and Schuler find correlations with the FFM fairly small, while correlations for some more specific traits, for example self-confidence, are greater.

AC dimension Personality ⇒	N	E	O	A	C
Communication	–	√	–	–	–
Consideration/awareness	–	–	–	√	–
Drive	–	–	–	–	√
Influencing others	–	√	–	–	–
Organising & planning	–	–	–	–	√
Problem solving	–	–	√	–	–
Stress tolerance	√	–	–	–	–

Figure 10.2   Links between seven generic AC dimensions, and the five-factor model of personality, according to experts. Data from Lievens *et al.* (2006).

Table 10.4 Summary of three meta-analyses of AC construct validity, correlating test with AC rating.

	Collins	Scholz	Meriac			
AC rating	overall	overall	overall	RS	AS	drive
Mental ability	0.65	0.43	0.26	0.21	0.30	0.23
Neuroticism	−0.34	−0.15	−0.03	−0.02	0.06	−0.04
Extraversion	0.47	0.14	0.14	0.14	0.09	0.25
Openness	0.23	0.09	0.10	0.10	0.12	0.08
Agreeableness	0.16	−0.07	0.09	0.06	0.06	0.13
Conscientiousness	nd	−0.06	0.04	0.04	0.07	0.09
Dominance		0.30				
Achievement motivation		0.40				
Social competence		0.41				
Self confidence		0.32				

RS – relational skills; AS – administrative skills.
Scholz & Schuler correct for reliability of both test and AC rating. Collins *et al.* correct for restricted range and AC rating reliability but not test reliability. Meriac *et al.* appear to correct for reliability of both test and AC rating.

- Collins *et al.* find much larger correlations than the other two meta-analyses. They corrected for restricted range which the other two did not.

Meriac *et al.* (2008) also report correlations between GMA and personality with their seven- and three-AC-dimension models (listed on page 000). They confirm a link with mental ability for all seven dimensions, between 0.20 and 0.32, strongest for organizing and planning and problem-solving, weaker for consideration/ awareness of others, which shows a degree of differentiation. Links with personality are much weaker. In the both three-dimensional and seven-dimensional accounts, the only correlation exceeding 0.20 is extraversion × drive.

Hoffman *et al.* (2015) include GMA test and PQs in their meta-analysis of five AC components (v.s.). They partly confirm their hypothesis that GMA will correlate better with case analysis and in tray exercises, which look 'more intellectual', but otherwise do not find much differentiation.

Incremental validity

Schmidt and Hunter (1998) cite Collins *et al.*'s estimate of 0.65 correlation between AC rating and mental ability (Table 10.4), and argue the incremental validity of ACs over GMA tests will be small. However, several empirical studies have shown ACs achieve better validity than psychological tests. Vernon (1950) found CSSB's test battery alone had poor predictive validity. Dayan, Kasten and Fox (2002) report data for the Israeli police force which show incremental validity of a very thorough AC over MA tests. They suggest that Schmidt and Hunter's pessimistic conclusions may only apply to management, not to entry-level selection, and may not apply either to work where dealing with people under very difficult circumstances is crucial. Krause *et al.* (2006) report similar incremental validity of AC over MA tests for senior German police officers. Note also that Collins *et al.*'s estimate of the correlation between AC rating and mental ability is far higher than those of Scholz and Schuler and Meriac *et al.*, which makes the estimate of incremental validity correspondingly lower.

Meriac *et al.* (2008) report a meta-analysis of 48 studies of incremental validity for Arthur *et al.*'s seven generic AC dimensions, and mental ability and personality tests. The seven AC dimensions achieve a validity (i.e. predicting work performance) of 0.40, compared to 0.32 for mental ability, or 0.45 for mental ability and personality. However, the combination of AC, mental ability and personality achieved significantly higher validity at 0.54, confirming that ACs have incremental validity. Dilchert and Ones (2009) use two very large datasets for middle and top-level managers from a range of US employers to estimate the incremental validity of ACs overall, and for each of Arthur *et al.*'s dimensions separately. They confirm that ACs have incremental validity on tests, and make the interesting suggestion that employers might sometimes consider assessing only one of the seven dimensions by AC, depending on what other tests they use, and what outcome they are trying to predict. AC assessment of influencing others has particularly good incremental validity on ability and personality tests.

RESEARCH AGENDA

- Meta-analysis of the intercorrelations between AC and other selection methods, besides tests (from which could be computed estimates of expected incremental validity).
- Review or meta-analysis of actual incremental validity achieved by different combinations of AC and other selection methods.

FAIRNESS AND THE ASSESSMENT CENTRE

The AC has been regarded as a fair and 'safe' selection method. However, meta-analysis by Dean, Roth and Bobko (2008) finds quite large adverse impact on African Americans ($d = 0.52$) and Hispanic Americans ($d = 0.40$). Dean *et al.*'s analysis confirmed earlier findings for gender, showing women tend to do slightly better in ACs ($d = 0.19$) than men. It appears that ACs will not entirely avoid adverse impact problems in the USA. Falk and Fox (2014) report an AC for education management in Israel which showed quite large adverse impact ($d = 0.64$) on Arab applicants, compared with Jewish applicants.

RESEARCH AGENDA

• Data on gender, ethnicity and age differences in AC performance in Britain and Europe.

KEY POINTS

In Chapter 10 you have learned the following:

• AC exercises can also be sorted into six or seven broad categories.
• Assessment centres (ACs) are tailor-made so can assess a range of dimensions by a range of exercises.
• ACs have a conceptual matrix linking dimensions to exercises.
• AC dimensions can be sorted into six or seven broad categories.
• ACs achieve fairly good validity, allowing for restriction of range.
• ACs are very complex, making it difficult to analyse how they work.
• AC validity may have an element of circularity because they tend to compare what management thinks of As during the AC with what management thinks of As subsequently 'on the job'.
• The small number of studies that have used 'objective' criteria may find lower validity.
• ACs are intended to assess dimensions as exhibited in a number of exercises (convergent validity), but appear in practice to assess global proficiency in a series of exercises.
• AC construct validity research shows ACs correlate quite strongly with mental ability, and to lesser extent with personality.
• ACs create adverse impact on minorities in the USA, but none by gender.

KEY REFERENCES

Anstey (1977) describes a long-term follow up of the British CSSB.

Becker et al. (2011) present a meta-analysis of AC validity in German-speaking regions.

Bowler & Woehr (2006) present a six-dimension by six-exercise framework for AC research, and describe some research on model fitting.

Bray & Grant (1966) describe the classic AT&T Management Progress Study.

Dean et al. (2008) present a meta-analysis of ethnicity and gender differences in AC ratings.

Gaugler et al. (1987) present an early meta-analysis and VGA of AC validity. (Hardison & Sackett's later meta-analysis has not yet been published in English).

Lance et al. (2000) argue that ACs do not work as planned and should be regarded as collections of work sample tests.

Lievens & Conway (2001) present a detailed structural equation modelling account of the AC convergent/discriminant validity problem (suitable for those interested in statistics).

Meriac, Hoffmann & Woehr (2014) present an analysis of AC dimensions.

Silvester & Dykes (2007) describe an AC used to select would-be Conservative MPs before the 2005 election.

Thornton & Rupp (2006) provide a detailed account of AC practice.

Woehr & Arthur (2003) discuss ways of solving the discriminant/convergent validity problem.

CHAPTER 11

Emotional intelligence and other methods

'Success in work is 80% dependent on emotional intelligence'

There are eight miscellaneous selection methods that do not fit neatly into any other main category: emotional intelligence, situational judgement, education, work samples, self-assessments, physical tests, drug-use testing, and social networks. Education is probably the oldest of these, having been used in Imperial China for many centuries to select public officials. Work samples can be traced back to Munsterburg's work in 1913 for the Boston streetcar system. An early situational judgement test was the George Washington Test of Social Intelligence of 1926. Formal physical tests have replaced more casual physical assessments since the 1970s to conform with fair employment legislation. Drug-use testing was introduced in the USA as part of President Reagan's 1986 drug-free workplace policy. Emotional intelligence can also be dated very precisely, to Goleman's (1995) book. The most recent arrival is the social network website, such as Facebook.

EMOTIONAL INTELLIGENCE

Being able to understand others and get along with them, it can be very plausibly claimed, is both a vital skill in work and one which very intelligent people often lack (what might be termed the 'geek hypothesis'). Since 1995 this supposed deficiency in the selector's library of tests has been filled by emotional intelligence (EI). Numerous measures have appeared; training schemes have been developed; EI has even been added to the school curriculum. EI is said to bring many benefits: finding better leaders, creating better teamwork, finding people who cope better with stress, even finding people who have morally superior values. EI is seen as trainable, so less fixed than GMA.

Assessing EI

There are actually two quite different types of EI measure, illustrated by the fictitious items in Table 11.1. The first type, in items 1 to 3, is a real 'test',

Personnel Selection: Adding Value Through People – A Changing Picture,
Sixth Edition. Mark Cook.
© 2016 John Wiley & Sons, Ltd. Published 2016 by John Wiley & Sons, Ltd.

Table 11.1   Some (fictitious) items for assessing emotional intelligence.

1. Someone you are talking to doesn't look you in the eye. What is a likely explanation of this?
   a. he/she is not telling the truth
   b. he/she respects you
   c. he/she likes you

2. Look at these three pictures of the same person. In which one does she look happy?
   A   B   C

3. What mood might be helpful when generating a lot of new ideas in a group?
   fear   very helpful   5   4   3   2   1   not at all helpful
   anger   very helpful   5   4   3   2   1   not at all helpful
   contentment   very helpful   5   4   3   2   1   not at all helpful

4. I take the lead in groups   always often sometimes occasionally never

5. I find it difficult to control my moods always often sometimes occasionally never

6. People listen to what I say   always often sometimes occasionally never

with right and wrong answers. It resembles a GMA test, but all the questions concern dealing with people. It may have a time limit. The main EI *test* is the Mayer–Salovey–Caruso Emotional Intelligence Test (MSCEIT). The second type of EI measure, in items 4 to 6, may look familiar. There are no right and wrong answers; there is no time limit; people are reporting their own thoughts, feelings and behaviour. This is an EI *questionnaire*, sometimes described as a 'mixed' EI measure. It also looks very much like a personality questionnaire. Joseph and Newman's (2010) meta-analysis found ability EI and mixed EI have a true correlation (corrected for error in both measures) of only 0.26, indicating they cannot be regarded as assessing the same thing.

VALIDITY OF EI MEASURES

Predictive validity

Joseph and Newman's (2010) meta-analysis correlated both ability and mixed EI with work performance, with surprising results; ability EI correlated relatively poorly with work performance (0.18), whereas mixed EI correlated very well (0.47). Joseph and Newman did not, however, recommend everyone to use mixed EI measures for selection; rather the opposite: 'we warn against their use due to their unknown content and theoretical value'. In a second meta-analysis (Joseph *et al.*, 2015) they add some new researches but exclude ones that had not defined work performance by supervisor ratings, and found a much lower validity of $p = 0.29$.

Construct validity

In their second paper Joseph *et al.* (2015) address the issue of the 'unknown content' of mixed EI measures they had raised in 2010, and explain why they had warned against their use, despite their apparently high validity. They note that mixed EI measures seem to have been produced by 'heterogeneous domain sampling'. *Domain sampling* means producing a new conscientiousness test by taking or adapting items from existing conscientiousness measures. *Heterogeneous domain sampling* means putting together a new test by taking items from a range of existing tests, to create what Joseph *et al.* describe as a 'grab bag' of questions. A similar phrase in Britain is 'cobbled together'. Joseph *et al.* note that discussion of the construct validity of mixed EI is made difficult by the fact that the tests' publishers do not allow any items to be quoted, making the tests something of a mystery, and buying them something of an act of faith. Joseph *et al.* examine what the tests' authors have said about EI, as well as item content; they look in particular for overlap with other tests and constructs that have already been shown to predict work performance. They find seven themes in all. The first four are very familiar: extraversion, conscientiousness, neuroticism, and general mental ability. The fifth is one their own 2010 meta-analysis had identified, ability EI (which correlates 0.26 with mixed EI). The remaining two are less familiar: general self-efficacy and self-rated work performance.

Self-efficacy was mentioned in Chapter 7: the belief that one is good at selling, or managing staff, or planning research. Chapter 7 noted that self-efficacy tests have direction of cause problems: do people sell a lot because they believe they are good at it? or do they believe they are good at it because they sell a lot? Generalized self-efficacy is the belief that one can succeed at things in general: co-operating with others, understanding others, having a positive self-image, etc.

The seventh construct is self-rated performance, in work or similar activities. Joseph and Nielsen note that some mixed EI test items are in effect self-reports of the person's own work performance, on the lines of (but not actually identical to): *I feel I can produce a lot of good work* or *I perform well in teams* or *I have accomplished many things in the last year*. As predictors of work performance, these are getting rather circular.

Joseph *et al.* offer some fairly critical observations on the role of some test publishers: 'Proprietary measurement is … a barrier to scientific progress' because it 'hides the survey items and thereby can hide the fact that a measure was derived by heterogeneous domain sampling' and that parts of the FFM are 'forced into anonymity by measurement copyrights'. They seem to be suggesting that some EI measures include a lot of material that is not all that new, and can be obtained much more cheaply by using existing personality tests.

Incremental validity

Joseph *et al.* (2015) conduct a series of new meta-analyses to estimate the correlations between mixed EI, the seven constructs, and work performance, then use MASEM analysis (Chapter 12, page 258) to estimate overlap and incremental validity. The analysis indicates mixed EI measures add nothing to the prediction that can be made from the seven constructs. It also shows that most of the overlap is with the three FFM personality factors. Critics' impression that many EI measures are little more than PQs, under a new name, seems to be confirmed.

Fakability

Grubb and McDaniel (2007) show that the Bar-On Emotional Quotient Inventory, a widely used PQ format EI measure, is easily faked; students directed to complete the EQI as if applying for a job increased their total 'EQ' by nearly one whole SD. European data show that applicants get much higher EI scores than present employees (in the same organization), suggesting that applicants may be faking good (Lievens, Klehe & Libbrecht, 2011).

The 'predictors' fallacy

Goleman made the famous claim that success at work is '80% dependent on emotional intelligence and only 20% on IQ'. It is true that GMA tests account for only 25% of the variance in work performance; it follows logically that something else accounts for the other 75%. But it does not follow logically that the something else is EI. Nor is it very likely; accounting for 75% of the variance requires EI to correlate with work performance 0.87, far higher than any test or set of tests has ever achieved. Landy (2005) suggests one basis for the popularity of EI may be the feeling that 'We can't perfectly explain behaviour so we need more predictors.' He also points to the snag with EI measures: 'But shouldn't these new predictors actually improve prediction?'

Adverse impact

EI is popular in part because people think it will avoid all the problems created by GMA tests, especially adverse impact on ethnic minorities. Information on ethnicity is as yet rather sparse; research on students by van Rooy, Alonso and Viswesvaran (2005) using an EIQ finds African Americans and Hispanic Americans score higher than white Americans, suggesting adverse impact may not be a problem.

Being able to get on with others at work is very important, and selectors do need some way of assessing it. Reinventing the PQ, and calling it EI, is unlikely to suit; the deficiencies of PQs were noted at some length in Chapter 7: low validity, fakability and lack of self-insight. Other approaches may prove more promising.

Other report

Table 5.1 (on page 95) shows the traditional reference is sometimes used to ask about human relations skills. EI may be assessable by ratings from peers or subordinates. Ford and Tisak (1983) devised a peer nomination measure for school pupils, for example, *Who in the class would be best at persuading the teacher to give less homework?*

Demonstration by test

Test format EI measures like the MSCEIT may have more promise, but may also have construct validity problems. EI tests have actually been around since the 1920s, under the name 'social intelligence'; they fell out of favour precisely because they correlated so well with GMA that they did not seem to be measuring anything new (Landy, 2005). Another possibility is the situational judgement test, discussed in the next section.

Behavioural demonstration

Group discussions and role plays can often assess important aspects of EI. For some jobs, work samples can be devised, for example dealing with a query or complaint by telephone. One can outline some possible, more elaborate behavioural tests of EI, and note the amount of research that would be needed to make them work. Negotiation is important in many managerial jobs: getting the best deal for the organization. One approach could be an elaborate simulation, with a cast of role players, who respond to the negotiator's every move with the 'right' response, for example if A gets aggressive, clam up. But what is the 'right' response? Detailed analysis of many real negotiations will be needed to generate a plausible script, based on what actually succeeds or fails in real negotiations. Real negotiations can last a long time so a very long and very complicated script will be needed. Or else researchers can analyse separate components of the negotiation process, for example non-verbal communication (receiving) – how good is A at recognizing wavering? – and NVC (sending) – how good is A at not giving anything away by tone of voice or facial expression? This research would take a long time, and cost a great deal to do properly. It would be so much quicker and easier to use a short EIQ with questions like *I am good at getting what I want* and *People say I can drive a hard bargain.*

RESEARCH AGENDA

There does not seem to be much need for any more research on EI, except perhaps to collect more data on gender and ethnicity differences.

SITUATIONAL JUDGEMENT TESTS

Table 11.2 shows a typical problem from a situational judgement test (SJT). SJT is a *method*, which can be used to study a wide range of *constructs*, including honesty, personality, or suitability for, for example, police work. SJTs also include various measures of supervisor judgement, dating back to the How Supervise? measure used in the 1940s.

There is an important difference between SJTs, and GMA tests. There is only one correct answer to '2 + 2' (except in Orwell's *Nineteen Eighty-Four*), but what of the question in Table 11.2? The 'right' answer today is 'negotiate' because that is what Western society values, and all the books on conflict resolution recommend. But it is easy to list societies, past and present, where answer (a) would be considered the 'right' one. Correct answers to SJTs are defined by expert panels, or sometimes by the consensus of the normative sample, which tends to make the test an exercise in conformity. (It also becomes impossible to include any 'difficult' questions.) The same issues arise with some emotional intelligence tests. SJTs can ask a different question, not *What is the best thing to do?* but *What would you do?* The former tends to make the SJT a test of ability, and nearly doubles its correlation with GMA; the latter makes it more a measure of personality and increases its correlation with the FFM (McDaniel *et al.*, 2007). Type of instruction does not affect correlation with work performance.

Sometimes rating formats are used. McDaniel, Kepes and Banks (2011) note that rating scales can introduce two problems in SJT scoring, arising from the fact that people who make more extreme ratings – 1 or 7 on a seven-point scale – tend to get poorer scores, because when they get the answer wrong, they get it more wrong. The first problem is that (some) people are coached not to give extreme ratings, thereby increasing their scores. The second problem is that African Americans on average use the ends of the scale more, so tend to get lower scores. A simple adjustment to the scoring system, called standardization (Box 11.1), can eliminate both problems.

Table 11.2   A fictitious situational judgement test question.

One of your team at work is taking a lot of time off, because he says his partner is unwell. You need him to work harder or your team will not reach its target.
What is the best thing to do? What is the worst thing to do?
a. Tell him to come to work on time every day or you will get him terminated.
b. Sympathize.
c. Seek to negotiate an agreement that he will reduce his absence by at least 50%.
d. Wait, because his partner will probably soon get better.

Alternative response formats:
A. What would you do?
B. Rate each each possibility on the scale 7 – very good idea to 1 – very bad idea.

Box 11.1   Standardization

Each person's set of scores is converted into standard scores, using that person's mean and standard deviation across all his/her ratings. This retains information about the person's ordering of the options, but removes the problematic effect of extreme rating values.

More elaborate SJTs have been devised, for example for police work in Germany, that use video rather than paper and pencil, and which 'branch' (Kanning *et al.*, 2006). Would-be police officers first choose what to do on encountering a group of football hooligans (confront/ignore/send for back-up). If they choose to confront, they are presented with a further set of choices for dealing with the resulting aggression. Lievens, De Corte and Westerveld (2012) describe an SJT for police work in Belgium that presents As with a filmed scenario, for example a domestic disturbance, possible fight, locked door, man shouting at the police to go away, at which point the action stops, and A has to make his/her reply. (Saying *OK I'll come back later* gets a very low mark.)

Validity

McDaniel *et al.*'s (2007) meta-analysis (Table 11.3) shows SJTs achieve a modest level of validity. Although SJTs have been used since the 1920s, not much was known until recently about what they measure, and why they predict work performance. McDaniel *et al.*'s meta-analysis also reports correlations between SJTs, GMA and personality. Table 11.3 shows SJTs correlate with GMA, and with three FFM factors. McDaniel *et al.* also estimate incremental validity of SJTs over GMA and FFM. They give some small incremental validity on PQ (ca 0.07) and GMA (ca 0.04) separately, but virtually none on the two combined.

Table 11.3   Meta-analysis of criterion and construct validity of SJTs.

	k	N	r	ρ
Work performance	118	24.8K	0.20	0.26
GMA	95	30.8K	0.29	0.32
Neuroticism	49	19.3K	−0.19	−0.22
Extraversion	25	11.4K	0.13	0.14
Openness	19	4.5K	0.11	0.13
Agreeableness	51	25.5K	0.22	0.25
Conscientiousness	53	31.3K	0.23	0.27

Data from McDaniel *et al.* (2007).
ρ = correlation corrected for reliability of work performance measure, or of GMA or FFM measure but not for range restriction.

Adverse impact

Whetzel, McDaniel and Nguyen (2008) report a meta-analysis of the adverse impact of SJTs in the USA. There is some adverse impact on African Americans, but less ($d = 0.38$) than for GMA tests. There is smaller adverse impact on Hispanic Americans ($d = 0.24$) and Asian Americans ($d = 0.29$). Women on average score slightly higher than men ($d = 0.11$). However, the size of the effect depends on whether the SJT is intended to assess ability or personality.

RESEARCH AGENDA

- More research on coachability of SJTs.
- Whether more elaborate SJTs using recorded scenarios achieve better validity, or greater acceptability, or reduced adverse impact, compared with simple paper-and-pencil forms.

EDUCATION

It is useful to distinguish amount, in years, and achievement, in marks or grades. Employers in Britain often specify a university degree; professional training schemes almost always do. American employers used to require high school graduation, but fewer do now. Ng and Feldman (2008) report a meta-analysis of links between amount of education and various indices of behaviour at work. More educated employees in North America do better work, are more creative, show more OCB, less drug use, less workplace aggression, and less absence. They do not differ in punctuality, training performance, or general CWB. The relationships are generally rather small: the largest correlation, corrected for restricted range and outcome reliability, is 0.28, and many are less than 0.10. Selecting for education level is quick and cheap, and across a large workforce can achieve substantial savings. The US military finds high school completion useful for predicting completion of basic training: people who 'drop out' of school also tend to drop out of training. (Sackett & Mavor, 2003). Roth et al. (1996) showed validity of GPA for predicting work performance decays very rapidly, falling from 0.45 one year after graduation to 0.11 six years after.

Education tests have fallen foul of American fair employment laws in a big way. Some US minorities do less well at school, so more fail to complete high school. Roth and Bobko (2000) reported an analysis of ethnicity differences in GPA for 7,000 students at an American university, which found a large difference that would create major adverse impact. The difference increased sharply from first to third year, where it amounted to $d = 0.78$. Adverse impact means the employer has to prove the job really needs the educational level or qualifications specified. This has often proved difficult. Meritt-Haston and

Wexley's (1983) review of 83 US court cases found educational requirements were generally ruled unlawful for skilled or craft jobs, supervisors, and management trainees, but were accepted for police and academics. Chapter 1 described systems of setting minimum qualifications, including education, designed to select suitable As without excluding people, especially minorities, who could do the job. In Britain using education as a selection method tends to be criticized as being tied up with social class.

Berry, Gruys and Sackett (2006) use the large and representative National Longitudinal Survey of Youth to check whether education makes a good substitute for tested mental ability. They confirm that GMA and years of education are highly correlated (0.63). Nevertheless, using amount of education (not grades) turns out to be a poor substitute for testing MA. The widely used high school diploma requirement only excludes the lowest 5% to 10% in tested MA. Even requiring the equivalent of a PhD, achieved by only 2% of people, only excludes the lower 70% of the MA distribution. However, Berry *et al.* do find selection by education creates less adverse impact on minorities than ability tests.

RESEARCH AGENDA

- Some British and European research on the relationship between amount of education, or educational achievement, and work performance.

WORK SAMPLE TESTS

A work sample test familiar to most adults is the driving test. It does not try to infer ability to drive from reaction time, or eye–hand co-ordination, or personality, or past behaviour. It places you in a car and requires you to drive it from A to B, while obeying all the rules in the Highway Code. Work samples are widely used for skilled and semi-skilled jobs. Work samples are observed and rated, using checklists. Work samples can usually achieve good inter-rater reliability: Lance *et al.* (2000) quoted 0.81 to 0.98. A specialized type of work sample is the simulation, for example of flying or nuclear power plant operation. These can assess, thoroughly, and safely, As' ability to cope with emergencies.

Validity

Roth, Bobko and McFarland (2005) report a new meta-analysis of work sample research, not so much because there has been a lot of new research – they found only 54 validities – but because they considered previous analyses lacking in detail, or over-inclusive. Roth *et al.* exclude job knowledge and situational judgement tests as not being true work samples. Average raw validity was 0.26, rising to 0.33 when corrected for reliability of work performance measure. This is, as they note, well below Hunter and Hunter's widely cited (1984) estimate of 0.54. Virtually all the studies use present employee samples, not applicant samples, so may suffer restricted range, and may underestimate validity for applicants. Roth *et al.* found an interesting moderator variable – date. Validity tended to be higher before 1982 than after. Recall that GATB validity and AC validity also seem to have fallen over time (Chapters 2 and 10).

Construct and incremental validity

Schmidt and Hunter (1998) reported a correlation of 0.38 between work samples and general mental ability. Roth *et al.*'s (2005) meta-analysis confirmed Schmidt and Hunter's estimate, finding work samples correlate with GMA moderately (0.32) and situational judgement tests slightly (0.13). There are little or no data for any other measure. Schmidt and Hunter concluded the incremental validity of work sample tests over GMA test will be high (0.12), one of the highest values they cite. The combination of work sample and GMA tests is one of the three that Schmidt and Hunter recommended employers to consider using. Roth *et al.* (2005) offer an estimate for incremental validity of work samples over GMA tests which is lower than Schmidt and Hunter's, at 0.06, but warn that their estimate makes a lot of assumptions and is not very safe.

Domain validity

Work samples can achieve domain validity in some circumstances. If HR can list every task in the job, and devise work samples to match, HR can then make statements along the lines of 'X has mastered 80% of the job's demands'. X is being compared with the job's requirements, not with other As. This avoids many problems. HR do not need large samples; X may be the one and only person who does that job but HR can still say X has mastered 80% of it. People who have only mastered 60% are given more training until they have mastered enough to be allowed to start work. Unfortunately many jobs cannot be analysed in sufficient detail for this approach.

True work samples can only be used if the person has already mastered the job's skills; it is clearly pointless (and dangerous) giving a driving test to someone who cannot drive. Three variations on the work sample theme can be used with inexperienced As.

Trainability tests

Trainability tests assess how well applicants can learn a new skill. The instructor gives standardized instructions and a demonstration, of , for example, using an industrial drilling machine, then rates A's efforts using a checklist: *does not tighten chuck sufficiently*, or *does not use coolant*. A meta-analysis of trainability test validity (Robertson & Downs, 1989) found they predicted training success quite well, job performance less well. Roth, Buster and Bobko (2011) say that it is widely supposed that trainability tests have good validity and create little adverse impact, the two things everyone in HR in the USA really wants. Bobko *et al.* are, however, somewhat sceptical and note the validity data suffer from small samples, and *criterion contamination*, which means essentially 'teaching the test'. They describe four American examples of trainability tests in the public sector which all generate large adverse impact on minority Americans, *d* ranging from 0.80 to 1.21, as large as is found in tests of GMA.

In-tray or in-basket tests

These are a management work sample: As deal with a set of letters, memos, notes, reports and phone messages (Figure 11.1). As' performance is usually rated both overall and item by item. Overall evaluation checks whether As sort items by priority, and notice any connections between items. Multiple choice form can speed up scoring and avoid rater error. IBTs are a *method*, which can be used to assess many different *constructs*. Whetzel, Rotenberry and McDaniel (2014) suggest IBTs may assess: decision-making, planning and organizing, and managing others, which includes delegation, directing subordinates, and consideration, but note that most studies 'only assert attributes measured', i.e. have no proof that IBTs actually do measure them – the same problem that many AC exercises suffer from. Whetzel *et al.*'s meta-analysis, however, only presents data on 'the validity of' the IBT, because there are not enough studies using IBTs to assess any particular named constructs to allow any comparison. Whetzel *et al.* find IBTs can be scored with reasonable reliability, and achieve an average corrected validity, across 24 studies, of 0.42.

IBT/1

From: V Wordy MICE CEMH FIME
                         Engineering Director

To: I Prior
                         Assistant General Manager

I am in receipt of your memorandum of 15th November concerning the necessity for more rapid progress on the revised layout of Number 4 Component Assembly Area and am fully cognisant of the urgency of this matter myself. My strenuous efforts in this respect are not however being assisted the calibre of some of the personnel allocated to myself for this purpose A particular obstacle with which I am currently faced lies in the persistent absenteeism of certain members of the workforce who appear to have little interest in contributing an effort commensurate with their present rates of pay and who make baseless complaints to the shop steward whenever any member of staff has the temerity to tell them to make more of an effort. The designated complement of shop floor workers for Assembly Area under the new establishment of 5th October is just adequate for the Area's requisites on the strict understanding that the full complement are in fact present and available for work as opposed to for example absenting themselves for lengthy smoking breaks in the male toilet facilities. Efforts on the part of myself and my foreman to instil a sense of purpose and discipline into a workforce sadly lacking any semblance of either have not so far, I am sorry to say, received what I would consider inadequate backing from the management. As your memorandum of 15th November has identified the implantation of the revised layout for Number 4 component Assembly Area as having a very high grade of priority and a target date for its completion which is can only be characterised as verging on the unrealistic, I find myself having no option but to take drastic action in order to conform with your present schedule. I have therefore dismissed with immediate effect two men found taking unauthorised breaks from work. I trust that I will receive your full backing for an action which I fully believe to be long overdue. At out next Interdepartmental Liaison Forum I will present my fifteen point plan for improving staff morale and discipline, based upon the principles of holistic integration coupled to an expansion of the static surveillance network.

Figure 11.1   A sample item from an in-tray test.

They correlate 0.26 with GMA, which suggests they are not simply disguised intelligence tests. Like most work samples, IBTs have high face validity, and are generally accepted by applicants.

Webcam tests

Webcam tests have become popular in recent years. Oostrom *et al.* (2011) present data from the Netherlands on a webcam test of leadership. Students are presented with a vignette of , for example, an underperforming employee who has been summoned into their presence, and who says 'You wanted to talk to me about something'. The person tested has to respond as if this were a real encounter. This is a role-play test, as used in many ACs, its distinguishing feature being that it can be administered over the Internet, which saves time and money. Oostrom *et al.* found the webcam test could predict actual leadership moderately well. Questions of faking or coaching do not arise with behavioural tests of assertiveness; if the A can act assertively, that is all the selectors need to know. The same may not hold true for all attributes.

Limitations of work sample tests

Work samples are necessarily job-specific so a streetcar system – like the Boston, Massachusetts, network that used the first work sample – will need different work samples for drivers, inspectors, mechanics, electricians, and so on, which will prove expensive. Work samples are best for specific concrete skills, and may not work so well where the work is diverse or abstract or involves other people. Work samples are usually administered one to one, and need expert raters, which makes them expensive.

Adverse impact

Roth *et al.* (2008) note that it is commonly assumed in the USA that work sample tests do not create any adverse impact on minorities, or at least not much. The 'not much' view derives from Schmitt, Clause and Pulakos (1996), and has three snags. Their *d* value was 0.38, which is quite large enough to cause some problems. It was derived from a combination of three different sorts of measures – work samples, job knowledge and situational judgement tests – which had been pooled because there was not enough research to analyse them separately. Most seriously, Schmitt *et al.*'s estimate falls into the Bobko–Roth fallacy of trying to estimate adverse impact on applicants by collecting data on differences in present employees. Roth *et al.* (2008) find enough research to compare present employees and applicants on work sample tests; their meta-analysis confirms the *d* of 0.38 for white/African American present employees, but finds a *d* of 0.73 in 21 samples of applicants who had not yet been screened by work sample or any other test. Using work sample tests on real applicants may create substantial adverse impact. Roth *et al.* found one moderator variable: the *constructs* the work sample *method* was being used to assess. Work samples intended to assess mental ability or job knowledge (for example examining engineering drawings) created large adverse impact, whereas work samples used to assess oral communication, leadership or persuasion (for example counselling a subordinate with a problem) created little. Chapter 13 shows work samples are readily accepted by applicants. Work samples are less often the subject of litigation in the USA (Terpstra, Mohamed & Kethley, 1999), and even less often the subject of successful litigation.

RESEARCH AGENDA

• Research on the validity of webcam tests.

SELF-ASSESSMENTS

Self-assessments are the simplest form of self-report. PQs ask up to 36 questions to estimate how dominant someone is; interviews last up to an hour. A self-assessment asks only for a rating on a seven-point scale: *How dominant are you?*

Validity

Mabe and West (1982) analysed 43 studies and reported an average operational validity of 0.36. They concluded self-assessments had highest validity when:

• They were given anonymously – not a lot of use in selection!
• People were told self-assessments would be compared with objective tests, which means either giving a test or lying to As.
• People were comparing themselves with fellow workers, which again tends to make them impractical for selection.

Dunning, Heath and Suls (2004) argue that workplace self-assessments are frequently wildly optimistic. They note especially that senior managers often have an inflated view of their own abilities to successfully enter new markets, to launch new products, or to identify properties or companies to acquire. Kruger and Dunning (1999) find that people who actually score in the bottom 25% on tests of logic or grammar place themselves around the 60th percentile, because they are unable to identify poor performance, in others or in themselves, which has been called the *Dunning–Kruger effect*.

RESEARCH AGENDA

• More research on the 'Dunning–Kruger effect' in self-assessments, in real selection.

PHYSICAL TESTS

Some jobs require strength, agility, or endurance. Some jobs require dexterity. For some jobs attractive appearance is, explicitly or implicitly, a requirement.

Strength

Measures of physique and physical performance are many, but intercorrelate very highly, so factor analysis concludes there are only three main factors: strength, endurance and movement quality, of which movement quality is more important in sport than work. Some research uses laboratory-type physical tests, designed to measure a single specific aspect of physical performance. Other research uses simulations of key job activities, for example *Run a quarter of a mile then wrestle a heavy object to the ground*, simulating a police officer chasing and catching a suspect, which involves many aspects of physical ability.

Validity

Schmitt *et al.*'s (1984) VGA yielded a raw validity of 0.32 for physical tests, used mainly to select unskilled labour. Physical tests also predict whether the employee can cope with the job without finding it too demanding, or even suffering injury. Chaffin (1974) found the greater the discrepancy between a worker's strength and the physical demands of the job, the more likely the worker is to suffer a back injury – a notorious source of lost output in industry.

Adverse impact

Courtright *et al.* (2013) report a new meta-analysis of sex differences in physical tests. They confirm that there are very large differences between men and women on Hogan's muscular strength and physical endurance dimensions: d values are 1.8 and 2.0. However, the analysis also finds that some aspects of muscular strength show much smaller differences, so it is possible some types of physical work can be done equally well by males and females. They compared specific physical tests, based on the Hogan dimensions, with global simulations, of the suspect-chasing variety, and found no difference in validity. The most interesting part of Courtright *et al.*'s meta-analysis was the effect of training, which improves physical performance by around $d = 1$, slightly more in women than men. Training does not eliminate the sex difference, but can raise women's performance sufficiently to meet a pass mark, and not be excluded from further consideration.

Disability discrimination laws make it essential to prove thoroughly that a job requires particular physical abilities. Terpstra *et al.*'s (1999) review of fair employment cases in the USA found physical tests featured three or four times as often as would be expected from their estimated frequency of use. Hence physical tests need to be carefully chosen and validated.

Rayson, Holliman and Belyavin (2000) described a physical testing programme for infantry soldiers in the British Army which encountered a serious problem. The army wants to recruit women into all branches, but also sets demanding physical standards. It first listed the main generic physical tasks the infantry soldier must be able to perform. These include the 'single lift', lifting a 44 kilogram box of ammunition from the ground to the back of truck, and the 'loaded march', covering 13 kilometres carrying a 25 kilogram pack. However, the core tasks could not be used as actual work samples on grounds of safety – suppose an applicant dropped the ammunition box on his/her foot – and practicality – the tests will be used in city centre recruiting offices, while route marches need open country and take too long. Accordingly tests of muscle strength, muscle endurance, body size, aerobic fitness, and fat-free mass were devised which were safe and practical; these proxy tests were intended to predict ability to complete the core tasks. Unfortunately some of the proxy tests showed differential validity: they worked well for men but not for women, which meant they could not be used.

Dexterity

Dexterity is needed for assembly work, which is generally semi-skilled or unskilled, and also for some professional jobs, notably dentistry and surgery. The general aptitude test battery (Chapter 6) includes two dexterity tests. Many work sample and trainability tests also assess dexterity. Ghiselli's (1966b) meta-analysis reported moderate validities of dexterity tests for vehicle operation, trades and crafts, and industrial work.

Physical attractiveness

Research on interviewing (Chapter 4) shows that appearance and attractive-ness often affect selectors' decisions. But is appearance or attractiveness a legitimate part of the person specification for any job? Acting and modelling certainly. Appearance or attractiveness is often an implicit requirement for receptionists; many advertisements specify 'smart appearance', 'pleasant manner', etc. Appearance, shading into 'charisma', is probably also important for selling, persuading, and influencing jobs.

RESEARCH AGENDA

- Whether height or attractiveness are legitimate requirements for any type of work.

DRUG USE TESTING

The 1990 (US) National Household Survey reports that 7% of adult employees use illegal drugs. In the USA testing applicants for illegal drug use is widely used, but controversial. The standard method is chemical analysis of urine samples. Large-scale research in the US Postal Service (Normand, Salyards, and Mahoney, 1990) found drug users more likely to be absent, or to suffer involuntary turnover, but not to have more accidents. Critics have argued that the link between drug use and work performance is tenuous. In correlational terms, relationships were very small (0.08 at best), and account for minute amounts of variance (0.6% at best). Critics argue this is nowhere near enough to justify the intrusion on As' privacy and civil rights. Other critics suggest many employers adopt drug-testing programmes to project an image, of control, or of corporate responsibility and concern for social problems, or as a convenient way to avoid employing 'dropouts'. Acceptability of drug testing depends on perceptions of danger (Murphy, Thornton and Prue, 1991); it is seen as fair for surgeons, police officers, or airline pilots, but not justified for janitors, farmworkers, or clerks.

RESEARCH AGENDA

• Whether drug use affects work performance, or behaviour in the workplace.

SOCIAL NETWORKING WEBSITES

Facebook and similar social networking sites (SNWs) allow people to describe themselves in words and images; many HR departments have started to use SNWs to screen applicants. This has many apparent advantages as a selection device: very cheap to use, instantly available, can be used to confirm CV and to see what others think of the applicant. It can reveal so-called 'faux pas': _ getting drunk, gambling, wearing a Nazi uniform. It can reveal information the prospective employer feels they ought to know: that the A 'bad mouths' his/her present employer, or discloses confidential information. However, assessing As through SNWs has many disadvantages, some obvious, others less so.

- Not everyone uses SNWs. Surveys show 90% in the 18–24 age range in the USA do, so the system will work well for graduate recruitment. Coverage will be less complete for older As, and for poorer As, which tends often to mean also ethnic minority As, which could raise issues of possible discrimination.
- SNW information is completely unstandardized: it is what the 'applicants' choose to tell you, in whatever form they choose, which makes comparing As very difficult.
- SNW information will often tell HR things they should not know at the sifting stage of selection: sex, race, age, disability.
- SNW information also gives scope for biases that do not break the law in most countries, but may lead to poor selection: physical appearance, including attractiveness, shared interests and pastimes, attitudes and politics.

- Presently SNW content is likely to be a mixture of some people describing themselves fairly frankly, for their own circle of friends, and of others presenting the image they think will help get them a job. HR, however, does not know which is which. In the longer term SNWs may become carefully crafted advertisements for oneself, like CVs, aided by careers advisory services who will tell the thoughtless or unwary that Nazi uniforms do not create a good impression
- Madera (2012) shows that using SNWs in selection is seen as unfair by students, and results in them expressing much less willingness to accept a job offer with a hypothetical employer. This suggests employers could lose good As, who can choose between jobs.
- SNW data may encourage the *fundamental attribution error*, meaning the belief that anything a person does reveals their true nature, so wearing a Nazi uniform means that person is a committed racist and fascist, rather than someone at a fancy dress party wearing the only costume they could get.

What SNWs are used to assess

In terms of Arthur and Villado's (2008) method/construct distinction, the SNW is definitely an assessment *method* that could be used to assess all sorts of different *constructs*. HR should draw up a coding scheme for SNW data based on the job description and person specification, if only because they might otherwise find it difficult to explain or defend their decisions if challenged. Roulin and Bangerter (2013) report Swiss data on what HR managers say they look for in SNWs; 19% look for faux pas, while 56% look at the personal information section. A minority look for aspects of personality. Roulin and Bangerter coded these using the FFM, and found most fell under conscientiousness and extraversion. This indicates the HR managers were looking for the 'right' information, given that conscientiousness does have the strongest link with actual work performance.

What SNWs could assess

Gosling *et al.* (2011) analysed correlations between tested personality and eight objective indices in Facebook, for example number of photographs included, number of wall posts, number of 'friends'. They found quite large correlations with extraversion, weaker ones with openness, but none at all for conscientiousness, agreeableness or neuroticism. These results do not strongly confirm that Facebook contains information that can be used to predict work performance. Kluemper, Rosen and Mosholder (2012) analyse ratings of the five factors of personality from Facebook. They find good inter-rater reliability, confirming Facebook does contain some information about personality that people can agree on. They also found ratings of personality from Facebook agree with PQ data to a modest extent, correlations ranging from 0.23 to 0.44, which shows Facebook contains some accurate information about personality.

They finally obtained supervisor ratings of work performance for some of their sample and found ratings of personality made from Facebook correlated with work performance, confirming that Facebook could be used a selection device. However, the aspects of personality that correlated with work performance were agreeableness and neuroticism, but not conscientiousness, which normally predicts work performance better.

Back *et al.* (2010) compared 'real' personality, assessed by PQs completed by American and German students and by four close acquaintances (an unusually thorough assessment), with personality rated from their SNW. They found moderate levels of agreement for extraversion and openness (0.41 and 0.39), less for agreeableness and conscientiousness (0.22 and 0.27), and none for emotional stability. More visible aspects of personality seem easier to rate from SNWs. Targets also completed ideal self-PQs, which were not related to personality as rated from SNW, suggesting people do not use SNWs to project an ideal self. These results indicate SNWs may contain some useful information about applicants. Recall, however, that PQs consist of statements like *I enjoy vigorous exercise* or *I like mixing with people*, which is the sort of information people offer in their SNWs, so there may be an element of circularity in Back *et al.*'s results. The PQ is a much more systematic, because it gives every A the same set of questions to answer.

Using SNWs in selection is rather like bugging someone's office or home, and as problematic. You might learn something tremendously important, or you might listen to hours of irrelevant chatter. If they realize you are doing it, they could sue you, or feed you disinformation.

RESEARCH AGENDA

- More research on what use is being made of SNW content in selection, and how As react to this.
- More research on real correlates of SNW content, in terms of personality and ability.

KEY POINTS

In Chapter 11 you have learned the following:

- Emotional intelligence is assessed by two types of measure: questionnaire and test.
- EI measures are far less successful at predicting work performance than has been claimed.
- Situational judgement tests are widely used and achieve moderately good validity.
- Educational achievement predicts some aspects of work performance to a limited extent.

- Educational achievement predicts work performance in the short term but not the long term.
- Educational achievement requirements create adverse impact in the USA.
- Work sample tests assess work performance directly and avoid inferences based on abilities or personality traits.
- Work samples may be less useful than is generally supposed, because new meta-analysis finds validity considerably lower, while adverse impact is much higher.
- Work samples tend to be limited to fairly specific skills.
- In-basket tests are useful in selection for management.
- Self-assessments can be valid indicators of performance but probably not in most selection contexts.
- Physical ability tests will create quite large adverse impact for gender, but can be used if carefully constructed, validated and normed.
- Drug-use testing needs to be thought about carefully: Who will be excluded, how and why? What will people think of it?
- Social networking websites may contain information that is useful in selection.

KEY REFERENCES

Back *et al.* (2010) report data on rating of personality from social networking websites, compared with personality assessed by PQ.

Berry *et al.* (2006) analyse the usefulness of educational attainment as a proxy for mental ability.

Bobko *et al.* (2005) argue that work sample tests create more adverse impact than is generally supposed.

Courtright *et al.* (2013) describe a meta-analysis of sex differences in physical ability in the selection context.

Joseph *et al.* (2015) present an analysis of the predictive validity and construct validity of emotional intelligence tests.

Landy (2005) gives an interesting historical account of social and emotional intelligence testing.

McDaniel *et al.* (2007) present a meta-analysis of the validity of situational judgement tests.

Ng & Feldman (2009) discuss how education can be linked to work performance in the USA.

Rayson *et al.* (2000) describe the problems faced by the British Army in devising physical tests for infantry soldiers.

Roth *et al.* (2005) present a new meta-analysis of the validity of work sample tests, suggesting it is lower than generally supposed.

Whetzel *et al.* (2014) present a meta-analysis of the validity of in-basket tests.

CHAPTER 12

Criteria of work performance

'the successful employee… does more work, does it better, with less supervision'

Bingham and Freyd (1926) summarized the criterion issue with a list of all the things employers typically want in successful new employees: 'He makes fewer mistakes and has fewer accidents … He ordinarily learns more quickly, is promoted more rapidly, and stays with the company.' Writing so long ago, they can be forgiven for appearing to assume the successful employee is also male. Validation compares a *predictor*, or selection test, with a *criterion*, or index of the employee's work performance. A good criterion should be:

- *Reliable*, meaning either stable (over time) or consistent (between observers).
- *Valid*. In one sense this is a tautology: the criterion defines success. But critics, and courts, often question criteria of work performance.
- *Unbiased*. The criterion should not result in unfair bias against women or ethnic minorities or any other protected group.
- *Practical*. Information can be obtained at reasonable cost, by procedures management and workers accept.

Validity

The validity of a criterion of work performance can be represented by an overlapping circles diagram, just like the validity of a selection test (Figure 2.3, page 35). In Figure 12.1 the right-hand circle represents true work performance, and the left-hand circle is the criterion of work performance.

- The shaded area in the middle is the overlap, the part of true performance that the criterion succeeds in measuring.
- The unshaded area of the right-hand circle is that part of true work performance the criterion does not succeed in measuring, sometimes referred to as *criterion deficiency*. For example performance standards for infantry soldiers that failed to include marksmanship or courage could be considered deficient.

Personnel Selection: Adding Value Through People – A Changing Picture,
Sixth Edition. Mark Cook.
© 2016 John Wiley & Sons, Ltd. Published 2016 by John Wiley & Sons, Ltd.

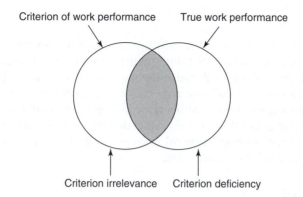

Criterion of work performance   True work performance

Criterion irrelevance   Criterion deficiency

Figure 12.1   Schematic representation of true work performance, and actual criterion.

- The unshaded area of the left-hand circle covers aspects of the criterion measures which are not part of true work performance, sometimes referred to as *criterion irrelevance*. Researchers are sometimes tempted to define success at work by something that is easy to quantify, but not actually very important. For example one could define the prime minister's success by the number of foreign heads of state entertained at 10 Downing Street, which is recorded in the Court Circular page in *The Times*. But is receiving visitors central to the prime minister's role?

Early research relied largely on supervisor rating of overall work performance, although some studies used 'objective' indices of work performance such as sales or output. Since 1980 research has broadened the definition of good work performance to include several 'new' criteria.

SUPERVISOR RATING

The supervisor rating criterion is very convenient to psychologists researching on selection, so long as they avoid reading the work of colleagues researching the same ratings under the heading of *performance appraisal*. Their colleagues' efforts document many problems: poor reliability, suspect validity, halo, leniency, and bias.

Reliability

Supervisor ratings have fairly poor reliability. Viswesvaran, Ones and Schmidt (1996) reported a meta-analysis of 40 samples covering 14,630 persons, and found an average inter-rater reliability of only 0.52. Rothstein (1990) plotted inter-rater reliability against length of acquaintance and found it eventually reaches 0.60, but only after 20 years.

Validity

Supervisor ratings are rarely criticized on grounds of their validity; for all their flaws, they have a satisfying finality about them. How do you know X is a better worker than Y? Because the supervisor says so. This is just as well, because attempts to validate supervisor ratings tend to fall into circularity. One strategy is to compare supervisor ratings with 'true' ratings produced by an expert panel, but if one expert panel does not agree with another, which has given the 'true' ratings? Several lines of research suggest supervisor rating may not always be very accurate.

Rater–rated

If five supervisors have each rated 500 workers, the data can be analysed by three sources of variance: supervisor (*rater*), worker (*ratee*), and interaction between rater and ratee. Ideally workers will account most of the variance, if the ratings are accurately describing true differences in performance. Interaction between rater and ratee may indicate gender or ethnicity bias, or more personal forms of favouritism. Identity of the supervisor ideally will account for little or none of the variation in the data, if supervisors are making careful, accurate, unbiased judgements of the workers. Unfortunately analyses of this sort, for example O'Neill, Goffin and Gellatly (2012), find rater accounts for the largest slice of the variance (58%), while identity of person rated, which represents true performance, accounts for much less (30%), with the potentially problematic interaction accounting for 12%.

Comparison with objective criteria

Meta-analysis confirms that supervisor ratings and objective criteria correlate poorly ($p = 0.39$), even correcting for error of measurement (Bommer *et al.*, 1995).

Comparison with peer rating

Viswesvaran, Schmidt and Ones (2005) reported a meta-analysis comparing supervisor and peer aka colleague aka co-worker rating of job performance. The correlation at first appears rather low, at 0.46, considering they are (meant to be) rating the same thing. However, Viswesvaran *et al.* noted that supervisor and peer ratings are both fairly unreliable; correcting for both sets of unreliability increased the correlation to a near-perfect 0.98. This suggests peer ratings could in theory make as good a measure of work performance as supervisor ratings.

Comparison with self-ratings

Heidemeier and Moser (2009) report a meta-analysis of self-ratings of work performance, comparing them with ratings by others, generally the customary supervisor rating. They find self and supervisor agree to a moderate extent – 0.34

corrected for unreliability of both sets of ratings – and that self-ratings tend to be more favourable to the extent of a d of 0.49. This suggests the two might not be interchangeable. Two-thirds of the research is North American, the rest European, apart from a few studies from further afield. European and North American studies do not differ on average.

Leniency

Supervisor ratings tend to display leniency. Appraisal ratings used to decide outcomes such as promotion are more lenient than ratings made especially for use in selection research (Murphy & Cleveland, 1995). Leniency is a problem in validation research, because it restricts range and reduces validity coefficients.

Murphy (2008) argues that supervisor ratings are a poor measure of work performance: he draws a crucial distinction between what supervisors see and *could* report, and what they *choose* to report, and offers a range of reasons why supervisors or managers might frequently give 'inaccurate' performance ratings:

- Some supervisors believe positive feedback will raise poor performance.
- Some believe telling poor performers their work is poor will damage the ability of group to function.
- Many managers will not say that some of their subordinates are poor performers because this reflects badly on their own competence as a manager.

More generally, Murphy argues that supervisor and managers have many reasons not to give their staff poor ratings, but no incentives at all to give poor ratings when these are merited. They are, according to Murphy, unlikely to get any thanks or reward for identifying poor performers.

Bias

Supervisor ratings are also known to be affected by a range of biases, discussed in a later section.

The last 10 years have seen some interest in *policy capturing* researches on ratings of work performance. Lee and Dalal (2011) prepared sets of data describing an employee's financial contribution to the organization week by week for six months, and asked informants to rate overall performance. The advantage of this format is allowing a range of other factors to be examined, besides simple level of work performance, such as upward trend, downward trend, or the presence of blips – weeks in which performance was unusually good, or unusually poor. A downward blip resulted in a poorer rating, but an upward blip did not produce a corresponding better rating.

OBJECTIVE CRITERIA

The first published validation study (Link, 1918) used an objective criterion: munitions output over a four-week period. Objective criteria divide into:

- Production, sales.
- Personnel criteria.
- Training grades.
- Work samples and 'walk throughs'.

Production

In some jobs there is a countable output: units produced, breakages, spoiled work, etc. However, output may not depend solely on how hard or well the worker works. A whole host of other factors may play a part: how well the machinery works, whether materials arrive in time, whether other workers do their bit, etc. For these sorts of reasons output criteria can have fairly low reliability. Production workers are often interdependent, each worker's output is regulated by the speed of the line, or socially by *output norms* (tacit agreements not to work too hard).

Output criteria have been used also for scientific work: inventions patented, papers published, or number of times work are cited by others. Scientists have been arguing for years whether publication and citation rates are good criteria of scientific output, some noting that neither Darwin nor Mendel published a lot. Murphy (2008) argues that objective measures almost always suffer from *criterion deficiency*, meaning they miss out important parts of the job. He gives an example which is highly topical in Britain at the time of writing: 'it is possible to count how many patients a physician sees in the course of a work-day but that would probably not be an adequate measure of his or her performance'. Public discussion of the work of general practitioners (family physicians) means everyone in Britain now knows GPs are expected to see one patient every 10 minutes on average (and most seem to agree with Murphy that this is not the best way to judge their effectiveness).

Sales

It can be argued that sales figures are central to the success of some organizations, so are the obvious criterion to use. They are also entirely objective. Some problems exist, however. It is easier to sell a good product, and easier to sell in an affluent area. Researchers can address this issue by standardizing sales figures. Suppose average sales are £340,000 in company A, and £430,000 in company B. Sales figures in both companies into converted into z scores (Box 6.2, page 114), using a mean of £340,000 in company A, and a mean of £430,000 in company B. A salesperson who sells £400,000 in company A is doing well, but in company B is below average. This assumes that it is easier to sell more in company B, which may be true if the company has a better product or more prosperous customers. But suppose company B employs better salespeople, which is why they sell more. In that case standardizing the sales figures for a validity study would be very misleading. Changes over time, such as a general recession, can also be dealt with by standardization.

Personnel criteria

These include: advancement/promotion, turnover, punctuality, absence, disciplinary action, accidents, sickness. They are easy to collect, but may be unreliable, or have skewed distributions. Many personnel criteria also exhibit multiple causation. An accident is unlikely to reflect nothing but the carelessness of the person concerned; it will depend also on others' behaviour, defects in equipment, company safety culture, etc. Some personnel criteria depend on subjective judgement, notably promotion.

Training grades

Training grades have been very widely used in American military selection research, where every one of many military occupational specialities has a training course which soldiers must pass to become tank mechanics, dog handlers, military police, etc. (Recall from Chapter 6 that a similar format in training tests and GMA tests may tend to build in some correlation.)

Work samples and 'walk-throughs'

Until recently validation research rarely used work samples as a criterion: they are so expensive to develop that employers prefer to use them for selection. The US Army's Project A (Campbell *et al.*, 1990) devised a set of *hands-on work-sample* criteria, designed to prove conclusively the army tests' validity in the face of Congressional criticism. Tank crews were observed and rated, in a real tank, repairing the radio, unjamming the gun, and driving the tank from A to B. The work-sample criterion can be used to validate less expensive *walk-through* criteria, in which the soldier stands in a mock-up tank, and explains how to unjam the gun, or describes how the vehicle is driven.

OTHER ASPECTS OF WORK PERFORMANCE

Work quality

Critics often complain that criteria used in selection overlook quality. Bommer *et al.* (1995) found that objective and subjective measures of quality agree even less well than objective and subjective measures of quantity.

Everyday vs. best performance, aka typical/maximum

Dubois *et al.* (1993) found that best performance in supermarket checkout operators correlated very poorly (0.11 to 0.32) with typical performance, and that ability tests correlate with best performance rather than typical. Supermarkets will usually be more interested in typical performance than best. On the other hand Sackett (2007) says the US military designs its selection to predict maximum performance, rather than typical. Beus and Whitman (2012) report a meta-analysis of the maximum vs typical performance distinction, and find the two are correlated, (ρ = 0.42), and that the correlation is greater in more complex work. Objective measures of work performance, for example sales, showed a smaller effect than ratings. The meta-analysis confirmed the hypothesis that mental ability is more strongly correlated with maximum performance than typical, but did not find any differences in personality.

NEW CRITERIA

What is sometimes referred as 'the criterion space' has been considerably extended over the last 25 years or so, under several headings, including organizational citizenship behaviour (OCB), counterproductive work behaviour (CWB), and adaptability. One aim is to widen the concept of a good worker; another (in the USA especially) is to reduce adverse impact.

Organizational citizenship

Katz and Kahn (1966) noted many years ago that 'an organization which depends solely upon its blueprint of prescribed behaviour is a very fragile social system'. Many employers in Britain in the 1960s and 1970s found how right Katz and Kahn were, when unions told their members to stick to the letter of their job description by 'working to rule'. The willingness to do more than one's prescribed tasks at work is called organizational citizenship (OC) or contextual performance (as opposed to task performance). As sometimes happens in industrial and organizational psychology, the concept of OCB has 'taken off' since around 1990. As the number of published researches grows enormously, the concept is extended and elaborated, eventually to the point when it seems to become so all-inclusive as to be in danger of losing focus. Mackenzie, Podsakoff and Podsakoff (2011) list 40 definitions of OCB, and a number of classifications into different types:

- Individual/organizational: OCB-I where the worker helps particular others, and OCB-O where the worker defends the organization's interests, image, etc.
- Affiliative/challenge (aka 'voice'). *Affiliative* means showing altruism, or courtesy to others, while *challenge* means identifying problems and suggesting change.

- Challenge can be further divided into *promotive*, suggesting new ideas, or *prohibitive*, covering 'principled organizational dissent', and 'whistle-blowing'.

Counterproductive work behaviour

There are lots of things employees do which employers wish they would not do. Gruys and Sackett (2003) listed no less than 66 separate examples of counterproductive work behaviour (CWB), some listed in the third column of Table 12.1. Bennett and Robinson (2000) report a survey which finds CWBs alarmingly frequent, from the employer's point of view: nearly 80% of employees admit taking longer breaks than they should or not working when they should, while more serious behaviours such as theft or falsifying expenses are admitted by a quarter.

One dimension? Ones and Viswesvaran (2003b) argue that CWB is a single dimension. They find six studies that correlate absenteeism with other counterproductive behaviours: aggression, alcohol use, antagonistic work behaviour, destruction of property, drug misuse, misuse of information, misuse of time and resources, substance abuse, theft, and unsafe behaviour. They calculate a weighted correlation of 0.44 between absence and other CWBs, rising to 0.58 when corrected for the reliability of both measures. Table 12.2 lists three

Table 12.1 Some examples of counterproductive behaviour, sorted into 11 classes, with number of CWBs in each class.

General category	N	Example(s)
Theft	10	Steal from customer
		Give away goods or services for free
Destruction of property	4	Deliberately sabotage production
Misuse information	5	Destroy or falsify records
		Lie to supervisor to cover up a mistake
Misuse time/resources	13	Work unnecessary overtime
		Use e-mail for personal purposes
Poor attendance	5	Leave early without permission
		Take sick leave when not really sick
Poor-quality work	3	Intentionally do work badly or incorrectly
Alcohol use	3	Come to work with a hangover
Drug use	3	Sell drugs at work
Inappropriate verbal behaviour	8	Argue or quarrel with customers
Inappropriate physical behaviour	7	Unwanted sexual advances to customer
		Physical attack on co-worker
Unsafe behaviour	4	Endanger colleagues by not following safety procedures
		Not read safety manuals

Data From Gruys & Sackett (2003).

Table 12.2 Estimated correlation between four individual types of CPB, and all other types of CPB.

	k^a	ρ
Absenteeism/withdrawal	9	0.58
Antagonistic behaviour/aggression/violence	4	0.55
Substance abuse	4	0.44
Theft/property violations	5	0.62

Data from Ones & Viswesvaran (2003b).
[a] estimated – some sources are meta-analyses.
ρ = correlation corrected for reliability of both measures.

parallel analyses for other CWBs. Quite large positive correlations are found for all four, suggesting a single underlying theme. The correlation for theft is highest, leading Ones and Viswesvaran to suggest it may serve as a marker for CWBs, which would be very convenient for HR as honesty tests exist to detect theft, and according to Ones, Viswesvaran and Schmidt's (1993) meta-analysis work very well (see Chapter 7).

An alternative view of the structure of CWB says the various behaviours listed in Table 12.1 may have nothing at all in common, except precisely that the employer objects to them. Sackett (2003) argues absence, lateness, disciplinary problems, theft, and accidents could 'have different underlying motives: greed, retaliation, laziness, inattention', so pooling them could be psychologically meaningless. This implies the idea of reducing CWB by selecting the right sort of people could be misguided.

It has also been suggested that OCB and CPB may be opposite ends of a single dimension. Dalal (2005) reported a meta-analysis of 49 correlations between OCB and CWB which found a corrected correlation of –0.32, which suggests they are related but not interchangeable.

Adaptability

Changes in work, such as new technology and globalization, require employees to be much more adaptable. Pulakos *et al.* (2002) propose an eight-dimensional model of adaptability, based on extensive critical incident research. Their dimensions include solving problems creatively, dealing with uncertainty, learning new technologies, interpersonal adaptability, cultural adaptability, handling stress, and handling emergencies. Pulakos *et al.* used the eight-dimensional model of adaptability in a conventional validation study on US soldiers, with rather disappointing results. When the eight dimensions are used on the conventional supervisor rating form as the criterion of work performance, the eight-dimensional structure fails to emerge. Pulakos *et al.* appear to miss the opportunity to compare adaptability with other measures of military work performance, which could show that adaptability is a separate aspect of work performance.

RESEARCH AGENDA

- More research to examine relationship between adaptability and other aspects of work performance, especially task performance, but also OCB, CWB.
- More research on criteria of adaptability at work.

STRUCTURE OF WORK PERFORMANCE

The last 10–15 years have seen an ongoing debate about multi-dimensional models of work performance, that list five or 10 or some other number of aspects of work performance. Some have proposed single-factor models that cover all aspects of work performance: OCB, CWB and task performance.

Multi-dimensional models of work performance

Critics argue that global criteria are oversimplified and misleading, because people succeed in many different ways. Therefore validation studies need multiple criteria. Several general models of work performance have been proposed, which usually list up to a dozen separate aspects that could be used as criteria. These include Viswesvaran's 10 dimensions, and Project A's five-dimensional criterion space.

Ten dimensions

Viswesvaran, Schmidt and Ones (2002) listed no less than 486 different job performance measures. Fortunately they were able to go on to show that all this confusing variety could be reduced to 10 basic categories, when sorted by experts (Table 12.3). Payne *et al.* (2008) analysed 282 researches of supervisor ratings, sorting them into Viswesvaran *et al.*'s headings. Their analysis finds the most frequently rated specific aspect of work performance is interpersonal competence. Payne *et al.* also found counterproductive work behaviour was rarely included in supervisor rating schedules.

Five dimensions – Project A

The revalidation of selection tests (Campbell *et al.*, 1990) for the American armed services, adopted a five-dimensional 'criterion space':

- Technical proficiency.
- General soldiering proficiency.
- Effort and leadership.
- Personal discipline.
- Fitness and military bearing.

Table 12.3   Viswesvaran *et al.*'s (2005) 10 dimensions of effective work performance, with examples for an academic psychologist.

Dimension	Academic example	%
Productivity	Publications, research grants	37
Effort	Working longer than 9-5	30
Job knowledge	Understanding latest version of SPSS	29
Interpersonal competence	Getting on well with colleagues and students	44
Administrative competence	Completing student records accurately and promptly	28
Quality	Marking student essays carefully	32
Communication competence	Giving clear lectures, writing papers that are clear	20
Leadership	Motivating research staff to find more participants	17
Compliance with rules	Only parking in permitted places	34
Overall job performance		76

% column indicates frequency of use in Payne *et al.*'s (2008) survey of supervisor ratings.

The five dimensions were derived from over 20 work-performance measures, including rating scales and personnel records, as well as measures more usually used as predictors: work samples, role plays, job knowledge tests, and situational judgement tests.

The monolithic hypothesis

Viswesvaran (Viswesvaran & Ones, 2005), having previously offered a 10-dimension model, argues that work performance is a unitary concept, and criticizes the 'Pollyanna-ish view of success' that 'every employee could be in the top 10% albeit in different dimensions of performance (evaluated by different sources)'. If work performance is 'monolithic', the criterion problem resolves itself, and HR's task becomes much easier: there really is such a class of person as the 'the good employee'. All HR need now is the perfect selection test – fast, cheap and infallible – to identify him or her. Viswesvaran's argument rests on complex analyses of two sets of data: supervisor and peer ratings of work performance, and his 1993 survey of a century's work performance research. The supervisor and peer rating data analysis is described in detail in Viswesvaran, Schmidt and Ones (2005), but the larger data set seems described in detail only in his unpublished PhD.

Rating data

There is no doubt that supervisor ratings of work performance contain a very large general factor. But is this true consistency of worker performance, or halo in the supervisor's judgement? Is there any way of telling the two apart?

Halo means different ratings intercorrelate strongly even though the scales are not conceptually related; the person who is rated polite is likely also to be rated well-adjusted, able, highly motivated, etc. This is a pervasive feature of all ratings made by human observers, and was first noted as long ago as 1907. Some researchers try to distinguish between *illusory halo*, where the rater treats dimensions as correlated when they are not, and *true halo*, where the rater is correct because the dimensions being rated really are correlated. It is of course very difficult to establish whether dimensions 'really' are correlated or not, when they can only be assessed by ratings which exhibit halo. Viswesvaran *et al.* (2005) proposed an analysis based on comparing supervisor and peer ratings. Ratings made by the same person exhibit halo, but ratings of different things by different people – they argued – do not. Therefore if supervisor ratings of Smith's *initiative* correlate with peer ratings of Smith's *helpfulness*, this is not halo but a true correlation. They use this analysis to conclude there a large 'real' factor running through supervisor ratings of work performance. Schneider, Hough and Dunnette (1996) are not convinced, and argue assumptions about dimensions being correlated could be shared by different raters, i.e. raters could all share same halo.

The larger dataset

Viswesvaran (described in part by Viswesvaran & Ones, 2005) assembled 2,600 correlations between work performance measures of all types, rating, objective, and 'personnel', and used MASEM analysis (see below) to conclude that 'a general factor exists across all measures of job performance used … over the past 100 years'. Schneider, Hough and Dunnette (1996) express doubt, and note that a lot of the correlations are less than 0.25, even after correction, which they argue is more consistent with a multi-dimensional model. (The dates are correct: Schneider *et al.* are citing Viswesvaran's unpublished PhD.) Viswesvaran (2002) has published a meta-analysis of absenteeism against four other outcomes (Table 12.4). People who are absent a lot produce less, of poorer quality, and are rated as making less effort, and being harder to get on with. Some relationships in Table 12.4 may have direction of cause problems; supervisors know who is absent a lot, and it would be odd if they gave them a high rating for effort.

Table 12.4   Meta-analysis of absence and four other work-performance measures.

Recorded absence X	k	N	ρ
Organizational records of productivity	7	1.8K	–0.21
Organizational records of quality	12	1.3K	–0.48
Supervisor rating of effort	10	1.6K	–0.54
Supervisor rating of interpersonal behaviour	15	2.8K	–0.33

Data from Viswesvaran (2002).
ρ = corrected for the reliability of both measures, but not range restriction.

Table 12.5 Meta-analytic estimates of true correlations between five aspects of work performance.

	OC	LT	AB	TN
Task performance (TP)	0.23	−0.26	−0.29	−0.15
Organizational citizenship (OC)		−0.15	−0.26	−0.22
Lateness (LT)			0.38	0.09
Absence (AB)				0.30
Turnover (TN)				

Data from Harrison *et al.* (2006).

Harrison, Newman and Roth (2006) report a MASEM analysis of the structure of work performance. They first assembled meta-analytic data on the intercorrelation of five work performance variables: task performance, organizational citizenship, lateness, absence and turnover (but not CWB or adaptability). Harrison *et al.* then tested the fit of three models to the correlations in Table 12.5. The model in which the five measures of performance are combined as individual effectiveness fits best, which is consistent with the monolithic hypothesis. A more old-fashioned view might focus on the table of correlations, and note that the average (median) correlation size is a modest 0.24, which does not seem particularly compelling evidence for the hypothesis that work performance is monolithic, and makes one wonder how well structural equation modelling distinguishes between 'best' fit, and 'least bad' fit.

MASEM

MASEM has apparently been around since Hunter's 1983 analysis of ability, job knowledge and work performance, described in Chapter 6. Harrison *et al.*'s data on five aspects of work performance (Table 12.5) illustrate its use. Harrison *et al.* assemble meta-analytic (MA) data on 10 correlations, then test models by structural equation modelling (SEM), hence MASEM. The particular point of MASEM is that each correlation can come from a different meta-analysis. The correlation for OCB × turnover is based on five samples with a total N of 578, and was calculated by Harrison *et al.*; the correlation between task performance and turnover comes from a 1997 meta-analysis of 72 samples with a total N of 25,234. Each is taken as an estimate of the true correlation between the two variables.

MASEM points to a change in opinion about how to analyse data. Each of the 10 meta-analytic correlations in Table 12.5 is based on a different set of between five and 72 researches, using different measures, on different sorts of workers, in different organizations. Before about 1980, regarding these 10 correlations as being capable of being interpreted as single dataset would have been dismissed as mistaken, even wrong. Why? Precisely *because* each is based on a different set of data: different people, different organizations, different measures. This is in effect another version of the 'chalk and cheese' argument, mentioned in Chapter 2, as the reason why meta-analysis was not performed before approximately 1980. Accept meta-analysis, and one has perhaps to accept the argument that each element in Table 12.5 – OCB × turnover, task performance × turnover – can be estimated from separate sets of data, then analysed overall.

The alternative way of answering questions about the structure of work performance would be to find an organization large enough to provide all the data summarized in Table 12.5 from the same set of workers. If such an organization could be found, questions might be asked about whether it was typical of all organizations (especially perhaps as the most likely candidate would be the US armed services). And in one respect this organization could not be typical – precisely size. Statisticians tend not to be happy with MASEM, for a range of technical reasons, one of which can be understood by non-statisticians: how can one state an N for the whole analysis, given each cell in Table 12.5 has a different N, ranging from 578 to 25,324 (Landis, 2013)? Other nagging doubts about MASEM include: How can one be sure OCB in the turnover × task performance dataset is the same thing as OCB in the OCB × absence dataset? The answer is to look at the measures used. But that requires getting hold of the 105 original researches, and then reading all the voluminous research on the construct validity of their OCB measures. Mackenzie *et al.* (2011) have commented on the number and variety of definitions of OCB (see page 252). Proponents of MASEM might argue that science cannot progress unless one is prepared to assume that constructs such as OCB exist, and can be measured, and used in models of work psychology, such as the monolithic hypothesis.

Hierarchical models

Some models are hierarchical, suggesting different aspects of work performance may correlate to some extent, while remaining conceptually and empirically distinct. Many years earlier Crites (1969) had suggested success may have a hierarchical structure, not unlike intellectual ability (Figure 12.2). At the

Figure 12.2 Possible hierarchical structure of work performance, suggested by Crites (1969).

highest level is the general factor, of overall vocational success. At the intermediate level are group factors: administrative skills and drive and initiative. At the level of specific factors are individual ratings such as company loyalty, and single objective criteria, such as scrap and waste.

Murphy (2008) is critical of the single factor/monolithic hypothesis because it justifies correction for low supervisor reliability estimates (0.52) which boost estimates of 'true' validity so much. If work performance is multi-factorial, then it can be argued that inter-rater disagreement is not necessarily just error, but may be a real effect where different supervisors are seeing different aspects of work performance. If inter-rater disagreement is not just error, there may be no justification for 'correcting' for it.

RESEARCH AGENDA

It is difficult to see where research should go next. The halo problem in supervisor ratings is insoluble, if Schneider *et al.*'s argument about shared halo is accepted.

Those who find MASEM slightly dubious might recommend collecting a sufficient quantity of work performance data from a single very large workforce, which would require very careful data collection, possibly over a very long period.

BIAS AND ASSESSMENT OF WORK PERFORMANCE

A survey of managers by Longenecker, Sims and Goia (1987) confirmed what many employees have probably always suspected: some managers allow bias to affect their ratings. In fact many in Longenecker's survey were quite blatant about using performance appraisals to send people messages, to work harder, to show more respect, or to get a job somewhere else. Supervisor bias can also affect apparently objective criteria, if supervisors 'overlook' absence, or petty delinquency, or substandard output, in favoured workers, but officially record it for employees they do not like. Bias can be idiosyncratic, for example hair that is too long/too short/too dyed, or it can be more systematic, and dangerous for the employer: ethnicity, gender, or age. Nandkeolyar *et al.* (2014) describe the problem of abusive supervision, aka undermining, bullying, incivility, harassment, and in the UK as 'picking on', as in 'The foreman is always picking on me'. It seems plausible to suggest that one form abusive supervision might take would be rating good workers down out of spite.

Liking bias

Sutton *et al.* (2013) report a meta-analysis of the link between liking and work-performance ratings. They find a very strong link of $\rho = 0.77$, which they note can be explained by two quite different directions of cause: supervisors give some workers better ratings because they like them more, *or* supervisors like some workers more because they do better work. The former is bias, while the latter could be seen as a legitimate preference based on accurate perception of better performance.

Age bias

Waldman and Avolio (1986) reported a meta-analysis of links between age and work performance showing that productivity objectively measured increases with age, whereas supervisory ratings tend to decrease with age, which implies possible bias in the ratings.

Gender bias

Roth, Purvis and Bobko (2012) report a new meta-analysis of gender differences in work performance, assessed by supervisor ratings, objective criteria and ratings of promotion potential. Both supervisor rating, and objective criteria show women on average do slightly better work ($d = 0.11$). The most striking result is for rating of promotion potential, where the sex difference is reversed: women get lower ratings for promotion potential, even though they get on average better rating for work performance. This effect was even found in six studies where both performance and potential were rated in the same sample. The research analysed seems mostly to have been done in the USA.

Ethnicity bias

Ethnicity bias is a major concern. If some white supervisors are biased again non-white employees, the whole validation paradigm could be undermined. However, simply finding a difference in supervisor rating of, for example, white and African Americans does not in itself prove bias, because supervisors could be reporting real differences in performance.

One line of research uses a within-groups design, where black and white supervisors rate the same set of black and white workers. Sackett and Dubois (1991) found some suitable data in the Project A and GATB databases, and reported that both black and white supervisors rate white workers higher, suggesting a true difference in performance, not bias. However, Stauffer and Buckley (2005) re-analyse the data, and disagree. They say that while it is true that both white and black supervisors rate white workers higher, there is an interaction between race of supervisor and race of worker. Figure 12.3 shows white supervisors see a much bigger difference between black and white workers than do black supervisors. This interaction suggests some white supervisors 'mark down' black workers, or that some black supervisors overlook poorer performance in black workers. Either way some supervisors' ratings may be biased by ethnicity.

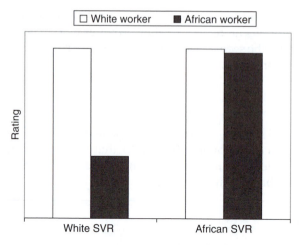

Figure 12.3   Average ratings by white and African American supervisors, of white and African American workers. Data from Stauffer & Buckley (2005).

Table 12.6   Four meta-analyses of differences in white and African Americans' work performance, assessed objectively and subjectively.

Assessment ⇒			Objective		Subjective	
			k	*d*	*k*	*d*
1986	Ford *et al.*		53	0.21	53	0.20
2002	Chung-Yan & Cronshaw		30	0.12	57	0.30
2003	Roth *et al.*	(quality of work)	8	0.24	10	0.20
		(quantity of work)	3	0.32	5	0.09
		(absence)	8	0.23	4	0.13
2006	McKay & McDaniel		62	0.22	510	0.28

Another approach compares rating of work performance with objective measures that are – in theory – unbiased. Four successive meta-analyses of white/African American differences in work performance have distinguished subjective measures, generally supervisor ratings, and a variety of objective measures (Ford, Kraiger & Schechtman, 1986; Chung-yan & Cronshaw, 2002; Roth, Huffcutt & Bobko, 2003; McKay & McDaniel, 2006). Note, however, that some data counted as 'objective' involve someone's opinion, for example promotion. Table 12.6 summarizes all four analyses, which reach conflicting conclusions:

- Ford *et al.* found no difference between objective and subjective.
- McKay and McDaniel found a small difference, in the direction of subjective measures showing a larger difference.

- Roth *et al.* found subjective measures show a smaller difference.
- Chung-Yan and Cronshaw found subjective measures show a larger difference.

Only Chung-Yan and Cronshaw's analysis can be seen as definite evidence of possible bias. The largest and most recent analysis, by McKay and McDaniel, finds little difference between subjective and objective measures, indicating an absence of bias in supervisor ratings. However, Roth *et al.* noted the possibility that raters these days may feel pressure not to generate ethnicity differences in performance ratings. It is easy to compute means of ratings for white and non-white employees, and a large difference might cast doubt on a supervisor's fairness or competence. McDaniel, McKay and Rothstein (2006) applied 'trim-and-fill' analysis for reporting bias to this area, and find evidence of a shortage of large differences in published research but not in unpublished, suggesting perhaps that some researchers are reluctant to publish data on ethnicity differences in work performance. An earlier meta-analysis (Kraiger & Ford, 1985) of 74 studies found a small but consistent *own-race bias*, where whites favour whites, and blacks favour blacks. There seem to be no published European data on these issues.

RESEARCH AGENDA

- Research on ethnicity differences in work performance measures, for different occupational groups, and for different combinations of subjective and objective criteria.
- Research on ethnicity differences in work performance measures, in countries outside North America.
- More research on subtler biases in supervisor ratings.

INGRATIATION AND REPUTATION

Critics have suggested supervisor ratings really measure *worker satisfactoriness*, not work performance. Worker satisfactoriness may include behaviours that please management as well as, or even instead of, good job performance.

- *Ingratiation.* Measure of Ingratiatory Behaviors in Organizational Settings (MIBOS) identifies many ways to please management (besides doing good work): tell them about your successes, compliment them on their successes, listen sympathetically to their problems, run errands for them, etc. (Kumar & Beyerlein, 1991).
- Plouffe and Grégoire (2011) introduce the concept of *Intraorganizational Employee Navigation*: knowing how to make the right contacts, and to work the system, including – according to their data – how to get a better rating from the supervisor.

- *Organizational fads and chairman's whims.* In the 1890s the Royal Navy valued 'spit and polish' so highly that some ship's captains were said to try to avoid gunnery practice in case the powder smoke spoiled their paintwork.
- *Pseudo-targets.* Higher management or politicians create a set of indicators against which performance will be assessed. For example, hospital managers are judged by length of waiting list for surgery, which can have unintended consequences, as when patients needing only minor, but quick, operations are given priority over patients with more serious illnesses, just to get the waiting list shortened.
- *First World War mentality.* Organizations occasionally exist in which subordinates gain credit for pushing ahead with management plans that are absurdly wrong, in pursuit of aims which are completely pointless, stifling criticism of either purpose or method with cries of 'commitment' and 'loyalty'.

Good reputation or good performance?

In many organizations supervisors rate reputation; a good reputation can be earned by good work, but many features of large organizations make it easy to earn one in other ways (Cook, 1995). Sometimes supervisors who rarely see the people they are rating may rely on reputation.

- *Social reality.* A company that manufactures gearboxes has its success defined externally and unambiguously by its sales figures. A university, by contrast, constructs its own social reality. A consensus of academics decides what issues are worth researching and teaching, and by implication whose work has merit. Where success is defined by the organization and its staff, greater scope exists for creating undeserved reputations.
- *Attributability problem.* Complex organizations and long time scales mean it can be hard to assign true responsibility for successes or failures, which opens the door for fast operators to steal the credit for successes, avoid the blame for failures, and build an undeserved reputation.
- *Empire-building.* In many organizations, success is defined in terms of increasing the size of one's department or budget. Services are provided for the sake of justifying the organization's expansion.
- *Reorganizations* create a perfect form of pseudo-work, divorced from external standards. The efforts of dozens, even hundreds, of workers are centred for months on something that has no end product and often serves no useful purpose, but is an ideal environment for the person who seeks to build a reputation. Reorganizations also blur responsibility for successes and failures.
- *Cover your back.* In cautious organizations a good reputation is built largely by not doing things: not making controversial decisions, not attracting complaints, not getting bad publicity.
- *It's who you know, not what you know.* A widely voiced observation, which implies one's time may be better spent creating a network of allies and contacts than doing any actual work.

- *The non-working day.* Only part of an academic's day is spent doing core job-description activities: teaching students, and conducting research. The rest of the day gets filled up by chattering, drinking coffee, tidying up, meetings, pointless paperwork, etc. The more of the working day is filled by non-work or semi-work, the more time there is to set about making oneself well thought of, without doing any good teaching or useful research.

DYNAMIC CRITERIA

Does work performance change over time? This could have important implications for selection, and validation. Suppose people take 12 months to settle into a new job. Collecting work performance data after three months might give very misleading results. Sturman, Cheramie and Cashen (2005) present a meta-analysis of 22 studies measuring work performance over time, on at least three occasions. They conclude work performance is stable over time, although the longer the time interval the lower the correlation. Over a six-month interval, the correlation is around 0.90; over a longer time span of three years, the correlation falls to 0.50. Consistency is less for objective measures like sales, than for ratings, and less for complex jobs (managers, academics, salespersons, securities brokers) than for simple jobs (machine workers, sewing machine operators, welders, bank clerks).

Qualitative shifts in work performance could create more of a problem for selection. Murphy (1989) argued for *transition* and *maintenance* stages in work performance. In transition, the worker is still learning the job, whereas in maintenance the job is very well learned and largely automatic. Ability tests will therefore predict performance during transition, i.e. in the short term, but not in the long term. Critics argue that 'real' jobs, as opposed to simple laboratory tasks, are always sufficiently complex to ensure that automatization does not happen. Farrell and McDaniel (2001) reported an analysis of the GATB database, examining the relationship between general intelligence and job performance over time spans of up to 10 years, and distinguishing between simple jobs that might become automatic and complex jobs that will not. The correlation for general intelligence generally remains positive, for both types of job, over the 10-year time span. It would be very valuable to replicate this study as a true follow-up; the GATB data are cross-sectional.

RESEARCH AGENDA

- A true follow-up of validity over a long time span.
- More research on qualitative shifts in work performance such as transition and maintenance.

CRITERIA, FAIRNESS AND THE LAW

Criterion ratings face some legal problems. They may be accused of bias, which often means racial bias. Research reviewed earlier in this chapter suggests there may be a problem. US fair employment agencies may also find fault with ratings that are unreliable, subjective, or too general. In the important *Albemarle* case (Chapter 13) criterion ratings were ruled unsatisfactory because they were vague, and their basis unclear. In the case of *Wade v Mississippi Co-operative Extension Service* the court ruled that supervisor ratings of attitude, personality, temperament, and habits had to be job-related:

> a substantial portion of the evaluation rating relates to such general characteristics as leadership, public acceptance, attitudes toward people, appearance and grooming, personal contact, outlook on life, ethical habits, resourcefulness, capacity for growth, mental alertness and loyalty to organization. As may be readily observed, these are traits which are susceptible to partiality and to the personal taste, whim or fancy of the evaluator.

Nor are objective criteria free from challenge. An employer cannot simply say 'high turnover' and leave it at that; it may be necessary to prove that high turnover creates problems, costs money, or results from employees' restlessness and not from the employer's behaviour.

PREDICTOR OR CRITERION?

The US Army's Project A used as criteria measures normally used as predictors: work samples, role plays, job knowledge tests, and situational judgement tests. The gist of Klimoski and Strickland's (1977) criticism of assessment centre validity was that assessment centres use the opinion of one set of managers (rating AC performance) to predict the opinion of another set of managers at a later point (rating performance on the job). The same could be said of interviews, especially traditional unstructured interviews. This raises some interesting questions about the whole selection exercise. Which assessments could not be used as a criterion? Personality inventories, or other generalized assessment of personality, tests of mental ability, biographical measures. Anything that assesses the individual as a person. Anything that relies on past behaviour or achievement.

Any measures of a particular skill or competence could logically be used as criterion as well as predictor. This implies some types of selection might becomes conceptually little more than exercises in retest reliability. If the recruit can show good situational judgement before joining the army, he/she will presumably show as much after a year in the army. Or else the second assessment of, for example, counselling a subordinate will reflect how effective the organization's training has been. Very specific assessments that predict very specific outcomes are useful to the employer, but have limitations. Such predictor criterion relationships will lack much if any general interest, or relevance in understanding success in various sorts of work. They might also have limited shelf life for the employer, if the job changes and different skills are required.

KEY POINTS

In Chapter 12 you have learned the following:

- Whatever criterion or measure of work performance is used will be imperfect.
- The most frequently used criterion is the supervisor rating, which is convenient, and inclusive, but frequently also biased.
- Objective criteria such as output, absence or sales, are complex, being shaped by many forces; they are also often unreliable.
- Increasing attention is being paid to other aspects of workplace behaviour, such as organizational citizenship, and counterproductive behaviour.
- Analysis of work performance measures have suggested models with five dimensions, or 10, or that there is only one underlying factor.
- Work performance changes over time, but remains constant enough to make selection a viable enterprise.

KEY REFERENCES

Cook (1995) discusses ways in which the supervisor rating criterion can be biased, or affected by irrelevant considerations.

Gruys & Sackett (2003) investigate the dimensionality of counterproductive work behaviours.

Harrison, Newman & Roth (2006) present a large dataset relating to the monolithic work performance hypothesis, analysed by the MASEM technique.

Hoffman, Nathan & Holden (1991) report research on quality as criterion in gas repair work.

McKay & McDaniel (2006) report the most recent analysis of ethnicity differences in work performance.

Murphy & Cleveland (1995) review research on performance appraisal.

Roth, Purvis & Bobko (2012) present a meta-analysis of gender differences in measures of work performance.

Sturman et al. (2005) analyse consistency of work performance over time. (Especially suitable for readers interested in statistics.)

Viswesvaran & Ones (2005) provides the most accessible account of the monolithic work-performance hypothesis.

CHAPTER 13

Minorities, fairness and the law

Getting the numbers right

The House of Commons of the British Parliament numbers 650 Members of Parliament. Following the 2015 election, there is a 'record number' of female MPs – 191, as well as 42 ethnic minority MPs.

Once upon a time employers could 'hire at will, and fire at will'. They could employ only fair-haired men, or red-haired women, or Baptists, or sycophants, or Freemasons, or football players. They could sack men who wore brown suits, or women who wore trousers. They might be forced out of business by more efficient competitors, who chose their staff more carefully and treated them better, but they were in no danger from the law. Employers could also indulge any racial stereotypes they happened to have: 'don't employ Fantasians because they are all too slow'; 'don't employ Ruritanians because they're unreliable', etc. Those bad old days are long past.

Fair employment legislation first appeared in the USA 50 years ago; the 1964 Civil Rights Act (CRA) prohibited discrimination in employment on grounds of race, colour, religion, or national origin (Table 13.1). CRA also prohibited discrimination on grounds of gender; it is said the US government did not originally intend to include women as a *protected minority*, but the scope of CRA was broadened by hostile senators who thought it would reduce the bill to an absurdity, and lead to its defeat. CRA was joined in 1967 by the Age Discrimination in Employment Act and in 1990 by the Americans with Disabilities Act. US government agencies were created to enforce the new laws, notably the Equal Employment Opportunities Commission (EEOC). In 1970 and 1978 EEOC issued *Uniform Guidelines on Employment Selection Procedures* which advise employers on how to achieve fair employment.

BRITISH LAW

In Britain two separate laws covered fair employment: the Race Relations Act (1976) and the Sex Discrimination Act (1975). In 1995 the Disability Discrimination Act extended protection to disabled people. Discrimination on grounds of

Personnel Selection: Adding Value Through People – A Changing Picture,
Sixth Edition. Mark Cook.
© 2016 John Wiley & Sons, Ltd. Published 2016 by John Wiley & Sons, Ltd.

Table 13.1 Key events in the development of fair employment legislation in Britain, USA, and European Union.

Year	USA	UK	European Union
1964	Civil Rights Act		
1967	Age Discrimination Act		
1970	First *Guidelines* published		
1971	*Griggs v Duke Power*		
1975	*Albemarle Paper Co. v Moody*	Sex Discrimination Act	
1976		Race Relations Act	Equal Treatment Directive
1978	Uniform *Guidelines* published		
1984		CRE Code published	
1985		EOC Code published	
1990	Americans with Disabilities Act	London Underground case	
		Paddington guards case	
1991	Civil Rights Act		
1995		Disability Discrimination Act	
1999		Disability Rights Commission	
2000			Employment Equality Framework Directive
			Racial Equality Directive
2003		Employment Equality (Sexual Orientation) Regulations	
		Employment Equality (Religion & Belief) Regulations	
2006		Employment Equality (Age) Regulations	
2007		Equality and Human Rights Commission	
2010		Equality Act	

religion, belief and sexual orientation became illegal in the UK in 2003, and on grounds of age from October 2006. All UK equal opportunities agencies merged into the Equality and Human Rights Commission (EHRC) in 2007. The 2010 Equality Act merged all previous legislation on fairness in employment, and extended its scope to cover gender reassignment, marriage and civil partnership, and pregnancy and maternity. The Equality Bill also permits an element of positive discrimination: employers may give preference to members of underrepresented groups so long as they are equally well qualified. (One wonders if the lawyers who drafted this had heard of error of measurement.)

EUROPEAN UNION LAW

The EU issued its Equal Treatment Directive in 1976, covering gender, and in 2000 the Racial Equality Directive, and the Employment Equality Framework Directive which covers disability, sexual orientation, religion or belief, and age. Individual European countries still retain their own laws relating to aspects of selection. For example in Germany and Austria, employers are required to provide references if employees ask for one.

OVERVIEW

Figure 13.1 shows how fair employment laws work in the USA. The American model has been followed in many other countries. If selection excludes more minorities than whites, or more women then men, it creates *adverse impact* (AI). The employer can remove AI by *quota hiring* to 'get the numbers right'. Or else the employer can try to demonstrate the selection test is *job-related*, i.e. valid. The employer who succeeds in proving the selection test is job-related faces one last hurdle – proving there is *no alternative* test that is equally valid but does not create AI.

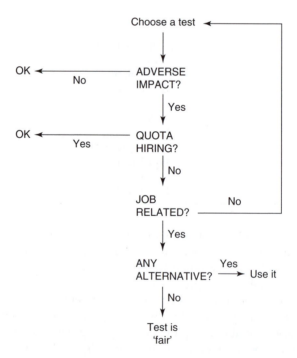

Figure 13.1 Stages in deciding whether a selection test is legally fair.

ADVERSE IMPACT

In Britain 8% of the population are ethnic minority, and half are female. If Members of Parliament were selected without regard to gender or ethnicity, Table 13.2 shows there would be 325 women MPs, and 52 minority MPs. ('Selection' as an MP has two stages: the constituency party selects a candidate, and the electorate choose whether to vote for him/her. Constituencies may come under pressure from party HQs to help secure a representative House of Commons.)

Adverse impact is not quite what the lay person thinks of as discrimination. AI does not mean turning away minorities in order to keep the job open for white males, or otherwise deliberately treating minorities differently. Adverse impact means the organization's recruitment and selection methods result in fewer women or ethnic minority persons being employed. The lack of women and minorities may not be intentional. Generally accepted ways of selecting staff may create unforeseen AI. For example, the case of *Green v Missouri Pacific Railroad* showed that excluding As with criminal records created adverse impact because some minorities had higher rates of being arrested or convicted. All that is needed to prove adverse impact is a statistical analysis of gender and ethnicity in the workforce, which makes it a very powerful tool in the hands of those seeking to prove discrimination.

Computing adverse impact

Are there fewer women or minority persons in the House of Commons than there 'should' be? Psychologists immediately think of calculating the chi-squared statistic, but the problem with chi-squared is that it is almost impossible not to find a significant discrepancy somewhere when analysing large numbers. No employer is likely to have a perfect balance of ethnicity and gender throughout a large workforce. In the USA the *Uniform Guidelines* introduced the four-fifths rule. If the selection ratio (selected/applied) for a protected minority is less than four-fifths of the highest ratio for any group, a 'presumption of discrimination' is established. Roth, Bobko and Switzer (2006) note that the four-fifths rule can give misleading results in small samples. For example, suppose the selection ratio is really the same, at 0.50, for both men and women, and that groups of 50 men and 50 women are assessed each week.

Table 13.2   Actual composition of the British House of Commons following the 2015 election, and expected composition, based on the assumption that MPs are selected regardless of gender and ethnicity.

	Actual	Expected	Expected (four-fifths rule)
Male	459	325	
Female	191	325	260
White	608		
Minority	42	52	42

Chance variations in such small groups will results in one in seven weeks' intakes appearing to break the four-fifths rule. Murphy and Jacobs (2012) note the four-fifths rule uses a ratio of ratios – *men hired/men rejected* compared with *women hired/ women rejected*, which makes it inherently unstable because chance variation in any of four elements can shift it. Murphy and Jacobs suggest the *d* statistic might make a better index of discrimination in selection, and suggest a cut-off of $d = 0.20$.

> The proportion of women in the Commons is obviously far less than four-fifths the number of men. The number of minority MPs however passes the four-fifths rule. Therefore 'recruitment and selection' for the Commons creates adverse impact on women, but not for minorities.

If there is no AI, the employer has no problem, but if AI is demonstrated, the burden of proof shifts to the employer to prove good business reasons, which essentially means proving the selection procedure is valid. Good business reasons do not include saying customers will be 'put off' by female or minority staff, so the shortage of female MPs could not be justified by claiming people would not vote for them. Employers whose 'numbers aren't right' are presumed guilty of discrimination until they succeed in proving their innocence. This can be difficult and expensive so most employers prefer to avoid creating adverse impact in the first place.

Adverse impact in Britain

Extensive data on adverse impact in graduate recruitment in Britain were reported by Scott (1997). Table 13.3 shows that overall, minority As are less successful, showing adverse impact. However, the minorities vary considerably, with Indian (South Asian) As being as successful as white applicants, and

Table 13.3   White and minority British applicants for graduate recruitment schemes (Scott, 1997).

	N	% selected for first interview	% selected for employment
White	49,370	23	3.4
Black African	648	13	1.7
Black Caribbean	162	19	1.9
Black other	88	18	2.3
All black As	1,001	13	1.6
Bangladeshi	142	21	1.4
Indian	1,706	28	3.2
Pakistani	530	20	2.1
All South Asian As	2,378	26	2.8
Chinese	457	26	5.4
Overall	6,462	18	1.9

Note: The total for minorities overall is higher than the total of specific minorities because some employers did not differentiate between minorities.

Chinese As considerably more successful than the white majority. The three Indian sub-continent groups differ considerably; parallel differences are found in average education and income levels for the three groups.

Adverse impact league tables

There is a trend, especially in the USA, to try to draw up league tables of AI, using the d statistic, for example Ployhart and Holtz (2008). These tables are intended to guide selectors in their choice of selection test. However, such analyses present considerable methodological problems, some obvious, others more subtle. Obvious problems include small and unrepresentative samples; it is clearly unwise to base statements about gender or ethnicity differences on any but very large and definitely representative samples. Another problem is the multiplicity of minorities. Even excluding the 'other' categories, the UK Census distinguishes six ethnic minority groups (see Table 13.3). Getting enough data to construct meaningful d statistic tables for six white/minority comparisons will be an enormous task. (Some employers cheat and pool all non-white groups when telling everyone there is no adverse impact in their selection.) League tables also tend to fall into the Bobko–Roth fallacy (described in Chapter 4, page 89) of using present employees to check for adverse impact, instead of applicants. This may underestimate AI, or miss it altogether. The Bobko–Roth fallacy seems to arise most often for tests that correlate positively with mental ability, which is the construct that creates the largest adverse impact problems in the USA.

Arthur *et al.* (2013) make the important point that adverse impact, and differences between subgroups, for example male and female, while closely linked, are not identical. Adverse impact applies to a particular workforce, or even a particular section of a workforce. The absence of a difference between American men and women in general, in, for example, ability to stand on your head, does not automatically mean the test of this used in XYZ Inc. will not find a difference in non-manual staff, and start a fair employment case. Nor can the employer necessarily rely on the proven absence of a general difference to justify the test's use when a local difference is found.

US research often seems preoccupied with finding tests or combinations of tests that will not go as far as eliminating AI altogether, but will reduce it sufficiently to pass the four-fifths rule. This sometimes seems to non-US observers possibly a little short-sighted, given that the rule is guidance not law, and could be tightened to, for example, nine-tenths if the fair employment agencies felt the time was right.

Combinations or composites of selection tests

Recently American researchers have been trying to solve the AI problem by using combinations of tests. Can a combination be found that will achieve good validity but not create too much adverse impact? Researchers have tried composites of ability and personality tests, with not very promising results.

Actually there is no need to conduct empirical research to demonstrate this. It follows logically that if two groups differ a lot in scores on a test used for selecting employees, then fewer members of the lower-scoring group will be selected. The effect can be diluted by using other measures that do not generate a score difference, but cannot be eliminated. The only way of eliminating AI based on mental ability would be to find another measure that produced an equally large difference but in the opposite direction, so the two differences cancelled each other out. This might still create problems: HR now have *two* differences to worry about.

Same construct – different method

Arthur *et al.* (2013) note that employers are often advised to resolve adverse impact problems by finding another way to measure something, in the hope of retaining validity while avoiding discrimination. If a test of GMA causes problems, try a structured interview or biodata focusing on intellectual achievement. In Arthur and Villado's (2008) terms, retain the *construct* (GMA) but change the *method*. Chapter 4 showed that interviews do measure GMA to some extent, but this is not the same as showing that interviews are as good at assessing GMA as GMA tests. It might be rather difficult to devise an interview that only assessed GMA, and nothing else. Arthur *et al.* argue that research is needed on assessing the same construct by different methods in same sample, and this research has not yet been done.

> Why has Parliament not been challenged over adverse impact? Because MPs are not employees, so are not covered by fair employment laws.

QUOTA HIRING

Employers who cannot prove good business reasons, or do not want to go to the trouble and expense of trying, must 'get their numbers right', which tends to mean quota hiring. Quotas can be hard or soft. A hard quota requires every other new employee to be from a minority; a soft quota tells the personnel department in effect 'try to find more minorities'. London's Borough of Lambeth, noted for its very progressive policies, announced in 1986 a soft quota for disabled black women in its road-mending teams.

Formal quotas

Some formal quota systems for mental ability test scores were discussed in Chapter 6. In *top-down quota*, the employer selects the best minority applicants even though they do not score as highly as the best white As. In *separate norming*, minority As' raw scores are converted to percentiles using a separate minority mean. In the 1980s the EEOC had favoured separate norms, but the Civil Rights Act of 1991 specifically prohibited them. Separate norms are not viewed with favour in Britain either. Presently *score banding* (Chapter 6) argues that people who do not differ reliably, in terms of error of measurement, could be treated as equal.

Affirmative action (AA)

Affirmative action is defined as 'the voluntary adoption of special programmes to benefit members of minority groups'. Kravitz (2008) describes many things employers can do to attract minority applicants, to make sure they do themselves justice in the selection. For example internship (work experience) programmes with local schools show minority pupils possible careers and prepare them for selection assessments.

Diversity

Diversity means adopting a policy of employing people from many different backgrounds, who vary in gender, ethnicity, age (dis)ability, etc. Many advantages are claimed, including making recruitment easier, reducing staff costs, reducing absence and turnover, improving flexibility and creativity, improving customer service, and creating a better public image. Critics note that conclusive proof of all this tends to be lacking, and note that diversity can have negative outcomes too. Sacco and Schmitt (2005) studied turnover in a US fast-food chain, across a quarter of a million workers in over 3,000 branches, and found the 'diverse' employee, the one who was not like his/her co-workers in age, gender, or ethnicity, tended to leave sooner. Thatcher and Patel (2011) analyse diversity under another, less comforting, name: *demographic faultlines*. Teams can split along a range of these: white/black, old/young, male/female, college educated/not. Thatcher and Patel's meta-analysis finds all types of faultline linked, quite strongly, to poorer team performance, less cohesion, greater conflict, and lower satisfaction.

RESEARCH AGENDA

- Research on assessing the same construct, for example general mental ability, by different methods, for example test or structured interview or biodata.
- Consequences of a more diverse workforce, in terms of output, morale, satisfaction and turnover.
- Consequences of a more diverse workforce, in terms outcomes for individual employees.

JOB-RELATEDNESS

If the test creates adverse impact and the employer wants to continue using it, the employer must prove the test is job-related, or valid. This is an area where work psychologists ought to be able to make a really useful contribution.

However, early court cases showed that lawyers and psychologists had different ideas about demonstrating test validity. Two events made the 1970s a very bad decade in the USA for selection in general, and psychological tests in particular: the 1971 Supreme Court ruling on *Griggs v Duke Power Company*, and EEOC's 1970 *Guidelines on Employee Selection Procedures*.

Griggs v Duke Power Company

Before CRA the Duke Power Company in North Carolina did not employ African Americans, except as labourers. When CRA came into effect the company changed its rules: non-labouring jobs needed a high school diploma or national high school graduate average scores on the Wonderlic Personnel and Bennett Mechanical Comprehension Tests, which 58% of white employees achieved, but only 6% of African Americans. The Supreme Court ruled that the company's new tests discriminated, not necessarily intentionally. The court's ruling attributed African Americans' lower scores on Wonderlic and Bennett tests to inferior education in segregated schools. The court said that 'The touchstone is business necessity. If an employment practice which operates to exclude negroes cannot be shown to be related to job performance, the practice is prohibited.' The ruling argued that high school education and high test scores were not necessary, because existing white employees with neither continued to perform quite satisfactorily. The *Griggs* case was very important for several reasons:

- *Griggs* established the principle of adverse impact. An employer could be proved guilty of discriminating by setting standards that made no reference to gender or ethnicity, and that were often well-established, 'common sense' practice.
- *Griggs* objected to assessing people in the abstract, and insisted all assessment be job-related. This implicitly extended the scope of the act; employers may not specify that employees be literate, or honest, or ex-army, or good-looking, just because they want that sort of person working for them.
- Business necessity means job-relatedness, which means validity. Duke Power had introduced new selection methods but done nothing to prove they were valid.

The *Griggs* case illustrates another important point about law and selection. Although the Civil Rights Act was passed in 1964, it was not until 1971 that its full implications became apparent. How a particular law will affect selection cannot be determined simply from reading what it says; what is crucial – and will cost employers a lot of time and money to discover – is how courts will interpret the law.

EEOC's *Guidelines*

The American Psychological Association (APA) had previously published its *Standards for Educational and Psychological Tests* which described ways of proving selection procedures were valid. When EEOC drew up the *Guidelines*, APA persuaded it to recognize its *Standards*. It seemed a good idea at the time but could be seen with hindsight as a mistake: APA's ideal standards for validation seemed to become EEOC's minimum acceptable, which made proving selection methods valid very difficult.

Albemarle Paper Co. v Moody

Four years after *Griggs* another court examined a 'hastily assembled validation study that did not meet professional standards' (Cronbach, 1980), and did not like it. *Albemarle* used the Wonderlic Personnel Test, validated against supervisor ratings. The court made a number of criticisms of both test and ratings.

- The supervisor ratings were unsatisfactory: 'there is no way of knowing precisely what criterion of job performance the supervisors were considering, whether each of the supervisors was considering the same criterion, or whether, indeed, any of the supervisors actually applied a focused and stable body of criteria of any kind'.
- Only white staff were rated, whereas applicants included minorities.
- The results were an 'odd patchwork'; sometimes Form A of the Wonderlic test predicted where the supposedly equivalent Form B did not. Local validation studies with smallish sample sizes often get 'patchy' results. Work psychologists accept this; *Albemarle* showed outsiders expected tests to do better.

PROVING SELECTION IS JOB-RELATED

Validation was discussed previously, in Chapter 2, from an exclusively psychological point of view. Now it is necessary to consider it again, adding a lawyer's perspective, using the three types of validation – content, criterion, and construct – mentioned by the APA's *Standards* and EEOC's *Guidelines*. The *Guidelines* expressed a preference for criterion validation.

Criterion validation

Miner and Miner (1979) described an ideal criterion validation study. The employer should:

- Test a large number of applicants.
- But not use the test scores in deciding whom to employ.
- Ensure there is a wide range of scores on the test.
- Wait for as long as necessary, then collect work performance data.
- Not use a concurrent design, where test data and work-performance data are collected at the same time.

It sounds quite easy – but there are several reasons why it is difficult, time-consuming and expensive in practice.

Criterion This 'must represent major or critical work behavior as revealed by careful job analysis' (*Guidelines*). Rating criteria may be accused of bias, especially if minorities or women get lower ratings. The *Guidelines* list acceptable criteria as production rate, error rate, tardiness, absenteeism, turnover, and training performance; note that this list does not include citizenship or 'attitude'. This could present a problem now that American employers are trying to broaden their concept of work performance, primarily to reduce adverse impact.

Sample size The correlation between test and outcome must be significant at the 5% level, yet the typical local validation study rarely has enough people to be sure of achieving this (Chapter 2). EEOC helps ensure the sample size is too small by insisting that differential validities for minorities be calculated, and that every job be analysed separately.

Concurrent/predictive validity The *Uniform Guidelines* favour predictive validity, which takes longer, and costs more.

Representative sampling and differential validity A representative sample contains the right proportion of minorities and women. The hypothesis of *differential validity* postulates that tests can be valid for whites or males but not for minorities or females. An employer with an all-white and/or all-male workforce cannot prove there is no differential validity without employing women and/or minorities, making this the 'Catch 22' of the *Guidelines*.

Critics may say psychologists have just been hoist with their own petard. They always claimed their tests were the best way to select staff. They always insisted validating tests was a highly technical business best left to the experts. But when American fair employment agencies took them at their word, the psychologists could not deliver an acceptable validity study. Their 50-year-old bluff had been called. In fact, fair employment legislation has done work psychologists a service, forcing them to prove more thoroughly that tests are valid and worth using, by validity generalization analysis (Chapter 2), utility analysis (Chapter 14), and differential validity research (v.i.).

Validity generalization analysis VGAs for general mental ability (GMA) tests imply that local validity studies are pointless, because GMA tests are valid predictors for every type of work. Accepting these conclusions would leave little or no scope for fair employment cases involving GMA tests, so it is not surprising that American civil rights lawyers do not seem keen to accept VGA. The *Guidelines* say nothing about meta-analysis or VGA, for the simple reason that the *Guidelines* have not been revised since 1978, when meta-analysis was very new, and VGA not yet invented. Landy (2003) notes that few legal cases have involved validity generalization. Landy draws the pessimistic conclusion that one of these cases – *Atlas Paper Box Co vs. EEOC* – means validity generalization is unlikely to prove acceptable to US courts. Harpe (2008) notes that EEOC requires either a local validity study or a transportability study using detailed job analysis to prove the two jobs really are the same. McDaniel, Kepes and Banks (2011) wonder if the EEOC prefers to make employers defend every case in exhaustive detail (rather than being willing to rely on validity generalization), with a hidden agenda of making it so difficult that employers will find it easier to hire their quota of protected groups.

Content validation

In 1964, when CRA was passed, content validity was virtually unheard of and not very highly regarded. Guion (1965) said: 'Content validity is of extremely limited utility as a concept for employment tests … [it] comes uncomfortably close to the idea of face validity unless judges are especially precise in their judgements'. Content validation became the favourite validation strategy after the *Guidelines* and the *Griggs* case, because criterion validation was impossibly difficult (v.s.), and the courts could not understand construct validation (v.i.). Content validation has three big advantages:

1. No criterion is required so it cannot be unsatisfactory. The test is its own justification.
2. There is no time interval between testing and validation. The test is validated before it is used.
3. Content-valid tests are easy to defend in court. Every item of the test is clearly relevant to the job.

Some US employers have tried to use content validity methods for assessing personality or general ability, usually in the hope of avoiding adverse impact problems. The *Guidelines* specifically block this: 'a content strategy is not appropriate for demonstrating the validity of selection procedures which purport to measure traits or constructs, such as mental ability, aptitude, personality, common-sense, judgement, leadership, and spatial ability'.

Construct validation

'A demonstration that (a) a selection procedure measures a construct (something believed to be an underlying human trait or characteristic, such as honesty) and (b) the construct is important for successful job performance' (*Guidelines*). Cronbach (1980) gives the example of high school graduation. A narrow approach might conclude employees do not need to write essays or do sums or even be able to read, so high school graduation is not job-related. The broader construct validity approach argues that it is a reasonable supposition that people who do well at school differ from those who do not, in more than just academic ability. Cronbach calls the something *motivation and dependability*. So an employer who does not want lazy, undependable employees could hope to exclude them by requiring a high school diploma. Cronbach's example shows very clearly why construct validation is not a promising approach. The constructs of motivation and dependability are exactly the sort of abstractions that are difficult to define, difficult to measure, and difficult to defend in court. In fact general education requirements are rarely accepted by American courts (Chapter 9). Harpe (2008) notes that US employers hardly ever rely on construct validity to defend selection.

McDaniel, Kepes and Banks (2011) argue the *Guidelines* are seriously out of date and need extensive revision in five main areas:

1. Continuing to subscribe to the long-disproved hypothesis of situational specificity of selection validity, and the consequent essential need for work analysis.
2. Remaining oblivious to sample size issues in test validation, and requiring local validation studies that most employers do have not sufficient employees to be able to do successfully. McDaniel *et al.* say at least 500 employees are needed for validation, but 84% of US employers do not employ that many in total, let alone doing the same job.
3. Not accepting meta-analysis and validity generalization analysis, which 'might change the litigation landscape' to 'the detriment of' employment attorneys, expert witnesses, employment testing consultants, and enforcement agencies'. McDaniel *et al.* seem to be suggesting that the *Guidelines* have created in the USA a self-perpetuating industry, that has just celebrated its fiftieth birthday.
4. Assuming – implicitly not explicitly – that adverse impact 'is an indication of a flawed test', and treating 'mean racial differences in employment tests' as *the elephant in the room* (i.e. a very large and obvious problem that is studiously ignored).
5. Regarding criterion, content and construct validity as three separate types of validity, rather than three ways of establishing validity.

Alternative tests

The 1970 *Guidelines* required employers to prove no alternative test existed that did not create AI, before they used valid tests that did create AI. Some time ago Reilly and Chao (1982) and Hunter and Hunter (1984) reviewed a range of alternative tests, and concluded that none achieved the same validity for selection as ability tests, except biodata and job tryouts. For promotion a wider range of alternative tests are as valid as ability tests: work samples, peer ratings, job knowledge tests, and assessment centres.

UK PRACTICE

The EHRC has issued seven volumes of *Guidance for Employers* (see the website section at the end of this chapter); volume 1 covers selection. The *Guidance* distinguishes between direct discrimination and indirect discrimination or adverse impact, but does not refer to the four-fifths rule, unlike its predecessor, the Commission for Racial Equality.

The *Guidance* says very little about tests, except that they should not require more ability to speak or read English than the job requires. There is no discussion of more technical issues such as validation of selection methods.

There are two prominent legal cases involving psychological tests in Britain, both dating back to the 1980s. In the *Centurion Managers* case, London Underground appointed 160 middle managers in such a rush, after the disastrous fire at King's Cross, that they did not find time to include all the tests psychologists had recommended, or to pre-test the ones they did use (CRE, 1990). The tests used, numerical and verbal reasoning and an interview, created adverse impact on minority As. In 1990 another case involving tests came to trial – the *Paddington Guards* case (CRE, 1996). British Rail guards (aka conductors aka train managers) seeking promotion to driver were tested on verbal reasoning, numerical reasoning, and clerical ability. A group of guards of Asian origin alleged unfair discrimination because the tests were not clearly job-related, but were harder for people whose first language was not English. A striking feature of the case was that British Rail had a work analysis for train drivers, done by Netherlands Railways, but did not use it to match tests to the job's needs. Both cases were settled out of court, and did not give rise to any legal rulings about test use in Britain.

Fair employment laws have not had the impact in Britain they had in the USA. The British government has not introduced *contract compliance*, although some local authorities have. English law does not provide for *class actions*, in which one person's test case can be used to enforce the rights of a whole class of others, for example female applicants. (This can be enormously expensive; in the *State Farm Insurance* case the employer had to pay $193,000, not just to the plaintiff, but to each of 812 other women as well). UK fair employment agencies have not concerned themselves with the technical detail of testing and validation, in marked contrast to the US EEOC. The EOC's notes for lawyers (Equal Opportunities Commission, 2005) included the interesting observation that 'tribunals seem disinclined to tangle with technicalities of testing and may ignore evidence where experts appear on each side'.

European law

'European law' means laws and directives of the European Community (EC), rather than laws of individual European states. The Community's Social Charter includes concerns with equal opportunities in employment, and for people 'excluded' from employment by disability or other reasons. The EC has accepted the idea of adverse impact as discrimination by results, and several European countries – Italy, Ireland, the Netherlands – have incorporated the concept into their legislation (Higuera, 2001).

DISABILITY

'Paper people' sifting research documents a paradoxical attitude to disability, in particular blindness. Blind applicants are evaluated more positively, which Wang, Barron and Hebl (2010) attribute to a norm to 'be-kind-to-the-disabled', but are not actually shortlisted. The Americans with Disabilities Act (ADA) was passed in 1990 and came into effect in 1992. ADA defines disability very broadly, to cover mental retardation, specific learning disabilities such as dyslexia, emotional or mental illness, AIDS/HIV, and 'morbid' obesity, as well as physical disability, blindness, and deafness. ADA does not cover non-'morbid' obesity, gambling, sexual deviations such as paedophilia, short-term illnesses or injuries, pregnancy, or common personality traits. Current illegal drug use is also excluded, but rehabilitated former drug users are covered. Alcoholism is covered by ADA, but employers can require employees to be sober during working hours. ADA covers discrimination against someone thought to have a disability, for example HIV/AIDS, but who in fact does not.

Work analysis

ADA distinguishes between *essential* and *marginal* job functions; ability to drive is essential for a bus driver, but marginal for most office workers. If a disabled person cannot perform an essential function, the employer may refuse to make an offer. Employers may ask if As can perform an essential function, and may ask As to demonstrate their ability. The essential/marginal distinction means careful work analysis is necessary. ADA also implies person specifications need to be more detailed. For example if the job needs someone who can handle stress well, the person specification should make this clear.

Medical examinations

Employers may only carry out medical examinations on people who have been offered a job, not as part of the selection process. 'Medical examination' seems to be interpreted fairly broadly, so may cover some selection tests. The MMPI, widely used in the USA to screen As for police work, was originally keyed to psychiatric diagnosis and gives its scales psychiatric-sounding names such as 'schizophrenia', which tends to make it look like a medical examination.

Accommodation

Employers must make *reasonable accommodation* for disabled persons, both as employees and applicants. This includes adapting selection methods by providing large-print question books, or someone to help the applicant. Time limits are sometimes changed to accommodate dyslexic As, or to allow for changes in format slowing As down. Changing the time limit for a timed test invalidates the norms, and so makes the results very hard to interpret. Research on educational testing reviewed by Geisinger, Boodoo and Noble (2002) has suggested allowing extra time can result in *over-predicting* subsequent college performance. There seems to be no workplace research on this issue. Given the diversity of disability, and the very large sample sizes needed to compare validities, no workplace research seems likely to be forthcoming. Employers may never know if allowing 50% or 100% or 200% extra time for a particular disability will make the test 'the same as for' someone without that disability.

One implication of ADA may be a need for more untimed tests. ADA has the usual collection of vague, but crucial, phrases like *'reasonable* accommodation' or *'undue* hardship' whose meaning for employers will only become apparent after a series of court cases.

DIFFERENTIAL VALIDITY AND TEST FAIRNESS

Critics often claim tests, especially mental ability tests, are valid for the white majority but not for minorities. This called *differential validity*, and should not be confused with *adverse impact*. Adverse impact refers to a difference in test scores between, for example, male and female, whereas differential validity refers to difference in the correlation between test and outcome. Differential validity can lead to a test being ruled legally 'unfair', which would prevent it being used. A series of meta-analyses of mostly American data in the 1970s eventually reached the comforting conclusion that differential validity was *not a problem*, and that tests worked equally well for white and non-white Americans.

However, Berry and Sackett (2008) argued that it is premature to dismiss differential validity. They noted that differences in validity have been found in both employment and educational testing. Hartigan and Wigdor (1989) found GATB validity 0.06–0.07 lower for African Americans. Three large American military studies, including Houston and Novick (1987), found correlation between test and training success 0.08 to 0.26 points lower for minorities. Berry and Sackett argue that the 1970s meta-analyses relied on comparing cor-relations in small samples, which has low statistical power. Berry and Sackett located a very large set (131,000) of Scholastic Assessment Test (SAT) data, predicting college grades, and found validity for African and Hispanic Americans was the same as for white Americans. Similarly extensive current data for employment testing would be highly desirable. (Recall that Chapter 2 notes that GATB validity seems to have shrunk over time, so data from the 1950s and 1960s may not reflect the current picture.) Te Nijenhuis and van der Flier (2000) report data for various immigrant groups in the Netherlands, and find little evidence of differential validity of ability tests. There are no published data on this important issue for Britain.

Gender and differential validity

Rothstein and McDaniel (1992) presented a meta-analysis of 59 studies where validity coefficients for males and females could be compared. Overall there was no difference. However the results suggested that where the work is usually done by one gender (e.g. most machinists are male), validity is higher for the majority gender. This trend is particularly marked for low-complexity jobs, where female validity for 'female' jobs was 0.20 higher than male validity. Rothstein and McDaniel suggest the result may reflect a bias in the supervisor rating criterion. Men who enter a low-complexity, and traditionally female, occupation may be seen by the (mostly female) supervisors as somehow out of the ordinary. Saad and Sackett (2002) analyse ABLE data for nine US Army specialist jobs and find the relationship between personality and work performance the same for male and female.

Test fairness

Critics often claim tests are not 'fair', meaning minorities do not score as well as whites. The technical meaning of test fairness is quite different; 'unfair' means the test does not predict the minority's productivity as accurately as it predicts majority productivity, which is *differential validity*. Several models of test fairness have been proposed; the most widely accepted is Cleary's model, which is based on regression lines. Figure 13.2 shows two types of unfair test, where there is differential validity.

- Figure 13.2a shows a *slope difference*, meaning the two regression lines are at different angles, reflecting the fact the test predicts productivity more accurately for one group than the other. This what Berry, Clark and McClure (2011) found in their analysis of white and African American GATB data.

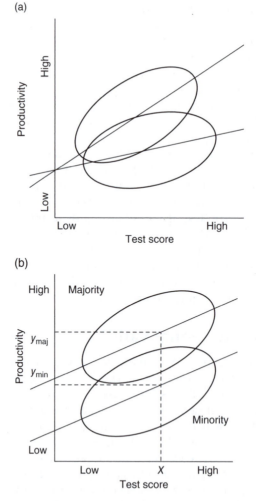

Figure 13.2   Two types of unfair test, showing (a) slope difference, and (b) intercept difference.

- Figure 13.2b shows an *intercept difference*. Minority and majority differ in test score but do not differ in productivity. Test scores under-predict minority persons' work performance; minority persons do better work than the test predicted.

Intercept differences and over-prediction

If test scores under-predicted work performance in, for example, African Americans, using the test might unfairly exclude minority applicants. The view that differential validity was 'not a problem' was therefore reinforced by the discovery that tests seemed to over-predict work performance for key American minorities (and so would not unfairly exclude any minority persons). However, Aguinis, Culpepper and Pierce (2010) questioned this, arguing that the usual computation overestimates subgroup intercept differences. Berry and Zhao (2015) present a new way of calculating intercept differences that avoids this, and is based on operational validity rather the uncorrected validity, and conclude that cognitive ability tests do generally over-predict job performance of African Americans, so, for the time being, there is not a problem.

Figure 13.3 shows a test which is fair, even though majority and minority averages differ. A regression line fitted to the two distributions has the same slope, and the same intercept, which means it forms one continuous straight line. Test scores predict productivity, regardless of minority or majority group membership.

RESEARCH AGENDA

- Large-scale investigation of differential validity in US employment testing.
- More research on possible differential validity by gender.
- Research on differential validity by gender and ethnicity in Britain, Europe, and elsewhere.

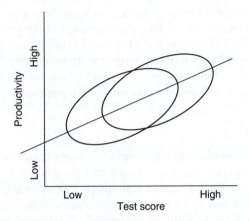

Figure 13.3 A fair test, in which test scores predict productivity equally accurately for minority and majority applicants.

THE SHAPE OF THINGS TO COME

Predictions about where fair employment practice might proceed in the near future seem to focus mostly on sections of the population who do not yet enjoy legal protection.

Sexual orientation

Legislation to prohibit discrimination in employment on grounds of sexual orientation – the Employment Non-Discrimination Act (ENDA) – has been introduced into every US Congress but one since 1994, but so far has always been rejected. Many US states and cities have local laws (Barron & Hebl, 2013). In Britain sexual orientation discrimination has been illegal since 2003, which makes this one area where Britain has moved before the USA, rather than five to 10 years behind, although the initiative actually came from the European Union.

Weight

Overweight people in the USA report widespread discrimination in employment, and have no legal protection, unless 'morbidly' obese (Fikkan & Rothblum, 2005).

Religion and marriage

Ruggs *et al.* (2013) list two minorities in the USA not covered by fair employment law: non-religious people and unmarried people. Apparently some Americans have a 'stark distrust' of atheists.

Attractiveness

No one seems yet to have suggested the physically unattractive as a minority needing protection in employment, although there is a large literature documenting the discrimination they experience in life in general.

Arthur *et al.*(2013) also say there is a move to recognize *intersectional discrimination*, for example black women. Arthur *et al.* note this would mean 11 groups in the USA who could be compared with white males. If age were added, to permit three-way intersections, the number of comparisons could double again.

The ungifted

While some psychologists and employers seem happy with the idea of differences in intelligence, the government and the general population seem either unaware or unreceptive. Characterizing people as unintelligent, or explaining their behaviour as linked to low intelligence, seems increasingly politically unacceptable. It seems unlikely that people of low intelligence would be listed directly as a protected minority, because that implies accepting the concept, and perhaps using the tests. However, it is possible that something closely linked to low intelligence might eventually confer protected minority status, perhaps low educational achievement.

CONCLUSIONS

Fair employment legislation is needed, because discrimination in employment on grounds of gender and ethnicity is clearly unacceptable, and would be rejected by most people these days. However, fair employment law has not primarily concerned itself with overt discrimination, but with adverse impact. In the USA, adverse impact places the burden of proof on employers, effectively requiring them to prove they are not discriminating if there are not 50% females and a certain percentage of ethnic minority persons throughout the entire workforce. It is less immediately obvious that this is entirely reasonable, or what the average person wants.

The effect of new fair employment laws typically takes some years to become apparent, and does not always seem to be quite what was intended. This creates prolonged periods of uncertainty, and costs employers large amounts. While it may be argued that fair employment laws have been a burden to American employers, it could also be argued they have indirectly helped work psychology, by forcing the profession to look much harder at issues like utility, validity and differential validity, to devise new techniques, like validity generalization or rational estimates, and to devise better selection methods.

KEY POINTS

In Chapter 13 you have learned the following:

- Fair employment law covers gender, ethnicity, disability, and age.
- Most fair employment selection cases involve adverse impact, not direct discrimination.
- Adverse impact means fewer minority persons are successful. If the success rate for minority persons is less than four-fifths that of the majority, adverse impact is established.
- Getting the numbers right, i.e. ensuring the correct proportions of women and minorities in the workforce, can be difficult as there are legal restrictions on how employers can achieve it.
- A selection method that creates adverse impact must be proved – in court – to be valid, which is expensive and uncertain.
- If the test is proved valid, the employer must also show there is no possible alternative that is equally valid but which will not create adverse impact.
- American researchers are trying sets of tests to try to find a combination that will prove valid but create no adverse impact.

- Differential validity means that a test has different validity for minority and majority persons.
- North American research on differential validity does not reach firm conclusions. Virtually no research has been reported on this issue outside North America.
- Disability discrimination legislation means employers must not use health-related enquiries as part of the selection process.
- Employers must try to adapt selection tests to disabled applicants.
- In Britain far fewer unfair selection cases have been brought, and the position is still much more open.
- Other countries, in Europe and elsewhere have adopted the same basic adverse impact model.

KEY REFERENCES

Berry & Zhao (2015) describe the latest development in the ongoing discussion of differential validity (Particularly suitable for those interested in statistical analysis.)

CRE (1990) describes the *Centurion Managers* case, one of the few fair employment cases involving psychological tests that have been tried in the UK.

Kravitz (2008) outlines ways of increasing minority representation by affirmative action.

Landy (2005) discusses legal aspects of validity generalization.

McDaniel, Kepes & Banks (2011) say why they consider the *Uniform Guidelines* are a 'detriment' to the field of personnel selection.

Roth, Bobko, Switzer & Dean (2001) discuss problems in assessing adverse impact.

Ruggs *et al.* (2013) outline likely future developments in fair employment.

te Nijenhuis & van der Flier (2000) present data on differential validity of psychological tests in the Netherlands.

Thatcher & Patel (2011) describe the effects of demographic faultlines in the workplace.

USEFUL WEBSITES

usdoj.gov/crt/ada. Official ADA site.
eeoc.gov. US government fair employment agency.
equalityhumanrights.com. (UK) Equality and Human Rights Commission. (Volume 1 of *Guidance for Employers* covers selection.)
hrhero.com. Interesting question-and-answer site on US fair employment.

CHAPTER 14

The value of good employees

The best is twice as good as the worst

In an ideal world, two people doing the same job under the same conditions will produce exactly the same amount. In the real world, some employees produce more than others. Which poses two questions:

- How much do workers vary in productivity?
- How much are these differences worth?

The short answer to both questions is 'a lot'. An answer to the first question is good workers do twice as much work as poor workers. An answer to the second question says the difference in value between a good worker and a poor one is roughly equal to the salary they are paid.

HOW MUCH DOES WORKER PRODUCTIVITY VARY?

Hull (1928) described ratios of output of best to worst performers in a variety of occupations. He reported that the best spoon polishers polished five times as many spoons as the worst. Ratios were less extreme for other occupations – between 1.5 to 1 and 2 to 1 for weaving and shoemaking jobs. Tiffin (1943) drew graphs of the distribution of output for various jobs, including hosiery loopers, who gather together the loops of thread at the bottom of a stocking to close the opening left in the toe (Figure 14.1); most workers fall between the extremes to form a roughly normal distribution of output. If the distribution is normal it can be summarized by its mean ($MEAN_p$) and standard deviation (SD_p). The standard deviation of the data in Figure 14.1 is the SD_p of hosiery looping.

For 95 samples of unskilled workers, Judiesch and Schmidt (2000) showed that SD_p is 18% of average output, indicating a substantial difference between good and poor performers. Defining 'the best' as 2 SDs above the mean, and 'the worst' as 2 SDs below, Judiesch and Schmidt's 18% average for SD_p

Personnel Selection: Adding Value Through People – A Changing Picture,
Sixth Edition. Mark Cook.
© 2016 John Wiley & Sons, Ltd. Published 2016 by John Wiley & Sons, Ltd.

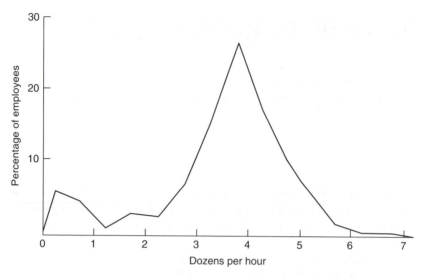

Figure 14.1   Distribution of productivity for 199 hosiery loopers (Tiffin, 1943).

confirmed neatly that the best, at 136%, is twice the worst, at 64%. Earlier analyses had suggested that paying people piece-rate, as is common in blue-collar jobs, compressed the distribution of output, but making allowance for error of measurement, Judiesch and Schmidt concluded that this does not happen. SD_p for low-level jobs is 18% whether people are paid by the hour or by output. SD_p is considerably higher for more complex work, being 27% for skilled craft jobs, 35% for clerical jobs that involve making decisions, and 46% for professional jobs. This implies the best/worst ratio in higher-level work will be much greater. Few professional jobs have been analysed, however, probably because it is far easier to count the output of soap wrappers or bicycle-chain assemblers than that of managers.

THE 'STAR' HYPOTHESIS

O'Boyle and Aguinis have recently challenged the proposition that work per-formance is normally distributed. Sometimes – they argue – it has a skewed distribution, with a few 'stars', whose performance is outstanding, and a long tail of average performers. Other names for this hypothesis include *the best and the rest*, *the necessary many and the vital few*, *the 80/20 principle* (80% of success achieved by 20% of workforce), and *the power law*.

In their first paper O'Boyle and Aguinis (2012) cite evidence from four groups: researchers, entertainers, politicians and sportsmen/women. Between 2000 and 2009 nearly half a million researchers published nearly 1 million papers in the five top journals in 54 fields of research from agriculture to zoology. This gives an overall average of two papers per researcher. The distribution of papers published was, however, markedly skewed: 66% of researchers produced less than the average, i.e. typically only one paper. The top 1% of researchers produced 10% of the papers, and the top 5% produced 26%. Similar results were obtained for the other three professions, success in entertainment being defined by awards (e.g. Oscars), in politics by number of times elected, and in sport by goals scored, medals won, etc. O'Boyle and Aguinis's four groups are, however, hardly typical of work in general. What other occupations will show the same pattern? Aguinis and O'Boyle (2014) mention chief executive officers, sales staff, scientists, and jobs with 'complex non-scripted duties', such as dentists, doctors, and lawyers, and also software engineers, consultants, and educators.

What occupations belong in the other type of work, where performance is normally distributed? O'Boyle and Aguinis mention manufacturing, noting that the interdependence of workers often limits the activities of potential 'stars', as does social pressure not to work harder than other people. They also mention industries and organizations that rely on manual labour, or have limited technology, as well as farmers and construction workers. They do not mention office work or retail, but these seem likely to belong in the non-'star' sector too.

Why is a non-normal distribution seen as a problem?

1. Psychologists like normal distributions because many of their favourite statistical analyses require them.
2. Normal distributions look 'more democratic'. Highly skewed distributions, where only the select few are any good, look very elitist. They may be acceptable in sport and the media, but are much less so in employment.
3. The Brogden equation (v.i.) for calculating the return on selection requires a standard deviation, of the value of employees' output, but standard deviations should not be calculated where the distribution is not normal.

Note that all four analyses of 'star' employees use objective measures of performance: papers in top journals, goals scored, etc. Sales is another key identifier of stars. Aguinis and O'Boyle argue that the most widely used index of work performance, the supervisor rating, tends to *create* a normal distribution. Managers are told performance is normally distributed; raters are told they are making rating errors if they do not generate one in their ratings. One of the reasons conventionally cited for not using sales figures as a criterion is precisely that they are skewed, with a few people selling a lot. This 'problem' can be dealt with by log transformation to make sales data normally distributed, or by discarding extreme values altogether as 'outliers' (or, as Aguinis and O'Boyle see it, throwing away the most important part of the data).

Implications for HR in general

Aguinis and O'Boyle discuss the possible implications of this different view of output for selection.

- 'Stars' should be paid five to 10 times more than the rest.
- HR practices that encourage the retention of the average worker will encourage the departure of 'stars'.
- 'Stars' should receive special treatment. called I (for idiosyncratic) deals, for example being allowed to spend two hours a day running their own business.

Implications for selection in particular

There are at least six:

1. There are two types of work: the everyday, and the elite, which need quite different selection methods.
2. Proposition 5 in the 2014 paper states: 'A firm's competitive advantage derives from "the best" [workers] not the average quality'. The success of selection should not be calculated from average workers but from "the best".'
3. Aguinis and O'Boyle say little about how to select 'stars'. Stars are identified by 'their exceptional output over time'; their 'definition of star performer is based on results, which does not consider the traits that workers possess or how they do the job'. This seems to imply 'stars' will be headhunted, or developed from existing employees, or will emerge from obscurity. They will not be identified by ability or personality tests
4. 'Stars' will never be numerous enough to do any of the usual HR things like developing person specifications, or test batteries, or prediction equations.
5. Different criteria will be needed. As Aguinis and O'Boyle note, supervisor rating will not serve at this level. In any case CEOs do not have supervisors. The criteria Aguinis and O'Boyle mention include sales, reputation, and outstanding achievements. Reputations, as noted in Chapter 12, can be manipulated, and may not always reflect 'true' performance. Company performance has many complex determinants, besides what the CEO does. Becoming a 'star' could be a complex process. Some people will have great natural abilities, for example to design new gadgets. Some people are good at developing, adapting, even stealing other peoples' ideas for new gadgets. Key questions might be how many stars fail, or to be precise how many people on a star track fail? How much damage do they cause? What determines failure? Can it be predicted?
6. The 'star' hypothesis reminds selection researchers that they have never had that much involvement in the selection of CEOs, nor of politicians, sports and media people, nor even – more surprisingly – of researchers.

Most readers in the US or UK will probably not find it too difficult to nominate political parties which are definitely more, or definitely less, likely to greet the 'star' hypothesis with enthusiasm. It has very clear political implications. The 'star' hypothesis is possibly more likely to meet with wider enthusiasm in the USA than in the European Union, which tends to favour social inclusion.

RESEARCH AGENDA

- Estimates of the normality of productivity and value distributions using more sophisticated methods.
- Survey of some samples of 'stars' to see if they can be distinguished from the mass by existing selection methods.

HOW MUCH IS A PRODUCTIVE WORKER WORTH?

If some workers produce more than others, an employer that succeeds in selecting them will make more money – but how much more? A lot of ingenious effort has gone into trying to put a cash value on the productive worker. Accountants can, at least in theory, calculate the value of each individual worker: so many units produced, selling at so much each, less the worker's wage costs, and a proportion of the company's overheads. In practice such calculations proved very difficult. But if accountants are unable to put a precise value on an individual production worker's output, how can they hope to do so for a manager, supervisor, or HR director?

Rational estimates

Work psychologists have devised a technique for putting a cash value on the people doing any job, no matter how varied and complex its demands, or how intangible its end products. Rational estimate (RE) technique was invented by Schmidt and Hunter, who argue that supervisors 'have the best opportunities to observe actual performance and output differences between employees on a day-to-day basis' (Schmidt *et al.*, 1979). So the best way to put a value on a good employee is simply to ask supervisors to judge the employee's worth. REs are collected using these instructions:

> *Based on your experience with [widget press operators] we would like you to estimate the yearly value to your company of the products and services provided by the average operator. Consider the quality and quantity of output typical of the average operator and the value of this output. … in placing a cash value on this output, it may help to consider what the cost would be of having an outside firm provide these products and services.*

Similar estimates are made for a good operator, and for a poor one. 'Good' is defined as an operator at the 85th percentile, one whose performance is better than 85% of his/her fellows. 'Poor' is defined as a operator at the 15th percentile. Why 15% and 85%? Because these values correspond roughly to one standard deviation either side of the mean. Therefore assuming the value of operators is

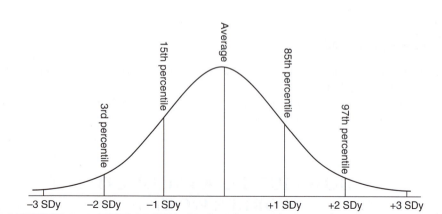

Figure 14.2 The distribution of employee productivity, showing the percentile points used in Rational Estimate technique to measure it.

normally distributed, the three estimates – 15th percentile, mean and 85th percentile – can be used to calculate the standard deviation of operator productivity, referred to as SDy. SDy summarizes the distribution in value to the employer of differences in output between employees (Figure 14.2). SDy tells the employer how much the workers' work varies in value. SDy is a vital term in the equation for estimating the return on a selection programme. The smaller SDy is, the less point there is putting a lot of effort and expense into selecting staff, because the less difference there is in value between good and poor staff. Note that the whole system depends on productivity, and value of output, being normally distributed, precisely the assumption that Aguinis and O'Boyle have challenged with their 'star' hypothesis.

A large number of supervisors make REs, then averages are calculated. Schmidt, Gast-Rosenberg and Hunter (1980) analysed REs for good, average, and poor computer programmers The differences between average and good, and average and poor, both around $10,000, did not differ significantly, which confirms the distribution is normal. Yoo and Muchinsky (1998) found that the more complex the job, in terms of either data analysis or interaction with other people, the greater SDy was, confirming Judiesch and Schmidt's (2000) finding for SD_p.

The 40–70% rule

SDy for computer programmers worked out at 55% of salary, which prompted Schmidt and Hunter to propose a rule of thumb:

SDy is between 40% and 70% of salary.

Good and poor workers are each one SDy from the average, so the difference between best and worst is two SDys. If SDy is 40% to 70% of salary, the difference between good and poor is between 80% and 140% of salary, which generates another rule of thumb:

> *The value of a good employee minus the value of a poor employee is roughly equal to the salary paid for the job.*

If salary for the job in question is £30,000, the difference in value between best and worst worker is roughly £30,000 too. Recall that good and poor, at the 85th percentile and 15th percentile, are far from being the extremes.

Are rational estimates valid?

Some critics think REs are dangerously subjective, and research has cast some doubt on their validity. Mathieu and Tannenbaum (1989) asked supervisors to explain how they generated REs and found most – especially the more experienced – based their estimates on salary. This makes some of Schmidt and Hunter's rules of thumb look suspiciously circular. If REs of SDy are based on salary, it is not surprising to find SDy closely related to salary.

CALCULATING THE RETURN ON SELECTION

It is fairly easy to calculate the cost of selection, although many employers only think of doing so when asked to introduce new methods; they rarely work out how much existing methods, such as day-long panel interviews, cost. It is much more difficult to calculate the return on selection. The formula was first stated by Brogden in 1946, but for many years had only academic interest because a crucial term in it could not be measured – SDy, the standard deviation of value of employee productivity. Until rational estimate technique was devised, there was no way of measuring how much more good employees are worth. Brogden's equation states:

$$\text{SAVING per EMPLOYEE per YEAR} = (r \times \text{SDy} \times Z) - (C / P)$$

where:

- r is the validity of the selection procedure (expressed as a correlation coefficient)
- SDy   is the standard deviation of employee value, in pounds, dollars or euros.
- Z is the calibre of recruits (expressed as their standard score on the selection test used).
- C is the cost of selection per applicant
- P is the proportion of applicants selected

Here is a worked example:

- The employer is recruiting in the salary range £40,000 p.a., so SDy can be estimated – by the 40% rule of thumb – at £16,000.
- The employer is using a test of mental ability whose validity is 0.45, so r is 0.45.
- The people recruited score on average 1 SD above the mean (for present employees), so Z is 1. This assumes the employer succeeds in recruiting high-calibre people.
- The employer uses a consultancy, who charge £750 per candidate.
- Of 10 applicants, four are appointed, so P is 0.40.

The SAVING per employee per year is:

$$(0.45 \times £16,000 \times 1) - (£750 / 0.40)$$
$$= £7,200 - £1,875$$
$$= £5,325$$

Each employee selected is worth some £5,000 a year more to the employer than one recruited at random. The four employees recruited will be worth in all £21,300 more to the employer each year. The larger the organization, the greater the total sum that can be saved by effective selection, hence the estimate in Chapter 1 of $18 million for the Philadelphia police force. Note also that SDy increases as test validity increases: using the latest (and highest) estimate of MA test validity, incorporating correction for indirect range restriction, means SDy increases to £9,325, and the saving for four recruits to £37,300.

Selection pays off better when:

- The calibre of recruits is high.
- Employees differ a lot in worth to the organization, i.e. SDy is high.
- The selection procedure has high validity.

Selection pays off less well when:

- Recruits are uniformly mediocre.
- SDy is low, i.e. workers do not vary much in value.
- The selection procedure has low validity.

Employers should have little difficulty attracting good recruits in periods of high unemployment (unless pay or conditions are poor). Rational estimate and other research shows SDy is rarely low. The third condition – zero validity – may apply quite often, when employers use poor selection methods. But if any of the three terms is zero, their product – the value of selection – is necessarily zero too. Only the right-hand side of the equation – cost – is never zero.

Utility analysis in practice

Other authors have pointed out that some utility theory estimates of savings achieved by good selection are over-optimistic.

- Brogden's equation overestimates the return on selection, because it assumes that everyone offered a job will accept it. Murphy (1986) pointed out that better applicants often reject offers so the calibre of the new employees – Z in the Brogden equation – is reduced, which in turn reduces the $ / £ / € return.
- At a more individual level, selecting the most capable may have hidden costs, if such individuals turn out to be divisive, verbally abusive, or bullying etc. This might reduce others' job satisfaction or even output, and result in people leaving the organization.
- Vance and Colella (1990) commented that utility theory makes the simplistic assumption that every worker works in isolation, whereas in reality much work is done by teams, where superhumans performing at the 95% percentile will be held back by slower mortals performing at the 50th percentile. Organizations in the Soviet Union had discovered this in the 1930s. They held up as a model a coalminer called Alexei Stakhanov who had exceeded his quota of coal many times over, and encouraged other workers to try to achieve enormous outputs. Some 'Stakhanovites' proved a liability; either because they produced far more of their product than was actually needed, or because the organization had to provide extra workers to bring in extra raw materials, and carry away the Stakhanovite's output.

Do utility estimates impress management?

Winkler, König and Kleinmann (2010) is the latest of several papers bemoaning the fact that utility estimates do not impress US management, and suggesting ways of presenting the information so that it will have an impact, and justify HR's existence. König *et al.* (2013) find utility analysis even less popular in Europe.

RESEARCH AGENDA

- Research on distribution of value of output in the UK, in a range of occupations, covering both private and public sectors.

PROVING SELECTION REALLY ADDS VALUE

Vance and Colella (1990) complained that utility estimates claim possible savings that dwarf the national debt, but that no one had actually proved any real savings were achieved. Recently some researches have provided proof, although it is probably still not as specific and definite as the critics would like.

Huselid, Jackson and Schuler (1997) correlated general HR effectiveness with employee productivity (net sales per employee), return on assets, and profitability, across 293 organizations. They reported weak (0.10 to 0.16) but significant correlations between HR effectiveness and capability, and return on assets and profitability, but not with employee productivity. Their measures of HR effectiveness and capability were, however, very global, including only a few specific references to selection and recruitment in a 41-item list. Their correlations may seem very low, but 0.10–0.20 is good by the standards of this type of research; it is difficult to demonstrate any relationship between how organizations operate and how well they do. Subsequently research in this area has burgeoned. Combs *et al.* (2006) report a meta-analysis of 92 studies, which find correlations of the same order of magnitude as Huselid's pioneering study. Most researches are similarly global, making it difficult to identify the contribution of better selection. Combs *et al.* separate out 15 studies which correlated *selectivity* with performance, finding a correlation of 0.14. Selectivity was coded from the number of selection tests the organization used or how many applicants were rejected, making it a fairly broad measure of selection.

Perhaps the most convincing data were provided by Terpstra and Rozell (1993). They correlated performance with selection practice across 201 organizations, and showed that organizations that used structured interviews, mental ability tests, biodata, analysis of recruiting source, and validation of selection methods had higher annual profits, more profit growth and more sales growth. The relationship was very strong (0.70–0.80) in sectors that arguably depend crucially on the calibre of their staff, such as service industry and the financial sector, but insignificant in sectors where capital equipment is possibly more important, such as manufacturing. (Or – as Aguinis and O'Boyle might argue – important in 'star'-type sectors, but not in normal distribution sectors.) Messersmith *et al.* (2011) report an analysis of HR practice and performance in 119 local government departments in Wales, which confirms a link, and suggests it is mediated by organizational citizenship, satisfaction, and commitment, i.e. that it works in part by changing the attitudes and behaviour of employees.

Most researches have taken a very broad view of HRM, on the argument that the whole pattern of HR matters, rather than specifics like selection. Most HR managers after all spend relatively little time on selection compared with training, performance management, employee relations, etc. It would nevertheless be useful to retain some specificity, to identify the contribution selection makes to organizational performance. In fact it would be useful to report even more specific analyses, looking for links between individual selection methods and organizational performance. Do organizations that use structured interviews make more money than ones that do not? Do organizations that rely on mental ability tests show higher productivity? Research has shown which methods have higher validity, in conventional validation research. But does a higher correlation between selection test and supervisor rating ultimately result in more profit for the organization? It should, but it would be useful to have confirmation. Perhaps some selection methods fail to realize their potential at the level of the 'bottom line'. Suppose personality tests put off many good applicants, or mental ability tests cause legal problems, or structured interviews fail to identify people who do not stay. The test's validity will not work through into better profitability or productivity. Critics note a serious flaw with this whole area of research: direction of cause. Most researches are cross-sectional, so data could be interpreted as showing that better-run companies are more profitable, and also use better HRM and selection methods. It does not follow that better HRM or selection creates greater profitability. For conclusive proof a longitudinal study is needed, showing that increased profitability follows changes in selection.

Human capital (HC) means – very broadly speaking – what the organization's workers have to offer in the way of abilities, experience, and expertise collectively rather than individually. The broad aim of selection is to increase the organization's HC. Crook *et al.* (2011) summarize 68 studies of HC and firm performance, and find an overall 0.21 correlation between HC and firm performance. HC measures tend to be very general, often just a global estimate of how good the organization thinks its staff are. Sometimes the measures are more specific, for example 'experience'. Rarely are they something that could be selected for; one study of the 68 mentioned mental ability as an index of HC. Kim and Ployhart (2014) report longitudinal analyses from Korea, covering the period 2000 to 2011, which includes the recession of December 2007 onward. They use a measure of 'selective staffing', which is simply the ratio of applicants to people appointed. Being able to choose from a large number of applicants, they argue, will tend to create better human capital, which will 'enable [company] flexibility and adaptation' in the difficult times of the recession; data from 359 companies confirm the hypothesis.

RESEARCH AGENDA

- More research at the organizational level, linking specific selection practices to profitability and productivity.
- More longitudinal study across organizations linking HR and selection to productivity.

THE APPLICANT'S PERSPECTIVE

Anderson (2004) comments how little notice selection research has taken the applicant's perspective, compared with the thousands of 'employer-centric' validation studies. One can list half a dozen good reasons why employers should ask themselves what As will make of their selection practices:

- Selection methods might put people off either applying or accepting an offer.
- Unhappy As may dissuade others from applying.

- Unhappy As may share their negative view of the organization with all their friends, and relatives, and colleagues – a sizeable number of people.
- Some rejected applicants may complain, perhaps even start a court case.
- Research has even suggested some disgruntled As cease buying the organization's products or services.
- Last but not least, abstract justice requires applicants be treated with respect.

Applicants' preferences for selection methods

Hausknecht, Day and Thomas (2004) meta-analysed 10 surveys of liking for nine selection methods. Figure 14.3 shows clearly that traditional methods of CV/résumé, reference and interview are favoured, graphology and personality questionnaires are not liked, and 'psychological tests' come in between. These results seem broadly stable across cultures, having been replicated in Europe and elsewhere (Anderson, Salgado & Hülsheger 2010). Hausknecht *et al.* suggested the data showed that people like methods that are face-valid and that give applicants the opportunity to perform well. Another interpretation could be that people like the familiar – CV, reference, interview – and do not trust psychologists' contributions.

Stone-Romero, Stone and Hyatt (2003) reported a US survey of perceived invasion of privacy by selection tests. Traditional tests, application form and interview, were seen as least invasive, lie detector and drug-use testing the most invasive. Psychological tests fell in between. Liking for methods and perceived (lack of) invasiveness seem closely linked. Sumanth and Cable (2011) focus on reactions to mental ability tests, and present US and UK data showing people are not attracted to employers who use MA tests, and are likely to feel insulted by being tested. This tendency is greater in 'high-status' people with

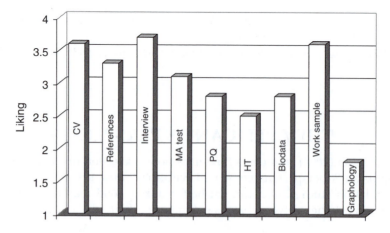

Figure 14.3   Favourability ratings of nine selection methods, across ten surveys. Data from Hausknecht *et al.* (2004).

established reputations. Note, however, that the research relies on self-report to assess reputation, with items like *People in my industry recognize my expertise*.

McCarthy *et al.* (2013) note that applicant reactions could be linked to selection and to subsequent job performance in two quite different ways:

1. Negative reactions reflect personality dispositions, for example higher neuroticism, which are also linked to poorer work performance (what one might call the 'disposition' hypothesis).
2. Negative reactions interfere with selection test performance, so result in lower test validity (the 'noise in selection' hypothesis).

McCarthy *et al.* analyse four datasets, and conclude the disposition hypothesis has some truth. They suggest that this implies employers need not worry too much about negative reactions to selection testing, especially if the job is stressful. They conclude there is no evidence that negative reactions result in lower selection validity.

Models of applicant reactions

Gilliland (1993) proposed an organizational justice model of reactions to selection, which has inspired a great deal of research. Organizational justice has two main aspects:

- Distributive justice – whether jobs go to those who deserve them. Relatively little research has been done on this aspect.
- Procedural justice – whether selection procedures are fair.

Gilliland listed nine aspects of procedural justice: assessment should:

- Be job-related.
- Be face-valid.
- Have perceived predictive validity.
- Give As the opportunity to perform well.
- Be consistently administered.
- Explain what is done and why.
- Be done by people who are pleasant and treat As with respect.
- Not ask improper questions.
- Provide opportunity for reconsideration.

Research has tended to focus on the first six of these. Hausknecht *et al.*'s (2004) meta-analysis showed that overall perceptions of procedural justice are shaped by job-relatedness, validity and opportunity to perform more than by consistency or explanation. Schleicher *et al.* (2006) note the paucity of research on opportunity to perform, which they argue is the most important procedural rule. Their data indicate people who were rejected for a real job complained afterwards of not having enough time, not being told clearly enough what to

Table 14.1 Correlation between procedural and distributive justice, and five outcomes.

	Procedural justice		Distributive justice	
	k	r	k	r
Attraction to organization	15	0.39	4	0.14
Intention to recommend	12	0.41	4	0.33
Intention to accept offer	12	0.25	1	0.44
Perceived performance in selection	8	0.47		
Actual performance in selection	14	0.11	3	0.26

Data from Hausknecht *et al.* (2004). NB excludes data collected from students rating hypothetical selections.

do, not being asked the right questions, etc. Other aspects of procedural justice, including job-relatedness, seemed less salient to them. Uggerslev, Fassina and Kraichy (2012) find a handful of studies relating to an aspect of perceived fairness mentioned in Gilliland's (1993) original paper, but largely overlooked since: fakability. Research confirms that applicants have a degree of preference for selection methods that cannot easily be faked.

Hausknecht *et al.* (2004) also meta-analysed the relationship between perceived justice, and five outcomes. Table 14.1 shows perceptions of procedural and distributive justice only weakly related to actual performance in selection. There were stronger links with how attracted As were to the organization, whether they would recommend it to others, and their intention to accept an offer. Hausknecht *et al.* found no usable research on links between perceived fairness and actual work performance, or applicant withdrawal. Uggerslev *et al.*'s (2012) second meta-analysis of the proliferating research confirms the link between attraction to an organization and its use of selection methods high in procedural justice.

Methodological problems

A lot of research on applicants' perception of selection is methodologically weak. Most studies collect all the information at the same time, from the same person, which creates problems of direction of cause. For example people who think the organization's selection methods unfair tend to say they are less likely to accept an offer. Do they decide not to accept an offer because they do not like the selection methods? Or do they form a dislike of the organization, so refuse the job offer, and incidentally find fault with the selection system? If researchers collected data on what people think of the selection system before they go through it, or before they find out whether they are successful, research would be in a stronger position to infer cause. Schleicher *et al.* (2006) asked people about selection methods twice, once after the assessment, then again three months after being told they had succeeded or failed. Rejection made people more critical of the selection's fairness. Too many studies use students, reacting to hypothetical selection, not real applicants for real jobs. Hausknecht *et al.* analysed students and real applicants separately, and found effects are stronger in student samples.

Other themes

While perceived fairness of selection is very important, there are other aspects of what applicants think that might usefully be researched: what applicants infer about the organization's likely success, or up-to-dateness, or whether they form expectations about how 'tight a ship' the organization will be. Schleicher *et al.* (2006) report one of very few studies to allow people to say what they think about selection, in their own words. Many comments concerned opportunity to perform, especially after people were told they had been turned down. Another theme was opportunity to interact with the assessors, which may explain why interviews are so popular. It might also be interesting to consider the perspective of not-so-good applicants (who nevertheless would like to get the job). They may not care much about accuracy or fairness. They may even prefer employers who use inaccurate selection methods because this gives them a better chance of getting the job.

Billsberry (2007) presents a completely open-ended survey of applicants' experiences of selection. Some accounts described experiences familiar to many: finding the shortlist includes an internal candidate who gets the job, leaving everyone else feeling – probably correctly – that they never had much chance, and were only there because the rules say five people must be interviewed. Another theme was deliberate misrepresentation, to get people to apply for, or accept, jobs which were not at all that applicants were led to believe. Several applicants mentioned failure to keep to schedule, interviewers who clearly had not read the application form, interviewers who seemed to have no idea how to conduct an interview, or made no attempt to conceal obvious, sometimes illegal, prejudices. Billsberry's data suggest many applicants see selection, or at least the selectors, in terms of competence, as well as fairness. Another theme in Billsberry's cases is malice: some applicants feel some managers see the interview as an opportunity to score points off applicants, or to be deliberately offensive. Wanberg *et al.* (2012) present some comments made by Americans searching for new jobs during the present (2007 onward) recession, which echo Billsberry's earlier UK observations: being interviewed by a very young HR person who did not seem to understand the questions he/she was asking which had presumably by supplied by someone else, being left waiting for a long time, having interviews cancelled at short notice, HR taking a very long time (six months) to do anything, misleading, inaccurate or vague job descriptions, and demographic discrimination, especially by age.

RESEARCH AGENDA

- More research on applicants' preferences, using real applicants with real experience of assessments.
- More longitudinal research on how applicants see selection.
- More open-ended exploratory research of how applicants view selection.

FIT

Most US selection research follows the 'predictivist' approach, focusing on selecting the most effective workers, who will maximize the organization's productivity. Workers are viewed in much the same way as raw materials, hence the name human *resource*. Utility theory and rational estimates exemplify this approach. Some Europeans prefer a different approach, seeing recruitment and selection as a social process, in which both worker and employer try to decide if the other is right for them – whether they 'fit' each other. Billsberry (2007) describes quite a few examples of applicants for jobs deciding during the selection process that this employer is not for them, sometimes even deciding because of the selection process. Others found the selection process well organized and the selectors fair and friendly, and were drawn to that employer. The worker is often at a considerable disadvantage here. Someone with scarce skills and a good track record (a possible 'star' in Aguinis and O'Boyle's terms), may be able to choose between several employers, and secure the job on favourable terms. Many workers have to take what they can get.

There is an extensive body of research on person organization fit (POF). Fit has been assessed in three ways:

- Direct – asking the person how well they fit the organization.
- Indirect subjective – the person describes his/her values, then the organization's values, and similarity is computed.
- Direct objective – the person describes his /her values, which are compared what the organization, in the shape of management or a consensus, says are its values.

Direct–subjective comparisons find a closer fit than direct–objective. Some people think they share more of the organization's values than they actually do. This could be a problem when, or if, they realize the discrepancy.

Kristof-Brown, Zimmerman and Johnson (2005) and Arthur *et al.* (2006) report meta-analyses of the extensive research on POF. The 'all studies' column of Table 14.2 finds POF weakly related to task performance, more strongly related to turnover and organizational citizenship, and very strongly related to (employer's) intent to hire. However, many studies collect all the data from the same source; finding employers do not intend to hire people they see as not sharing their values is not especially surprising. The conservative studies column of Table 14.2 contains only studies where the information comes from different sources. Relationships are much lower, but are still present for turnover, intent to hire, job satisfaction and commitment. Note also that there is not all that much research on POF and job performance that uses independent data on performance.

POF as selection test?

POF seems to predict turnover to a worthwhile extent, so could possibly be worth selecting for. Chapter 4 noted interviews are sometimes used to assess fit.

Table 14.2   Relationship of person–organization fit to six outcomes.

	All studies		Conservative studies	
	k	ρ	k	ρ
Task performance	17	0.13	9	0.04
Organizational citizenship	13	0.27	3	0.06
Turnover	8	0.24	6	0.23
Intent to hire	9	0.61	3	0.18
Job offer	8	0.32	6	0.03
Job satisfaction	65	0.44	19	0.29
Organizational commitment	44	0.51	12	0.27

Data from Kristof-Brown *et al.* (2005) and Arthur *et al.* (2006).

Selecting for 'fit' could lead to cloning, which Chapter 7 noted can be dangerous. 'Fit' could also be a code word for bias, even illegal discrimination. An alternative approach, outside the 'predictivist' perspective, might be to give applicants extensive, and candid, information about the organization, and rely on them to decide if they will 'fit'. Billsberry *et al.* (2005) note that POF has generally been defined in terms of values, meaning the organization's values; they suggest a less 'employer-centric' approach, allowing employees or applicants to say what they mean by fit, in their own words.

RESEARCH AGENDA

- More research linking fit, assessed by comparing employee's view with organization's, to work performance, and employer's intention to hire.
- Exploration of applicants' and employees' ideas about fit.

KEY POINTS

In Chapter 14 you have learned the following:

- People vary in the amount of work they do, and in the value of their work to the organization.
- Earlier theories argued that productivity of individual workers followed a normal distribution.
- The 'star' hypothesis argues the distribution is highly skewed, such that most people are average while a few 'stars' are outstanding.
- How much people vary in productivity can be calculated using various techniques including rational estimates.
- Utility analysis tries to put a cash value to choice of selection method, in terms of how much value good employees will add.

- Utility estimates do not seem to impress managers all that much.
- Some evidence suggests good selection may improve an organization's profitability.
- Applicants prefer some selection methods to others.
- Applicants' perceptions have been explained by an organizational justice perspective.
- Fit is related to turnover, but not to work performance.

KEY REFERENCES

Aguinis & O'Boyle (2014) argue the case for the 'star' hypothesis.

Billsberry (2007) presents 52 case studies of applicants' experience of selection.

Hausknecht *et al.* (2004) report a meta-analysis of applicant reactions to selection procedures.

Judiesch & Schmidt (2000) review research on individual differences in productivity.

Kim & Ployhart (2014) examine links between selection and productivity during the recent recession.

Kristof-Brown *et al.* (2005) review research on person–organization fit.

Terpstra & Rozell (1993) present data showing better selection may be linked to increased profitability.

Vance & Colella (1990) criticize utility theory estimates as unrealistic.

CHAPTER 15

Conclusions

Calculating the cost of smugness

We find everywhere a type of organization (administrative, commercial, or academic) in which the higher officials are plodding and dull, those less senior are active only in intrigue … and the junior men are frustrated and frivolous. Little is being attempted, nothing is being achieved.

C. Northcote Parkinson (1958)

In some organizations the costs of selecting ineffective staff mount indefinitely, because the organization lacks the mechanism, or the will, to dispense with their services. Naturally morale in such organizations suffers, driving out the remaining efficient workers, until only the incompetent remain, creating the state of terminal sickness so graphically described by Northcote Parkinson. Staff wander aimlessly about, 'giggling feebly', losing important documents, coming alive only to block the advancement of anyone more able, 'until the central administration gradually fills up with people stupider than the chairman'. Other diagnostics include surly porters and telephonists, out-of-order lifts, a proliferation of out-of-date notices, and smugness, especially smugness. The organization is doing a good job, in its own modest way; anyone who disagrees is a troublemaker who would probably be happier somewhere else. Parkinson advises that smugness is most easily diagnosed in the organization's refectory. The terminally smug do not just consume an 'uneatable, nameless mess'; they congratulate themselves on having catering staff who can provide it at such reasonable cost – 'smugness made absolute'.

Selectors sometimes often see their task as avoiding mistakes, minimizing error. They bring in psychologists as the final check the applicant is 'safe'. So long as the year's gone by, with no obvious disasters, and no complaints, HR have done their job. This negative approach to selection is wrong. Chapter 14 showed there is a continuous distribution of productivity from the very best to the very worst; selection is not as simple as avoiding mistakes – not employing a small minority of obvious incompetents or troublemakers. The employer who succeeds in employing average staff has not succeeded in employing good staff; the employer who finds good staff has not found excellent staff.

Personnel Selection: Adding Value Through People – A Changing Picture, Sixth Edition. Mark Cook.

HOW TO SELECT

Chapter 2 listed six criteria for judging selection tests:

- *reliable*   giving a consistent account of applicants (As)
- *valid*   selecting good As and rejecting poor ones
- *fair*   complying with equal opportunities legislation
- *acceptable*   to As as well as the organization
- *cost-effective*   saving the organization more than it costs to use
- *easy to use*   fitting conveniently into the selection process

Validity

Validity is the most important criterion. Unless a test can predict work performance, there is little point using it. (Unreliable tests cannot achieve high validity.) Table 15.1 collates the results of the various meta-analyses and VGAs discussed in earlier chapters. The earlier analyses, by Dunnette, Schmitt *et al.*, Reilly and Chao, and Hunter and Hunter, remain in some cases the main source of information. Later meta-analyses for graphology, interviewing, biographical measures, psychomotor tests, job knowledge tests, personality testing, projective tests, assessment centres, and work sample and trainability tests, generally confirm the conclusions of the earlier meta-analyses. Research on personality questionnaires confirms they generally predict job proficiency fairly poorly, but other research – not included in Table 15.1 – suggests PQs may predict organizational citizenship, leadership, and absence of counter-productive work behaviour more successfully. Note, however, that trim-and-fill analysis (Chapter 2) has cast some doubt on meta-analytic conclusions; re-analysis may result in downward revision of some validity estimates.

Fairness

Fairness in the legal sense. Table 15.2 summarizes the relative merits of 12 selection methods, against five criteria (subsuming reliability under validity). Ratings for fairness in Table 15.2 are primarily based on US experience. (Things may be different in other countries: recall that König, Jöri and Knüsel (2011) say the law seems to have little impact on selection in Switzerland). As time passes, selection methods tend to acquire poorer ratings under this heading. For example, personality tests were listed as 'untested' in the second edition of this book, but from the fourth edition were listed as 'some doubts' because the US *Soroka* case had raised, but not settled, the issue of invasion of privacy. Since the fourth edition, new meta-analyses and distinguishing between adverse impact in applicants and present employees has thrown doubt on work samples and assessment centres, which used to be thought 'safe'. Bobko and Roth (1999) have challenged the generally accepted view that structured interviews and biodata cause no adverse impact. Consequently no test now has a 'no problem' rating.

Table 15.1 Summary of the validity of different selection tests for work performance.

	Early analyses				Later analyses				Specific analyses
	Dun	R&C	H&H	SGN	W&C	H&A	McD	HCW	
Reference									
Interview									
unstructured	16	18[uc]	26		47	37	47		40 Schmidt & Rader (1999)
structured		19[uc]	14		31	20	33		62 Salgado et al. (2003)
empirical					62	57	44		66[irr] Schmidt, Oh & Le (2006)
General mental ability	45		53	25				70[irr]	66[irr] Kramer (2009)
Psychomotor ability	35								42 Salgado (1998)

	Early analyses				Later analyses				
	Dun	R&C	H&H	SGN	B&M	TJR	Sal	BMJ	S&P
Personality questionnaire	08								
Neuroticism					-07	-22	-13	-11	-27[cx]
Extraversion					10	16	08	11	25[cx]
Openness					-03	27	06	04	19[cx]
Agreeableness					06	33	01	09	24[cx]
Conscientiousness					23	18	15	20	30[cx]

	Early analyses				Later analyses	
	Dun	R&C	H&H	SGN	C&O	OWM
Others' report						
Neuroticism					-17	-18
Extraversion					11	24
Openness					22	22
Agreeableness					17	26
Conscientiousness					28	32

(Continued)

Table 15.1 (Continued)

	Early analyses				Later analyses					Specific analyses
	Dun	R&C	H&H	SGN	C&O	OWM	Bli	Fun	Dra	
Projective tests	"little"	18[uc]								Martinussen & Torjussen (1993) — 20[uc]; Collins et al. (2004) — 16–20[uc]; Hoffman et al. (2011) — 19; Norton (1992) — 58; Neter & Ben-Shakar (1989) — zero
Peer ratings		37[uc]		49						
Graphology		"none"								
Biodata	34	35	37	24						
Assessment centre			43	41		47	30[uc]		21[uc]	Gaugler et al. (1987) — 37; Hardison & Sackett (2007) — 26; Becker et al. (2011) — 40
Emotional intelligence										Joseph et al. (2015) — 29
Situational judgement test										McDaniel et al. (2007) — 26
Self-assessment										Mabe & West (1982) — 08–45
Physical test			32							
Education		14	10							Roth et al. (1996) — 33
Work sample test			54	38						Roth, Bobko & McFarland (2005) — 33
Trainability test										Robertson & Downs (1989) — 20–24[uc]
In-tray test										Whetzel, Rotenberry & McDaniel (2014) — 42

Dun   R&C   H&H   SGN

^α contextualized PQs
^{uc} uncorrected validity

^{irr} corrected for indirect range restriction

Bli	Bliesener (1996)	BMJ	Barrick, Mount & Judge (2001)

Bli   Bliesener (1996)
B&M   Barrick & Mount (1991)
Dra   Drakeley, in Gunter et al. (1993)
Fun   Funke et al. (1987)
H&H   Hunter & Hunter (1984)
McD   McDaniel et al. (1994)
R&C   Reilly & Chao (1982)
S&P   Shaffer & Postlethwaite (2012)
TJR   Tett, Jackson & Rothstein (1991)

BMJ   Barrick, Mount & Judge (2001)
C&O   Connelly & Ones (2010
Dun   Dunnette (1972)
H&A   Huffcutt & Arthur (1994)
HCW   Huffcutt, Culbertson & Weyhrauch (2014)
OWM   Oh, Wang & Mount (2011)
Sal   Salgado (1997)
SGN   Schmitt et al. (1984)
W&C   Wiesner & Cronshaw (1988)

Table 15.2   Summary of 12 selection tests by five criteria.

	Validity	Legal fairness	Acceptability	Cost	Practicality
Interview	Low	Uncertain	High	Med/high	High
Structured IV	High	Some doubts	Some doubts	High	? Limited
References	Moderate	Some doubts	Medium	Very low	High
Others' ratings	High	Untested	Low	Very low	Very limited
Biodata	High	Some doubts	Low	High/low	High
Ability test	High	Major problems	Low	Low	High
Psychomotor	High	Untested	Untested	Low	Moderate
Job knowledge	High	Some doubts	Untested	Low	High
PQ	Variable	Some doubts	Low	Low	Fair
AC	High	Some doubts	High	Very high	Fair
Work sample	High	Some doubts	High	High	Moderate
Education	Moderate	Major doubts	Untested	Nil	High

Diversity-validity dilemma

Ployhart and Holtz (2008) describe the problem facing HR in the USA. They want to use valid tests to select, but must also do so to achieve a diverse, or representative, workforce. Unfortunately validity and diversity seem to some extent inversely related; the most valid tests tend to create the most adverse impact. Ployhart and Holtz review 16 varied attempts to solve this dilemma, such as score banding, emphasis on personality rather than ability, and modifying ability tests, all discussed in previous chapters. They suggest using interview, situational judgement tests, and biodata, either supplementing ability tests or replacing them, reducing reading and mental ability requirements as far as possible, and using face-valid methods such as interviews to try to ensure applicants see the selection process as fair.

One gets the strong impression that public opinion in Britain will think diversity much more important than validity, and that employers who press for greater validity in selection at the expense of less diversity could attract some very negative publicity. It might be worth someone's while to commission a survey of public opinion on this issue, in both the USA and Britain, differentiating respondents by occupational level.

Cost

Cost tends to be accorded too much weight by selectors. Cost is not an important consideration, so long as the test has validity. A valid test, even the most elaborate and expensive, is almost always worth using. Chapter 13 showed the return on selection is often considerable, far outweighing its cost. In Table 15.2 interview costs are given as medium/low, because interviews vary so much, and because they're so much taken for granted that few estimates of their cost have been made. Structured interview costs are high, because they have to be written specially for each job. Biodata costs are given as high or low; the cost is high if the inventory has to be specially written for the employer, but might be lower if a 'ready-made' consortium biodata could be used. The cost of using educational qualifications is given as nil, because the information is routinely collected through application form or software. Checking what As say will cost a small amount.

Practicality

Practicality means the test is not difficult to introduce, because it fits into the selection process easily. Ability and personality questionnaires are very practical because they can be given over the Internet, or to groups of applicants. References are very practical because everyone is used to giving them. Assessment centres are only fairly practical, because they need a lot of organizing. Peer assessments are highly impractical because they require applicants to spend a long time with each other, or need some means of contacting applicants' families, friends, or former work colleagues and persuading them to provide accurate information. Structured interviews may have limited practicality, because managers may resist the loss of autonomy involved. Work sample and psychomotor tests have limited practicality, because candidates have to be tested individually, not in groups

Acceptability

Acceptability to applicants is important, especially in times of full employment. Ratings are largely based on Hausknecht, Day and Thomas's (2004) meta-analysis of various surveys, described in Chapter 14.

Taking validity as the overriding consideration, there are seven classes of test with high validity: peer ratings, biodata, structured interviews, ability tests, assessment centres, work sample tests, and job knowledge tests. Three of these have limited scope. Peer ratings can rarely be used in selection, while work sample and job knowledge tests only work for jobs where specific skills or knowledge are central. This leaves biodata, structured interviews, MA tests and assessment centres.

- Biodata do not achieve quite such good validity as ability tests, and are not as transportable, which makes them more expensive.
- Structured interviews have excellent validity but limited transportability, and are expensive to set up.
- MA tests have excellent validity, can be used for all sorts of job, are readily transportable, are cheap and easy to use, but fall foul of the law in the USA, and might one day do the same in Britain or Europe.
- Assessment centres have excellent validity, can be used for most grades of staff, but are difficult to install, expensive, and may create adverse impact.
- Work samples have excellent validity, and are easy to use, but are expensive, because they are necessarily specific to the job, and may create adverse impact.

Most other tests in Tables 15.1 and 15.2 have lower validity – but not zero validity. Tests with validities below 0.10–0.20 can be worth using, if they are cheap, or if they contribute new information. Hence the only test in Table 15.1 that can be definitely dismissed as never worth using is graphology.

- Personality questionnaires achieve poor validity for predicting work performance, but may prove more useful for predicting other aspects of the applicant's contribution to the organization.
- References have only moderate validity, but are cheap to use. Legal cautions, however, are tending to limit their value.

Incremental validity

The big gap in present knowledge is the validity of combinations of tests. Schmidt and Hunter (1998) made estimates based on intercorrelations of predictors, and argue that many other tests add little to mental ability tests. Empirical research on actual incremental validity is as yet relatively thin. Chapter 7 shows that personality tests do contribute incremental validity, when used with MA tests. Chapter 11 shows that in-tray exercises contribute incremental validity to tests of mental ability. There remain, however, a large number of possible combinations of selection methods where no information about incremental validity is available. Do reference checks improve on personality inventories? Is there anything to be gained adding peer ratings to work samples and MA tests? What combination of the methods listed in Tables 15.1 and 15.2 will give the best results, and how good will that 'best' be?

Positive manifold

Murphy, Dzieweczynski and Zhang (2009) advance the hypothesis of positive manifold: 'a consistent pattern of positive correlations among tests and of positive correlations between tests and criteria'. Positive manifold implies that 'the match or mismatch between the content of those tests and the content of the jobs will have little impact on the criterion-related validity of test batteries'. Chapter 6 showed that tests of mental ability are generally highly correlated even when they are using different types of items – verbal, abstract, numerical, clerical – to assess different types of ability. Murphy et al. suggest this extends to other tests as well, mentioning structured interviews, biodata, work samples, situational judgement tests, psychomotor and spatial tests. One type of test, however, does not show the positive manifold effect: personality measures. One consequence of positive manifold is 'flat validities': any combination of the tests, except of personality, will give much the same result. This has two implications. It implies synthetic validity will not work and that careful matching of the job's characteristics to the content of the test will not increase validity. More broadly it suggests the entire traditional model of selection – work analysis determining choice of tests to use – may not be all that vital, or all that useful. Their analysis, however, confined itself to the 10 subtests of the Armed Services Vocational Aptitude Battery (ASVAB), which

Ree and Earles (1991) had shown not to add much to a general mental ability score (see Chapter 6). The positive manifold hypothesis implies validity may not be greatly improved by matching test to job, but matching will help meet claims of unfairness, and make the tests acceptable. Positive manifold perhaps also implies that the incremental validity attainable by adding more tests will always be fairly limited, unless they are of personality.

Incompetence + jealousy = 'injelitance'?

The discussion has assumed that all employers genuinely want the best applicants; Northcote Parkinson thinks this very naive: 'if the head of an organization is second rate, he will see to it that his immediate staff are all third-rate: and they will, in turn, see to it that their subordinates are fourth rate'. Such organizations suffer *injelitance* – 'a disease of induced inferiority', compounded equally of incompetence and jealousy. The 'injelitant' organization does not fill up with stupid people accidentally: dull, smug people at its core deliberately recruit even duller, smugger people, to protect their own positions. And what better way is there to perpetuate incompetence than the traditional interview? Mediocrities can be selected and promoted, using the code words 'soundness', 'teamwork', and 'judgement'. And what greater threat to injelitant organizations can there be than objective tests of ability which might introduce unwelcome, disruptive, 'clever' people? Parkinson thinks injelitance a terminal illness of organizations, which can only be cured by dismissing all the staff, and burning the buildings to the ground; he does suggest, however, that 'infected personnel' might be 'dispatched with a warm testimonial to such rival institutions as are regarded with particular hostility'.

THE FUTURE OF SELECTION

This final section offers a number of suggestions about likely trends, under five headings.

Technical refinements

Voice recognition and transcription Voice recognition and transcription software may soon make it possible to generate transcripts of interviews, group discussions and other AC exercises very quickly and cheaply. This could prove useful in cases of dispute about improper interview questions, for quality checks on interviewers, and to extract far more information, and more accurate information, from interviews and group exercises.

Computer simulations Computers can now generate realistic images of people moving and talking; this is already done in computer games and in the cinema. It may be possible to generate role plays or other exercises using computer-generated 'customers', 'complainants' or 'appraisees'. These would be more convenient and economical to use, and could be more consistent than a human role player. The problem with simulations is not so much generating the images and sounds, but providing a plausible and realistic script, and devising software that can characterize the assessee's responses, so that the system can react to them.

Short-term trends in assessment

Testing Grade inflation, in school and university exams, may devalue educational qualifications, and encourage more employers to use ability tests. Already some universities are considering whether to use tests to select students, saying the school exams do not differentiate. Some employers are saying the same about university degrees.

Attributes assessed

Assessing the applicant as a person, rather than assessing specific abilities that are very closely job-related, may become more common. Employers need people who can adapt to new skills, fill a variety of roles, etc. Some employees need to be able to cope with stress. Others need to be able to cope with aggressive or violent customers. Increasing globalization might make it necessary to assess more specifically the ability to fit into other cultures, or work 'away from home', an issue that arises already with expatriate staff. Increasing emphasis on 'security' may create a need to assess for 'security risk', which may prove very difficult, for several reasons: faking good and concealment, links with ethnicity, and a low base rate (e.g. one person in 10,000), hence a lot of false positives (people labelled a risk when they are not).

Changes in the law

Limits on what HR can assess people by Brenkert (1993) argues that the 'commercial relationship does not entitle [the employer] to probe the attitudes, motives, and beliefs of the person beyond their own statements, record of past actions and the observations of others'. Brenkert's argument would restrict assessment to educational achievement and work experience, results of technical and cognitive tests, 'in-tray' exercises, role playing, group exercises, as well as references and interview structured around the candidate's job knowledge. This links to the idea that HR should only assess the specific ability to carry out the job activities, and should therefore only assess specific knowledge and skills. Applicants should not be assessed on any 'non-job-relevant' activities, which excludes leisure interests, lifestyle, possibly also personality. This would severely restrict most 'sifting' systems, which often rely heavily on non-work activity.

Privacy The idea of a right to privacy is gaining ground, and could have implications for selection assessments. Personality tests in particular may be especially vulnerable because they can appear very intrusive to applicants, as well as not sufficiently job-related.

Data protection Employees now have some rights of access to personnel files. Applicants have some right of access to interview notes, test data, and references. Some organizations list specified materials, for example interview notes, that should be retained in case applicants want to see them (and assessors are warned not to write down anything unsuitable). Suppose assessors were required to keep a detailed record of the whole process, including possibly a record of discussions about which of two equally matched applicants gets the job and why.

Factors that might limit legal controls on selection

Globalization Developed countries like Britain and the USA have to compete with countries where wages are lower, and employers less regulated. Organizations that find it too expensive or onerous to employ people in Europe or North America may move their operations to cheaper, less extensively regulated countries.

'Emergencies' In wartime, people's rights tend to be suddenly and drastically curtailed. During the Second World War the British government quickly gave itself powers to direct people into any employment where they were needed. The elaborate system of fair employment legislation could disappear very quickly if it seemed to be hindering a country's ability to cope with an external threat.

Broader strategic issues

Over-optimistic expectations One sometimes gets the impression that more and more people are coming to believe that almost anyone can do almost any job. Politicians and the media seem to encourage this view, and talk of structuring the education system to ensure that it works. It would end the need for personnel selection and render this book obsolete. It would be worth testing the hypothesis by unselected intakes into some selected jobs, where nothing could go horribly wrong if the hypothesis turned out to be incorrect.

However, the research reviewed in this book tends to disprove the hypothesis. Some jobs require abilities that not everyone possesses, and perhaps not everyone can acquire. This implies some people's career aspirations are not going to be met. It could also mean that some jobs end up being done by people who are not able to do them very well, because the pressure to fill them is too great.

Psychological contract Once upon a time employees and employers had a 'psychological contract': the employee gave loyalty and commitment, and in exchange the employer provided a job for life, with training and promotion, etc. In the hard times of the 1980s many employees found the psychological contract 'wasn't worth the paper it wasn't written on'. When employers needed to, they broke the contract and made people redundant, in large numbers. The breaking of the psychological contract should make employees view the organization differently, perhaps more realistically. Employees might be less willing to go beyond their contractual obligations. This might reduce the scope for personality measures, because individual differences in organizational citizenship might be less important, or less readily translated into differences in performance.

Power balance In Britain since 1979 the power of the trade unions has declined greatly, which has correspondingly increased the power of management. Organizations are free to pursue productivity and profitability. Unsatisfactory or superfluous employees can be 'released'. It could be argued that the easier it is terminate unsatisfactory staff, the less vital effective selection becomes.

Rising unemployment An employer who succeeds in recruiting able, productive workers needs fewer of them. If all employers use highly accurate tests to select very productive workers, the number of jobs will shrink, creating more unemployment. If employers start exchanging information, the ungifted could find themselves never even being shortlisted. This has some alarming implications:

- A steadily growing, unemployed, disillusioned, and resentful underclass.
- What will all those unemployed people do? Will the government have to bring in work programmes to keep them occupied and out of trouble?
- At the other end of the distribution of ability, a shrinking workforce, of more able people, works harder and longer to maximize productivity. In the process, they wear themselves out, and have no time left to enjoy life.
- If fewer and fewer people produce more and more, who is going to buy it? How are they going to pay for it?

References

Aamodt M G, Bryan D A & Whitcomb A J (1993) Predicting performance with letters of recommendation. *Public Personnel Management*, **22**, 81–90.

Agerström J, Björklund F, Carlsson R & Rooth D-O (2012) Warm and competent Hassan = cold and incompetent Erik: a harsh equation of real-life hiring discrimination. *Basic and Applied S ocial Psychology*, **34**, 359–366.

Agerström J & Rooth D-O (2011) The role of automatic obesity stereotypes in real hiring decisions. *Journal of Applied Psychology*, **96**, 790–805.

Aguinis H, Culpepper S A & Pierce C A (2010) Revival of test bias research in preemployment testing. *Journal of Applied Psychology*, **95**, 648–680.

Aguinis H, Mazurkiewicz M D & Heggestad E D (2009) Using web-based frame-of-reference training to decrease biases in personality-based job analysis: an experimental field study. *Personnel Psychology*, **62**, 405–438.

Aguinis H & O'Boyle E (2014) Star performers in twenty-first century organisations. *Personnel Psychology*, **67**, 313–350.

Allen T D, Facteau J D & Facteau C L (2004) Structured interviewing for OCB: construct validity, faking, and the effects of question type. *Human Performance*, **17**, 1–24.

Anderson N (2004) Editorial – the dark side of the moon: applicant perspectives, negative psychological effects (NPEs), and candidate decision making in selection. *International Journal of Selection and Assessment*, **12**, 1–8.

Anderson N, Salgado J F & Hülsheger U R (2010) Applicant reactions in selection: comprehensive meta-analysis into reaction generalisation versus situational specificity. *International Journal of Selection and Assessment*, **18**, 291–304.

Anderson V V (1929) *Psychiatry in Industry*. Henry Holt, New York.

Andler E C & Herbst D (2002) *The Complete Reference Checking Handbook*, 2nd edn. Amacom, New York.

Anstey E (1977) A 30–year follow-up of the CSSB procedure, with lessons for the future. *Journal of Occupational Psychology*, **50**, 149–159.

Arneson J J, Sackett P R & Beatty A S (2011) Ability-performance relationships in education and employment settings: critical tests of the more-is-better and the good-enough hypotheses. *Psychological Science*, **22**, 1336–1342.

Arthur W, Bell S T, Villado A J & Doverspike D (2006) The use of person-organization fit in employment decision making: an assessment of its criterion-related validity. *Journal of Applied Psychology*, **91**, 786–901.

Arthur W, Day E A, McNelly T L & Edens P S (2003) A meta-analysis of the criterion-related validity of assessment center dimensions. *Personnel Psychology*, **56**, 125–154.

Arthur W, Day E A & Woehr D J (2008) Mend it, don't end it: an alternate view of assessment center construct-related validity evidence. *Industrial and Organizational Psychology* **1**, 106–111.

Arthur W, Doverspike D, Barrett G V & Miguel R (2013) Chasing the Title VII holy grail: the pitfalls of guaranteeing adverse impact elimination. *Journal of Business Psychology*, **28**, 473–485.

Personnel Selection: Adding Value Through People – A Changing Picture,
Sixth Edition. Mark Cook.
© 2016 John Wiley & Sons, Ltd. Published 2016 by John Wiley & Sons, Ltd.

Arthur W & Villado A J (2008) The importance of distinguishing between constructs and methods when comparing predictors in personnel selection and practice, *Journal of Applied Psychology*, **93**, 435–442.

Arthur W, Woehr D J, Akande A & Strong M H (1995) Human resource management in West Africa: practices and perceptions. *International Journal of Human Resource Management*, **6**, 347–367.

Arvey R D & Begalla M E (1975) Analysing the homemaker job using the Position Analysis Questionnaire. *Journal of Applied Psychology*, **60**, 513–517.

Avolio B J & Waldman D A (1994) Variations in cognitive, perceptual, and psychomotor abilities across the working life span: examining the effects of race, sex, experience, education, and occupational type. *Psychology and Ageing*, **9**, 430–442.

Back M B, Stopfer J M, Vazire S, Gaddis S, Schmukle S C, Egloff B & Gosling S D (2010) Facebook profiles reflect actual personality, not self-idealization, *Psychological Science*, **21**, 372–374.

Bangerter A, König C J, Blatti S & Salvisberg A (2009) How widespread is graphology in personnel selection practice? A case study of a job market myth. *International Journal of Selection and Assessment*, **17**, 219–230.

Banks G C, Kepes S & McDaniel M A (2012) Publication bias: a call for improved meta-analytic practice in the organizational sciences. *International Journal of Selection and Assessment*, **20**, 182–196.

Barge B N & Hough L M (1986) Utility of biographical data for predicting job performance. In L M Hough (ed.) *Utility of Temperament, Biodata and Interest Assessment for Predicting Job Performance: A Review of the Literature*. Army Research Institute, Alexandria, VA.

Barrett G V, Polomsky M D & McDaniel M A (1999) Selection tests for firefighters: a comprehensive review and meta-analysis. *Journal of Business and Psychology*, **13**, 507–514.

Barrick M R & Mount M K (1991) The big five personality dimensions and job performance: a meta-analysis. *Personnel Psychology*, **44**, 1–26.

Barrick M R, Mount M K & Judge T A (2001) Personality and performance at the beginning of the new millennium: what do we know and where do we go next? *International Journal of Selection and Assessment*, **9**, 9–30.

Barrick M R, Shaffer J A & DeGrassi S W (2008) A meta-analysis of the relationship between peripheral information and employment interview outcomes. Paper presented at 23rd Annual Conference of SIOP, San Francisco.

Barrick M R, Shaffer J A & DeGrassi S W (2009) What you see may not be what you get: relationships among self-presentation tactics and ratings of interview and job performance. *Journal of Applied Psychology*, **94**, 1394–1411.

Barrick M R & Zimmerman R D (2005) Reducing voluntary, avoidable turnover through selection. *Journal of Applied Psychology*, **90**, 159–166.

Barron L G & Hebl M (2013) The force of law: the effects of sexual orientation antidiscrimination legislation on interpersonal discrimination in employment. *Psychology, Public Policy & Law*, **19**, 191–205.

Barthell C N & Holmes D S (1968) High school yearbooks: a nonreactive measure of social isolation in graduates who later became schizophrenics. *Journal of Abnormal Psychology*, **73**, 313–316.

Bartram D (2000) Internet recruitment and selection: kissing frogs to find princes. *International Journal of Selection and Assessment*, **8**, 261–274.

Bartram D (2005) The great eight competencies: a criterion-centric approach to validation. *Journal of Applied Psychology*, **90**, 1185–1203.

Baxter J C, Brock B, Hill P C & Rozelle R M (1981) Letters of recommendation: a question of value. *Journal of Applied Psychology*, **66**, 296–301.

Beatty A S, Barratt C L, Berry C N & Sackett P R (2014) Testing the generalizability of indirect range restriction corrections. *Journal of Applied Psychology*, **99**, 587–598.

Becker N, Hoft S, Holzenkamp M & Spinath F M (2011) The predictive validity of assessment centers in German-speaking regions: a meta-analysis. *Journal of Personnel Psychology*, **10**, 61–69.

Becker T E & Colquitt A L (1992) Potential versus actual faking of a biodata form: an analysis along several dimensions of item type. *Personnel Psychology*, **45**, 389–406.

Becker W C (1960) The matching of behavior rating and questionnaire personality factors. *Psychological Bulletin*, **57**, 201–212.

Bell S T (2007) Deep-level composition variables as predictors of team performance: a meta-analysis. *Journal of Applied Psychology*, **92**, 595–615.

Bennett R J & Robinson S L (2000) Development of a measure of workplace deviance. *Journal of Applied Psychology*, **85**, 349–360.

Bernard L C, Walsh P & Mills M (2005) The Motivation Analysis Test: an historical and contemporary evaluation. *Psychological Reports*, **96**, 464–492.

Bernerth J B, Taylor S G, Walker H J & Whitman D S (2012) An empirical investigation of dispositional antecedents and performance-related outcomes of credit scores. *Journal of Applied Psychology*, **97**, 469–478.

Berry C M, Clark M A & McClure T K (2011) Racial/ethnic differences in the criterion-related validity of cognitive ability tests: a qualitative and quantitative review. *Journal of Applied Psychology*, **96**, 881–906.

Berry C M, Cullen M J & Meyer J M (2014) Racial/ethnic differences in cognitive ability test range restriction: implications for differential validity. *Journal of Applied Psychology*, **99**, 21–37.

Berry C M, Gruys M L & Sackett P R (2006) Educational attainment as proxy for cognitive ability in selection: effects on levels of cognitive ability and adverse impact. *Journal of Applied Psychology*, **91**, 696–705.

Berry C M, Ones D S & Sackett P R (2007) Interpersonal deviance, organizational deviance, and their common correlates: a review and meta-analysis. *Journal of Applied Psychology*, **92**, 410–424.

Berry C M & Sackett P R (2008) Toward understanding race differences in validity of cognitive ability tests. Paper presented at 23rd Annual Conference of Industrial and Organizational Psychology, San Francisco.

Berry C M & Sackett P R (2009) Faking in selection: tradeoffs in performance versus fairness resulting from two cut-score strategies. *Personnel Psychology*, **62**, 835–863.

Berry C M, Sackett P R & Landers R N (2007) Revisiting interview-cognitive ability relationships: attending to specific range restriction mechanisms in meta-analysis. *Personnel Psychology*, **60**, 837–874.

Berry C M, Sackett P R & Tobares V (2010) A meta-analysis of conditional reasoning tests of aggression. *Personnel Psychology*, **63**, 361–384.

Berry C M, Sackett P R & Wiemann S (2007) A review of recent developments in integrity test research. *Personnel Psychology*, **60**, 271–301.

Berry C M & Zhao P (2015) addressing criticisms of existing bias research: cognitive ability test scores still overpredict African-Americans' job performance. *Journal of Applied Psychology*, **100**, 162–179.

Bertrand M & Mullainathan S (2004) Are Emily and Greg more employable than Lakisha and Jamal? A field experiment on labor market discrimination. *American Economic Review*, **94**, 991–1013.

Beus J M, Dhahani L Y & McCord M A (2015) A meta-analysis of personality and workplace safety: addressing unanswered questions. *Journal of Applied Psychology*, **100**, 481–498.

Beus J M & Whitman D S (2012) The relationship between typical and maximum performance: a meta-analytic examination. *Human Performance*, **25**, 355–376.

Billsberry J (2007) *Experiencing Recruitment and Selection*. Wiley, Chichester.

Billsberry J, Ambrosini V, Moss-Jones J & Marsh P (2005) Some suggestions for mapping organizational members' sense of fit. *Journal of Business and Psychology*, **19**, 555–570.

Bing M N, Stewart S M, Davison H K, Green P D, McIntyre M D & James L R (2007) An integrative typology of personality assessment for aggression: implications for predicting counterproductive workplace behavior. *Journal of Applied Psychology*, **92**, 722–744.

Bingham W V & Freyd M (1926) *Procedures in Employment Psychology*. Shaw, Chicago.

Birkeland S A, Manson T M, Kisamore J L, Brannick M T & Smith M A (2006) A meta-analytic investigation of job applicant faking on personality measures. *International Journal of Selection and Assessment*, **14**, 317–335.

Bliesener T (1996) Methodological moderators in validating biographical data in personnel selection. *Journal of Occupational and Organizational Psychology*, **69**, 107–120.

Bobko P & Roth P L (1999) Derivation and implications of a meta-analytic matrix incorpo-rating cognitive ability, alternative predictors, and job performance. *Personnel Psychology*, **52**, 561–589.

Bommer W H, Johnson J L, Rich G A, Podsakoff P M & MacKenzie S B (1995) On the interchangeability of objective and subjective measures of employee performance: a meta-analysis. *Personnel Psychology*, **48**, 587–605.

Borkenau P & Liebler A (1993) Convergence of stranger ratings of personality and intelligence with self-ratings, partner ratings, and measured intelligence. *Journal of Personality and Social Psychology*, **65**, 546–553.

Borkenau P, Riemann R, Angleitner A & Spinath F M (2001) Genetic and environmental influences on observed personality: evidence from the German Observational Study of Adult Twins. *Journal of Personality and Social Psychology*, **80**, 655–668.

Bowler M C & Woehr D J (2006) A meta-analytic evaluation of the impact of dimension and exercise factors on assessment center ratings. *Journal of Applied Psychology*, **91**, 1114–1124.

Bozionelos N (2005) When the inferior candidate is offered the job: the selection interview as a political and power game. *Human Relations*, **58**, 1605–1631.

Bray D W & Grant D L (1966) The assessment center in the measurement of potential for business management. *Psychological Monographs*, **80** (17, whole No. 625).

Brenkert G G (1993) Privacy, polygraphs and work. In T White (ed.) *Business Ethics: A Philosophical Reader*. Macmillan, New York.

Brown S H (1981) Validity generalisation and situational moderation in the life insurance industry. *Journal of Applied Psychology*, **66**, 664–670.

Brtek M D & Motowidlo S J (2002) Effects of procedure and outcome accountability on interview validity. *Journal of Applied Psychology*, **87**, 185–191.

Brummel B J, Rupp D E & Spain S M (2009) Constructing parallel simulation exercises for assessment centers and other forms of behavioral assessment. *Personnel Psychology*, **62**, 137–170.

Buffardi L C, Fleishman E A, Morath R A & McCarthy P M (2000) Relationships between ability requirements and human errors in job tasks, *Journal of Applied Psychology*, **85**, 551–564.

Bureau of National Affairs (1995) Hiring. *Personnel Management*, **201**, 284–285.

Burns G N & Christiansen N D (2006) Sensitive or senseless: on the use of social desirability measures in selection and assessment. In R L Griffith & M H Peterson (eds.) *A Closer Examination of Applicant Faking Behavior*. Information Age Publishing, Greenwich, CT.

Burns G N & Christiansen N D (2011) Methods of measuring faking behaviour. *Human Performance*, **24**, 358–372.

Buss D M & Craik K H (1983) The act frequency approach to personality. *Psychological Review*, **90**, 105–126.

Buster M A, Roth P L & Roth P (2005) A process for content validation of education and experience-based minimum qualifications: an approach resulting in federal court approval. *Personnel Psychology*, **58**, 771–799.

Callender J C & Osburn H G (1981) Testing the constancy of validity with computer-generated sampling distributions of the multiplicative model variance estimate: results for petroleum industry validation research. *Journal of Applied Psychology*, **66**, 274–281.

Campion M A, Fink A A, Ruggeberg B J, Carr L, Phillips G M & Odman R B (2011) Doing competencies well: best practices in competency modelling. *Personnel Psychology*, **64**, 225–262.

Carlson K D, Scullen S E, Schmidt F L, Rothstein H & Erwin F (1999) Generalizable bio-graphical data validity can be achieved without multi-organizational development and keying. *Personnel Psychology*, **52**, 731–753.

Carlsson R, Agerström J, Björklund F, Carlsson M & Rooth D-O (2014) Testing for backlash in hiring: a field experiment on agency, communion, and gender. *Journal of Personnel Psychology*, **13**, 204–214.

Carroll S J & Nash A N (1972) Effectiveness of a forced-choice reference check. *Personnel Administration*, **35**, 42–146.

Carter N T, Daniels M A & Zickar M J (2013) Projective testing: historical foundations and uses for human resources management. *Human Resource Management Review*, **23**, 205–218.

Cattell R B (1936) *The Fight for our National Intelligence*. P S King, London.

Cattell R B & Warburton F W (1967) *Objective Personality and Motivation Tests*. University of Illinois Press, Urbana.

Cervantes M (1607/1950) *Don Quixote*. Penguin, Harmondsworth.

Chaffin D B (1974) Human strength capability and low back pain. *Journal of Occupational Medicine*, **16**, 248–254.

Chiaburu D S, Oh I-S, Berry C M, Li N & Gardner R G (2011) The five-factor model of personality traits and organizational citizenship behaviors: a meta-analysis. *Journal of Applied Psychology*, **96**, 1140–1166.

Christiansen N D, Goffin R D, Johnston N G & Rothstein M G (1994) Correcting the 16PF for faking: effects on criterion-related validity and hiring decisions. *Personnel Psychology*, **47**, 847–860.

Chung-yan G A & Cronshaw S F (2002) A critical re-examination and analysis of cognitive ability tests using the Thorndike model of fairness. *Journal of Occupational and Organizational Psychology*, **75**, 489–510.

CIPD (Chartered Institute of Personnel and Development) (2006) *Annual Survey Report 2006: Recruitment, Retention and Turnover*. CIPD, London.

Colarelli S M, Hechanova-Alampay R & Canali K G (2002) Letters of recommendation: an evolutionary perspective. *Human Relations*, **55**, 315–344.

Collins C J, Hanges P J & Locke E A (2004) The relationship of achievement motivation to entrepreneurial behavior: a meta-analysis. *Human Performance*, **17**, 95–177.

Collins J M, Schmidt F L, Sanchez-Ku M, Thomas L, McDaniel M A & Le H (2003) Can basic individual differences shed light on the construct meaning of assessment center evaluations? *International Journal of Selection and Assessment*, **11**, 17–29.

Combs J, Yongmei L, Hall A & Ketchen D (2006) How much do high-performance work practices matter? A meta-analysis of their effects on organizational performance. *Personnel Psychology*, **59**, 501–528.

Connelly B S & Ones D S (2010) Another perspective on personality: meta-analytic integration of observers' accuracy and predictive validity. *Psychological Bulletin*, **136**, 1092–1122.

Connelly B S, Ones D S, Ramesh A & Goff M (2008) A pragmatic view of assessment center exercises and dimensions. *Industrial and Organizational Psychology*, **1**, 121–124.

Consiglio C, Alessandri G, Borgogni L & Piccolo R F (2013) Framing work competencies through personality traits: the big five competencies grid. *European Journal of Psychological Assessment*, **29**, 162–170.

Conte J M, Dean M A, Ringenbach K L, Moran S K & Landy F J (2005) The relationship between work attitudes and job analysis ratings: do rating scale type and task discretion matter? *Human Performance*, **18**, 1–21.

Converse P D, Oswald F L, Gillespie M A, Field K A & Bizot E B (2004) Matching individuals to occupations using abilities and the O*NET. *Personnel Psychology*, **57**, 451–487.

Conway J M & Huffcutt A I (1997) Psychometric properties of multisource performance ratings: a meta-analysis of subordinate, supervisor, peer, and self-ratings. *Human Performance*, **10**, 331–360.

Conway J M, Jako R A & Goodman D F (1995) A meta-analysis of interrater and internal consistency reliability of selection interviews. *Journal of Applied Psychology*, **80**, 565–579.

Conway J M, Lombardo K & Sanders K C (2001) A meta-analysis of incremental validity and nomological networks for subordinate and peer ratings. *Human Performance*, **14**, 267–303.

Cook M (1995) Performance appraisal and true performance. *Journal of Managerial Psychology*, **10**, 3–7.

Cook M (2013) *Levels of Personality*, 3rd edn. Cambridge University Press, Cambridge.

Cook M, Cripps B, Eysenck H J & Eysenck S B G (2007) *Eysenck Cripps Cook Occupational Scales: Technical Manual*. ECCOS Partnership, Dartington.

Correll S J, Benard S & Paik I (2007) Getting a job: is there a motherhood penalty. *American Journal of Sociology*, **112**, 1297–1338.

Cortina J M, Goldstein N B, Payne S C, Davison H K & Gilliland S W (2000) The incremental validity of interview scores over and above cognitive ability and conscientiousness scores. *Personnel Psychology*, **53**, 325–352.

Courtright S H, McCormick B W, Postlethwaite B E, Reeves C K & Mount M K (2013) A meta-analysis of sex differences in physical ability: revised estimates and strategies for reducing differences in selection contexts. *Journal of Applied Psychology*, **98**, 623–641.

Coward W M & Sackett P R (1990) Linearity of ability-performance relationships: a reconfirmation. *Journal of Applied Psychology*, **75**, 297–300.

CRE (Commission for Racial Equality) (1990) *Lines of Progress: An Enquiry into Selection and Equal Opportunities in London Underground*. CRE, London.

CRE (Commission for Racial Equality) (1996) *A Fair Test? Selecting Train Drivers at British Rail*. CRE, London.

Crites J O (1969) *Vocational Psychology*. McGraw Hill, New York.

Cronbach L J (1970) *Essentials of Psychological Testing*, 3rd edn. Harper and Row, New York.

Cronbach L J (1980) Selection theory for a political world. *Public Personnel Management Journal*, **9**, 37–50.

Crook T R, Todd S Y, Combs J G, Woehr D J & Ketchen D J (2011) Does human capital matter? A meta-analysis of the relationship between human capital and firm performance. *Journal of Applied Psychology*, **96**, 443–456.

Cucina J M, Caputo P M, Thibodeaux H F & Maclane C N (2012) Unlocking the key to biodata scoring: a comparison of empirical, rational, and hybrid approaches at different sample sizes. *Personnel Psychology*, **65**, 385–428.

Cucina J M, Caputo P M, Thibodeaux H F, Maclane C N & Bayless J M (2013) Scoring biodata: is it rational to be quasi-rational? *International Journal of Selection and Assessment*, **21**, 226–232.

Dalal R S (2005) A meta-analysis of the relationship between organizational citizenship behavior and counterproductive work behavior. *Journal of Applied Psychology*, **90**, 1241–1255.

Dany F & Torchy V (1994) Recruitment and selection in Europe: policies, practices and methods. In C Brewster & A Hegewisch (eds.) *Policy and Practice in European Human Resource Management: The Price Waterhouse Cranfield Survey*. Routledge, London.

Davison H K & Burke M J (2000) Sex discrimination in simulated employment contexts: a meta-analytic investigation. *Journal of Vocational Behavior*, **56**, 225–248.

Dayan K, Kasten R & Fox S (2002) Entry-level police candidate assessment center: an efficient tool or a hammer to kill a fly? *Personnel Psychology*, **55**, 827–849.

Dean M A, Roth P L & Bobko P (2008) Ethnic and gender subgroup differences in assessment center ratings: a meta-analysis. *Journal of Applied Psychology*, **93**, 685–691.

Deary I J, Whiteman M C, Starr J M, Whalley L J & Fox H C (2004) The impact of childhood intelligence in later life: following up the Scottish Mental Surveys of 1932 and 1947. *Journal of Personality and Social Psychology*, **86**, 130–147.

de Meijer L A L, Born M P, Terlouw G & van der Molen H T (2006) Applicant and method factors related to ethnic score differences in personnel selection: a study at the Dutch police. *Human Performance*, **19**, 219–251.

Derous E, Ryan A M & Nguyen H-H D (2012) Multiple categorisation in resume screening: examining effects on hiring discrimination against Arab applicants in field and lab settings. *Journal of Organizational Behavior*, **33**, 544–570.

Dick P & Nadin S (2006) Reproducing gender inequalities? A critique of realist assumptions underpinning personnel selection and practice. *Journal of Occupational and Organizational Psychology*, **79**, 481–498.

Dierdorff E C & Morgeson F P (2009) Effects of descriptor specificity and observability on incumbent work analysis ratings. *Personnel Psychology*, **62**, 601–628.

Dierdorff E C & Wilson M A (2003) A meta-analysis of job analysis reliability. *Journal of Applied Psychology*, **88**, 635–646.

Dilchert S & Ones D S (2009) Assessment center dimensions: individual differences correlates and meta-analytical incremental validity. *International Journal of Selection and Assessment*, **17**, 254–270.

Di Milia, L (2004) Australian management selection practices: closing the gap between research findings and practice. *Asia Pacific Journal of Human Resources*, **42**, 214–228.

Ding V J & Stillman J A (2005) An empirical investigation of discrimination against over-weight female job applicants in New Zealand. *New Zealand Journal of Psychology*, **34**, 139–145.

Dirk F (2007) Fairness reactions to selection methods: an Italian study. *International Journal of Selection and Assessment*, **15**, 197–205.

Dunnette M D (1972) *Validity Study Results for Jobs Relevant to the Petroleum Refining Industry*. American Petroleum Institute.

Dunning D, Heath C & Suls J M (2004) Flawed self assessment: implications for health, education, and the workplace. *Psychological Science in the Public Interest*, **5**, 69–106.

Duval S J (2005) The trim and fill method. In H R Rothstein, A J Sutton, & M Borenstein (eds.) *Publication Bias in Meta Analysis: Prevention, Assessment and Adjustments*. Wiley, Chichester.

Dwight S A & Donovan J J (2003) Do warnings not to fake reduce faking? *Human Performance*, **16**, 1–23.

Earnest D R, Allen D G & Landis R S (2011) Mechanisms linking realistic job previews with turnover: a meta-analytic path analysis. *Personnel Psychology*, **64**, 865–897.

Ekman P & O'Sullivan M (1991) Who can catch a liar? *American Psychologist*, **46**, 913–920.

Ellingson J E, Heggestad E D & Makarius E E (2012) Personality testing for managing intentional distortion. *Journal of Personality and Social Psychology*, **102**, 1063–1076.

Ellingson J E, Sackett P R & Connelly B S (2007) Personality assessment across selection and development contexts: insights into response distortion. *Journal of Applied Psychology*, **92**, 386–395.

Ellingson J E, Sackett P R & Hough L M (1999) Social desirability corrections in personality measurement: issues of applicant comparison and construct validity. *Journal of Applied Psychology*, **84**, 155–166.

Elliott S, Lawty-Jones M & Jackson C (1996) Effect of dissimulation on self-report and objective measures of personality. *Personality and Individual Differences*, **21**, 335–343.

Ellis A P J, West B J, Ryan A M & DeShon, R P (2002) The use of impression management tactics in structured interviews: a function of question type? *Journal of Applied Psychology*, **87**, 1200–1208.

Equal Opportunities Commission (EOC) (2005). *Discrimination in Recruitment Methods*. www.eoc-law.org.uk.

Eysenck H J (1967) *The Biological Basis of Personality*. C C Thomas, Springfield IL.

Falk A & Fox S (2014) Gender and ethnic composition of assessment centers and its relationship to participants' success. *Journal of Personnel Psychology*, **13**, 11–20.

Farrell J N & McDaniel M A (2001) The stability of validity coefficient over time: Ackerman's (1988) model and the General Aptitude Test Battery. *Journal of Applied Psychology*, **86**, 60–79.

Farrell S & Hakstian A R (2001) Improving salesforce performance: a meta-analytic investigation of the effectiveness and utility of personnel selection procedures and training interventions. *Psychology and Marketing*, **18**, 281–316.

Fast L A & Funder D C (2008) Personality as manifest in word use: correlations with self-report, acquaintance report, and behavior. *Journal of Personality and Social Psychology*, **94**, 334–346.

Feigelson M E & Dwight S A (2000) Can asking questions by computer improve the candidness of responding? *Consulting Psychology Journal: practice and research*, **52**, 248–255.

Ferguson C J & Brannick M T (2012) Publication bias in psychological science: prevalence, methods for identifying and controlling, and implications for the use of meta-analysis. *Psychological Methods*, **17**, 120–128.

Fikkan J & Rothblum E (2005) Weight bias in employment. In K D Brownell, R M Puhl, M B Schwartz & L Rudd (eds.) *Weight Bias: Nature, Consequences, and Remedies*. Guilford Press, New York.

Flanagan J C (1946) The experimental validation of a selection procedure. *Educational and Psychological Measurement*, **6**, 445–466.

Flanagan J C (1954) The critical incident technique. *Psychological Bulletin*, **51**, 327–358.

Fleenor J W & Brutus S (2001) Multisource feedback for personnel decisions. In D W Bracken, C W Timmreck, & A H Church (eds.) *The Handbook of Multisource Feedback: The Comprehensive Resource for Designing and Implementing MSF Processes*. Jossey Bass, San Francisco.

Foldes H J, Duehr E E & Ones D S (2008) Group differences in personality: meta-analyses comparing five U.S. racial groups. *Personnel Psychology*, **61**, 579–616.

Ford J K, Kraiger K & Schechtman S L (1986) Study of race effects in objective indices and subjective evaluations of performance: a meta-analysis of performance criteria. *Psychological Bulletin*, **99**, 330–337.

Ford L A, Campbell R C, Campbell J P, Knapp D J & Walker C B (1999) *21st Century Soldiers and Non-Commissioned Officers: Critical Predictors of Performance* (FR-EADD-99–45). HumRRO, Alexandria, VA.

Ford M E & Tisak M S (1983) A further search for social intelligence. *Journal of Educational Psychology*, **75**, 196–206.

Frieder R E, van Iddekinge C H & Raymark P H (2015) How quickly do interviewers reach decisions? An examination of interviewers' decision-making times across applicants. *Journal of Occupational and Organizational Psychology*.

Funder D C (2007) *The Personality Puzzle*, 4th edn. Norton, New York.

Funke U, Krauss J, Schuler H & Stapf K H (1987) Zur Prognostizierbarkeit wissenschaftlich-technischer Leistungen mittels Personvariablen: eine Metaanalyse der Validität diagnostischer Verfahren im Bereich Forschung und Entwicklung. *Gruppendynamik*, **18**, 407–428.

Gaugler B B, Rosenthal D B, Thornton G C & Bentson C (1987) Meta-analysis of assessment center validity. *Journal of Applied Psychology*, **72**, 493–511.

Gaugler B B & Thornton G C (1989) Number of assessment center dimensions as a determinant of assessor accuracy. *Journal of Applied Psychology*, **74**, 611–618.

Geisinger K F, Boodoo G & Noble J P (2002) The psychometrics of testing individuals with disabilities. In R B Ekstrom & D K Smith (eds.) *Assessing Individuals with Disabilities in Educational, Employment and Counseling Settings*. APA, Washington DC.

Ghiselli E E (1966a) The validity of a personnel interview. *Personnel Psychology*, **19**, 389–394.

Ghiselli E E (1966b) *The Validity of Occupational Aptitude Tests*. Wiley, New York.

Ghiselli E E (1973) The validity of aptitude tests in personnel selection. *Personnel Psychology*, **26**, 451–477.

Gibbons A M & Rupp D E (2009) Dimension consistency as an individual difference: a new (old) perspective on the assessment center validity problem. *Journal of Management*, **35**, 1154–1180.

Gibson W M & Caplinger J A (2007) Transportation of validation results. In S M McPhail (ed.) *Alternative Validation Strategies: Developing New and Leveraging Existing Validity Evidence*. Wiley, New York.

Gill C M & Hodgkinson G F (2007) Development and validation of the Five Factor Model Questionnaire (FFMQ): an adjectival-based personality inventory. *Personnel Psychology*, **60**, 731–766.

Gilliland S W (1993) The perceived fairness of selection systems: an organizational justice perspective. *Academy of Management Review*, **18**, 694–734.

Glennon J R, Albright L E & Owens W A (1962) *A Catalog of Life History Items*. American Psychological Association, Chicago.

Goertz W, Hülsheger U R & Maier G W (2014) The validity of specific cognitive abilities for the prediction of training success in Germany: a meta-analysis. *Journal of Personnel Psychology*, **13**, 123–133.

Goffin R D, Rothstein M G, Rieder G, Poole A, Krajewski F T, Powell D M, Jelly R B, Boyd A & Mestdagh T (2011) Choosing job-related personality traits: developing valid personality-oriented job analysis. *Personality and Individual Differences*, **51**, 646–651.

Goheen H W & Mosel J N (1959) Validity of the Employment Recommendation Questionnaire: II. Comparison with field investigations. *Personnel Psychology*, **12**, 297–301.

Goldsmith D B (1922) The use of a personal history blank as a salesmanship test. *Journal of Applied Psychology*, **6**, 149–155.

Goldstein I L (1971) The application blank: how honest are the responses? *Journal of Applied Psychology*, **55**, 491–492.

Goleman D (1995) *Emotional Intelligence*. Bantam, New York.

Gonzalez-Mulé E, Mount M K & Oh I-S (2014) A meta-analysis of the relationship between general mental ability and nontask performance. *Journal of Applied Psychology*, **99**, 1222–1243.

Gosling S D, Augustine A A, Vazire S, Holtzman N & Gaddis S (2011) Manifestations of personality in online social networks: self-reported Facebook-related behaviors and observable profile information. *Cyberpsychology, Behavior and Social Networking*, **14**, 483–488.

Gosling S D, John O P, Craik K H & Robins R W (1998) Do people know how they behave? Self-reported act frequencies compared with on-line codings by observers. *Journal of Personality and Social Psychology*, **74**, 1337–1349.

Gottfredson L S (1997) Why g matters: the complexity of everyday life. *Intelligence*, **24**, 79–132.

Gottfredson L S (2003) Dissecting practical intelligence theory: its claims and evidence. *Intelligence*, **31**, 343–397.

Graham K E, McDaniel M A, Douglas E F & Snell A E (2002) Biodata validity decay and score inflation with faking: do other attributes explain variance across items. *Personnel Psychology*, **16**, 573–592.

Griffeth R W, Hom P W & Gaertner S (2000) A meta-analysis of antecedents and correlates of employee turnover: update, moderator tests, and research implications for the next millennium. *Journal of Management*, **26**, 463–488.

Griffith R L, Chmielowski T & Yoshita Y (2007) Do applicants fake? An examination of the frequency of applicant faking behavior. *Personnel Review*, **36**, 341–355.

Grote C L, Robiner W N & Haut A (2001) Disclosure of negative information in the letters of recommendation: writers' intentions and readers' experience. *Professional Psychology – research and practice*, **32**, 655–661.

Grubb W L & McDaniel M A (2007) The fakability of Bar-On's Emotional Quotient Inventory short form: catch me if you can. *Human Performance*, **20**, 43–59.

Gruys M L & Sackett P R (2003) Investigating the dimensionality of counterproductive work behavior. *International Journal of Selection and Assessment*, **11**, 30–42.

Guilford J P (1959) *Personality*. McGraw-Hill, New York.

Guion R M (1965) *Personnel Testing*. McGraw-Hill, New York.

Guion R M & Gottier R F (1965) Validity of personality measures in personnel selection. *Personnel Psychology*, **18**, 135–164.

Gunter B, Furnham A & Drakeley R (1993) *Biodata: Biographical Indicators of Business Performance*. Routledge, London.

Hardison C M & Sackett P R (2007) Kriterienbezogene Validität des Assessment Centers: Lebendig und wohlauf? In H Schuler (ed.) *Assessment Center zur Potenzialanalyse*. Hogrefe, Göttingen.

Harold C N, McFarland L A & Weekley J A (2006) The validity of verifiable and non-verifiable biodata items: an examination across applicants and incumbents. *International Journal of Selection and Assessment*, **14**, 336–346.

Harpe L D G (2008) Test validity: a multiple stakeholder approach, enforcement agency perspective. Paper presented at 23rd Annual Conference of SIOP, San Francisco.

Harris L (2000) Procedural justice and perceptions of fairness in selection practice. *International Journal of Selection and Assessment*, **8**, 148–157.

Harris M M, Dworkin J B & Park J (1990) Pre-employment screening procedures: how human resource managers perceive them. *Personnel Psychology*, **4**, 279–292.

Harrison D A, Newman D A & Roth P L (2006) How important are job attitudes? Meta-analytic comparisons of integrative behavioural outcomes and time sequences. *Academy of Management Journal*, **49**, 305–325.

Hartigan J A & Wigdor A K (1989) *Fairness in Employment Testing*. National Academy Press, Washington DC.

Hartshorne H & May M A (1928) *Studies in the Nature of Character. I Studies in Deceit.* Macmillan, New York.

Harvey-Cook J E & Taffler R J (2000) Biodata in professional entry level selection: statistical scoring of common format applications. *Journal of Occupational and Organizational Psychology*, **73**, 103–118.

Hausknecht J P (2010) Candidate persistence and personality test practice effects: implications for staffing system management. *Personnel Psychology*, **63**, 299–324.

Hausknecht J P, Day D V & Thomas S C (2004) Applicant reactions to selection procedures: an updated model and meta-analysis. *Personnel Psychology*, **57**, 639–683.

Hausknecht J P, Halpert J A, Di Paolo N T & Gerrard M O M (2007) Retesting in selection: a meta-analysis of coaching and practice effects for tests of cognitive ability. *Journal of Applied Psychology*, **92**, 373–385.

Hebl M R, Foster J B, Mannix L M & Dovidio J F (2002) Formal and interpersonal discrimination: a field study of bias toward homosexual applicants. *Personality and Social Psychology Bulletin*, **28**, 815–825.

Hebl M R & Mannix L M (2003) The weight of obesity in evaluating others: a mere proximity effect. *Personality and Social Psychology Bulletin*, **29**, 28–38.

Heidemeier H & Moser K (2009) Self-other agreement in job performance ratings: a meta-analytic test of a process model. *Journal of Applied Psychology*, **94**, 353–370.

Henle C A (2004) Case review of the legal status of banding. *Human Performance*, **17**, 415–432.

Herrnstein R J (1973) *IQ in the Meritocracy.* Allen Lane, London.

Herrnstein R J & Murray C (1994) *The Bell Curve: Intelligence and Class Structure in American Life.* Free Press, New York.

Hershcovis M S, Turner N, Barling J, Arnold K A, Dupre, K E, Inness M, LeBlanc M M & Sivanathan N (2007) Predicting workplace aggression: a meta-analysis. *Journal of Applied Psychology*, **92**, 228–238.

Higuera L A (2001) Adverse impact in personnel selection: the legal framework and test bias. *European Psychologist*, **6**, 103–111.

Hirsh H R, Northrop L C & Schmidt F L (1986) Validity generalisation results for law enforcement occupations. *Personnel Psychology*, **39**, 399–420.

Hitt M A & Barr S H (1989) Managerial selection decision models: examination of configural cue processing. *Journal of Applied Psychology*, **74**, 53–61.

Hoffman B J, Blair C A, Meriac J P & Woehr D J (2007). Expanding the criteria domain? A quantitative review of the OCB literature. *Journal of Applied Psychology*, **92**, 555–566.

Hoffman B J, Gorman C A, Blair C A, Meriac J P, Overstreet B & Atchley E K (2012) Evidence for the effectiveness of an alternative multisource performance rating methodology. *Personnel Psychology*, **65**, 531–563.

Hoffman B J, Kennedy C L, Lance C E, LoPilato A C & Monahan E L (2015) A review of the content, criterion-related, and construct-related validity of assessment center exercises. *Journal of Applied Psychology*, **100**, 1143–1168.

Hoffman B J, Melchers K G, Blair C A, Kleinmann M & Ladd R T (2011) Exercises and dimensions are the currency of assessment centers. *Personnel Psychology*, **64**, 351–395.

Hoffman B J, Woehr D J, Maldagen-Youngjohn R & Lyons B D (2011) Great man or great myth? A quantitative review of the relationship between individual differences and leader effectiveness. *Journal of Occupational and Organizational Psychology*, **84**, 347–381.

Hoffman C C, Holden L M & Gale K (2000) So many jobs, so little 'n': applying expanded validation models to support generalisation of cognitive test validity, *Personnel Psychology*, **53**, 955–991.

Hoffman C C, Nathan B R & Holden L M (1991) A comparison of validation criteria: objective versus subjective performance and self- versus supervisor ratings. *Personnel Psychology*, **44**, 601–619.

Hofstede G (2001) *Culture's Consequences.* Sage, Thousand Oaks CA.

Hogan J, Barrett P & Hogan R (2007) Personality measurement, faking, and employment selection. *Journal of Applied Psychology*, **92**, 1270–1285.

Hogan J & Holland B (2003) Using theory to evaluate personality and job-performance relations: a socioanalytic perspective. *Journal of Applied Psychology*, **88**, 100–112.

Hogan R, Chamorro-Premuzic T & Kaiser R B (2013) Employability and career success: bridging the gap between theory and reality. *Industrial and Organizational Psychology*, **6**, 3–16.

Holden R R & Hibbs N (1995) Incremental validity of response latencies for detecting fakers on a personality test. *Journal of Research in Personality*, **29**, 362–372.

Holden R R, Wood L L & Tomashewski L (2000) Do response time limitations counteract the effect of faking on personality inventory validity? *Journal of Applied Psychology*, **81**, 160–169.

Hoque K & Noon M (1999) Racial discrimination in speculative applications: new optimism six years on? *Human Resource Management Journal*, **9**, 71–83.

Hosoda M, Nguyen L T & Stone-Romero E F (2012) The effect of Hispanic accents on employment decisions. *Journal of Managerial Psychology*, **27**, 34–364.

Hough L M (1992) The 'big five' personality variables – construct confusion: description versus prediction. *Human Performance*, **5**, 139–155.

Hough L M (1998) Personality at work: issues and evidence. In M Hakel (ed.) *Beyond Multiple Choice: Evaluating Alternatives to Traditional Testing for Selection*. Lawrence Erlbaum, Mahwah, NJ.

Hough L, Barge B & Kamp J (2001) Assessment of personality, temperament, vocational interests, and work outcome preferences. In J P Campbell & D J Knapp (eds.) *Exploring the Limits of Personnel Selection and Classification*. Lawrence Erlbaum, Mahwah NJ.

Hough L M, Eaton N K, Dunnette M D, Kamp J D & McCloy R A (1990) Criterion-related validities of personality constructs and the effect of response distortion on those validities. *Journal of Applied Psychology*, **75**, 581–595.

Hough L M, Oswald F L & Ployhart R E (2001) Determinants, detection and amelioration of adverse impact in personnel selection procedures: issues, evidence and lessons learned. *International Journal of Selection and Assessment*, **9**, 152–194.

Houston W M & Novick M R (1987) Race-based differential prediction in Air Force technical training programs. *Journal of Educational Measurement*, **24**, 309–320.

Huang L, Frideger M & Pearce J L (2013) Political skill: explaining the effects of nonnative accent on managerial hiring and entrepreneurial investment decisions. *Journal of Applied Psychology*, **98**, 1005–1017.

Huffcutt A I & Arthur W (1994) Hunter and Hunter (1984) revisited: interview validity for entry-level jobs. *Journal of Applied Psychology*, **79**, 184–190.

Huffcutt A I, Conway J M, Roth P L & Klehe U C (2004) The impact of job complexity and study design on situational and behavior description interview validity. *International Journal of Selection and Assessment*, **12**, 262–273.

Huffcutt A I, Conway J M, Roth P L & Stone N J (2001) Identification and meta-analytic assessment of psychological constructs measured in employment interviews. *Journal of Applied Psychology*, **86**, 897–913.

Huffcutt A I, Culbertson S S & Weyhrauch W S (2014) Moving forward indirectly: reanalysing the validity of employment interviews with indirect range restriction methodology, *International Journal of Selection and Assessment*, **22**, 297–309.

Huffcutt A I, Roth P L & McDaniel M A (1996) A meta-analytic investigation of cognitive ability in employment interview evaluations: moderating characteristics and implications for incremental validity. *Journal of Applied Psychology*, **81**, 459–473.

Huffcutt A I & Woehr D J (1999) Further analyses of employment interview validity: a quantitative evaluation of interviewer-related structuring methods. *Journal of Organizational Behavior*, **20**, 549–560.

Hughes J F, Dunn J F & Baxter B (1956) The validity of selection instruments under operating conditions. *Personnel Psychology*, **9**, 321–423.

Hull C L (1928) *Aptitude Testing*. Harrap, London.

Hülsheger U R, Maier G W & Stumpp T (2007) Validity of general mental ability for the prediction of job performance and training success in Germany: a meta-analysis. *International Journal of Selection and Assessment*, **15**, 3–18.

Hunter A E, Vasilopous N L, Marton N R & Cucina J M (2008) Revisiting P = f (A×M): the roles of tenure and performance domain. Paper presented at 23rd Annual Conference of SIOP, San Francisco.

Hunter D R & Burke E F (1994) Predicting aircraft pilot-training success: a meta-analysis of published research. *International Journal of Aviation Pychology*, **4**, 297–313.

Hunter J E (1983) A causal analysis of cognitive ability, job knowledge, and supervisory ratings. In F Landy, S Zedeck & J Cleveland (eds.) *Performance Measurement and Theory.* Lawrence Erlbaum, Hillsdale NJ.

Hunter J E (1986) Cognitive ability, cognitive aptitudes, job knowledge, and job performance. *Journal of Vocational Behavior*, **29**, 340–362.

Hunter J E & Hunter R F (1984) Validity and utility of alternate predictors of job performance. *Psychological Bulletin*, **96**, 72–98.

Hunter J E & Schmidt F L (1996) Intelligence and job performance: economic and social implications. *Psychology, Public Policy & Law*, **2**, 447–472.

Hunter J E & Schmidt F L (2004) *Methods of Meta-Analysis: Correcting Error and Bias in Research Findings*, 2nd edn. Sage, Thousand Oaks, CA.

Huo Y P, Huang H J & Napier N K (2002) Divergence or convergence: a cross-national comparison of personnel selection practices. *Human Resource Management*, **41**, 31–44.

Hurtz G M & Donovan J J (2000) Personality and job performance: the big five revisited. *Journal of Applied Psychology*, **85**, 869–879.

Huselid M A, Jackson S E & Schuler R S (1997) Technical and strategic human resource management effectiveness as determinants of firm performance. *Academy of Management Journal*, **40**, 171–188.

Hyde J S (2005) The gender similarities hypothesis. *American Psychologist*, **60**, 581–592.

Isaacson J A, Griffith R L, Kung M C, Lawrence A & Wilson K A (2008) Liar, liar: examining background checks and applicants who fail them. Paper presented at 23rd Annual Conference of SIOP, San Francisco.

Jackson M (2009) Disadvantaged through discrimination: the role of employers in social stratification. *British Journal of Sociology*, **69**, 669–692.

Janz T (1982) Initial comparisons of patterned behavior description interviews versus unstructured interviews. *Journal of Applied Psychology*, **67**, 577–580.

Jeanneret P R (1992) Application of job component / synthetic validity to construct validity. *Human Performance*, **5**, 81–96.

Jeanneret P R & Strong M H (2003) Linking O*NET job analysis information to job requirement predictors: an O*NET application. *Journal of Applied Psychology*, **56**, 465–492.

Johnson J W, Steel P, Scherbaum C A, Hoffman C C, Jeanneret P R & Foster J (2010) Validation is like motor oil: synthetic is better. *Industrial and Organizational Psychology*, **3**, 305–328.

Johnson R E, Tolentino A L, Rodopman O B & Cho E (2010) We (sometimes) know not how we feel: predicting job performance with an implicit measure of trait affectivity. *Personnel Psychology*, **63**, 197–219.

Jones A & Harrison E (1982) Prediction of performance in initial officer training using reference reports. *Journal of Occupational Psychology*, **55**, 35–42.

Jones D P & Gottschalk R J (1988) Validation of selection procedures for electric utility construction and skilled trades occupations: literature review and meta-analysis of related validation studies. Edison Electric Institute, Washington, DC.

Jones R G, Sanchez J I, Parameswaran G, Phelps J, Shoptaugh C, Williams M & White S (2001) Selection or training? A two fold test of the validity of job -analytic ratings of trainability. *Personnel Psychology*, **15**, 363–389.

Joseph D L, Jin J, Newman D A & O'Boyle E H (2015) Why does self-reported emotional intelligence predict job performance? A meta-analytic investigation of mixed EI. *Journal of Applied Psychology*, **100**, 298–342.

Joseph D L & Newman D A (2010) Emotional intelligence: an integrative meta-analysis and cascading model. *Journal of Applied Psychology*, **95**, 54–78.

Judge T A, Bono J E, Ilies R & Gerhardt M W (2002) Personality and leadership: a qualitative and quantitative review. *Journal of Applied Psychology*, **87**, 765–780.

Judge T A & Cable D M (2004) The effect of physical height on workplace success and income: preliminary test of a theoretical model *Journal of Applied Psychology*, **89**, 428–441.

Judge T A, Colbert A E & Ilies R (2004) Intelligence and leadership: a quantitative review and test of theoretical propositions. *Journal of Applied Psychology*, **89**, 542–552.

Judge T A & Higgins C A (1998) Affective disposition and the letter of reference. *Organizational Behavior and Human Decision Processes*, **75**, 207–221.

Judge T A, Ilies R & Dimotakis N (2010) Are health and happiness the product of wisdom? The relationship of general mental ability to educational and occupational attainment, health, and well being. *Journal of Applied Psychology*, **95**, 454–468.

Judge T A, Klinger R L & Simon L S (2010) Time is on my side: time, general mental ability, human capital, and extrinsic career success. *Journal of Applied Psychology*, **95**, 92–107.

Judge T A, Rodell J B, Klinger R L, Simon L S & Crawford E R (2013, September 9) Hierarchical representations of the five-factor model of personality in predicting job performance: integrating three organizing frameworks with two theoretical perspectives. *Journal of Applied Psychology*, **98**, 875–925.

Judiesch M K & Schmidt F L (2000) Between-worker variability in output under piece-rate versus hourly pay systems. *Personnel Psychology*, **14**, 529–551.

Kanning U P, Grewe K, Hollenberg S & Hadouch M (2006) From the subjects' point of view: reactions to different types of situational judgment items. *European Journal of Psychological Assessment*, **22**, 168–176.

Katz D & Kahn R L (1966) *The Social Psychology of Organisations*. John Wiley & Sons, New York.

Keenan T (1997) Selection for potential: the case of graduate recruitment. In N Anderson & P Herriott (eds.) *International Handbook of Selection and Appraisal*. John Wiley & Sons, Chichester.

Kepes S, Banks G C & Oh I-S (2014) Avoiding bias in publication bias research: the value of 'null' findings. *Journal of Business and Psychology*, **29**, 183–203.

Kethley R B & Terpstra D E (2005) An analysis of litigation associated with the use of the application form in the selection process. *Personnel Psychology*, **34**, 357–375.

Kim Y & Ployhart R E (2014) The effects of staffing and training on firm productivity and profit growth before, during, and after the Great Recession. *Journal of Applied Psychology*, **99**, 361–389.

Kinslinger H J (1966) Application of projective techniques in personnel psychology since 1940. *Psychological Bulletin*, **66**, 134–150.

Kish-Gephart J J, Harrison D A & Treviño L K (2010) Bad apples, bad cases, and bad barrels: meta-analytic evidence about sources of unethical decisions at work. *Journal of Applied Psychology*, **95**, 1–31.

Klehe U-C, König C J, Richter G M, Kleinmann M & Melchers K G (2008) Transparency in structured interviews: consequences for construct and criterion-related validity. *Human Performance*, **21**, 107–137.

Klimoski R J & Strickland W J (1977) Assessment centers – valid or merely prescient? *Personnel Psychology*, **30**, 353–361.

Kline P & Cooper C (1984) A construct validation of the Objective-Analytic Test Battery (OATB) *Personality and Individual Differences*, **5**, 328–337.

Kluemper D H, Rosen P A & Mossholder K W (2012) Social networking websites, personality ratings, and the organizational context: more than meets the eye? *Journal of Applied Social Psychology*, **42**, 1143–1172.

Kluger A N, Reilly R R & Russell C J (1991) Faking biodata tests: are option-keyed instruments more resistant? *Journal of Applied Psychology*, **76**, 889–896.

König C J, Klehe U-C, Berchtold M & Kleinmann M (2010) Reasons for being selective when choosing personnel selection procedures. *International Journal of Selection and Assessment*, **18**, 17–27.

König C J, Jöri E & Knüsel P (2011) The amazing diversity of thought: a qualitative study on how human resource practitioners perceive selection procedures. *Journal of Business Psychology*, **26**, 437–452.

König C J, Bösch F, Reshef A & Winkler S (2013) Human resources managers' attitudes towards utility analysis: an extended and refined update from Switzerland. *Journal of Personnel Psychology*, **12**, 152–156.

Kraiger K & Ford J K (1985) A meta-analysis of ratee race effects in performance ratings. *Journal of Applied Psychology*, **70**, 56–65.

Kramer J (2009) Allgemeine Intelligenz und beruflicher Erfolg in Deutschland: vertiefende und weiterführende Metaanalysen. *Psychologische Rundschau*, **60**, 82–98.

Krause D E & Thornton G C (2009) A cross-cultural look at assessment center practices: survey results from Western Europe and North America. *Applied Psychology: an International Review*, **58**, 557–585.

Krause D E, Kersting M, Heggestad E D & Thornton G C (2006) Incremental validity of assessment center ratings over cognitive ability tests: a study at the executive management level. *International Journal of Selection and Assessment*, **14**, 360–371.

Kravitz D A (2008) The diversity-validity dilemma: beyond selection – the role of affirmative action. *Personnel Psychology*, **61**, 173–193.

Kristof-Brown A L, Zimmerman R D & Johnson E C (2005) Consequences of individuals' fit at work: a meta-analysis of person-job, person-organization, person-group, and person-supervisor fit. *Personnel Psychology*, **58**, 281–342.

Kruger J & Dunning D (1999) Unskilled and unaware of it: how difficulties in recognizing one's own incompetence lead to inflated self-assessment. *Journal of Personality and Social Psychology*, **77**, 1121–1134.

Krzystofiak F, Newman J M & Anderson G (1979) A quantified approach to measurement of job content: procedures and payoffs. *Personnel Psychology*, **32**, 341–357.

Kumar K & Beyerlein M (1991) Construction and validation of an instrument for measuring ingratiatory behaviors in organisational setting. *Journal of Applied Psychology*, **76**, 619–627.

Kuncel N R & Borneman M J (2007) Toward a new method of detecting deliberately faked personality tests: the use of idiosyncratic item responses. *International Journal of Selection and Assessment*, **15**, 220–231.

Kuncel N R, Klieger D M, Connelly B S & Ones D S (2013) Mechanical versus clinical data combination in selection and admissions decisions: a meta-analysis. *Journal of Applied Psychology*, **98**, 1060–1072.

Kuncel N R, Kochevar R J & Ones D S (2014) A meta-analysis of letters of recommendation in college and graduate admissions: reasons for hope. *International Journal of Selection and Assessment*, **22**, 101–107.

Kuncel N R & Sackett P R (2014) Resolving the assessment center construct validity problem (as we know it). *Journal of Applied Psychology*, **99**, 38–47.

Kuncel N R & Tellegen A (2009) A conceptual and empirical reexamination of the measurement of the social desirability of items: implications for detecting desirable response style and scale development. *Personnel Psychology*, **62**, 201–228.

Kutcher E J & Bragger J D (2004) Selection interviews of overweight job applicants: can structure reduce the bias? *Journal of Applied Social Psychology*, **34**, 1993–2022.

Lahuis D M, Martin N R & Avis J M (2005) Investigating nonlinear conscientiousness–job performance relations for clerical employees. *Human Performance*, **18**, 199–212.

Lance C E (2008) Why assessment centers do not work the way they are supposed to. *Industrial and Organizational Psychology*, **1**, 84–97.

Lance C E, Johnson C D, Douthitt S S, Bennett W & Harville G L (2000) Good news: work sample administrators' global performance judgements are (about) as valid as we've suspected. *Human Performance*, **13**, 253–277.

Lance C E, Lambert T A, Gewin A G, Lievens F & Conway J M (2004) Revised estimates of dimension and exercise variance components in assessment center postexercise dimension ratings. *Journal of Applied Psychology*, **89**, 377–385.

Lance C E, Newbolt W H, Gatewood R D, Foster M S, French N R & Smith D E (2000) Assessment center exercise factors represent cross-situational specificity, not method bias. *Human Performance*, **12**, 323–353.

Landers R N & Sackett P R (2012) Offsetting performance losses due to cheating in unproctored internet-based testing by increasing the applicant pool. *International Journal of Selection and Assessment*, **20**, 220–228.

Landers R N, Sackett P R & Tuzinski K A (2011) Testing after initial failure, coaching rumors, and warnings against faking in online personality measures for selection. *Journal of Applied Psychology*, **96**, 202–210.

Landis R S (2013) Successfully combining meta-analysis and structural equation modeling: recommendations and strategies. *Journal of Business Psychology*, **28**, 251–261.

Landy F J (2003) Validity generalization: then and now. In K R Murphy (ed.) *Validity Generalization: A Critical Review*. Lawrence Erlbaum, Mahwah, NJ.

Landy F J (2005) Some historical and scientific issues related to research on emotional intelligence. *Journal of Organizational Behavior*, **26**, 411–424.

Lang J W B & Bliese P D (2009) General mental ability and two types of adaptation to unforeseen change: applying discontinuous growth models to the task-change paradigm. *Journal of Applied Psychology*, **94**, 411–428.

Lang J W B, Kersting M, Hülsheger U R & Lang J (2010) General mental ability, narrower cognitive abilities, and job performance: the perspective of the nested-factors model of cognitive abilities. *Personnel Psychology*, **63**, 595–640.

Latham G P, Saari L M, Pursell E D & Campion M A (1980) The situational interview. *Journal of Applied Psychology*, **65**, 422–427.

Latham G P & Wexley K N (1981) *Increasing Productivity through Performance Appraisal*. Addison Wesley, Reading MA.

Lawshe C H (1952) Personnel selection. *Personnel Psychology*, **6**, 31–34.

LeBreton J M, Burgess J R D, Kaiser R B, Atchley E K & James L J (2003) The restriction of variance hypothesis and interrater reliability and agreement: are ratings from multiple sources really dissimilar? *Organizational Research Methods*, **6**, 80–128.

Le H, Oh I-S, Robbins S B, Ilies R, Holland E & Westrick P (2011) Too much of a good thing: curvilinear relationships between personality traits and job performance. *Journal of Applied Psychology*, **96**, 113–133.

Lee H & Dalal R S (2011) The effects of performance extremities on ratings of dynamic performance. *Human Performance*, **24**, 99–118.

Lent R H, Aurbach H A & Levin, L S (1971) Predictors, criteria, and significant results. *Personnel Psychology*, **24**, 519–533.

Levashina J & Campion M A (2006) A model of faking likelihood in the employment interview. *International Journal of Selection and Assessment*, **14**, 299–316.

Levine E L, Spector P E, Menon S, Narayan L & Cannon-Bowers J (1996) Validity generalisation for cognitive, psychomotor, and perceptual tests for craft jobs in the utility industry. *Human Performance*, **9**, 1–22.

Lievens F (2001a) Assessor training strategies and their effects on accuracy, interrater reliability and discriminant validity. *Journal of Applied Psychology*, **86**, 255–264.

Lievens F (2001b) Assessors and use of assessment center dimensions: a fresh look at a troubling issue. *Journal of Organizational Behavior*, **22**, 203–221.

Lievens F & Burke E (2011) Dealing with the threats inherent in unproctored Internet testing of cognitive ability: results from a large-scale operational test program. *Journal of Occupational and Organizational Psychology*, **84**, 817–824.

Lievens F, Chasteen C S, Day E A & Christiansen N D (2006) Large-scale investigation of the role of trait activation theory for understanding assessment center convergent and discriminant validity. *Journal of Applied Psychology*, **91**, 247–258.

Lievens F & Conway J M (2001) Dimension and exercise variance in assessment center scores: a large scale evaluation of multitrait-multimethod studies. *Journal of Applied Psychology*, **86**, 1202–1222.

Lievens F, De Corte W & Westerveld L (2012) Understanding the building blocks of selection procedures: effect of response fidelity on performance validity. *Journal of Management*.

Lievens F & De Paepe A (2004) An empirical investigation of interviewer-related factors that discourage the use of high structure interviews. *Journal of Organizational Behavior*, **25**, 29–49.

Lievens F, Highhouse S & DeCorte W (2005) The importance of traits and abilities in supervisors' hirability decisions as function of method of assessment. *Journal of Occupational and Organizational Psychology*, **78**, 453–470.

Lievens F, Klehe U C & Libbrecht N (2011) Applicant versus employee scores on self-report emotional intelligence measure. *Journal of Personnel Psychology*, **10**, 89–95.

Lievens F & Patterson F (2011) The validity and incremental validity of knowledge tests, low-fidelity simulations, and high fidelity simulations for predicting job performance in advanced-level high-stakes selection. *Journal of Applied Psychology*, **96**, 927–940.

Lievens F & Peeters H (2008) Interviewers' sensitivity to impression management tactics in structured interviews. *European Journal of Psychological Assessment*, **24**, 174–180.

Lievens F, Reeve C I & Heggestad E D (2007) An examination of psychometric bias due to restesting on cognitive ability tests in selection settings. *Journal of Applied Psychology*, **92**, 1672–1682.

Lievens F & Sanchez J I (2007) Can training improve the quality of inferences made by raters in competency modeling? A quasi-experiment. *Journal of Applied Psychology*, **92**, 812–819.

Lievens F, Sanchez J I, Bartram D & Brown A (2010) Lack of consensus among competency ratings of the same occupation: noise or substance? *Journal of Applied Psychology*, **95**, 562–571.

Link H C (1918) An experiment in employment psychology. *Psychological Review*, **25**, 116–127.

Little B L & Sipes D (2000) Betwixt and between; the dilemma of employee references. *Employee Responsibilities and Rights Journal*, **12**, 1–8.

Locke E L (1961) What's in a name? *American Psychologist*, **16**, 607.

Loher B T, Hazer J T, Tsai A, Tilton K & James J (1997) Letters of reference: a process approach. *Journal of Business and Psychology*, **11**, 339–355.

Longenecker C O, Sims H P & Goia D A (1987) Behind the mask: the politics of employee appraisal. *Academy of Management Executive*, **1**, 183–193.

Lyons B D, Hoffman B J & Michel J W (2009) Not much more than g? An examination of the impact of intelligence on NFL performance. *Human Performance*, **22**, 225–245.

Mabe P A & West S G (1982) Validity of self-evaluation of ability: a review and meta-analysis. *Journal of Applied Psychology*, **67**, 280–296.

Macan T (2009) The employment interview: a review of current studies and directions for future research, *Human Resource Management Review*, **19**, 203–218.

Machwirth U, Schuler H & Moser K (1996) Entscheidungsprozesse bei der Analyse von Bewerbungsunterlagen. *Diagnostica*, **42**, 220–241.

Mackenzie S C, Podsakoff P M & Podsakoff N P (2011) Challenge oriented organizational citizenship behaviors and organisational effectiveness: do challenge oriented behaviors really have an impact on the organization's bottom line. *Personnel Psychology*, **64**, 559–592.

Madera J M (2012) Using social networking websites as a selection tool: the role of selection process fairness and job pursuit intentions. *International Journal of Hospitality Management*, **31**, 1276–1282.

Madera J M, Hebl M R & Martin R C (2009) Gender and letters of recommendation for academia: agentic and communal differences. *Journal of Applied Psychology*, **94**, 1591–1599.

Mael F A & Ashworth B E (1995) Loyal from day one: biodata, organisational identification, and turnover among newcomers. *Personnel Psychology*, **48**, 309–333.

Mael F A & Hirsch A C (1993) Rainforest empiricism and quasi-rationality: two approaches to objective biodata. *Personnel Psychology*, **46**, 719–738.

Martinussen M (1996) Psychological measures as predictors of pilot performance: a meta-analysis. *International Journal of Aviation Psychology*, **6**, 1–20.

Martinussen M & Torjussen T (1993) Does DMT (Defense Mechanism Test) predict pilot performance only in Scandinavia? In R S Jensen & D Neumeister (eds.) *Proceedings of the Seventh International Symposium on Aviation Psychology*. Avebury Aviation, Aldershot.

Mathieu J E & Tannenbaum S I (1989) A process-tracing approach toward understanding supervisors' SD_y estimates: results from five job classes. *Journal of Occupational Psychology*, **62**, 249–256.

Matthews G E, Roberts R D & Zeidner M (2006) What is this thing called emotional intelligence? In K R Murphy (ed.) *A Critique of Emotional Intelligence: What Are the Problems and How Can They Be Fixed?* Lawrence Erlbaum, Mahwah, NJ.

Maurer T J, Solamon J M, Andrews K D & Troxtel D D (2001) Interviewee coaching, preparation strategies and response strategies in relation to performance in situational employment interviews: an extension of Maurer, Solamon, & Troxtel (1998) *Journal of Applied Psychology*, **86**, 709–717.

McCarthy J M & Goffin R D (2001) Improving the validity of letters of recommendation: an investigation of three standardised reference forms. *Military Psychology*, **13**, 199–222.

McCarthy M J & Goffin R (2004) Measuring job interview anxiety: beyond weak knees and sweaty palms. *Personnel Psychology*, **57**, 607–637.

McCarthy J M, van Iddekinge C H & Campion M A (2010) Are highly structured jobs interviews resistant to demographic similarity effects? *Personnel Psychology*, **63**, 325–359.

McCarthy J M, van Iddekinge C H, Lievens F, Kung M-C, Sinar E F & Campion M A (2013) Do candidate reactions relate to job performance or affect criterion-related validity? A multi-study investigation of relations among reactions, selection test scores and job performance. *Journal of Applied Psychology*, **98**, 701–719.

McClelland D C (1971) *The Achieving Society*. Van Nostrand, Princeton, NJ.

McCormick E J, Jeanneret P R & Mecham R C (1972) Study of job characteristics and job dimensions as based on the position analysis questionnaire (PAQ). *Journal of Applied Psychology*, **56**, 347–368.

McDaniel M A, Douglas E F & Snell A F (1997) A survey of deception among job seekers. Paper presented at 12th Annual Conference of SIOP, St Louis, MO.

McDaniel M A, Hartman N S, Whetzel D L & Grubb W L (2007) Situational judgment tests, response instructions, and validity: a meta-analysis. *Personnel Psychology*, **60**, 63–91.

McDaniel M A & Kepes S (2012) Spearman's hypothesis is a model for understanding alternative g tests. Paper presented at 27th Annual Conference of SIOP, San Diego.

McDaniel M A, Kepes S & Banks G C (2011) The *Uniform Guidelines* are a detriment to the field of personnel selection. *Industrial and Organizational Psychology*, **4**, 494–514.

McDaniel M A, McKay P & Rothstein H R (2006b). Publication bias and racial effects on job performance: the elephant in the room. Paper presented at 21st Annual Conference of SIOP, Dallas TX.

McDaniel M A, Rothstein H R & Whetzel D L (2006a) Publication bias: a case study of four test vendors. *Personnel Psychology*, **59**, 927–953.

McDaniel M A, Schmidt F L & Hunter J E (1988) A meta-analysis of the validity of methods for rating training and education in personnel selection. *Personnel Psychology*, **41**, 283–314.

McDaniel M A, Whetzel D L, Schmidt F L & Maurer S (1994) The validity of employment interviews: a comprehensive review and meta-analysis. *Journal of Applied Psychology*, **79**, 599–616.

McEvoy G M & Buller P F (1987) User acceptance of peer appraisals in an industrial setting. *Personnel Psychology*, **40**, 785–797.

McFall R M & Marston A (1970) An experimental investigation of behavioral rehearsal in assertive training. *Journal of Abnormal Psychology*, **76**, 295–303.

McGinnity F & Lunn P D (2011) Measuring discrimination facing ethnic minority job applicants: an Irish experiment. *Work, Employment and Society*, **25**, 693–708.

McHenry J J, Hough L M, Toquam J L, Hanson M A & Ashworth S (1990) Project A validity results: the relationship between predictor and criterion domains. *Personnel Psychology*, **43**, 335–354.

McKay P F & McDaniel M A (2006) A re-examination of black-white mean differences in work performance: more data, more moderators. *Journal of Applied Psychology*, **91**, 538–554.

McKinney A P, Carlson K D, Mecham R L, D'Angelo N C & Connerley M L (2003) Recruiters' use of GPA in initial screening decisions: higher GPAs don't always make the cut. *Personnel Psychology*, **56**, 823–845.

McManus M A & Kelly M L (1999) Personality measures and biodata: evidence regarding their incremental predictive value in the life insurance industry. *Personnel Psychology*, **52**, 137–148.

Meehl P E (1954) *Clinical versus Statistical Prediction*. University of Minnesota Press, Minneapolis.

Merenda P F (1995) Substantive issues in the Soroka v. Dayton-Hudson case. *Psychological Reports*, **77**, 595–606.

Meriac J P, Hoffman B J & Woehr D J (2014) A conceptual and empirical review of the structure of assessment center dimensions. *Journal of Management*, **40**, 1269–1296.

Meriac J P, Hoffman B J, Woehr D J & Fleisher M S (2008) Further evidence for the validity of assessment center dimensions: a meta-analysis of the incremental criterion related validity of dimension ratings. *Journal of Applied Psychology*, **93**, 1042–1052.

Meritt-Haston R & Wexley K N (1983) Educational requirements: legality and validity. *Personnel Psychology*, **36**, 743–753.

Messersmith J S, Patel P C, Lepak D P & Gould-Williams J S (2011) Unlocking the black box: exploring the link between high-performance work systems and performance. *Journal of Applied Psychology*, **96**, 1105–1118.

Meyer R D, Dalal R S & Bonaccio S (2009) A meta-analytic investigation into the moderating effects of situational strength on the conscientiousness-performance relationship. *Journal of Organizational Behavior*, **30**, 1077–1102.

Miner J B (1971) Personality tests as predictors of consulting success. *Personnel Psychology*, **24**, 191–204.

Miner M G & Miner J B (1979) *Employee Selection within the Law*. Bureau of National Affairs, Washington, DC.

Mischel W (1968) *Personality and Assessment*. Wiley, New York.

Mitchell T W & Klimoski R J (1982) Is it rational to be empirical? A test of methods for scoring biographical data. *Journal of Applied Psychology*, **67**, 411–418.

Mls J (1935) Intelligenz und fähigkeit zum kraftwagenlenken. *Proceedings of The Eight International Conference of Psychotechnics*, Prague. pp 278–284.

Mol S T, Born M P, Willemsen M E & van der Molen H T (2005) Predicting expatriate job performance for selection purposes: a quantitative review. *Journal of Cross-Cultural Psychology*, **36**, 590–620.

Monahan E L, Hoffman B J, Lance C E, Jackson D J R & Foster M R (2013) Now you see them, now you do not: the influence of indicator-factor ratio on support for assessment center dimensions. *Personnel Psychology*, **66**, 1009–1047.

Morgan W B, Walker S S, Hebl M R & King E B (2013) A field experiment: reducing interpersonal discrimination toward pregnant job applicants. *Journal of Applied Psychology*, **98**, 799–809.

Morgeson F P & Campion M A (2012) A framework of potential sources of inaccuracy in job analysis. In M A Wilson, W Bennett, S G Gibson & G M Alliger (eds.) *The Handbook of Work Analysis*. Routledge, New York.

Morgeson F P, Campion M A, Dipboye R L, Hollenbeck J R, Murphy K & Schmitt N (2007) Reconsidering the use of personality tests in personnel selection contexts. *Personnel Psychology*, **60**, 683–729.

Morgeson F P, Delaney-Klinger K, Mayfield M S, Ferrara P & Campion M A (2004) Self-presentation processes in job analysis: a field experiment investigating inflation in abilities, tasks and competencies. *Journal of Applied Psychology*, **89**, 674–686.

Morgeson F P & Dierdorff E C (2011) Work analysis: from technique to theory. In S Zedeck (ed.) *APA Handbook of Industrial and Organizational Psychology*, vol. 2: *Selecting and Developing Members for the Organization*. American Psychological Association, Washington, DC.

Morgeson F P, Reider M H, Campion M A & Bull R A (2008) Review of research on age discrimination in the employment interview. *Journal of Business and Psychology*, **22**, 223–232.

Morris B S (1949) Officer selection in the British Army 1942–1945. *Occupational Psychology*, **23**, 219–234.

Mosel J N (1952) Prediction of department store sales performance from personal data. *Journal of Applied Psychology*, **36**, 8–10.

Mosel J N & Goheen H W (1959) The validity of the Employment Recommendation Questionnaire. III Validity of different types of references. *Personnel Psychology*, **12**, 469–477.

Moser K & Rhyssen D (2001) Referenzen als eignungsdiagnostische Methode. *Zeitschrift für Arbeits- und Organisationspsychologie*, **45**, 40–46.

Mount M K & Barrick M R (1995) The big five personality dimensions: implications for research and practice in human resources management. *Research in Personnel and Human Resources Management*, **13**, 153–200.

Mount M K, Barrick M R & Stewart G L (1998) Five-factor model of personality and performance in jobs involving interpersonal interaction. *Human Performance*, **11**, 145–165.

Mount M K, Barrick M R & Strauss J P (1999) The joint relationship of conscientiousness and ability with performance: test of the interaction hypothesis. *Journal of Management*, **25**, 707–721.

Mount M K, Witt L A & Barrick M R (2000) Incremental validity of empirically keyed bio-data scales over GMA and the five factor personality constructs. *Personnel Psychology*, **53**, 299–323.

Muchinsky P M & Raines (2013) The overgeneralized validity of validity generalisation. *Journal of Organizational Behavior*, **34**, 1057–1060.

Muchinsky P M (2004) When the psychometrics of test development meets organizational realities: a conceptual framework for organizational change, examples, and recommendations. *Personnel Psychology*, **57**, 175–209.

Mumford M D & Owens W A (1987) Methodology review; principles, procedures, and findings in the applications of background data measures. *Applied Psychological Measurement*, **11**, 1–31.

Murphy K R (1986) When your top choice turns you down: effect of rejected offers on the utility of selection tests. *Psychological Bulletin*, **99**, 133–138.

Murphy K R (1989) Is the relationship between cognitive ability and job performance stable over time? *Human Performance*, **2**, 183–200.

Murphy K R (2008) Explaining the weak relationship between job performance and ratings of job performance. *Industrial and Organizational Psychology*, **1**, 148–160.

Murphy K R & Cleveland J N (1995) *Understanding Performance Appraisal: Social, Organisational, and Goal-Based Perspectives.* Sage, Thousand Oaks, CA.

Murphy K R, Dzieweczynski J L & Zhang Y (2009) Positive manifold limits the relevance of content-matching strategies for validating selection test batteries. *Journal of Applied Psychology*, **94**, 1018–1031.

Murphy K R & Jacobs R R (2012) Using effect size measures to reform the determination of adverse impact in equal employment litigation. *Psychology, Public Policy & Law*, **18**, 477–499.

Murphy K R, Thornton G C & Prue K (1991) Influence of job characteristics on the acceptability of employee drug testing. *Journal of Applied Psychology*, **76**, 447–453.

Murphy N (2006) Testing the waters: employers' use of selection assessments. *IRS Employment Review*, **852**, 42–48.

Mussel P, Berhmann M & Schuler H (2008) Explaining the psychometric qualities of structured and unstructured interviews. Paper presented at 23rd Annual Conference of SIOP, San Francisco.

Nandkeolyar A K, Shaffer J A, Li A, Ekkirala S & Bagger J (2014) Surviving an abusive supervisor: the joint roles of conscientiousness and coping strategies. *Journal of Applied Psychology*, **99**, 138–150.

Nathan B R & Alexander R A (1988) A comparison of criteria for test validation: a meta-analytic investigation. *Personnel Psychology*, **41**, 517–535.

Neter E & Ben-Shakhar G (1989) The predictive validity of graphological inferences: a meta-analytic approach. *Personality and Individual Differences*, **10**, 737–745.

Newman D A, Jacobs R R & Bartram D (2007) Choosing the best method for local validity estimation: relative accuracy of meta-analysis versus a local study versus Bayes-analysis. *Journal of Applied Psychology*, **92**, 1394–1413.

Newman D A & Lyon J S (2009) Recruitment efforts to reduce adverse impact: targeted recruiting for personality, cognitive ability, and diversity. *Journal of Applied Psychology*, **94**, 298–317.

Ng T W H, Eby L T, Sorenson K L & Feldman D C (2005) Predictors of objective and subjective career success: a meta-analysis. *Personnel Psychology*, **58**, 367–408.

Ng T W H & Feldman D C (2008) The relationship of age to ten dimensions of job performance. *Journal of Applied Psychology*, **93**, 392–423.

Ng T W H & Feldman D C (2012) Evaluating six common stereotypes about older workers with meta-analytical data. *Personnel Psychology*, **65**, 821–858.

Nguyen H-H D & Ryan A M (2008) Does stereotype threat affect test performance of minorities and women? A meta-analysis of experimental evidence. *Journal of Applied Psychology*, **93**, 1314–1334.

Nicklin J M & Roch S G (2009) Letters of recommendation: controversy and consensus from expert perspectives. *International Journal of Selection and Assessment*, **17**, 76–91.

Nielsen M L & Kuhn K M (2005) Late payments and leery applicants: credit checks as a selection test. *Employee Rights and Responsibilities Journal*, **21**, 116–130.

Noe R A, Hollenbeck J R, Gerhart B & Wright P M (2000) *Human Resource Management*. 3rd edn. McGraw-Hill/Irwin, New York.

Normand J, Salyards S D & Mahoney J J (1990) An evaluation of preemployment drug testing. *Journal of Applied Psychology*, **75**, 629–639.

Norton S M (1992) Peer assessments of performance and ability: an exploratory meta-analysis of statistical artifacts and contextual moderators. *Journal of Business and Psychology*, **6**, 387–399.

O'Boyle E & Aguinis H (2012) The best and the rest: revisiting the norm of normality of individual performance. *Personnel Psychology*, **65**, 79–119.

O'Boyle E H, Forsyth D R, Banks G C & McDaniel M A (2012) A meta-analysis of the dark triad and work behavior: a social exchange perspective. *Journal of Applied Psychology*, **97**, 557–579.

O'Brien J & Rothstein M (2008) Selection interviewer judgment and personal fear of invalidity. Paper presented at 23rd Annual Conference of SIOP, San Francisco.

Oh I S, Postlethwaite B E, Schmidt F L, McDaniel M A & Whetzel D L (2007) Do structured and unstructured interviews have nearly equal validity? Implications of recent developments in meta-analysis. Paper presented at 22nd Annual Conference of SIOP, New York.

Oh I-S, Wang G & Mount M K (2011) Validity of observer ratings of the five-factor model of personality traits: a meta-analysis. *Journal of Applied Psychology*, **96**, 762–773.

O'Neill T A, Goffin R D & Gellatly I R (2012) The use of random coefficient modelling for understanding and predicting job performance ratings: an application with field data. *Organizational Research Methods*, **15**, 436–462.

Ones D S & Anderson N (2002) Gender and ethnic group differences on personality scales in selection: some British data. *Journal of Occupational and Organizational Psychology*, **75**, 255–277.

Ones D S, Dilchert S, Viswesvaran C & Salgado J F (2010) Cognitive abilities. In J L Farr & N T Tippins (eds.) *Handbook of Employee Selection*. Routledge, New York.

Ones D S & Viswesvaran C (1998) The effects of social desirability and faking on personality and integrity assessment for personnel selection. *Human Performance*, **11**, 245–269.

Ones D S & Viswesvaran C (2003a) Job-specific applicant pools and national norms for personality scales: implications for range-restriction corrections in validation research. *Journal of Applied Psychology*, **88**, 570–577.

Ones D S & Viswesvaran C (2003b) The big-5 personality and counterproductive behaviours. In A Sagie, S Stashevsky & M Koslowsky M (eds.) *Misbehaviour and Dysfunctional Attitudes in Organizations*. Palgrave Macmillan, Basingstoke.

Ones D S, Viswesvaran C & Reiss A D (1996) Role of social desirability in personality testing for personnel selection: the red herring. *Journal of Applied Psychology*, **81**, 660–679.

Ones D S, Viswesvaran C & Schmidt, F L (1993) Comprehensive meta-analysis of integrity test validities: findings and implications for personnel selection and theories of job performance. *Journal of Applied Psychology*, **78**, 679–703.

Oostrom J K, Born M P, Serlie A W & van der Molen H T (2011) A multimedia situational test with a constructed-response format: its relationship with personality, cognitive ability, job experience, and academic performance. *Journal of Personnel Psychology*, **10**, 78–88.

Orwell G (1949/1984) *Nineteen Eighty-Four*. Clarendon Press, Oxford.

OSS Assessment Staff (1948) *Assessment of Men*. Rinehart, New York.

Owens W A & Schoenfeldt L F (1979) Toward a classification of persons. *Journal of Applied Psychology*, **65**, 569–607.

Pannone R D (1984) Predicting test performance: a content valid approach to screening applicants. *Personnel Psychology*, **37**, 507–514.

Parkes K R & Razavi T D B (2004) Personality and attitudinal variables as predictors of voluntary union membership. *Personality and Individual Differences*, **37**, 333–347.

Parkinson C N (1958) *Parkinson's Law*. John Murray, London.

Parry G (1999) A legal examination of two cases involving employment reference. *Educational Management and Administration*, **27**, 357–364.

Payne S C, Horner M T, Deshpande S S & Wynne K T (2008) Supervisory performance ratings: what have we been measuring? Paper presented at 23rd Annual Conference of SIOP.

Pearlman K & Sanchez J I (2010) Work analysis. In J L Farr & N T Tippins (eds.) *Handbook of Employee Selection*. Routledge, New York.

Pearlman K, Schmidt F L & Hunter J E (1980) Validity generalisation results for tests used to predict job proficiency and training success in clerical occupations. *Journal of Applied Psychology*, **65**, 373–406.

Peres S H & Garcia J R (1962) Validity and dimensions of descriptive adjectives used in reference letters for engineering applicants. *Personnel Psychology*, **15**, 279–286.

Piotrowski C & Armstrong T (2006) Current recruitment and selection practices: a national survey of Fortune 1000 firms. *North American Journal of Psychology*, **8**, 489–496.

Plouffe C R & Grégoire Y (2011) Intraorganizational employee navigation and socially derived outcomes: conceptualization, validation, and effects on overall performance. *Personnel Psychology*, **64**, 693–738.

Ployhart R E & Holtz B C (2008). The diversity-validity dilemma: strategies for reducing racioethnic and sex subgroup differences and adverse impact in selection. *Personnel Psychology*, **61**, 153–172.

Pollack J M & McDaniel M A (2008) An examination of the Previsor™ Employment Inventory for publication bias. Paper presented at 23rd Annual Conference of SIOP, San Francisco.

Prewett-Livingston A J, Feild H S, Veres J G & Lewis P M (1996) Effects of race on interview ratings in a situational panel interview. *Journal of Applied Psychology*, **81**, 178–186.

Pulakos E D, Schmitt N, Dorsey D W, Arad S, Hedge J W & Borman W C (2002) Predicting adaptive performance: further tests of a model of adaptability. *Human Performance*, **15**, 299–323.

Putka D J & Hoffman B J (2013) Clarifying the contribution of assessee-, dimension-, exercise-, and assessor-related effects to reliable and unreliable variance in assessment center ratings. *Journal of Applied Psychology*, **98**, 114–133.

Putka D J & McCloy R A (2004) Preliminary AIM validation based on GED Plus program data. In D J Knapp, E D Heggestad & M C Young (eds.) *Understanding and Improving the Assessment of Individual Motivation (AIM) in the Army's GED Plus Program*. US Army Institute for the Behavioral and Social Sciences, Alexandria, VA.

Quist J S, Arora A & Griffith R L (2007) Social desirability and applicant faking behaviour. Paper presented at 23rd Annual Conference of SIOP, San Francisco.

Raymark P H, Schmit M J & Guion R M (1997) Identifying potentially useful personality constructs for employee selection. *Personnel Psychology*, **50**, 723–736.

Rayson M, Holliman D & Belyavin A (2000) Development of physical selection procedures for the British Army. Phase 2: relationship between physical performance test and criterion tasks. *Ergonomics*, **43**, 73–105.

Ree M J & Earles J A (1991) Predicting training success: not much more than g. *Personnel Psychology*, **44**, 321–332.

Reeve C L & Schultz L (2004) Job-seeker reactions to selection process information in job ads. *International Journal of Selection and Assessment*, **12**, 343–355.

Reilly R R & Chao G T (1982) Validity and fairness of some alternative employee selection procedures. *Personnel Psychology*, **35**, 1–62.

Reiter-Palmon R & Connelly M S (2000) Item selection counts: a comparison of empirical key and rational scale validities in theory-based and non-theory-based item pools. *Journal of Applied Psychology*, **85**, 143–151.

Reynolds D H & Dickter D N (2010) Technology and employee selection. In J L Farr & N T Tippins (eds.) *Handbook of Employee Selection*. Routledge, New York.

Roberts B W, Harms P D, Caspi A & Moffitt T E (2007) Predicting the counterproductive employee in a child-to-adult prospective study. *Journal of Applied Psychology*, **92**, 1427–1436.

Robertson I T & Downs S (1989) Work-sample tests of trainability: a meta-analysis. *Journal of Applied Psychology*, **74**, 402–410.

Robie C, Schmit M J, Ryan A M & Zickar M J (2000) Effects of item context specificity on the measurement equivalence of a personality inventory. *Organizational Research Methods*, **3**, 348–365.

Robinson D D (1972) Prediction of clerical turnover in banks by means of a weighted application blank. *Journal of Applied Psychology*, **56**, 282.

Roth P L, Bevier C A, Bobko P, Switzer F S & Tyler P (2001b) Ethnic group difference in cognitive ability in employment and educational settings: a meta-analysis. *Personnel Psychology*, **54**, 297–330.

Roth P L, Bevier C A, Switzer F S & Schippman J S (1996) Meta-analyzing the relationship between grades and job performance. *Journal of Applied Psychology*, **81**, 548–556.

Roth P L & Bobko P (2000) College grade point average as a personnel selection device: ethnic group differences and potential adverse impact. *Journal of Applied Psychology*, **85**, 399–406.

Roth P L, Bobko P & McFarland L A (2005) A meta-analysis of work sample test validity: updating and integrating some classic literature. *Personnel Psychology*, **58**, 1009–1037.

Roth P, Bobko P, McFarland L & Buster M (2008) Work sample tests in personnel selection: a meta-analysis of black-white differences in overall and exercise scores. *Personnel Psychology*, **61**, 637–662.

Roth P L, Bobko P & Switzer F S (2006) Modeling the behavior of the 4/5ths rule for determining adverse impact: reasons for caution. *Journal of Applied Psychology*, **91**, 507–522.

Roth P L, Bobko P, Switzer F S & Dean M A (2001a) Prior selection causes biased estimates of standardized ethnic group differences: simulation and analysis. *Personnel Psychology*, **54**, 591–617.

Roth P L, Buster M A & Bobko P (2011) Updating the trainability tests literature on black-white subgroup differences and reconsidering criterion-related validity. *Journal of Applied Psychology*, **96**, 34–45.

Roth P L & Huffcutt A I (2013) A meta-analysis of interviews and cognitive ability: back to the future? *Journal of Personnel Psychology*, **12**, 157–169.

Roth P L, Huffcutt A I & Bobko P (2003) Ethnic group differences in measures of job performance: a new meta-analysis. *Journal of Applied Psychology*; **88**, 694–706.

Roth P L, Purvis K L & Bobko P (2012) A meta-analysis of gender group differences for measures on job performance in field studies. *Journal of Management*, **38**, 719–739.

Roth P L, van Iddekinge C H, Huffcutt A I, Eidson C E & Bobko P (2002) Corrections for range restriction in structured interview ethnic group differences: the values may be larger than researchers thought. *Journal of Applied Psychology*, **87**, 369–376.

Roth P L, van Iddekinge C H, Huffcutt A I, Eidson C E & Schmit M J (2005) Personality saturation in structured interviews. *International Journal of Selection and Assessment*, **13**, 261–273.

Rothstein H R (1990) Interrater reliability of job performance ratings: growth to asymptote level with increasing opportunity to observe. *Journal of Applied Psychology*, **75**, 322–327.

Rothstein H R & McDaniel M A (1992) Differential validity by sex in employment settings. *Personnel Psychology*, **7**, 45–62.

Rothstein H R, Schmidt F L, Erwin F W, Owens W A & Sparks C P (1990) Biographical data in employment selection: can validities be made generalisable? *Journal of Applied Psychology*, **75**, 175–184.

Rotundo M & Sackett P R (2004) Specific versus general skills and abilities: a job level examination of relationships with wage. *Journal of Occupational and Organizational Psychology*, **77**, 127–148.

Roulin N & Bangerter A (2013) Social networking websites in personnel selection: a signaling perspective on recruiters' and applicants' perceptions. *Journal of Personnel Psychology*, **12**, 143–151.

Roulin A, Bangerter A & Yerly E (2011) The uniqueness effect in selection interviews. *Journal of Personnel Psychology*, **10**, 43–47.

Rubenzer S J, Faschingbauer T R & Ones D S (2000) Assessing the U.S. presidents using the revised NEO Personality Inventory. *Assessment*, **7**, 403–420.

Rudolph C W, Wells C L, Weller M D & Baltes B B (2008) Weight-based bias and evaluative workplace outcomes: a meta-analysis. Paper presented at 23rd Annual Conference of SIOP, San Francisco.

Ruggs E N, Hebl M R, Law C, Cox C B, Roehling M V, Wiener R L & Barron L (2013) Gone fishing: I-O psychologists' missed opportunities to understand marginalized employees' experiences with discrimination. *Industrial and Organizational Psychology*, **6**, 39–60.

Russell C J, Mattson J, Devlin S E & Atwater D (1990) Predictive validity of biodata items generated from retrospective life experience essays. *Journal of Applied Psychology*, **75**, 569–580.

Russell C J, Settoon R P, McGrath R N, Blanton A E, Kidwell R E, Lohrke F T, Scifres E L & Danforth G W (1994) Investigator characteristics as moderators of personnel selection research: a meta-analysis. *Journal of Applied Psychology*, **79**, 163–170.

Ryan A M, McFarland L, Baron H & Page R (1999) An international look at selection practices: nation and culture as explanation for variability in practice. *Personnel Psychology*, **52**, 359–391.

Saad S & Sackett P R (2002) Investigating differential prediction by gender in employment-oriented personality measures. *Journal of Applied Psychology*, **87**, 667–674,

Sacco J M & Schmitt N (2005) A dynamic multilevel model of demographic diversity and misfit effects. *Journal of Applied Psychology*, **90**, 203–231.

Sackett P R (2003) The status of validity generalization research: key issues in drawing inferences from cumulative research findings. In K R Murphy (ed.) *Validity Generalization: A Critical Review*. Lawrence Erlbaum, Mahwah, NJ.

Sackett P R (2007) Revisiting the origins of the typical-maximum performance distinction. *Human Performance*, **20**, 179–185.

Sackett P R (2011) Integrating and prioritizing theoretical perspectives on applicant faking of personality measures. *Human Performance*, **24**, 379–385.

Sackett P R, Bornemann M J & Connelly B S (2008) High-stakes testing in higher education and employment; appraising the evidence for validity and fairness. *American Psychologist*, **63**, 215–227.

Sackett P R & Dreher G F (1982) Constructs and assessment center dimensions: some troubling empirical findings. *Journal of Applied Psychology*, **67**, 401–410.

Sackett P R & Dubois C L Z (1991) Rater-ratee race effects on performance evaluation: challenging meta-analytic conclusions. *Journal of Applied Psychology*, **76**, 873–877.

Sackett P R, Gruys M L & Ellingson J E (1998) Ability-personality interactions when predicting job performance. *Journal of Applied Psychology*, **83**, 545–556.

Sackett P R & Mavor A (2003) *Attitudes, Aptitudes, and Aspiration of American Youth: Implications for Military Recruiting*. National Academies Press, Washington DC.

Sackett P R & Ostgaard D J (1994) Job-specific applicant pools and national norms for cognitive ability tests: implications for range restriction correction in validation research. *Journal of Applied Psychology*, **79**, 680–684.

Sackett P R & Schmitt N (2012) On reconciling meta-analytic findings regarding integrity validity. *Journal of Applied Psychology*, **97**, 550–556.

Sackett P R, Schmitt N, Ellingson J E & Kabin M B (2001) High-stakes testing in employment, credentialing, and higher education: prospects in a post-affirmative-action world. *American Psychologist*, **56**, 302–318.

Salgado J F (1998) Big five personality dimensions and job performance in army and civil occupations: a European perspective. *Human Performance*, **11**, 271–289.

Salgado J F (2002) The Big Five personality dimensions and counterproductive behaviors. *International Journal of Selection and Assessment*, **10**, 117–125.

Salgado J F & Anderson N (2002) Cognitive and GMA testing in the European Community: issues and evidence. *Human Performance*, **15**, 75–96.

Salgado J F & Anderson N (2003) Validity generalisation of GMA tests across countries in the European Community. *European Journal of Work and Organizational Psychology*, **12**, 1–17.

Salgado J F, Anderson N, Moscoso S, Bertua C, de Fruyt F & Rolland J P (2003) A meta-analytic study of general mental ability validity for different occupations in the European Community. *Journal of Applied Psychology*, **88**, 1068–1081.

Salgado J F, Anderson N & Tauriz G (2015) The validity of ipsative and quasi-ipsative forced-choice personality inventories for different occupational groups: a comprehensive meta-analysis. *Journal of Occupational and Organizational Psychology*, **88**, 797–834.

Salgado J F & Moscoso S (2002) Comprehensive meta-analysis of the construct validity on the employment interview. *European Journal of Work and Organizational Psychology*, **11**, 299–324.

Sanchez J I, Prager I, Wilson A & Viswesvaran C (1998) Understanding within-job title variance in job-analytic ratings. *Journal of Business and Psychology*, **12**, 407–418.

Schleicher D J, van Iddekinge C H, Morgeson F P & Campion M A (2010) If at first you don't succeed, try, try again: understanding race, age, and gender difference in retesting score improvement. *Journal of Applied Psychology*, **95**, 603–617.

Schleicher D J, Venkataramani V, Morgeson F P & Campion M A (2006) So you didn't get the job … Now what do you think? Examining opportunity-to-perform fairness perceptions. *Personnel Psychology*, **59**, 559–590.

Schmid Mast M, Frauendorfer D & Popovic L (2011) Self-promoting and modest job applicants in different cultures. *Journal of Personnel Psychology*, **10**, 70–77.

Schmidt F L (2002) The role of general cognitive ability and job performance: why there cannot be a debate. *Human Performance*, **15**, 187–210.

Schmidt F L, Gast-Rosenberg I & Hunter J E (1980) Validity generalisation results for computer programmers. *Journal of Applied Psychology*, **65**, 643–661.

Schmidt F L & Hunter J E (1977) Development of a general solution to the problem of validity generalisation. *Journal of Applied Psychology*, **62**, 529–540.

Schmidt F L & Hunter J E (1995) The fatal internal contradiction in banding: its statistical rationale is logically inconsistent with its operational procedures. *Human Performance*, **8**, 203–214.

Schmidt F L & Hunter J E (1998) The validity and utility of selection methods in personnel psychology: practical and theoretical implications of 85 years of research findings. *Psychological Bulletin*, **124**, 262–274.

Schmidt F L & Hunter J (2004) General mental ability in the world of work: occupational attainment and job performance, *Journal of Personality and Social Psychology*, **86**, 162–173.

Schmidt F L, Hunter J E, McKenzie R C & Muldrow T W (1979) Impact of valid selection procedures on work-force productivity. *Journal of Applied Psychology*, **64**, 609–626.

Schmidt F L, Hunter J E, Pearlman K & Hirsh H R (1985b) Forty questions about validity generalisation and meta-analysis. *Personnel Psychology*, **38**, 697–798.

Schmidt F L, Ocasio B P, Hillery J M & Hunter J E (1985a) Further within-setting empirical tests of the situational specificity hypothesis in personnel selection. *Personnel Psychology*, **38**, 509–524.

Schmidt F L & Oh I-S (2010) Can synthetic validity methods achieve discriminant validity? *Industrial and Organizational Psychology*, **3**, 344–350.

Schmidt F L, Oh I S & Le H (2006) Increasing the accuracy of correction for range restriction: implications for selection procedure validities and other research results. *Personnel Psychology*, **59**, 281–305.

Schmidt F L & Rader M (1999) Exploring the boundary conditions for interview validity: meta-analytic validity findings for a new interview type. *Personnel Psychology*, **52**, 445–465.

Schmidt F L & Rothstein H R (1994) Application of validity generalisation to biodata scales in employment selection. In G S Stokes, M D Mumford & W A Owens (eds.) *Biodata Handbook: Theory, Research and Use of Biographical Information in Selection and Performance Prediction*. Consulting Psychology Press, Palo Alto, CA.

Schmidt F L, Shaffer J & Oh I S (2008) Increased accuracy for range restriction corrections: implications for the role of personality and general mental ability in job and training performance. *Personnel Psychology*, **61**, 827–868.

Schmidt F L & Zimmerman R D (2004) A counterintuitive hypothesis about employment inter-view validity and some supporting evidence. *Journal of Applied Psychology*, **89**, 353–361.

Schmidt-Atzert L & Deter B (1993) Intelligenz und Ausbildungserfolg: eine Untersuchung zur prognistischen Validität des I-S-T 70. *Zeitschrift für Arbeits- und Organisationspsychologie*, **37**, 52–63.

Schmit M J & Ryan A M (1993) The big five in personnel selection: factor structure in applicant and nonapplicant populations. *Journal of Applied Psychology*, **78**, 966–974.

Schmitt N (2007) The value of personnel selection; reflections on some remarkable claims. *Academy of Management Perspectives*, **3**, 19–23.

Schmitt N, Clause C S & Pulakos E D (1996) Subgroup differences associated with different measures of some common job-relevant constructs. *International Review of Industrial and Organizational Psychology*, **11**, 115–139.

Schmitt N, Gooding R Z, Noe R A & Kirsch M (1984) Metaanalyses of validity studies, published between 1964 and 1982 and the investigation of study characteristics. *Personnel Psychology*, **37**, 407–422.

Schmitt N & Kunce C (2002) The effects of required elaboration of answers to biodata questions. *Personnel Psychology*, **55**, 569–587.

Schneider R J, Hough L M & Dunnette M D (1996) Broadsided by broad traits: how to sink science in five dimensions or less. *Journal of Organizational Behavior*, **17**, 639–655.

Scholz G & Schuler H (1993) Das nomologische Netzwerk des Assessment Centers: eine Metaanalyse. *Zeitschrift für Arbeits- und Organisationspsychologie*, **37**, 73–85.

Schrader A D & Osburn H G (1977) Biodata faking: effects of induced subtlety and position specificity. *Personnel Psychology*, **30**, 395–404.

Schuler H (2008) Improving assessment centers by the trimodal concept of personnel assess-ment. *Industrial and Organizational Psychology*, **1**, 128–130.

Schuler H, Hell B, Trapmann S, Schaar H & Boramir I (2007) Die Nutzung psychologischer Verfahren der externen Personalauswahl in deutschen Unternehmen: ein Vergleich über 20 Jahre. *Journal of Personnel Psychology*, **6**, 60–70.

Schuler H & Moser K (1995) Die validität des multimodalen interviews. *Zeitschrift für Arbeits- und Organisationspsychologie*, **39**, 2–12.

Scott S J (1997) Graduate selection procedures and ethnic minority applicants. MSc thesis, University of East London.

Shaffer J & Postlethwaite B E (2012) A matter of context: a meta-analytic investigation of the relative validity of contextualized and non-contextualized personality measures, *Personnel Psychology*, **65**, 445–494.

Sharf J C (1994) The impact of legal and equal employment opportunity issues on personal history enquiries. In G S Stokes, M D Mumford & W A Owens (eds.) *Biodata Handbook: Theory, Research, and Use of Biographical Information in Selection and Performance Prediction*. Consulting Psychology Press, Palo Alto CA.

Sheehan E P, McDevitt T M & Ross H C (1998) Looking for a job as a psychology professor? Factors affecting applicant success. *Teaching of Psychology*, **25**, 8–11.

Shermis M D, Falkenberg B, Appel V A & Cole R W (1996) Construction of a faking detector scale for a biodata survey instrument. *Military Psychology*, **8**, 83–94.

SHRM (Society for Human Resource Management) (1998) *SHRM Reference Checking Survey*. SHRM, Alexandria VA.

Siers B P & Christiansen N D (2013) On the validity of implicit association measures of per-sonality traits. *Personality and Individual Differences*, **54**, 361–366.

Silvester J & Dykes C (2007) Selecting political candidates: a longitudinal study of assess-ment centre performance and political success in the 2005 UK General Election. *Journal of Occupational and Organizational Psychology*, **80**, 11–25.

Silvester J, Mohammed A R, Anderson-Gough F & Anderson N (2002) Locus of control, attributions and impression management in the selection interview. *Journal of Occupational and Organizational Psychology*, **75**, 59–78.

Sitzmann T & Yeo G (2013) A meta-analytic investigation of the within-person self-efficacy domain: is self-efficacy a product of past performance or a driver of future performance? *Personnel Psychology*, **66**, 531–568.

Sliter K A & Christiansen N D (2012) Effected of targeted self-coaching on applicant distortion of personality measures. *Journal of Personnel Psychology*, **11**, 169–175.

Spain S M, Harms P & Lebreton J M (2014) The dark side of personality at work. *Journal of Organizational Behavior*, **35**, S41–S60.

Sparrow J, Patrick J, Spurgeon P & Barwell F (1982) The use of job component analysis and related aptitudes in personnel selection. *Journal of Occupational Psychology*, **55**, 157–164.

Springbett B M (1958) Factors affecting the final decision in the employment interview. *Canadian Journal of Psychology*, **12**, 13–22.

Spychalski A C, Quinones M A, Gaugler B B & Pohley K (1997) A survey of assessment center practices in organizations in the United States. *Personnel Psychology*, **50**, 71–90.

Stauffer J M & Buckley M R (2005) The existence and nature of racial bias in supervisory ratings. *Journal of Applied Psychology*, **90**, 586–591.

Stedman J M, Hatch J P & Schoenfeld L S (2009) Letters of recommendation for the predoctoral internship in medical school and other settings: do they enhance decision making in the selection process. *Journal of Clinical Psychology in Medical Settings*, **16**, 339–345.

Steffens M C & König S S (2006) Predicting spontaneous big five behavior with implicit association tests. *European Journal of Psychological Assessment*, **22**, 13–30.

Stewart G L, Darnold T C, Zimmerman R D, Barrick M R, Parks L & Dustin S L (2008). Exploring how response distortion of personality measures affects individuals. Paper presented at 23rd Annual Conference of SIOP, San Francisco.

Stokes G S, Hogan J B & Snell A F (1993) Comparability of incumbent and applicant samples for the development of biodata keys: the influence of social desirability. *Personnel Psychology*, **46**, 739–762.

Stone D L, Lukaszewski K M, Stone-Romero E F & Johnson T L (2013) Factors affecting the effectiveness and acceptance of electronic selection systems. *Human Resource Management Review*, **23**, 50–70.

Stone-Romero E F, Stone D L & Hyatt D (2003) Personnel selection procedures and invasion of privacy. *Journal of Social Issues*, **59**, 343–368.

Sturman M C, Cheramie R A & Cashen L H (2005) The impact of job complexity and performance measurement on the temporal consistency, stability, and test-retest reliability of employee job performance ratings. *Journal of Applied Psychology*, **90**, 269–283.

Sulea C, Fine S, Fischmann G, Sava F A & Dumitru C (2013) Abusive supervision and counterproductive work behaviors: the moderating effects of personality. *Journal of Personnel Psychology*, **12**, 196–200.

Sumanth J J & Cable D M (2011) Status and organizational entry: how organizational and individual status affect justice perceptions on hiring systems. *Personnel Psychology*, **64**, 963–1000.

Super D E & Crites J O (1962) *Appraising Vocational Fitness by Means of Psychological Tests.* Harper and Row, New York.

Sutton A W, Baldwin S P, Wood L & Hoffman B J (2013) A meta-analysis of the relationship between rater liking and performance ratings. *Human Performance*, **26**, 409–429.

Taylor P, Keelty Y & McDonnell B (2002) Evolving personnel selection practices in New Zealand organisations and recruitment firms. *New Zealand Journal of Psychology*, **31**, 8–18.

Taylor P J, Pajo K, Cheung G W & Stringfield P (2004) Dimensionality and validity of a structured telephone reference check procedure. *Personnel Psychology*, **57**, 745–772.

Taylor P J & Small B (2002) Asking applicants what they would do versus what they did do: a meta-analytic comparison of situational and past behaviour employment interview questions. *Journal of Occupational and Organizational Psychology*, **74**, 277–294.

Te Nijenhuis J & van der Flier H (2000) Differential prediction of immigrant versus majority group training performance using cognitive and personality measures. *International Journal of Selection and Assessment*, **8**, 54–60.

Terpstra D E & Kethley R B (2002) Organizations' relative degree of exposure to selection discrimination litigation. *Personnel Psychology*, **31**, 277–292.

Terpstra D E, Mohamed A A & Kethley R B (1999) An analysis of Federal court cases involving nine selection devices. *International Journal of Selection and Assessment*, **7**, 26–34.

Terpstra D E & Rozell E J (1993) The relationship of staffing practices to organizational level measures of performance. *Personnel Psychology*, **46**, 27–48.

Terpstra D E & Rozell E J (1997) Why potentially effective staffing practices are seldom used. *Public Personnel Management*, **26**, 483–495.

Tett R P, Jackson D N & Rothstein M (1991) Personality measures as predictors of job performance. *Personnel Psychology*, **44**, 407–421.

Tett R P, Jackson D N, Rothstein M & Reddon J R (1999) Meta-analysis of bidirectional relations in personality-job performance research. *Human Performance*, **12**, 1–29.

Thatcher S M B & Patel P C (2011) Demographic faultlines: a meta-analysis of the literature. *Journal of Applied Psychology*, **96**, 1119–1139.

Thornton G C & Gibbons A (2009) Validity of assessment centers for personnel selection. *Human Resource Management Review*, **19**, 169–187.

Thornton G C & Rupp D R (2006) *Assessment Centers in Human Resource Management: Strategies for Prediction, Diagnosis and Development*. Mahwah NJ, Lawrence Erlbaum.

Tiffin J (1943) *Industrial Psychology*. Prentice Hall, New York.

Tross S A & Maurer T J (2008) The effect of coaching interviewees on subsequent interview performance in structured experience-based interviews. *Journal of Occupational and Organizational Psychology*, **81**, 589–605.

Trull T J, Widiger T A, Useda J D, Holcomb J, Doan B T, Axelrod S R, Stern B L & Gershuny B S (1998). A structured interview for the assessment of the Five Factor model of personality. *Psychological Assessment*, **10**, 229–240.

Tupes E C & Christal R E (1992) Recurrent personality factors based on trait ratings. *Journal of Personality*, **60**, 224–251.

Uggerslev K L, Fassina N E & Kraichy D (2012) Recruiting through the stages: a meta-analytic test of predictors of applicant attraction at different stages of the recruiting process. *Personnel Psychology*, **65**, 597–660.

Van Iddekinge C H, Eidson C E, Kudisch J D & Goldblatt A M (2003) A biodata inventory administered via interactive voice response (IVR) technology: predictive validity, utility, and subgroup differences. *Journal of Business and Psychology*, **18**, 145–156.

Van Iddekinge C H, Raymark P H & Eidson C E (2011) An examination of the validity and incremental value of needed-at-entry ratings for a customer service job. *Applied Psychology: an International Review*, **60**, 24–45.

Van Iddekinge C H, Raymark P H & Roth P L (2005) Assessing personality with a structured employment interview: construct-related validity and susceptibility to response inflation. *Journal of Applied Psychology*, **90**, 536–552.

Van Iddekinge C H, Raymark P H, Eidson C E & Attenweiler W J (2004) What do structured selection interviews really measure? The construct validity of behavior description interviews. *Human Performance*, **17**, 71–93.

Van Iddekinge C H, Roth P L, Putka D J & Lanivich S E (2011) Are you interested? A meta-analysis of relations between vocational interests and employee performance and turnover *Journal of Applied Psychology*, **96**, 1167–1194.

Van Iddekinge C H, Roth P L, Raymark P H & Odle-Dusseau H N (2012a) The criterion-related validity of integrity tests: an updated meta-analysis. *Journal of Applied Psychology*, **97**, 499–530.

Van Iddekinge C H, Roth P L, Raymark P H & Odle-Dusseau H N (2012b) The critical role of the research question, inclusion criteria, and transparency in meta-analyses of integrity research: a reply to Harris et al. (2012) and Ones, Viswesvaran, and Schmidt (2012). *Journal of Applied Psychology*, **97**, 543–549,

Van Iddekinge C H, Sager C E, Burnfield J L & Heffner T S (2006) The variability of criterion-related validity estimates among interviewers and interview panels. *International Journal of Selection and Assessment*, **14**, 193–205.

Van Rooy D L, Alonso A & Viswesvaran C (2005) Group differences in emotional intelligence scores: theoretical and practical implications. *Personality and Individual Differences*, **38**, 689–700.

Vance R J & Colella A (1990) The futility of utility analysis. *Human Performance*, **3**, 123–139.

Vasilopoulos N L, Cucina J M & Hunter A E (2007) Personality and training proficiency: issues of bandwidth-fidelity and curvilinearity. *Journal of Occupational and Organizational Psychology*, **80**, 109–131.

Vasilopoulos N L, Cucina J M & McElreath J M (2005) Do warnings of response verification moderate the relationship between personality and cognitive ability. *Journal of Applied Psychology*, **90**, 306–322.

Vernon P E (1950) The validation of Civil Service Selection Board procedures. *Occupational Psychology*, **24**, 75–95.

Vernon P E & Parry J B (1949) *Personnel Selection in the British Forces*. University of London Press, London.

Vinchur A J, Schippmann J S, Switzer F S & Roth P L (1998) A meta-analytic review of predictors of job performance for sales people. *Journal of Applied Psychology*, **83**, 586–597.

Viswesvaran C (2002) Absenteeism and measures of job performance: a meta-analysis. *International Journal of Selection and Assessment*, **10**, 53–58.

Viswesvaran C & Ones D (1999) Meta-analyses of fakability estimates: implications for personality measurement. *Educational and Psychological Measurement*, **59**, 197–210.

Viswesvaran C & Ones D S (2000) Measurement error in 'big five factors' of personality assessment: reliability generalisation across studies and measures. *Educational and Psychological Measurement*, **60**, 224–238.

Viswesvaran C & Ones D S (2005) Job performance: assessment issues in personnel selection. In A Evers, N Anderson & O Voskuijl (eds.) *The Blackwell Handbook of Personnel Selection*. Blackwell, Oxford.

Viswesvaran C, Ones D S & Schmidt F L (1996) Comparative analysis of the reliability of job performance ratings. *Journal of Applied Psychology*, **81**, 557–574.

Viswesvaran C, Schmidt F L & Ones D S (2005) Is there a general factor in ratings of job performance? A meta-analytic framework for disentangling substantive and error influences. *Journal of Applied Psychology*, **90**, 108–131.

Wagner R (1949) The employment interview: a critical summary. *Personnel Psychology*, **2**, 17–46.

Wai J, Lubinski D & Benbow C P (2005) Creativity and occupational accomplishments among intellectually precocious youths: an age 13 to age 33 longitudinal study. *Journal of Educational Psychology*, **97**, 484–492.

Waldman D A & Avolio B J (1986) A meta-analysis of age differences in job performance. *Journal of Applied Psychology*, **71**, 33–38.

Wanberg C, Basbug G, van Hooft E A J & Samtani A (2012) Navigating the black hole: explicating layers of job search context and adaptational responses. *Personnel Psychology*, **65**, 887–926.

Wang K, Barron L G & Hebl M R (2010) Making those who cannot see look best: effects of visual resume formatting on ratings of job applicants with blindness. *Rehabilitation Psychology*, **55**, 68–73.

Wee S, Newman D A & Joseph D L (2014) More than g: selection quality and adverse impact implications of considering second stratum abilities. *Journal of Applied Psychology*, **99**, 547–563.

Weiss B & Feldman R S (2006) Looking good and lying to do it: deception as an impression management strategy in job interviews. *Journal of Applied Social Psychology*, **36**, 1070–1086.

Weller I, Holtom B C, Matiaske W & Mellewigt T (2009) Level and time effects of recruitment sources on early voluntary turnover. *Journal of Applied Psychology*, **94**, 1146–1162.

Whetzel D L, McDaniel M A & Nguyen N T (2008) Subgroup differences in situational judgement test performance: a meta-analysis. *Human Performance*, **21**, 291–309.

Whetzel D L, Rotenberry P F & McDaniel M A (2014) In-basket validity: a systematic review. *International Journal of Selection and Assessment*, **22**, 62–79.

White L, Nord R D, Mael F A & Young M C (1993) The assessment of background and life experiences (ABLE). In T Trent and J H Laurence (eds.) *Adaptability Screening for the Armed Forces*. Office of Assistant Secretary of Defense, Washington, DC.

Whitney D J & Schmitt N (1997) Relationship between culture and responses to biodata employment items. *Journal of Applied Psychology*, **82**, 113–129.

Wiens A N, Jackson R H, Manaugh T S & Matarazzo J D (1969) Communication length as an index of communicator attitude: a replication. *Journal of Applied Psychology*, **53**, 264–266.

Wiesner W H & Cronshaw S F (1988) A meta-analytic investigation of the impact of interview format and degree of structure on the validity of the employment interview. *Journal of Occupational Psychology*, **61**, 275–290.

Wilk S L & Sackett P R (1996) Longitudinal analysis of ability, job complexity fit and job change. *Personnel Psychology*, **49**, 937–967.

Williamson L G, Malos S B, Roehling M V & Campion M A (1997) Employment interview on trial: linking interview structure with litigation outcomes. *Journal of Applied Psychology*, **82**, 900–912.

Wilson N A B (1948) The work of the Civil Service Selection Board. *Occupational Psychology*, **22**, 204–212.

Winkler S, König C J & Kleinmann M (2010) Single-attribute utility analysis may be futile, but this can't be the end of the story: causal chain analysis as an alternative. *Personnel Psychology*, **63**, 1041–1065.

Witt L A & Ferris G R (2003) Social skill as moderator of the conscientiousness-performance relationship: convergent results across four studies. *Journal of Applied Psychology*, **88**, 809–820.

Woehr D J & Arthur W (2003) The construct-related validity of assessment center ratings: a review and meta-analysis of the role of methodological factors. *Journal of Management*, **29**, 231–258.

Wunder R S, Thomas L L & Luo Z (2010) Administering assessments and decision-making. In J L Farr & N T Tippins (eds.) *Handbook of Employee Selection*. Routledge, New York.

Yoo T Y & Muchinsky P M (1998) Utility estimates of job performance as related to the Data, People, and Things parameters of work. *Journal of Organizational Behavior*, **19**, 353–370.

Zeidner M (1988) Cultural fairness in aptitude testing revisited: a cross-cultural parallel. *Professional Psychology: Research and Practice*, **19**, 257–262.

Zeidner M, Matthews G & Roberts R D (2004) Emotional intelligence in the workplace: a critical review. *Applied Psychology: an International Review*, **53**, 371–399.

Zibarras L D & Woods S A (2010) A survey of UK selection practices across different organisation sizes and industry sectors. *Journal of Occupational and Organizational Psychology*, **83**, 499–511.

Zhao H & Seibert S E (2006) The big five personality dimensions and entrepreneurial status: a meta-analytical review. *Journal of Applied Psychology*, **91**, 259–271.

Zickar M J (2001) Using personality inventories to identify thugs and agitators: applied psychology's contribution to the war against labor. *Journal of Vocational Behavior*, **59**, 149–164.

Zickar M J & Drasgow F (1996) Detecting faking on a personality instrument using appropriateness measurement. *Applied Psychological Measurement*, **20**, 71–87.

Zickar M J & Gibby R E (2006) A history of faking and socially desirable responding on personality tests. In R L Griffith & M H Peterson (eds.) *A Closer Examination of Applicant Faking Behavior*. Information Age Publishing, Greenwich, CT.

Zickar M J & Robie C (1999) Modeling faking good on personality items: an item-level analysis. *Journal of Applied Psychology*, **84**, 551–563.

Zimmerman R D (2008) Understanding the impact of personality traits on individuals' turnover decisions: a meta-analytic path model. *Personnel Psychology*, **61**, 309–348.

Zimmerman R D, Triana M C & Barrick M R (2010) Predictive criterion-related validity of observer ratings of personality and job-related competencies using multiple raters and multiple performance criteria. *Human Performance*, **23**, 361–378.

Zottoli M A & Wanous J P (2000) Recruitment source research: current status and future directions. *Human Resource Management Review*, **10**, 353–382.

Index